QuickBooks Online

2014

The Handbook

By Lisa Newton

Intuit Certified ProAdvisor

QuickBooks Online Help

First published in 2014 by Boogles Bookkeeping Ltd

Ground Floor, Unit PG04, 23-28 Penn Street,

London N1 5DL, United Kingdom

Tel: 0844 8844 622. Fax: 08712 449 500

Email : admin@boogles.co.uk

Web : www.QuickBooksOnlineHelp.com

Lisa Newton has asserted her right to be identified as the author of this work in accordance with sections 77 and 78 of the Copyright, Designs and Patents Act 1988.

All rights reserved. No part of the work may be reproduced or stored in an information retrieval system (other than for purposes of review), or transmitted in any form or by any means, electronic, mechanical, photocopying, recording or otherwise, without the express permission of the publisher in writing.

ISBN-13: 978-1492969303

First edition 2014

Printed and bound by Amazon Creates

NOTE: The material contained in this book is set out in good faith for general guidance and no liability can be accepted for loss or expense incurred as a result of relying in particular circumstances on statements made in this book. Laws and regulations are complex and liable to change, and readers should check the current positions with the relevant authorities in their country of origin before making personal arrangements.

This book is available online and at all good bookstores.

© Copyright 2014 Lisa Newton

CONTENTS

1: GETTING STARTED 8

1.1 Introducing QuickBooks 8
1.2 Free Trial 10
1.3 System Requirements 10
1.4 Getting around in QuickBooks 10
1.5 All the accounting you need to know 11
1.6 Using Lists 13
1.7 Using Registers 13
1.8 Getting around in QuickBooks 14
1.9 Help! 15
1.10 Accounting Terminology 16

2: SETTING UP QUICKBOOKS 26

2.1 Creating a QuickBooks Company 26
2.2 Entering company information 27
2.3 Chart of Accounts 39
2.4 Setting up QuickBooks preferences 46
2.5 Setting up income accounts 51
2.6 Entering opening balances 54
2.7 Setting up payroll 57
2.8 Getting help whilst using QuickBooks 58

3: WORKING WITH LISTS 61

3.1 Using QuickBooks lists 61
3.2 Editing the chart of accounts 62
3.3 Working with the Customer: sub-customer list 69

3.4 Working with the Employee list 73
3.5 Working with the Supplier list 74
3.6 Working with Other Lists (Terms, Payment, Classes) 76
3.7 Adding custom fields 88
3.8 Managing lists 91

4: WORKING WITH BANK AND CREDIT CARD ACCOUNTS 95

4.1 Writing a QuickBooks cheque 95
4.2 Using bank account registers 102
4.3 Entering a handwritten cheque 105
4.4 Transferring money between accounts 107
4.5 Reconciling bank accounts 109
4.6 Tracking credit card transactions 121

5: USING OTHER ACCOUNTS IN QUICKBOOKS 135

5.1 Other account types in QuickBooks 135
5.2 Working with asset accounts 136
5.3 Working with liability accounts 143
5.4 Understanding equity accounts 149
5.5 Working with journal entries 150

6: ENTERING SALES AND INVOICES 153

6.1 Using sales forms in QuickBooks 153
6.2 Filling in a sales form 155
6.3 Memorising a sale 159
6.4 Entering a new service item 162

7: RECEIVING PAYMENTS AND MAKING DEPOSITS 164

7.1 Recording customer payments 164

7.2 Making deposits 175

8: ENTERING AND PAYING BILLS 180

8.1 Handling bills in QuickBooks 180
8.2 Using QuickBooks for accounts payable..180
8.3 Entering bills 181
8.4 Memorising bills...184
8.5 Paying bills 186

9: ANALYSING FINANCIAL DATA 191

9.1 Reports and graphs help you to understand your business............191
9.2 Creating QuickReports 192
9.3 Creating and customising preset reports 194
9.4 Saving report settings..204
9.5 Printing reports 208
9.6 Exporting reports to Microsoft Excel...210
9.7 Creating QuickInsight graphs 212

10: SETTING UP STOCK..215

10.1 Turning on the stock control feature 215
10.2 Entering products into stock 216
10.3 Ordering products 217
10.4 Receiving stock and entering the bill 219
10.5 Manually adjusting stock 221
10.6 Stock Valuation 222

11: TRACKING, REPORTING AND PAYING VAT 223

11.1 Overview of VAT in QuickBooks 223
11.2 Setting up VAT 224

11.3 Viewing the VAT Control Account 232
11.4 Paying VAT to HM Revenue and Customs 235
11.5 VAT Reports 238

12: DOING PAYROLL 240

12.1 Overview of payroll tracking 240
12.2 Setting up the payroll 241
12.3 Setting up employee payroll information 243
12.4 Paying employees 253
12.5 Tracking your tax liabilities 260
12.6 Paying employees 263
12.7 Paying payroll taxes 265
12.8 Paying over payroll deductions 266
12.9 Leavers – p45 269
12.10 Processing payroll at year end 271

13: BANKING 273

13.1 Banking 273
13.2 Bank Deposit 283
13.3 Transfer 286
13.4 Bank Reconciliation 287
13.5 Credit Cards 290

14: CUSTOMISING FORMS 297

14.1 About QuickBooks forms 297
14.2 Customising an invoice 297
14.3 Customising an estimate or sales receipt 301
14.4 Customising email for sales forms 302
14.5 Creating A Statement 303

15: USING SALES ORDERS AND ESTIMATES 306

15.1 Creating Estimates (sales orders) 306
15.2 Creating an invoice from an estimate 308
15.3 Delayed charge 308
15.3 Delayed credits 310
15.5 Displaying reports for estimates 312

16: TRACKING TIME 313

16.1 Tracking time 313
16.2 Weekly Timesheet 316
16.3 Invoicing a customer from a timesheet 318
16.4 Single Time Activity 321
16.5 Displaying project reports for time tracking 322

17: USING MULTIPLE CURRENCIES 324

17.1 Turning on multicurrency 324
17.2 Updating the Currency list 325
17.3 Setting up foreign accounts (Customers) 326
17.4 Creating foreign suppliers 328
17.5 Creating a foreign invoice 328
17.6 Entering and paying foreign bills 330
17.7 Exchange rate gain and losses report 333

18: TRACKING FINANCE 335

18.1 Tracking finances 335
18.2 Budgeting 336
18.3 Searching transactions 343

19: APPS 345

19.1 Available Apps...345
19.2 Import Data...347

APPENDIX **351**

INDEX **376**

ABOUT THE AUTHOR **379**

OTHER BOOKS BY THE AUTHOR **380**

How To Start Your Own Bookkeeping Business 380
97 Ways To Market Your Accountancy Business 380
The 21st Century Business Model 380
Cosmic Ordering With Vision Boards..381
Make The Most of Your Money 381
Money Maths With Boogles: Workbook 1: Getting To Know Your Numbers: 5-6 yrs...381

1: Getting Started

> *Summary of what is in this chapter:*
> 1.1 Introducing QuickBooks
> 1.2 Free trial
> 1.3 System Requirements
> 1.4 Getting around in QuickBooks
> 1.5 All the accounting you need to know
> 1.6 Using Lists
> 1.7 Using Registers
> 1.8 Getting around in QuickBooks
> 1.9 Help!
> 1.10 Accounting Terminology

1.1 Introducing QuickBooks

This handbook is to help you get to grips with QuickBooks Online 2014 edition. If you are already familiar with the desktop versions – QuickBooks Pro, QuickBooks Premier or QuickBooks Premier Accountant, then making the transition to online shouldn't be too painful. Be aware that some features are hidden, some aren't quite where you'd expect them to be and some don't exist at all (yet). It's all a work in progress, and the information and screen shots included in this book are correct as at May 2014 at the time of going to print.

Online systems are more fluid than desktop releases, and changes can be made overnight and ongoing without the need for anyone to 'upgrade' or 'get the latest version'. By the time you get to the end of this handbook, you'll have a very good idea of all that QuickBooks Online can do, and will be familiar with the most common tasks that users perform. It's written with the non-financial manager in mind. But if you are a bookkeeper or an accountant – then this should still provide useful material for you.

If you are the owner-manager, whether it's an SME (small-medium sized enterprise) or you are currently a solopreneur – if you have any intention to use QuickBooks Online at all... take this book, read it from cover to cover & get a free trial set up - visit our site for our latest special offers on the software: http://www.booglesltd.com/QuickBooks_Online.html, and work with me through the modules, so that you 'use the system' and 'read the manual' at the same time. QuickBooks is a tool you can use to make your bookkeeping task much easier. It is well named in that it certainly DOES make doing the books *quick*! So whether you need to invoice your customers, send them out a reminder statement, keep track of and pay your supplier bills, track your stock or just run a few reports to see how well your business is doing... QuickBooks has the solution for you. I've (personally) been an avid user of the software for over ten years, and have been a QuickBooks Pro Advisor for most of those years. I've ran many training courses on this software, (and other accounting systems) and I have to say that it is one of the easier and 'more intuitive' types that I've (personally) come across. I hope after the end of this book, that you'll be a raving fan and happy user too.

1.2 Free Trial

To make this more 'hands on' I'd suggest you get a free trial of the software (if you haven't already). For this, you'll need access to the internet. For the latest special Boogles (free) offers on this software, see:
http://www.booglesltd.com/QuickBooks_Online.html

1.3 System Requirements

One of the biggest advantages of QuickBooks Online (compared to the desktop versions) is that you can access you accounts from anywhere in the world (as long as you have an internet connection), and it doesn't matter whether you have a PC or a MAC (which was an issue before).
http://www.intuit.co.uk/QuickBooks- accounting- software.jsp

Three Options
There is Simple Start, Essentials and Plus. The most popular option is the middle option – the Online Essentials.

1.4 Getting around in QuickBooks

To log into QuickBooks, go to: https://uk.qbo.intuit.com
Enter the user name (often an email) and password which you've set up.

QuickBooks Online Help

User name: _____

Password: _____

Use this book by either reading cover to cover from start to end, or look in the index at the back and jump to the part that you need.

1.5 All the accounting you need to know

QuickBooks doesn't require you to know debits and credits or the accounting equation, trigonometry or high-tech maths ... or anything like that (that's the good news).

Throughout this book we'll be using the example of Megzina Ltd, a property maintenance company. When you log in, you'll see this as the home page.

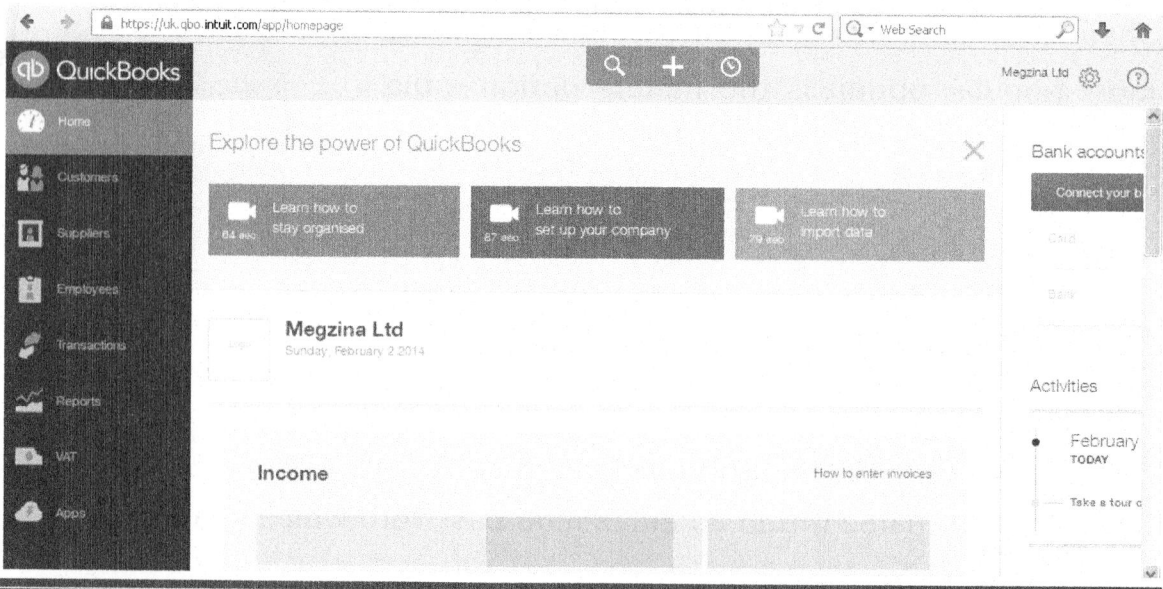

You record most of your daily business transactions on a QuickBooks form, which looks just like a paper form. Below is an example of the form to use when you want to record an expense. The form is intuitive – you already know how to fill in a form. QuickBooks, simply does the accounting for you in the background. The drop-down menu options make it easy for you to click and choose.

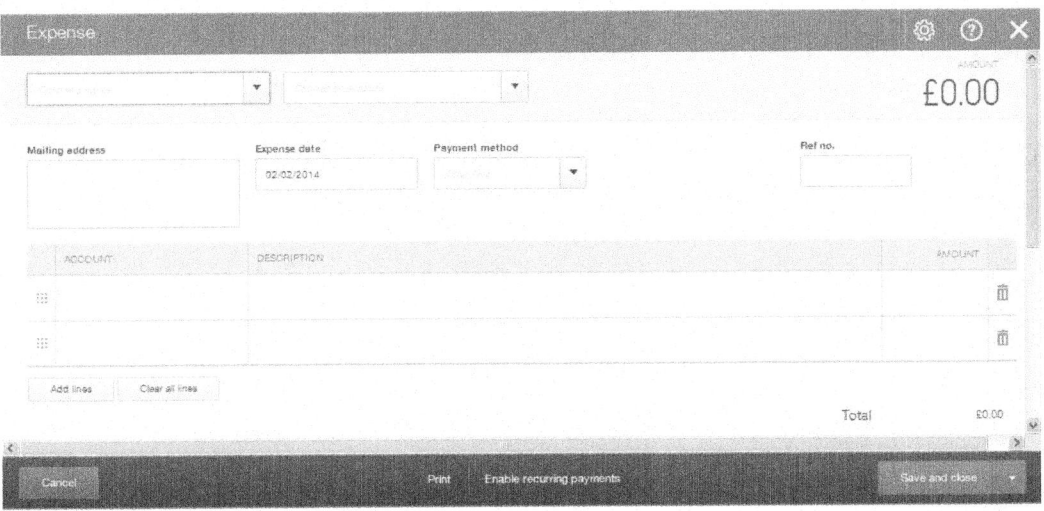

When you fill out the invoice form, and you select a customer name from the Customer list, QuickBooks not only fills in the name, email, billing address, terms & VAT. Here is an example of the Customer Invoice form:

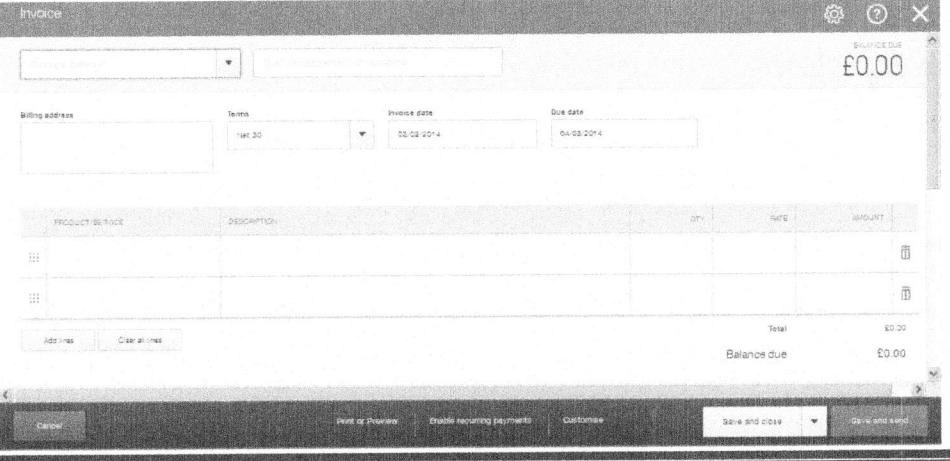

1.6 Using Lists

The list is another basic QuickBooks feature. You fill in most QuickBooks forms by selecting entries from a list. QuickBooks has lists where you can store information about suppliers, customers, employees, terms, classes, items or services you sell etc., Lists can save you time as you just choose the correct entry from the drop down menu, which helps you to enter information consistently and correctly.

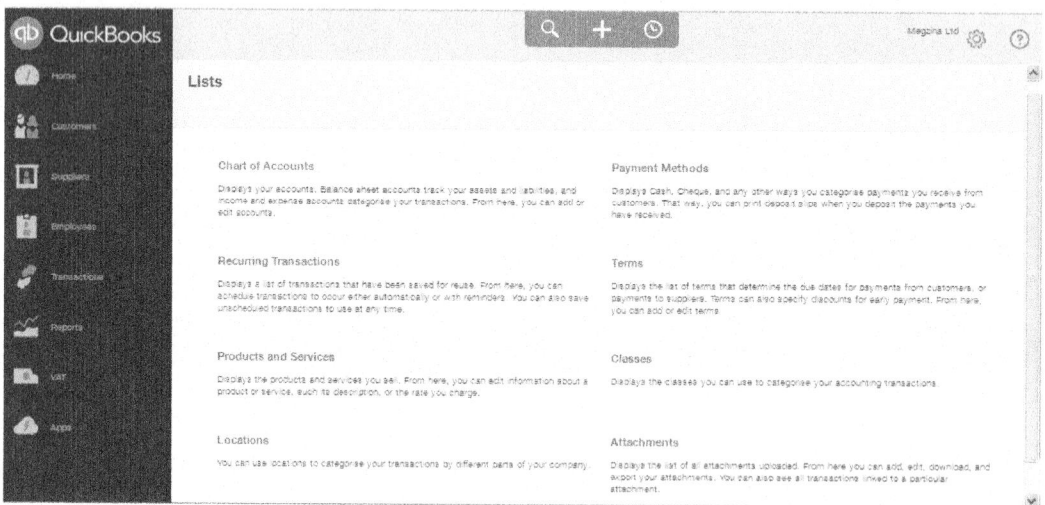

1.7 Using Registers

In addition to forms and lists, you'll also work with registers in QuickBooks. Just as you can use your bank statement to see a record of all the transactions in your current account i.e. cheques you've written, direct debits, standing orders, online bank payments, other withdrawals you've made from your account, and deposits – a QuickBooks register contains a record of all the activity in one account. Almost every QuickBooks account has its own register. Here is an example of the register for an Accounts Receivable account:

1.8 Getting around in QuickBooks

As soon as you log into the system, and land on the home page, click on the cog / wheel in the top right hand corner of the page - which will open up further options to explore. In addition, there is the navigation menu to the left hand side.

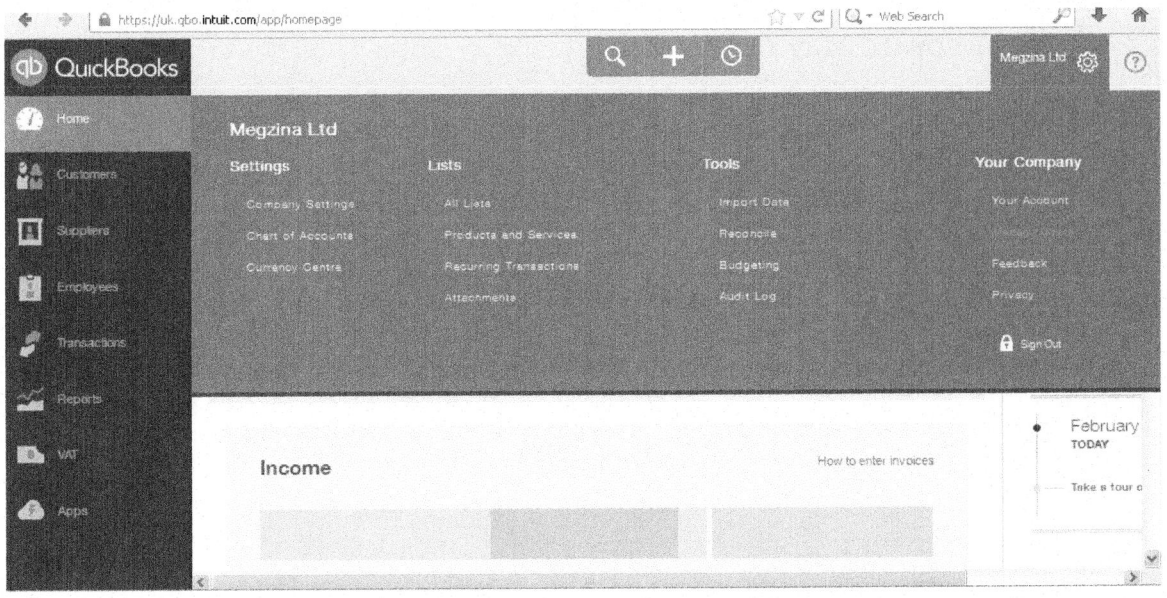

Whenever you click on the '+' icon, this too opens up further options.

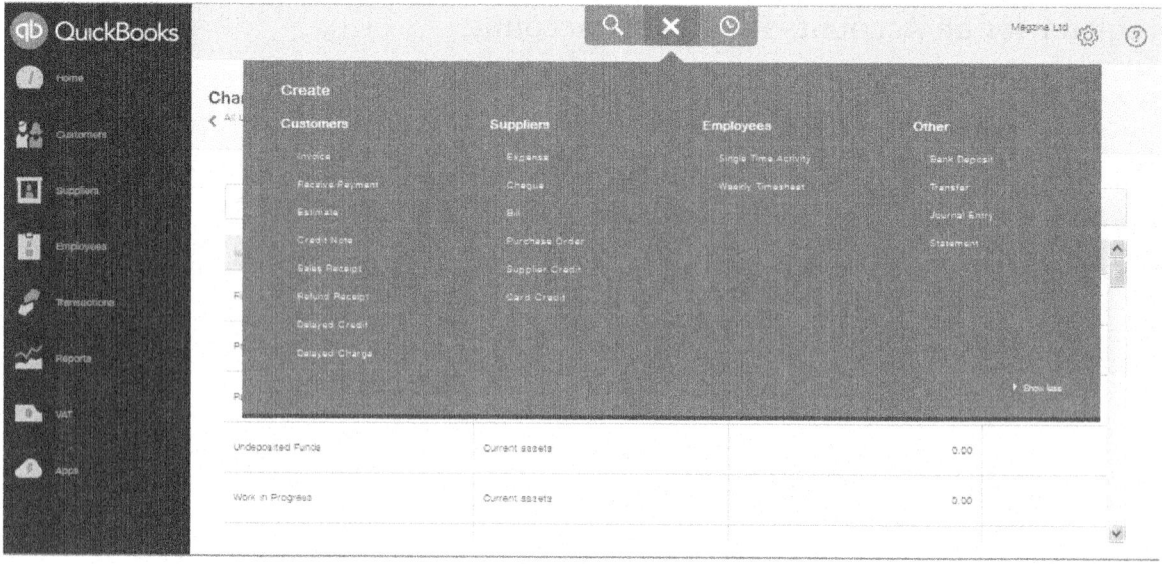

1.9 Help!

If you're new to QuickBooks, then as soon as you log in, you'll see some (very short) videos which you can watch to help you to get started.
- Learn how to stay organised
- Learn how to set up your company
- Learn how to import data

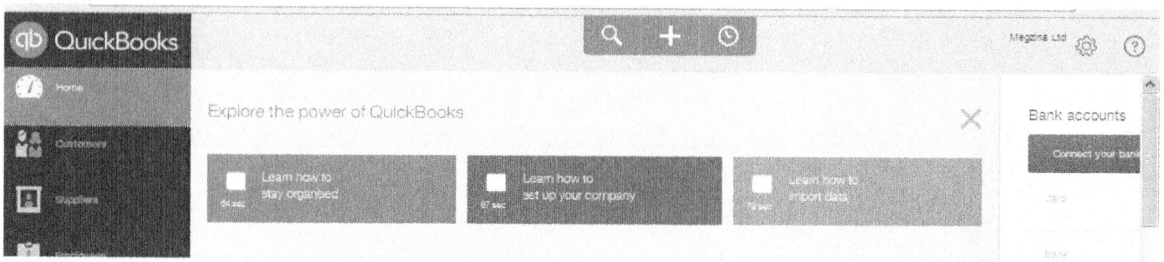

In addition, in the top left hand corner – on whatever page you are on, if you see the '?' icon, you can click on this to get help.

Clicking on the icon, expands the menu option and you can type your question in to search bar. QuickBooks will find the best answer for your question.

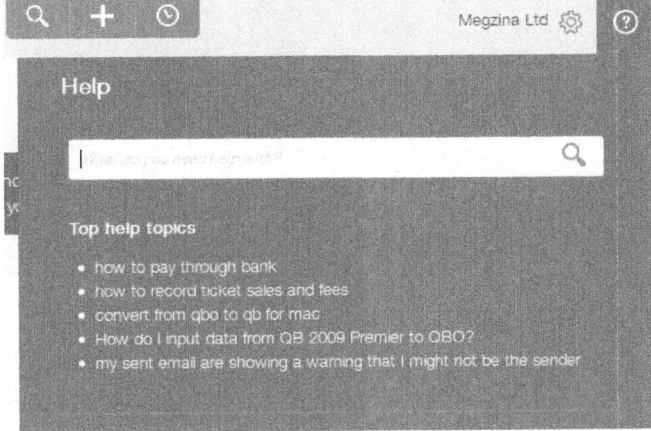

1.10 Accounting Terminology

QuickBooks uses some accounting terms, which are handy to know.

Chart of Accounts
When you keep books for a company, you need to track where the money (income) comes from, where you put it, what your expenses are for, and

what you use to pay them. You track this flow of money through a list of accounts called the chart of accounts.

To display the chart of accounts

1. From the COG (top right hand corner of the screen), click once to display further options.
2. Under 'Settings' choose *Chart of Accounts*, and click once.

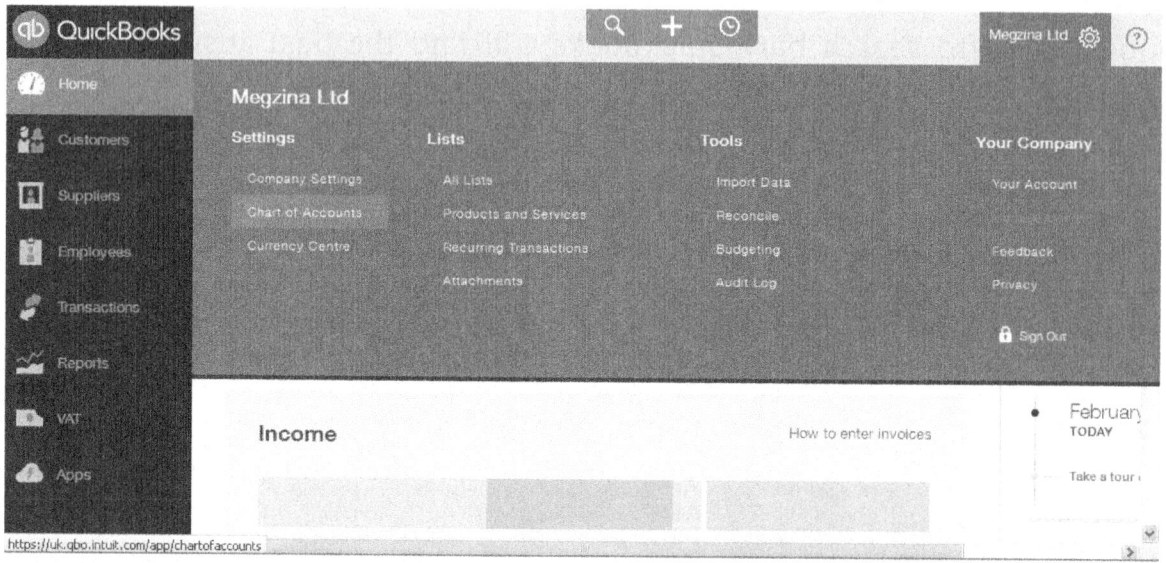

The chart of accounts is then displayed. The system comes with a set of accounts already pre-populated. Notice that the list is sorted by TYPE. The *Current Assets* are displayed first, followed by the *Tangible Assets*, and then *Equity* and *Income, Cost of Sales, Expenses* etc.,

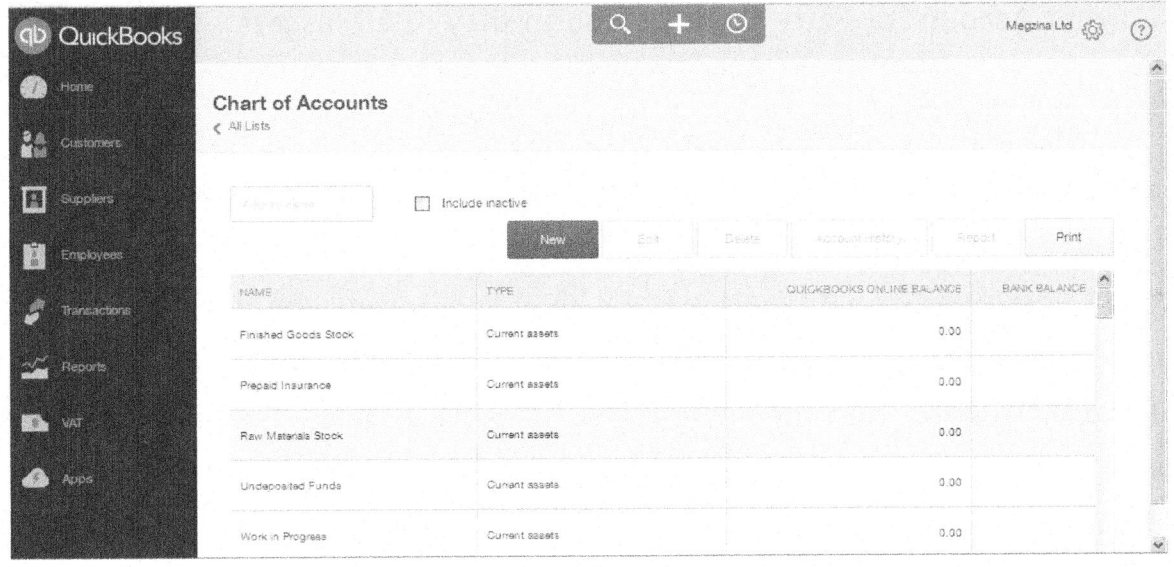

About Assets, Liabilities & Equity

Assets

Assets include both what you have e.g. *Bank, Petty Cash, Stock, Equipment* and what other people owe you e.g. *Prepayments, Debtors*. The money that people (i.e. your customers) owe you is called your *Accounts Receivable*, or *A/R* for short. *Fixed Assets* (such as equipment, furniture or vehicles) are items which are used IN the business to RUN the business. They're less 'fluid' i.e. readily convertible into cash (unlike *Current Assets*). *Undeposited funds* are money that you've received from your customer, but not yet deposited into the bank.

When adding new items to the Chart of Accounts (COA), you need to be aware of the type of item it is. But QuickBooks does provide examples. Be aware, that when adding a new 'bank' account – e.g. Savings Account,

Current Account or Petty Cash (although they're all 'assets', in the COA's they're classed as "bank" type accounts.

Even within 'asset' types, there are still further distinctions which can be made. A 'Current' Asset is deemed as something about to be turned into Cash within 12 months e.g. *Stock*. A *Non-Current Asset* is something which won't be turned into cash within 12 months. E.g. a *License* or a *Security Deposit*. And then there are *'Tangible Assets'* – I.e. things which you can touch… an example of a *'Tangible Fixed Asset'* is *Premises* (building), and an *'Intangible Asset'* could be *Stocks/Shares Investments*, or *Goodwill*.

Liabilities

Liabilities are what your company owes to other people. They money you owe for unpaid bills is your *Accounts Payable* or *A/P* for short. QuickBooks uses an accounts payable account to track the money you owe to different people for bills. A liability can be a formal loan, an unpaid bill or taxes you owe to the government.

Even within 'liability' types, there are still further distinctions which can be made. A 'Current' Liability is deemed as something due to be paid within 12 months e.g. *Tax & National Insurance*. Other examples on the system include *insurance payable, line of credit, loan payable, and short term borrowings*. And then there is *Credit Card* – which is a current liability, but in a separate category on the system. A *Non-Current Liability* is something which isn't due to be paid within 12 months. E.g. a *long term borrowings* or *Shareholder notes payable*.

Equity

Equity is the difference between what you have (your assets) and what you owe (your liabilities):

Equity = Assets – Liabilities

If you sold all of your assets today, and paid off your liabilities using the money received from the sale of your assets, the money you'd have left would be your equity. Your equity reflects the health of your business, since it is the amount of money left after you satisfy all your debts. Equity comes from three sources:

1. Money invested in the company by its owners
2. Net profit from operating the business during the current accounting period
3. Retained earnings – net profits from earlier periods that haven't been distributed to the owners

You as the owners can also take money out of the business – this withdrawal is called owners drawings, which reduces the business equity. On the system there are many sub-accounts of Equity including *called up share capital, ordinary shares, owners equity, paid-in capital or surplus, preference shares, partners equity.*

If you run a *Balance Sheet* report – you can check the value of the business equity.

Cash vs Accrual Bookkeeping

When you begin your business, you should decide which bookkeeping method to use. The bookkeeping method determines how you report income and expenses on your tax forms. Check with your accountant or HMRC before choosing a bookkeeping method for tax purposes. The key is consistency. Choose one and be consistent.

Cash basis

Many small businesses record income when they receive the money and expenses when they pay the bills. This method is known as bookkeeping on a cash basis. If you've been recording the deposits of your customer payments but have not been including the money customers owe as part of your income, you've been using the cash basis. In the same way, if you've been tracking expenses at the time you pay them and not at the time when you first receive the bills – you've been using the cash basis.

Accrual basis

With the accrual basis of bookkeeping – you record the income at the time the invoice is sent, not at the time you receive the payment. Similarly, you enter expenses when you receive the bill – not when you pay for it.

Most accountants feel that the accrual method gives you a truer picture of your business finances because EVERYTHING is being taken into account.

How your bookkeeping method affects QuickBooks

When you use the cash or accrual method, you enter transactions the same way into QuickBooks.

QuickBooks is automatically set up to do your reports on an accrual basis, i.e. it shows income on a profit and loss statement for invoices as soon as you enter them, even if the customer hasn't paid yet. It shows expenses, even if they're unpaid.

You can see any report (except transaction reports) on a cash basis by changing the reporting preference. From the left hand menu, chose *Reports*, and then choose the report e.g. *Profit and Loss account*. Choose *customise*.

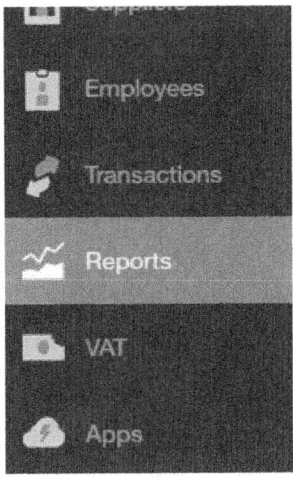

Under the accounting method, you can choose between Accrual and Cash.

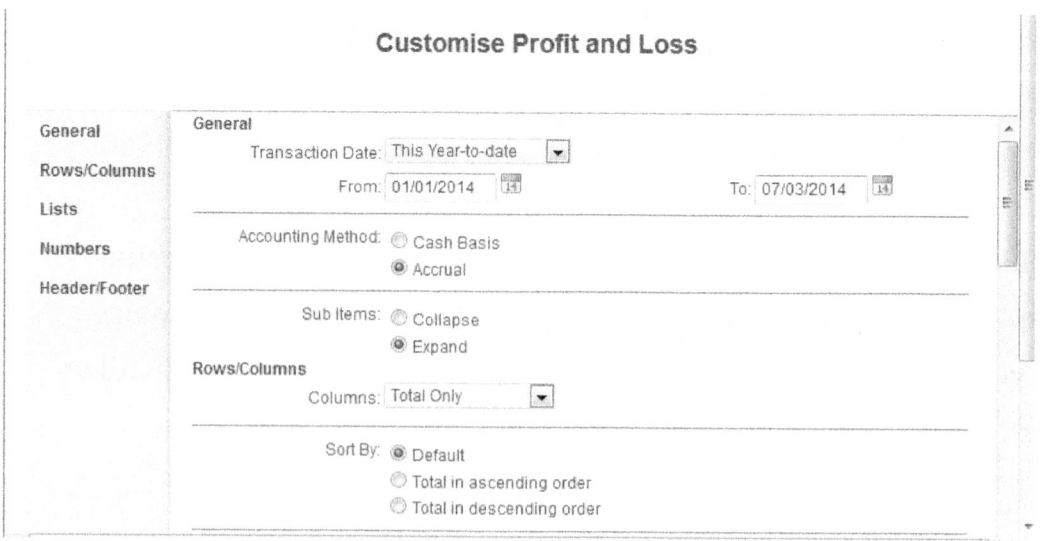

Measuring Business Profitability

Two of the most important reports for measuring the profitability of your business are the balance sheet and the profit and loss statement (also called an income statement). These are the reports most often requested by accountants and financial advisors (e.g. your bank manager may request both of these reports when applying for a loan).

The balance sheet

The balance sheet is a financial snapshot of your company on one date it's like an X-ray. It shows:

- What you have (assets)
- What people owe you (accounts receivable)
- What your business owes to other people (liabilities and accounts payable)
- The net worth of your business (equity)

To run a balance sheet report:

1. From the Reports menu, choose run *Balance Sheet.*

The profit and loss statement

A profit and loss statement, also called an income statement, shows your income, expenses, and net profit or loss (equal to income minus expenses). The QuickBooks profit and loss statement summarises the revenue and expenses of your business by category (first income, then expenses).

To run the profit and loss report:

1. From the Reports menu, choose run *Profit and Loss account.*

The statement of cash flows

Another report that the accountant may be interested in is the statement of cash flows report. A statement of cash flows shows your receipts and payments during a specific accounting period.

To run the statement of cash flows report:

1. From the Reports menu, choose from the dropdown menu *Statement of Cash Flows.*

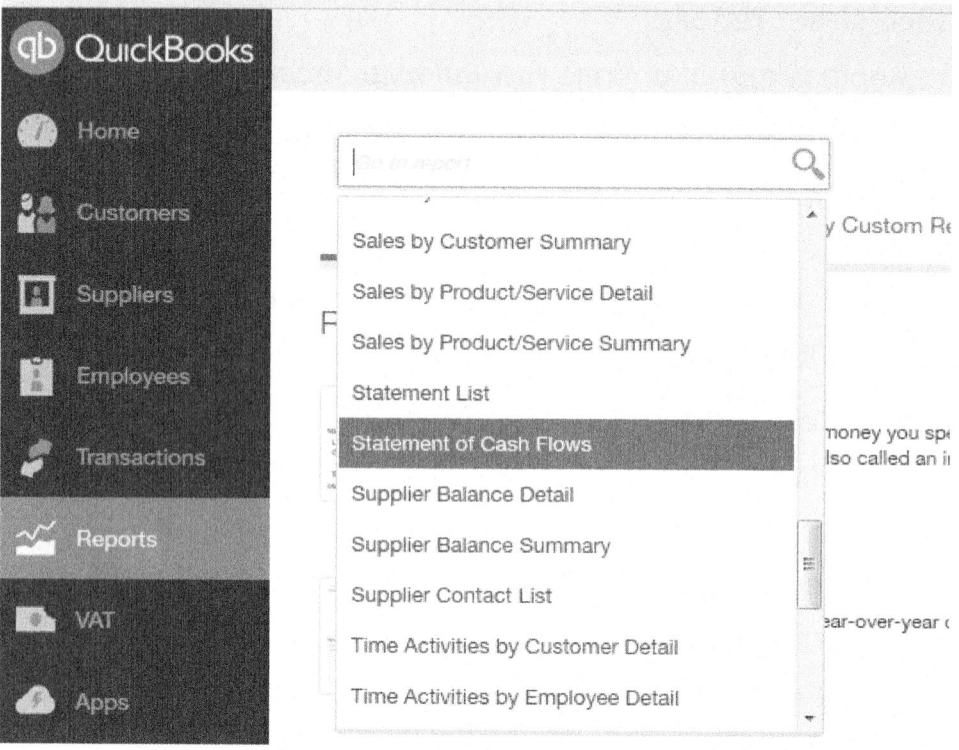

Exiting QuickBooks

QuickBooks online saves your data as you go along. It will automatically log you off the system after a period of inactivity.

To exit QuickBooks:

- From the top right hand corner, click on the cog icon and then click *Sign Out*.

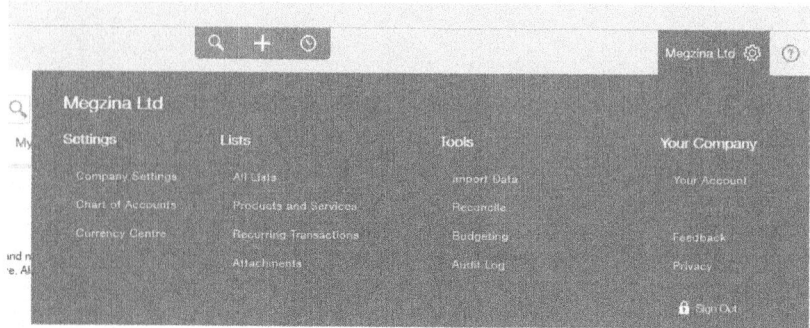

2: Setting up QuickBooks

> *Summary of what is in this chapter:*
> 2.1 Creating a QuickBooks Company
> 2.2 Entering company information
> 2.3 Chart of Accounts
> 2.4 Setting up QuickBooks preferences
> 2.5 Setting up income accounts
> 2.6 *Entering* opening balances
> 2.7 Setting up payroll
> 2.8 Getting help whilst using QuickBooks

2.1 Creating a QuickBooks Company

A QuickBooks company contains all the financial records for a single business. Before you can use QuickBooks, you need to tell QuickBooks about your company so that it can create a proper company profile. If you've been using the desktop version of QuickBooks, or have existing data from another system e.g. Sage desktop and want to transfer data onto the system, QuickBooks have a solution for you to be able to do this. Go to www.MoveMyBooks.co.uk to find out more.

How many companies should you set up?
If you run more than one business, each 'business' needs its own set of accounts so it's usually best to set up a separate QuickBooks company for each. If you are a sole trader, but under your name, operate different

businesses (and sell different things), then you could put everything under your name, and use different 'classes' to track each business separately – more on setting up classes this later.

Quickstart Helpful Videos

As you log in, on the Home page, there are three short videos to watch which guide you through the process of setting up your business on QuickBooks.

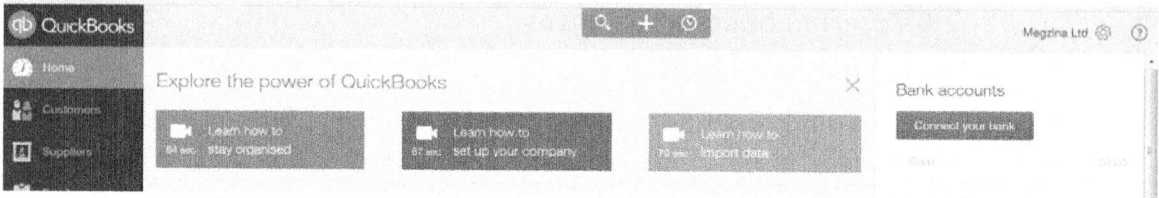

There are three videos:
- Learn how to stay organised;
- Learn how to set up your company;
- Learn how to import data.

2.2 Entering company information

To enter your company information onto the system, go to the top right hand corner cog/wheel picture, and under company name click *company settings*.

QuickBooks Online Help

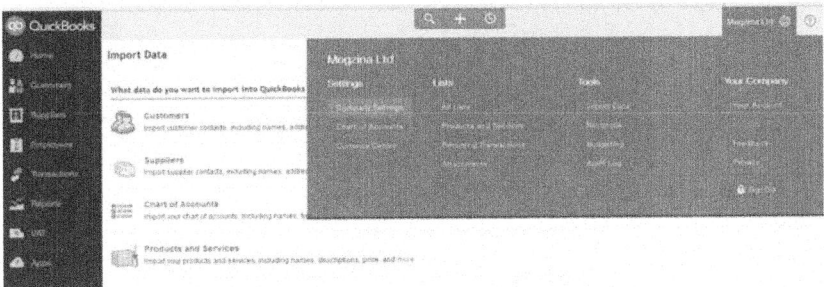

This screen will then pop up.

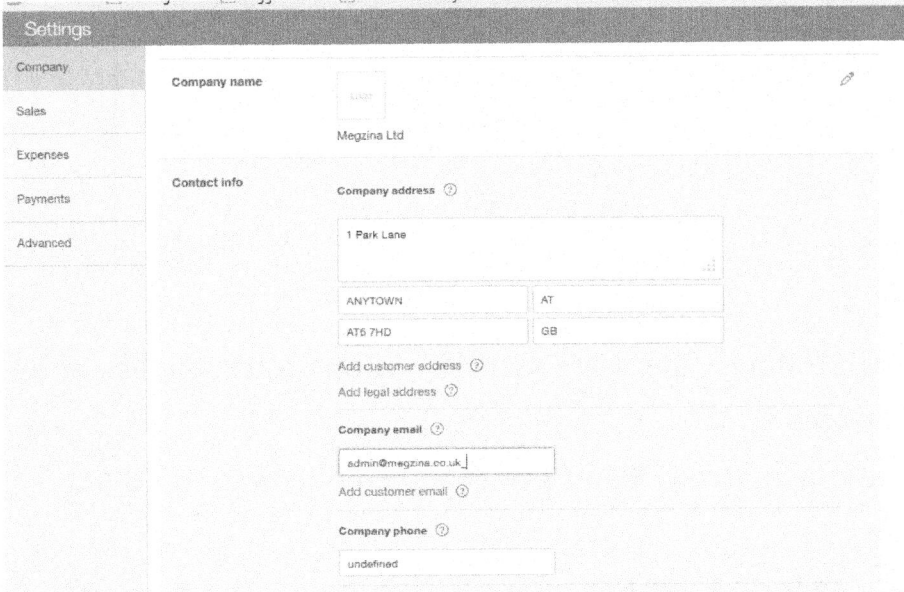

Click on the pen icon to change/update any of the information.

Company Name

1 Company name – click on the edit (pen) icon.

2 Click *Customise logo.*

3 Click *upload logo.*

4 Choose the location of where your logo can be found.

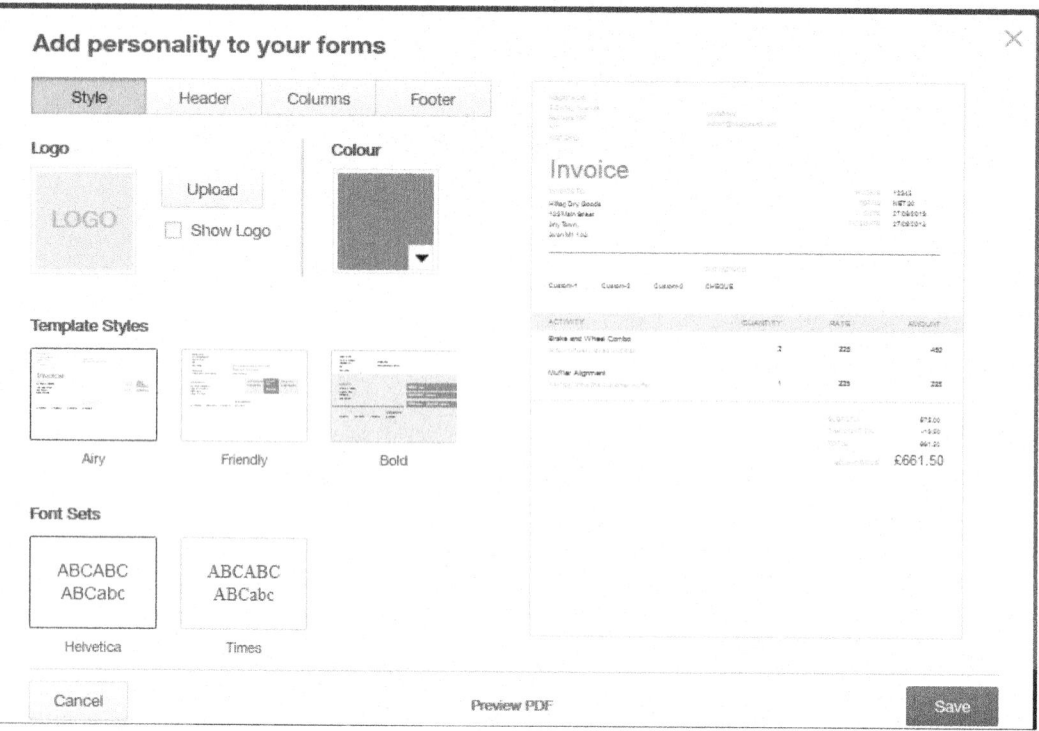

5 On the page which follows, there are further options to customise your forms – *Invoice Format*.

6 Colour – click the down arrow ▼ and select the colour that you'd like your invoices to be.

7 Template Styles – choose from Any, Friendly and Bold – the invoice preview on the right side will change.

8 Font Sets – choose from Helvetica and Times.

9 This is the style options set. Next, click on *Header* to customise it.

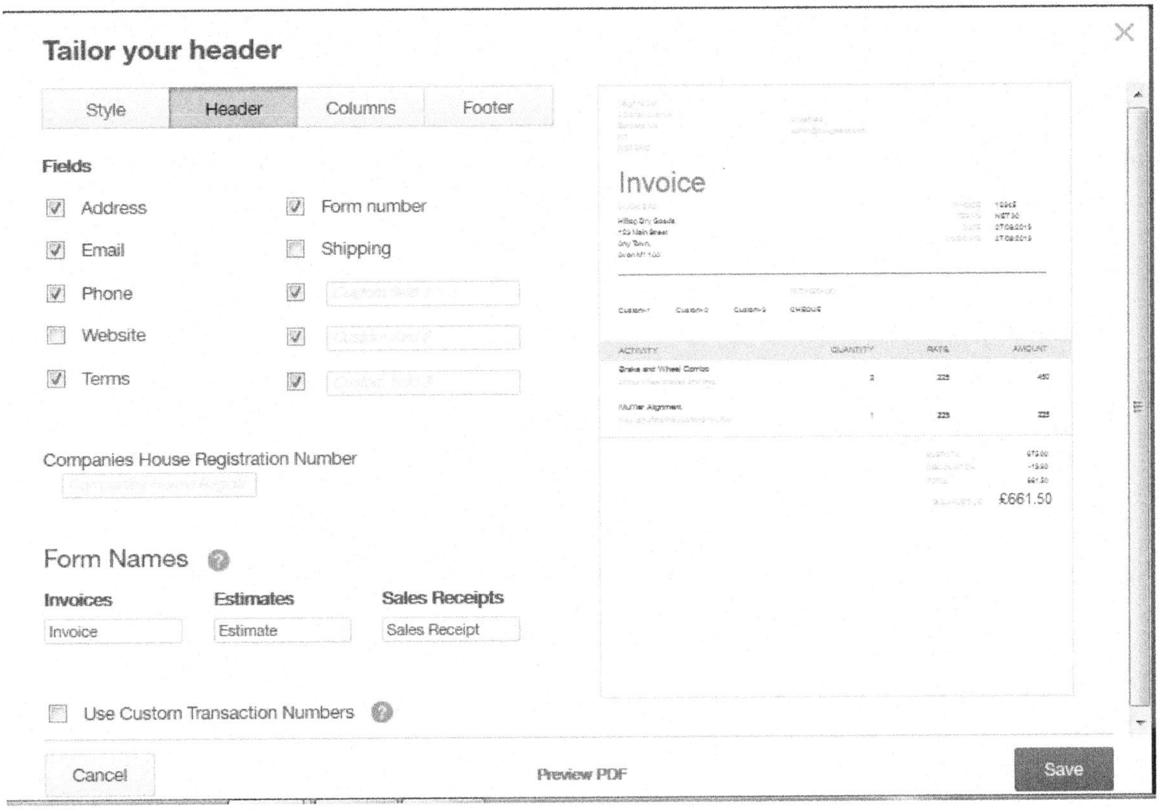

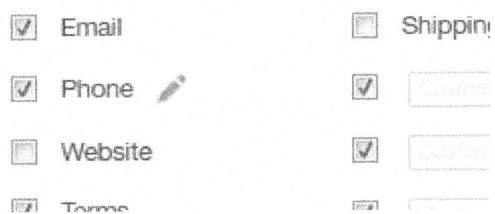

10 If you don't want your Website address to appear on your invoices, untick the box, and it won't appear.

11 If you want to amend any of the Fields, e.g. Phone, hover the mouse over the word phone, and the pen icon will appear.

Click on the pen and make your amendments.

12 The screen will pop up – type in the phone number of your business and click the blue *Save* button.

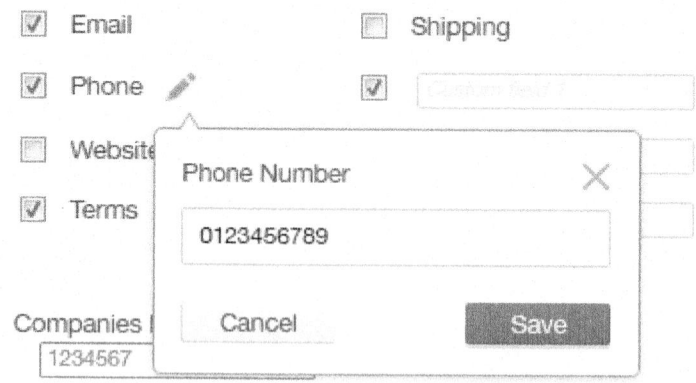

13 If you want to change the names of the forms (Invoices, Estimates, Sales Receipts) as given by QuickBooks, then you can, by typing in the preferred name in the box.

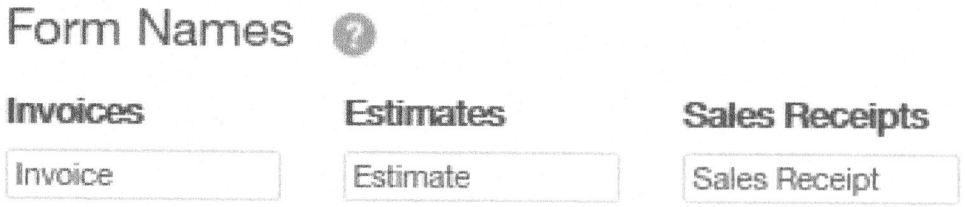

14 If you are ever in doubt about what something means, and there is the blue '?' icon, then you can click on the question mark, and an explanation will pop up on the screen.

15 Use custom transaction numbers – select this if you want to create your own custom numbers for your sales form. Or, leave it cleared and QuickBooks will assign the numbers for you.

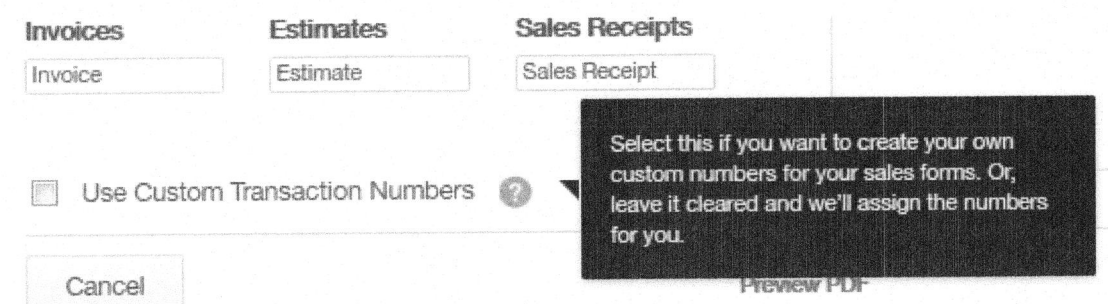

16 Next, click on *Columns* to customise them.

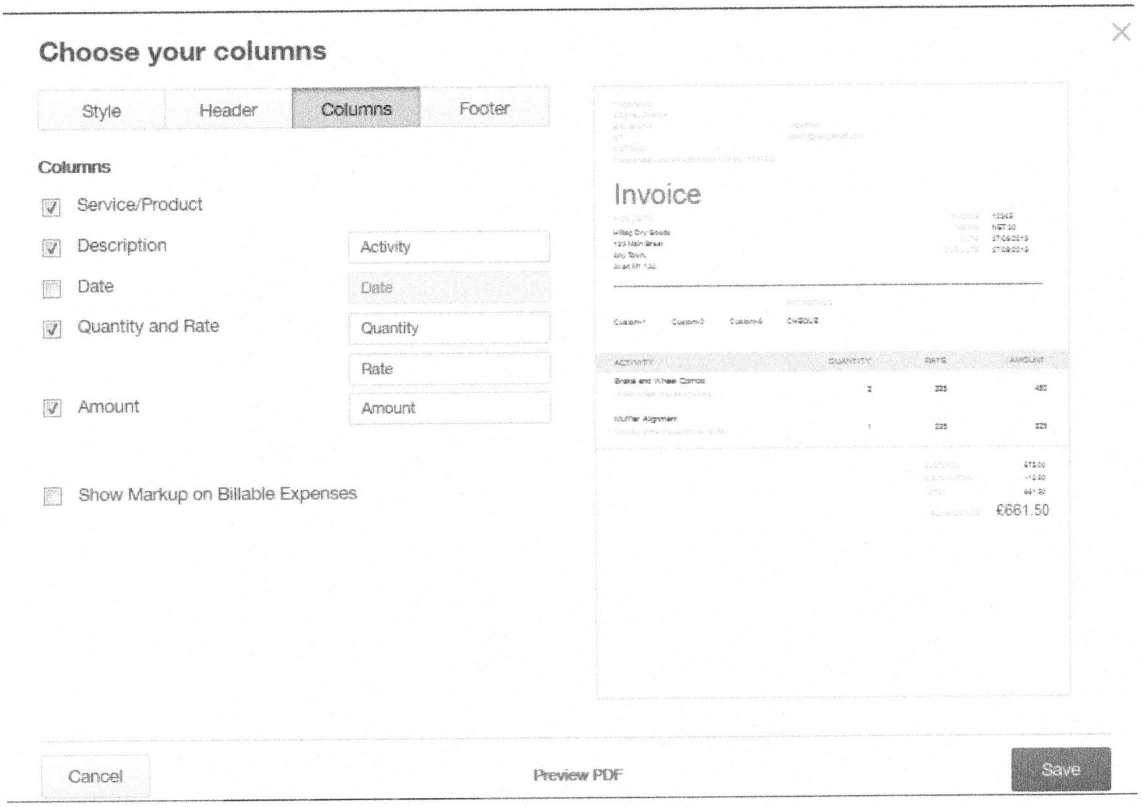

17 If you want to change the description of any items on the invoice, edit the description in the box by typing straight into the box.

18 Next, click on *Footer* to customise it.

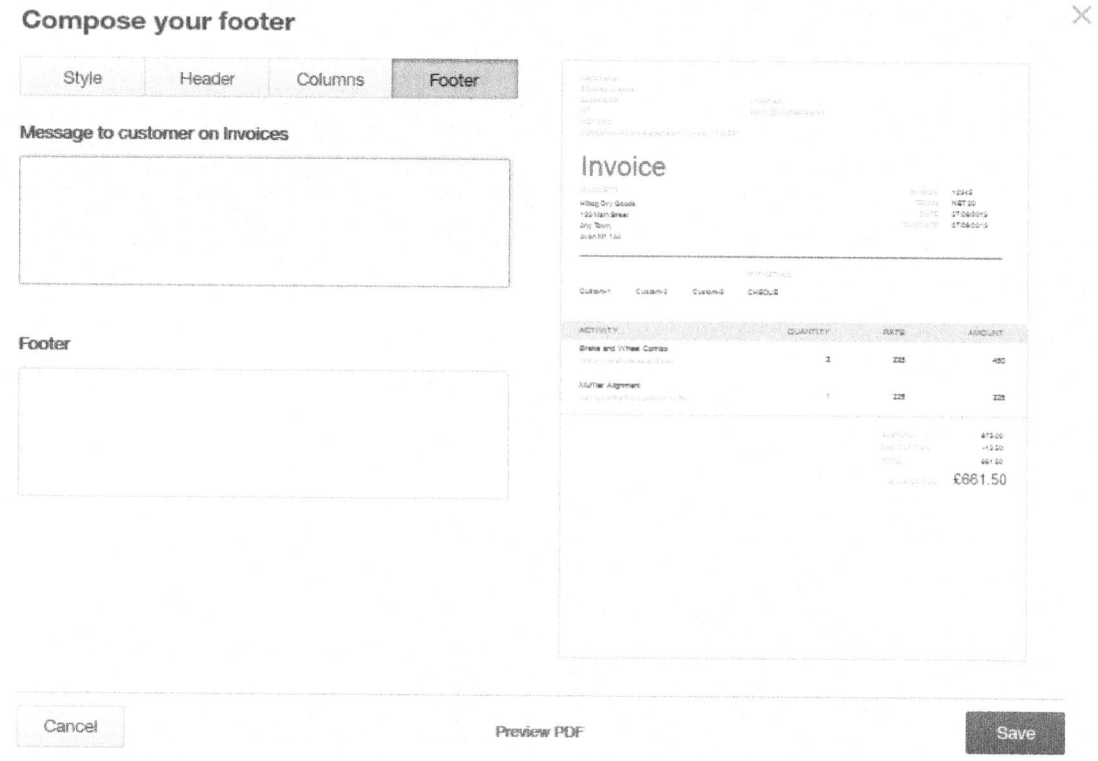

19 You can type any message that you want to appear on your Invoice, straight into the box. An example of a message might be 'Thank you for your business' or 'Please make cheques payable to Megzina Ltd, or if paying online, Sort: 00-00-00, Account No: 87654321.'

20 As you do this, you'll see the Invoice change.

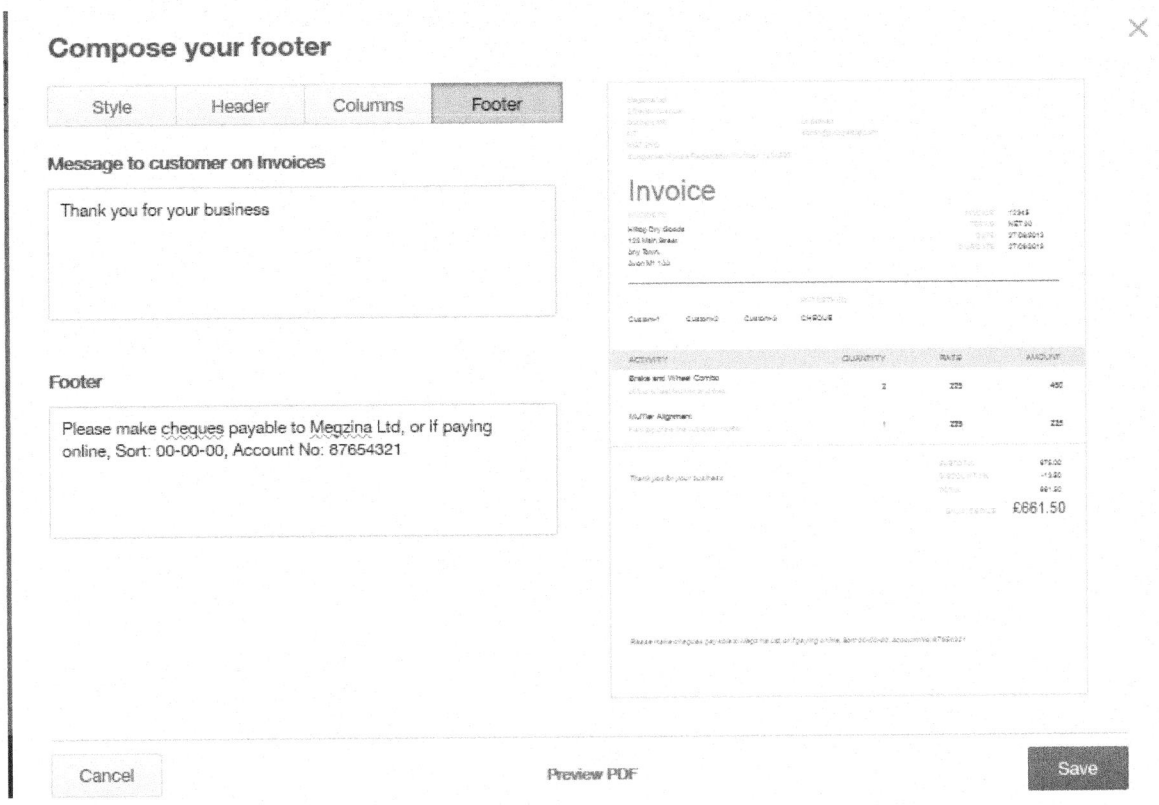

21 Once you are happy with the amendments, click *save*.

This will take you back to the contact page. To amend the company's address click on the pen icon.

Contact Info

1 Contact info – click on the *edit* (pen) icon.

2 Add the customer address (if there is one). Note this is the address where customers contact you or send payments. It's shown on sales forms. If left blank, the company address is used.

3 Add the legal address (if there is one). Note this is the address used for filing taxes. If left blank, the company address is used.

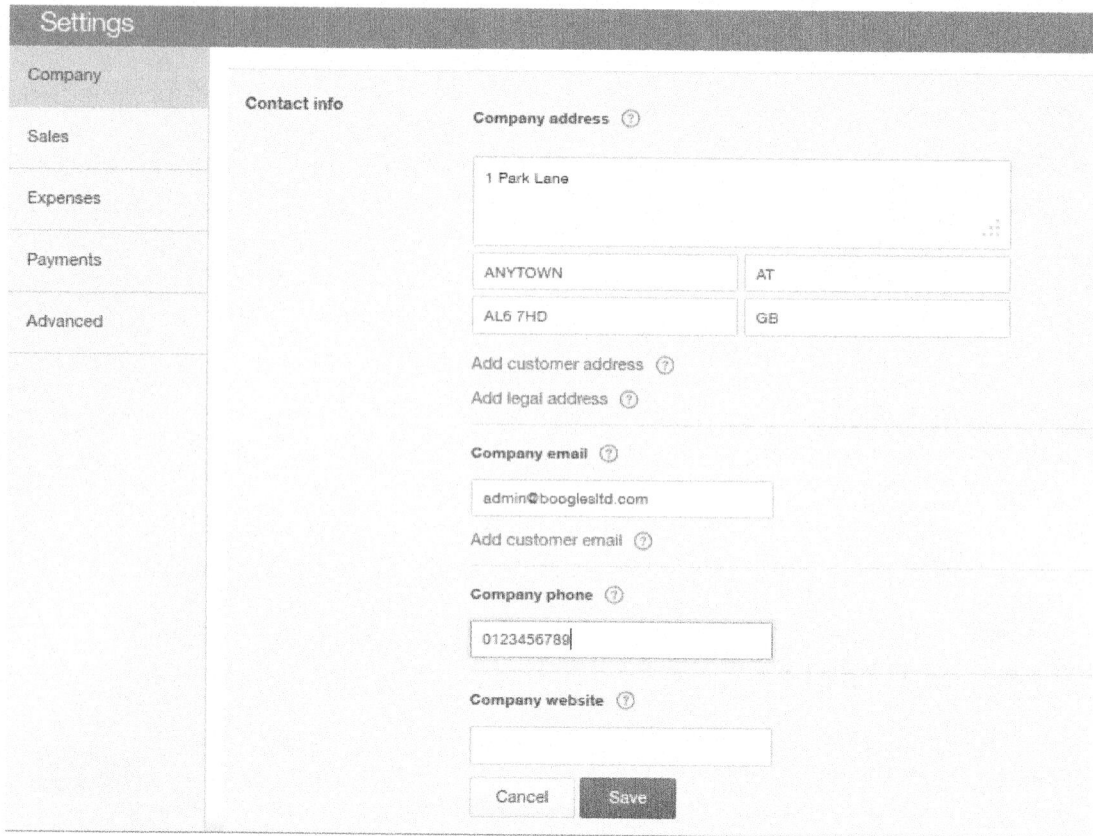

4 Amend the company email if necessary.

5 Add customer email – this is the email where customers can contact you. If left blank, company email is used.

6 Add company website – this is shown on sales forms.

7 Click *Save*.

This will take you back to the contact page. To amend accounting method click on the pen icon.

Accounting Method

1 Accounting Method – click on the *edit* (pen) icon

QuickBooks Online Help

2 Select one of the options in the dropdown box – either accrual or cash. Choose Accrual to report income when you bill a customer; choose Cash to report income when you receive payment from a customer. If you're not sure, consult your accountant or bookkeeper. If you are looking for bookkeeping help, take a look at www.FindMeABookkeeper.com.

3 Click *save.*

This will take you back to the contact page. To amend the Companies House Registration number click on the pen icon.

Companies House Registration Number

1 Companies House Registration number – click on the *edit* (pen) icon.
2 Type in the number.
3 Click *save.*

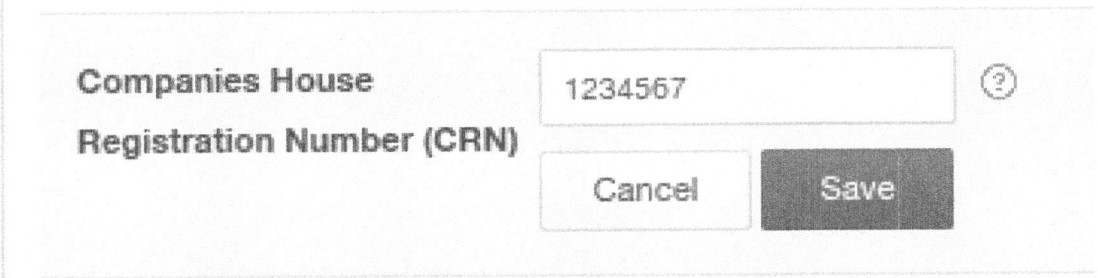

This will take you back to the contact page. To amend the Categories click on the pen icon.

Categories

1 Categories – click on the *edit* (pen) icon
2 Tick, to switch on, if you want to track classes or track locations. Track Classes - adds a Class field on forms so you can assign transactions to

different segments like departments, locations, and product lines. Track Locations - adds a Location field on forms so you can assign transactions to different locations like stores, sales regions, and counties.

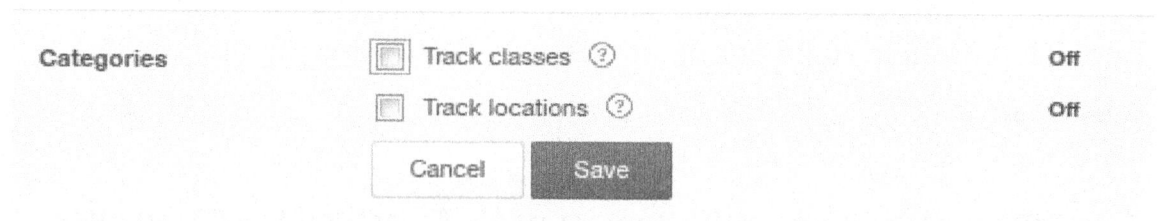

3 If Tracking classes is ticked on, there's a further two options. Firstly, if you want QuickBooks to warn you every time you enter a transaction which isn't assigned a class, then tick the box. Secondly, you can assign classes as one to entire transaction OR one to each row in a transaction. If you are likely to enter items e.g. a bill (or an invoice) which is likely to be split over more than one class – go for the second option, and allocate a class to each row.

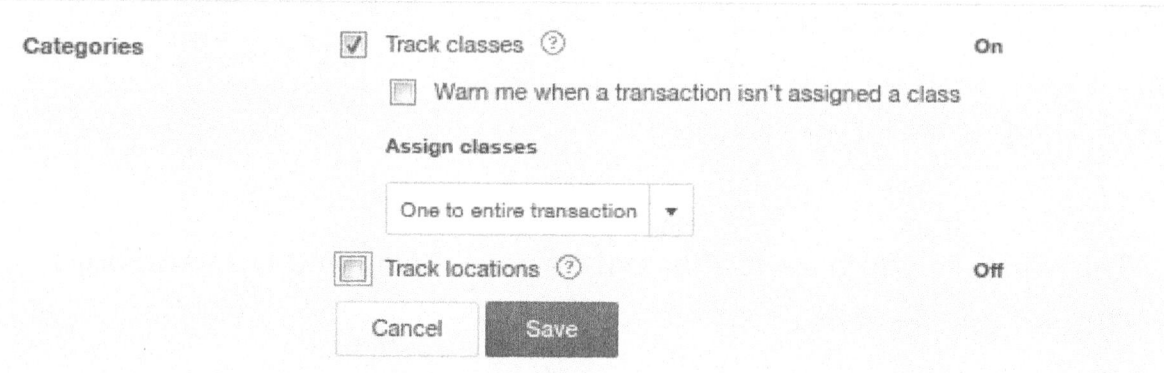

4 Click *save*.

This will take you back to the contact page. The Language is set to English and QuickBooks doesn't give you the option to amend it.

To amend the Currency click on the pen icon

Currency

1 Currency – click on the *edit* (pen) icon.

2 Click on the drop down box to reveal the list of currencies available. 3 Choose your currency and click *save*.

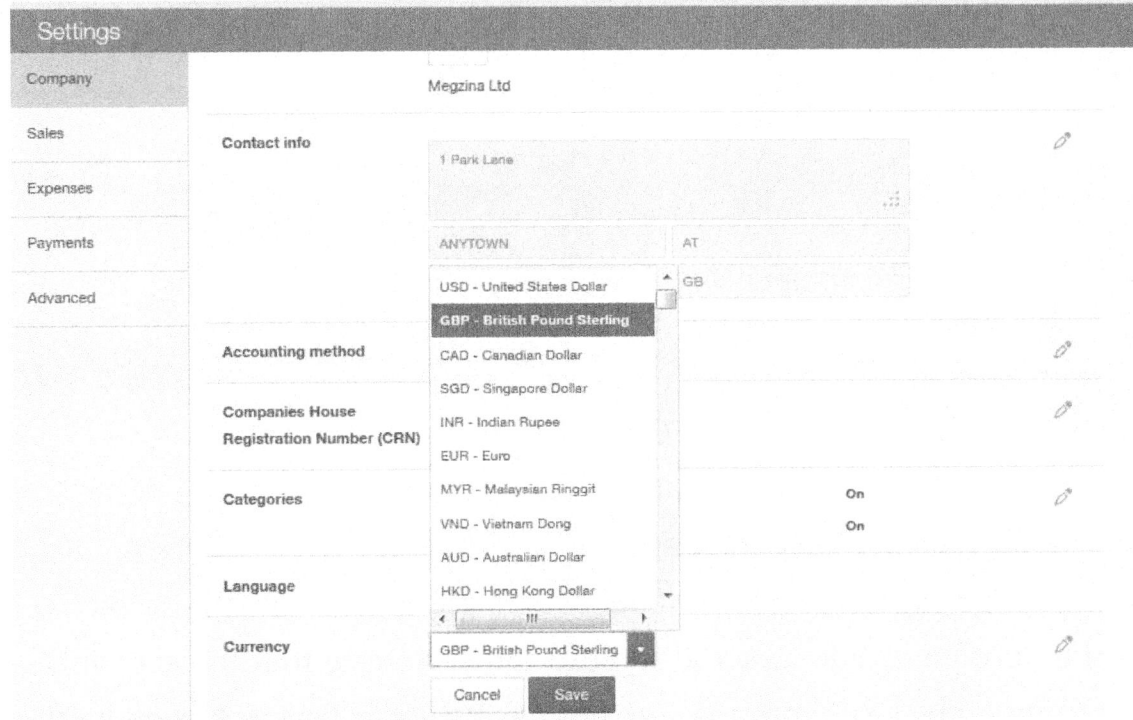

This will take you back to the contact page.

Click DONE in the bottom right-hand corner of the page.

2.3 Chart of Accounts

The chart of accounts lists balance sheet accounts, income accounts, and expense accounts. QuickBooks comes with the accounts already set up for you, but you can amend it. To get to the chart of accounts, click the cog /wheel in the top right hand corner of the screen, and under Settings, choose *Chart of Accounts.*

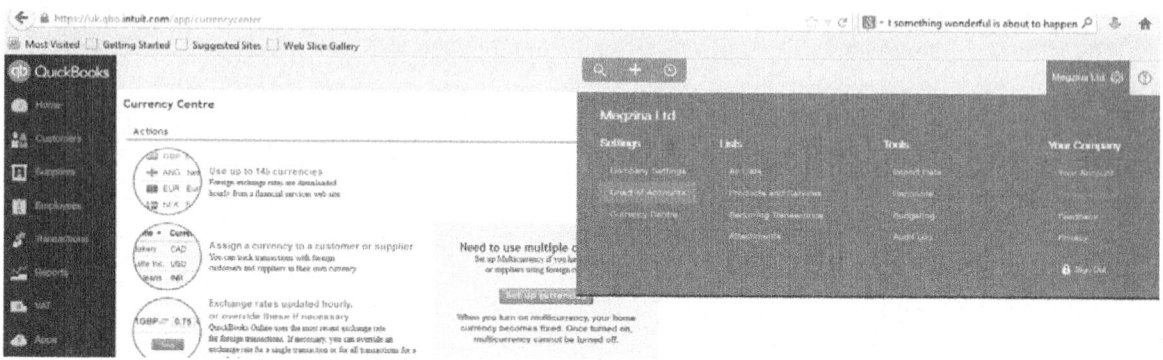

To amend the Chart of Accounts

1 Familiarise yourself which what accounts are there – use the scroll bar on the right hand side to scroll right to the end. Note that the accounts are arranged by TYPE with the Current Assets listed first, followed by the Tangible Assets.... right through to Other Expenses.

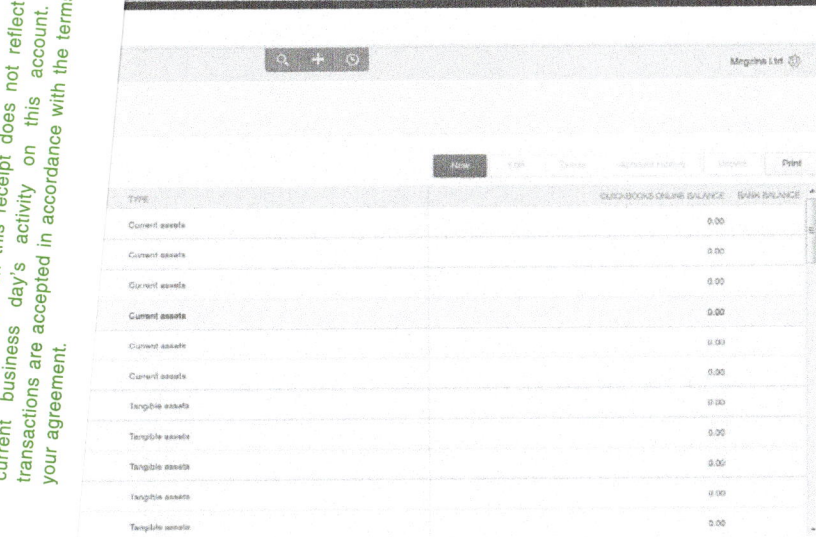

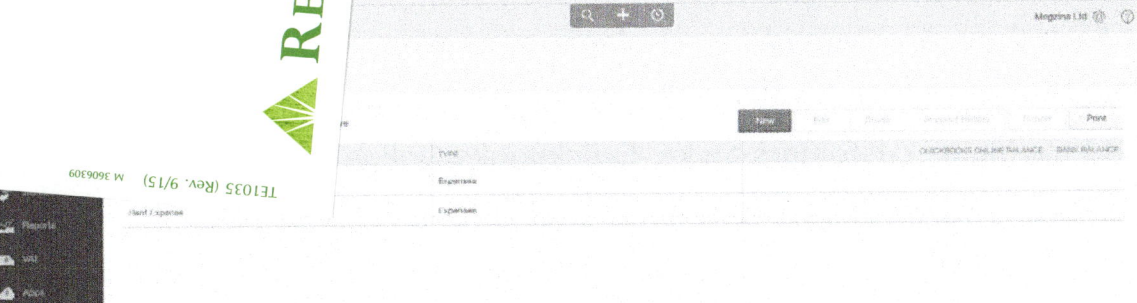

:ount is there, type it into the top left hand box. in 'rent' – this will filter by name, and the two
ent Rental and Rent Expense.

2 If you want to add an account, click on the blue '*New*' button – and a screen will pop up with a drop down list of options

3 From the Category Type – scroll down the list – there's 15 options to choose from: Debtors, Current Assets, Cash at Bank and In Hand, Tangible assets, Non-current assets, Creditors, Credit Card, Current Liabilities, Non-current liabilities, Equity, Income, Other income, cost of sales, expenses, other expenses.

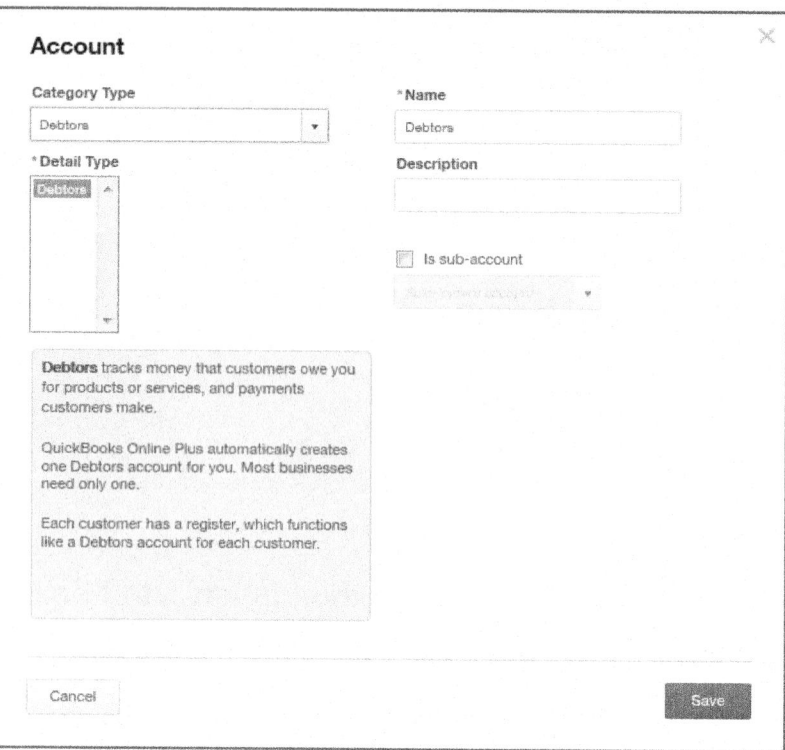

4 Each Category Type has an explanation of what it is. So for example, **Debtors** tracks money that customers owe you for products or services, and payments customers make. QuickBooks Online Plus automatically creates one Debtors account for you. Most businesses need only one. Each customer has a register, which functions like a Debtors account for each customer.

5 Some Category Types have further sub-types. For example Cash at Band and In Hand has 6 detail types – cash on hand, client trust account, current, money market, rents held in trust and savings.

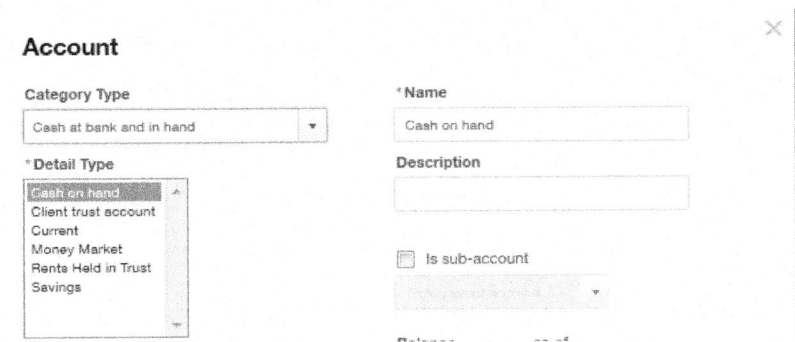

6 Decide on the CATEGORY TYPE of account that you want to add and then look at the DETAIL TYPE to find the account which most closely matches what you want to add.

7 For example choose *Cash on hand* and in the Name box type *Petty Cash*, and repeat in the Description box (type in *petty cash*)

8 If you have a the petty cash amount, and want to enter an opening bank balance as at a set date, enter that in, otherwise leave it blank.

9 *Save*

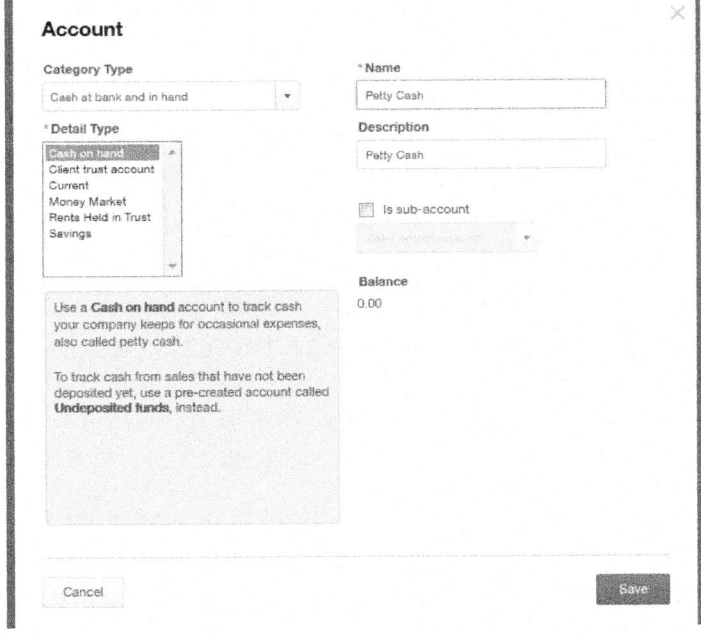

Your new account will now be listed in the Chart of Accounts.

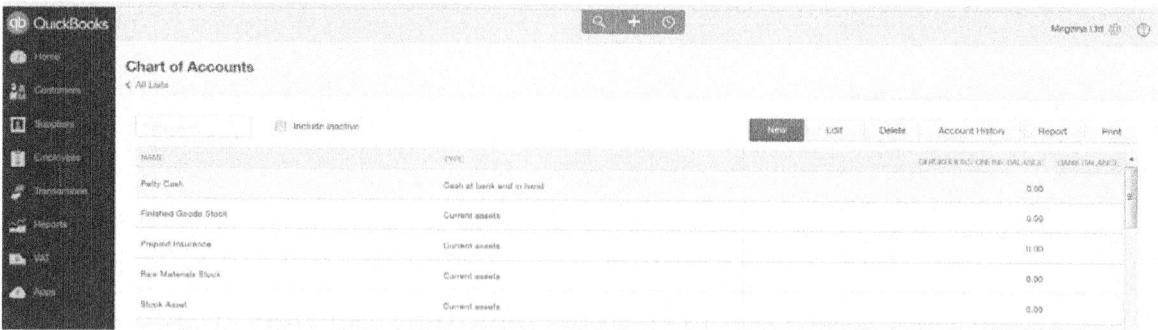

Deleting Accounts

If you scroll down the list and decide that there is an account that you don't need, you can DELETE it.

1 Scroll through the list and click on *Land*.

2 In the top right hand corner click *delete*.

3 A warning box will pop up – Are you sure you want to delete this?

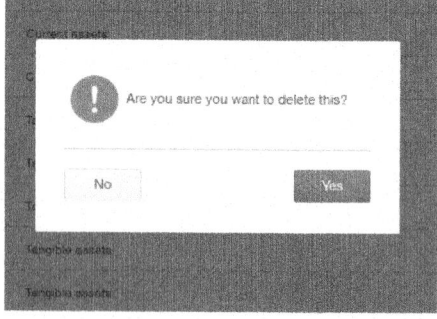

4 Click *Yes*

5 You'll be returned to the chart of accounts page – and the Land account will be deleted

Editing Accounts

If you just want to just EDIT the name of the account:

1 Scroll through the list to the account that you want to change e.g. *Vehicles*.

2 Click on the account.

3 In the top right hand corner click *edit*.

4 In the *Name box it says Vehicles, amend it to *Vehicles – car*.

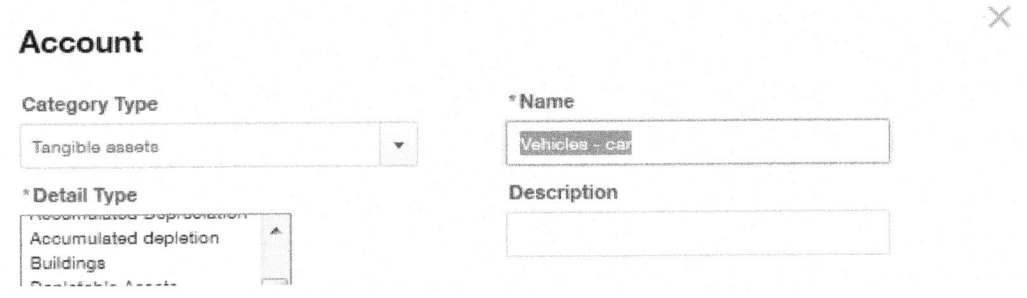

5 Click *save*.

6 On the chart of accounts, you'll now see the amended name.

Sub - Accounts

You can create sub-accounts, to customise the Chart of Accounts to make it more relevant to your business. For example, if you scroll through the list to the Expense accounts, there is Utilities. You can further divide this (if it's helpful to your business)

1 Click on *New*.

2 From the Category Type choose *Expenses*.

3 From the Detail Type choose *Utilities*.

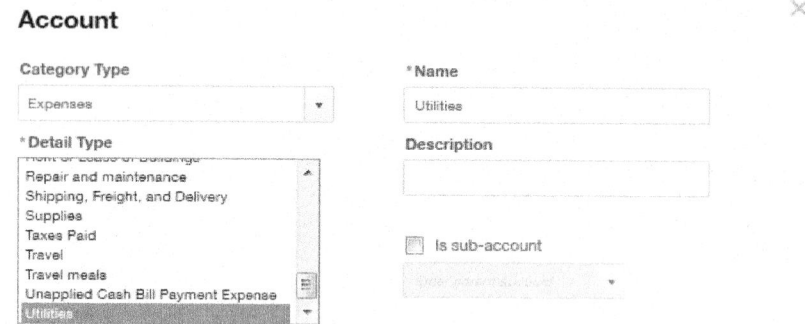

4 In the Name box remove 'Utilities' and type in *Electric*.

5 Tick the box is sub-account.

6 From the dropdown box choose *Utilities*.

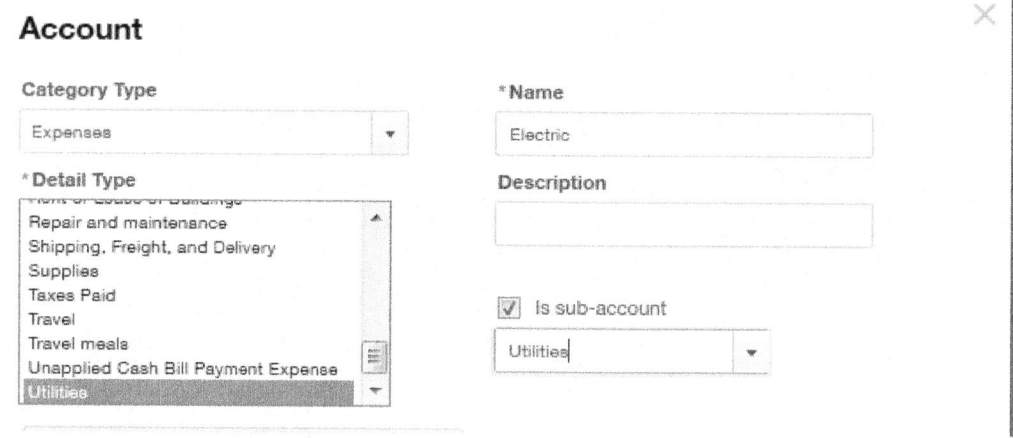

7 *Save*.

8 Repeat steps 1-3 above.

9 In the Name box remove 'Utilities' and type in *Gas*.

10 Tick the box is sub-account

11 From the dropdown box choose *Utilities*.

12 *Save*.

When you return to the chart of accounts page, you'll now see under Utilities, there are two sub-accounts.

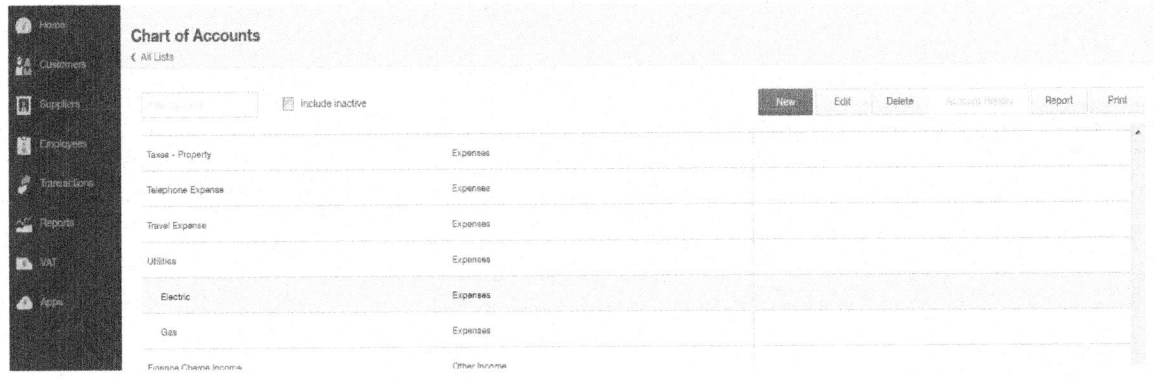

2.4 Setting up QuickBooks preferences

You can customise various features in QuickBooks:
- Multicurrency
- VAT
- Customise the look and feel of forms – (Estimates, Sales Receipts, Invoices)
- Time tracking
- Bill entry
- Reminders

Enabling Multicurrency

If you do business in currencies other than your home currency e.g. sterling, you can enable the QuickBooks multicurrency feature. Note – once it's turned on, it can't be turned off. Multicurrency lets you to set up all the bank, credit card, receivables and payables accounts needed for transactions with foreign customers and suppliers. QuickBooks integrates multicurrency dealings with the rest of your accounts, tracking foreign-exchange gains and losses. The benefits of the online system are that up to 145 currencies are available, Foreign exchange rates are downloaded hourly from a financial services web site, you can assign a currency to a customer or supplier, and you can see the value of your foreign transactions in your home currency.

To enable Multicurrency:
1 On the top right-hand corner of the screen click on the cog/wheel.
2 Under settings, choose *currency centre*.
3 Click the blue button – *set up currencies*.
4 Follow the steps.

Entering VAT information
If you are registered for VAT, you need to turn on VAT tracking.

To turn on VAT tracking:
1 From the home page, on the left hand side of the page – click *VAT*.
2 Click *Set-up VAT*.
3 Answer the following questions – you'll need to know your VAT number, which month your current VAT period begins, select your current accounting scheme (standard or cash), your vat filing frequency (monthly, quarterly, half-yearly, yearly)
4 Click *set-up*.

Set up VAT

As you are located in **United Kingdom**, we have selected **HM Revenue & Customs (VAT)** for you

Agency	HM Revenue & Customs (VAT)
Your VAT Registration Number	
Your current VAT period begins	January ▼
Your VAT Accounting Scheme	Standard ▼
Your VAT filing frequency	Monthly ▼

[Set up]

Choosing remaining preferences

To set up the rest of the company preferences is just a matter of answering some questions.

1 Click the cog/wheel in the top right hand corner.

2 Under settings, choose *Company Settings.*

3 On the left hand side of the page, click *Sales.*

4 Click the blue button to customise the look and feel of your sales forms.

5 Edit the sales form content, product and services (some features can be turned on and off), add a default message or email message to a sales form, select online delivery options (e.g. send the invoice as a PDF attachment, show sales form summary or detail), statement options

6 Click *Done.*

7 Repeat steps 1-2 above, on the left hand side click *Expenses.*

8 Edit the bills and expenses (features can be turned on and off)

9 Purchase orders – to use them or not – this feature can be switched on or off.

Settings			
Company	Bills and expenses	Show items table on expense and purchase forms	Off
Sales		Track expenses and items by customer	Off
Expenses		Make expenses and items billable	Off
		Default bill payment terms	
Payments	Purchase orders	Use purchase orders	Off
Advanced			

10 Click *Done*.

11 Repeat steps 1-2 above, on the left hand side click *Payments*.

12 If you already have an Intuit Pay account with Intuit (you may know it as GoPayment), connect it to your QuickBooks. Click *connect* and follow the steps.

13 Click *Done*.

14 Repeat steps 1-2 above, on the left hand side click *Advanced*.

15 Edit the features which you want to switch on and off – customise the features to suit you.

16 Click *Done*.

Settings				
Company	Accounting	First month of financial year	January	
Sales		First month of tax year	Same as financial year	
Expenses		Close the books	Off	
Payments	Chart of accounts	Account numbers	Off	
Advanced	Automation	Pre-fill forms with previously entered content	On	
		Automatically apply credits	On	
		Copy estimates to invoices	On	
		Automatically apply bill payments	On	
	Time tracking	Add Service field to timesheets	Off	
		Add Customer field to timesheets	On	
	Miscellaneous	Warn if duplicate cheque number is used	On	
		Warn if duplicate bill number is used	Off	
		Sign me out if inactive for	1 hour	
		Date format	dd/MM/yyyy	
		Number format	123,456.00	

Choosing a start date

Before you start entering your financial data, you need to choose a QuickBooks start date. This is the starting point you want to use for all your QuickBooks accounts. Once you decide on a start date, enter all the company's transactions *since* that date. Many business owners choose the last day of a financial period as their start date, such as the end of last financial year, last quarter, or last month. You need to enter all historical transactions from the day *after* your start date up to today. Eg. If you decided on a start date of 31 December, you would enter your historical transactions from 1 January until today.

To set the company start date:
1 Click the cog/wheel in the top right hand corner.
2 Under settings, choose *Company Settings*.

3 Click *advanced.*

4 Under accounting edit the first month of the financial year.

5 *Save.*

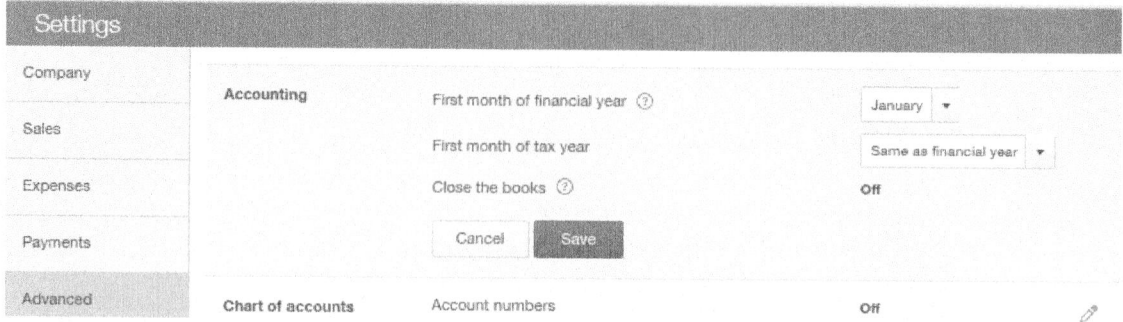

2.5 Setting up income accounts

We've already seen how to add new accounts in the chart of accounts, and that QuickBooks online comes with a preset list of Income and Expense accounts. Go to the Chart of Accounts (Click cog/wheel in the top right hand corner, click Chart of Accounts) – there's 3 income accounts already set up (sales, sales discounts, sales of product income). This may be appropriate for you, or you may want to split your sales income further.

For example, if you ran a 'Property Management' business, you may want to split the different types of income e.g. inventory income, tenants registration, rental income… making them all a sub-type under the sales category. You may sell 'fire safety packs' and put the sales income of these items under 'sales of product income'. Likewise, if you ran an 'Events Management' business, you may split the different types of income into e.g. weddings, birthdays, bar mitzvahs, funerals, christenings etc., You may receive commission income from 'photographers' if you recommend certain companies to your clients, who win the job – they pay you 10% of the fee.

Linking Products & Services to the Income account

1 In the top right hand corner, click on the wheel / cog icon.
2 Select under Lists, *Products and Services*.
3 By default, two are already set up: Hours & Sales.

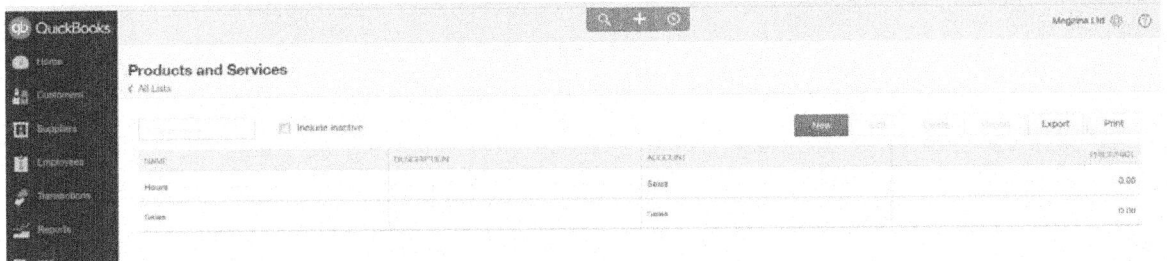

4 Click *New*.
5 Type in the Name of your service, description on sales forms and price/rate.
6 The Income Account – choose from the drop down menu of Sales etc.,
7 *Save*.

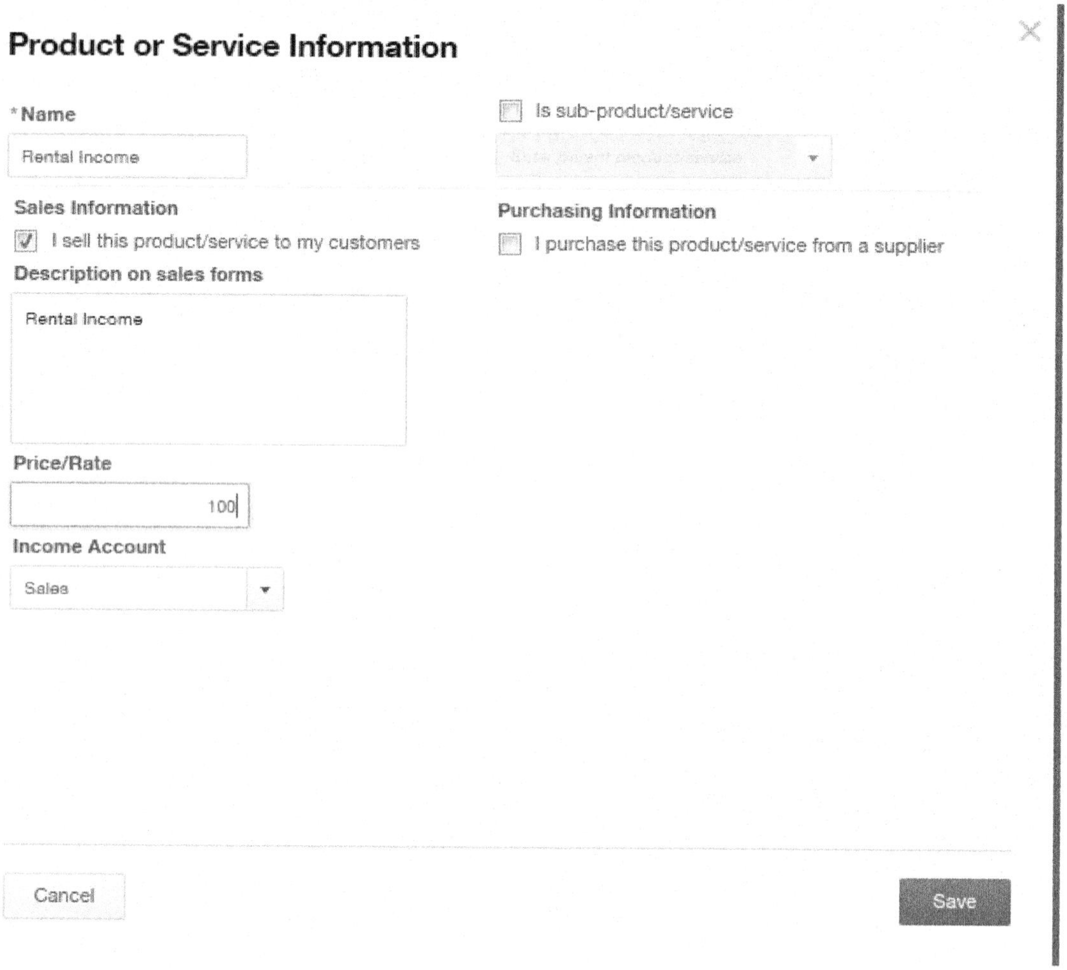

Product or Service Information

*Name

Rental Income

☐ Is sub-product/service

Sales Information

☑ I sell this product/service to my customers

Description on sales forms

Rental Income

Purchasing Information

☐ I purchase this product/service from a supplier

Price/Rate

100

Income Account

Sales

Cancel   Save

The List of Products and Services now include the new item e.g. Rental Income.

2.6 Entering opening balances

You can enter Opening Balances – amounts owed by you to suppliers or owed to you by customers, as well as the balances in your balance sheet accounts, as at your start date. The balance sheet accounts in the chart of accounts begin with an opening balance of zero. Before you begin working in QuickBooks, you need to enter an opening balance for each balance sheet account as at your start date.

The opening balance is important because QuickBooks can't give you an accurate balance sheet (what your company owes and what it owes) without it. Also, if you start with an accurate balance as at a specific date, you can reconcile your QuickBooks bank accounts with your bank statements, and your QuickBooks bank accounts will show the actual amount of money you have in the bank.

The easiest way to determine an account's opening balance is to work from an accurate balance sheet. If you have a balance sheet as at your start date, you can take the opening balance from there.

To enter the Current Bank account opening balance:
1 Click the cog/wheel (top right hand corner), click *Chart of Accounts.*
2 Click *New.*
3 Category Type: *cash at bank and in hand,* Detail Type: *Current,* Name: *Current.* Description - type in the bank name and account number.
4 Find the bank statement covering the date that you want the system to start from. Enter the opening balance and date. *Save.*

QuickBooks Online Help

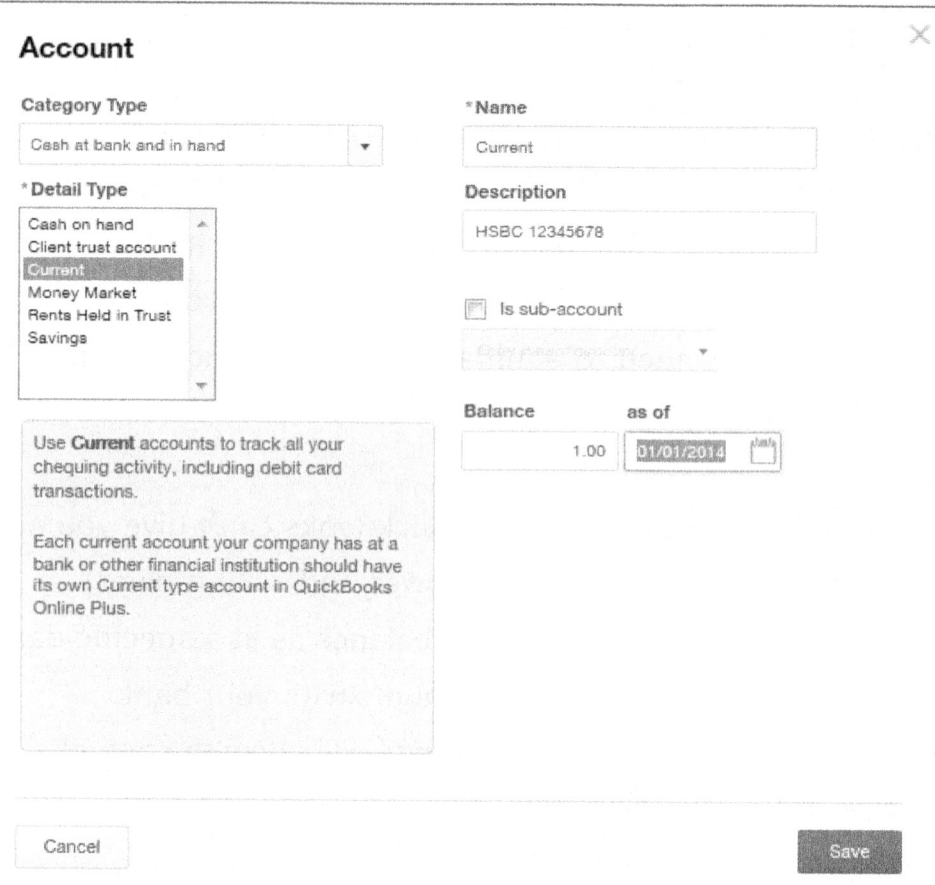

To enter the Customer account opening balance:

1 Click *Customers* on the left hand side of screen.

2 Click *New Customers* in the right hand corner of the screen.

3 Fill in the Customer Information form with your customer details e.g. Sally Jones – the more information you can fill in, the better. If you include an email address, later options means you can send invoices and statements by email.

4 Click on the tab – payment and billing.

5 Enter the customer opening balance as of (date) here.

6 *Save*

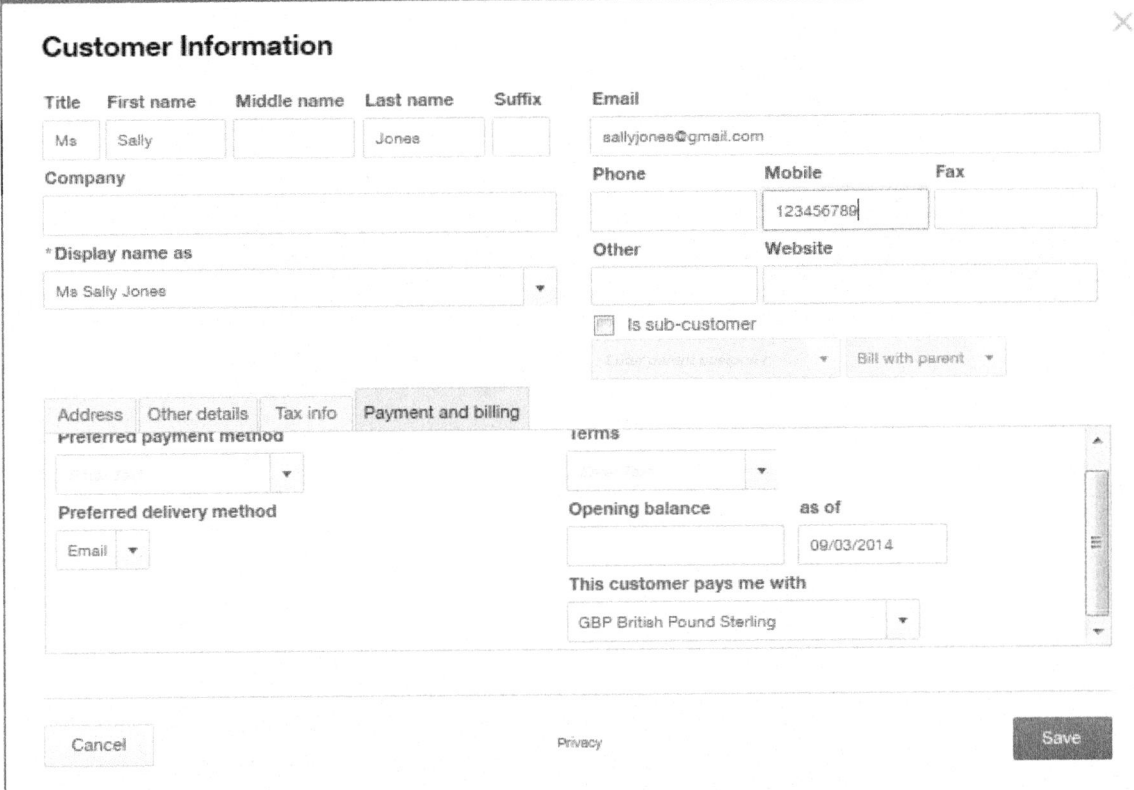

To enter the Suppliers account opening balance:

1 Click *Suppliers* on the left hand side of screen.

2 Click *New Suppliers* in the right hand corner of the screen.

3 Fill in the Supplier Information form with your Supplier details e.g. Bob Building Ltd – the more information you can fill in, the better. If you include an email address, later options means you can send remittance advices by email.

4 Enter the supplier opening balance as of (date) here.

5 *Save*

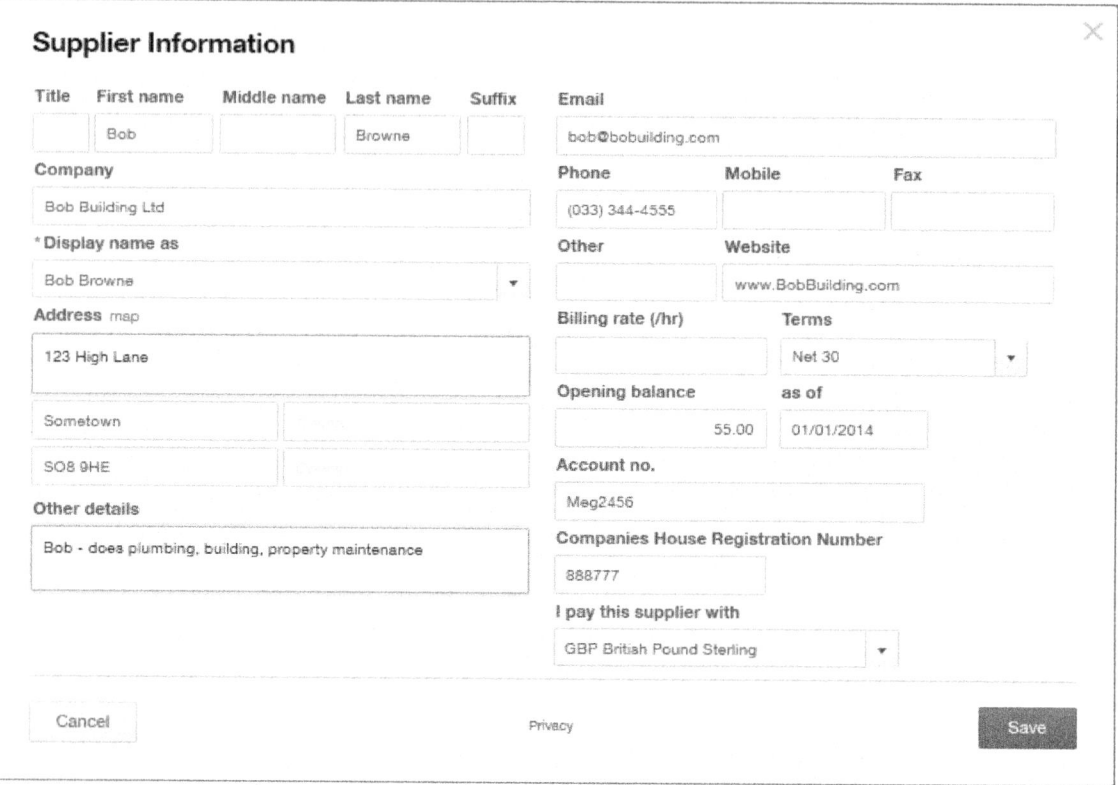

2.7 Setting up payroll

QuickBooks online has the option to run payroll within the system; or, you can use other programmes to run the payroll, and just journal the entries in. Plus, there is an employee's section.

To set up employees:

1 Click *Employees* on the menu bar on the left hand side of the screen.

2 Click *New Employee* in the right hand corner of the screen.

3 Fill in the Employee Information form with your Employee details e.g. Megzina Magic – the more information you can fill in, the better.

4 *Save*

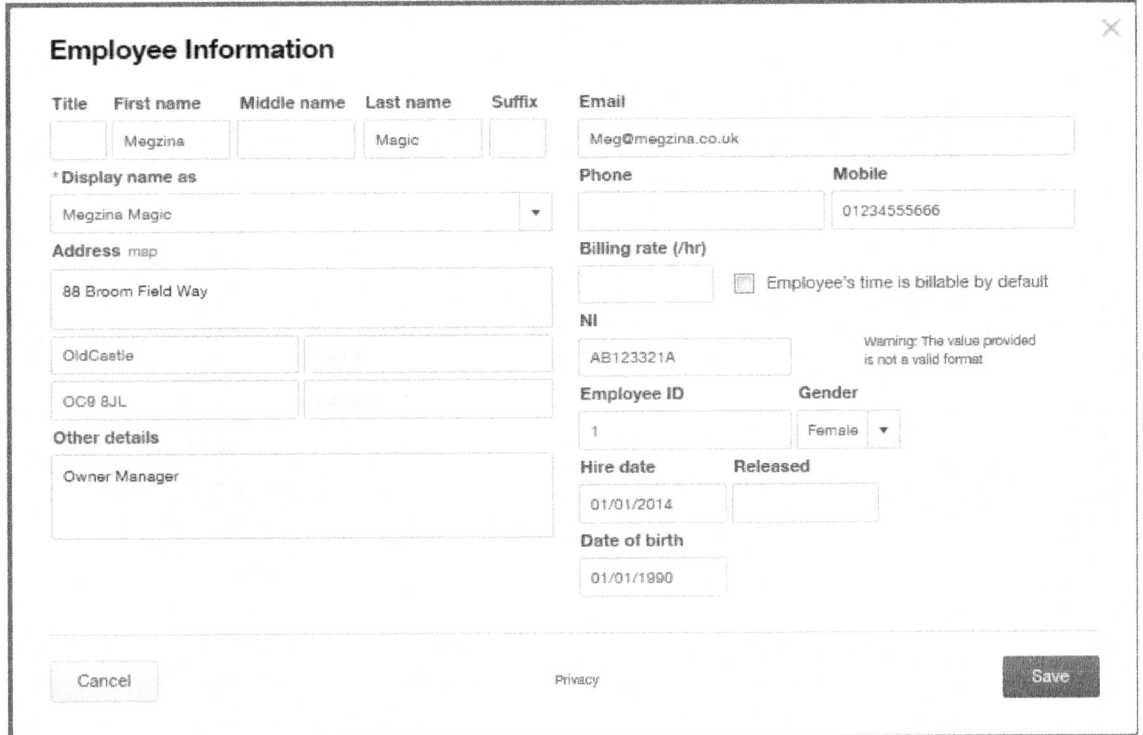

2.8 Getting help whilst using QuickBooks

When you have questions, QuickBooks provides a lot of help in various formats:

- Explanations as you go along, by clicking on '?' the question mark icons when you see them.

- Step-by-step instructions, available from the Help and How Do I? Menus and ask fields.
- You can ask the Community Online.
- You can chat (Live) with an operator online Open: 9am-5:30pm (GMT) Mon-Fri, email support with your question and get you an answer within 1 business day! Or call QuickBooks support 0808 234 5337 - Open: 8am-8pm (GMT) Mon-Fri. The US number is 1-800-756-3485. During UK bank holiday times, the call is likely to be transferred to QuickBooks support abroad.

Finding a topic in the onscreen Help Index

1 Click the question mark icon in the top right hand corner of the screen.

2 Type your question into the white bar e.g. *How do I add a new supplier?*
3 A list of possible answers will be displayed

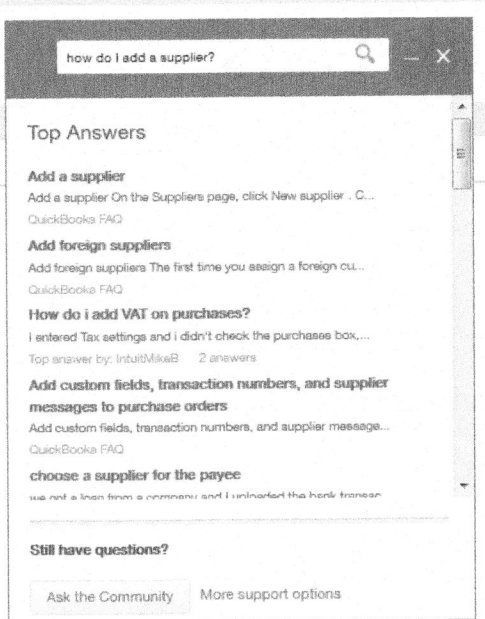

3: Working with Lists

Summary of what is in this chapter:

3.1 Using QuickBooks lists

3.2 Editing the chart of accounts

3.3 Working with the Customer: sub-customer list

3.4 Working with the Employee list

3.5 Working with the Supplier list

3.6 Working with Other Lists (Terms, Payment, Classes)

3.7 Adding custom fields

3.8 Managing lists

3.1 Using QuickBooks lists

QuickBooks lists organises different information, including data on customers, suppliers, terms, payment classes, products and services and more. Lists save you time by helping you enter information on a list - you enter it once and never need to retype it. Think about how many names, addresses and other information you use more than once in your business:

- Customers who purchase from you on a regular basis
- Suppliers from whom you purchase your supplies
- Products or services you sell again and again

Simply enter repetitive information into a list once, and then use it over and over on cheques, on invoice forms, and in other daily transactions. You don't have to enter all the information from your company's lists before you begin working with QuickBooks. You can add information to lists as you go along.

3.2 Editing the chart of accounts

The chart of accounts is your most important list, because it shows how much your business has, how much it owes, how much money you have coming in, and how much you're spending.

To display the chart of accounts:
1 Click the cog /wheel in the top right hand corner of the screen, and under Settings, choose *Chart of Accounts.*

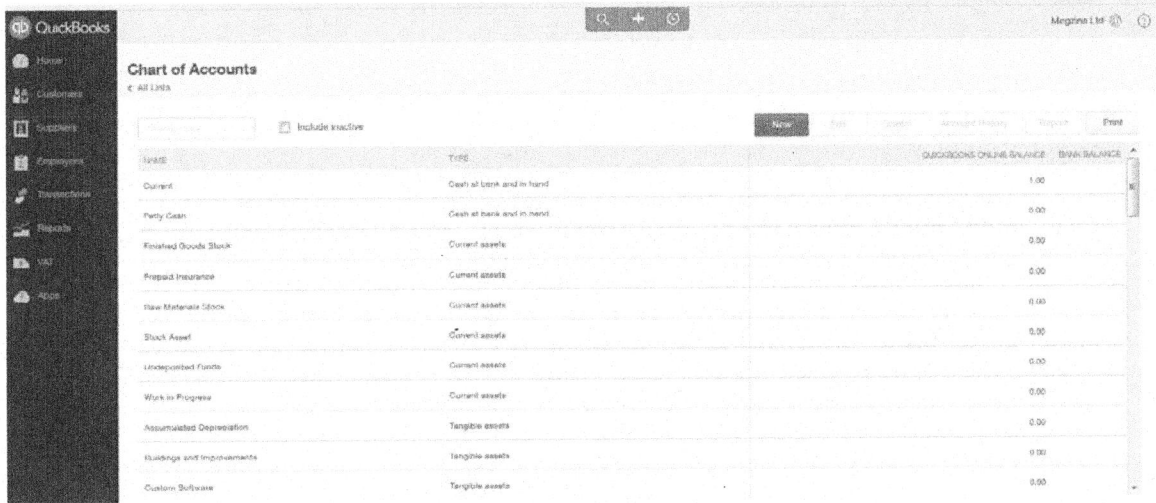

QuickBooks Online Help

Overview of the Chart of Account Options

1 *Debtors*
- Debtors

2 *Current Assets*
- Allowance for bad debts
- Called up share capital not paid
- Development costs
- Employee cash advances
- Investments-other
- Loans to officers
- Loans to others
- Loans to shareholders
- Other current assets
- Prepaid expenses
- Retainage
- Stock
- Undeposited funds

3 *Cash at Bank and In Hand*
- Cash on hand
- Client trust account
- Current
- Money market
- Rents held in trust
- Savings

4 *Tangible assets*
- Accumulated amortisation
- Accumulated depreciation
- Accumulated depletion
- Buildings
- Depletable assets
- Furniture & fixtures
- Leasehold improvements
- Machinery and equipment
- Other tangible assets
- Vehicles

5 Non-current assets

- Accumulated amortisation of noncurrent assets
- Deferred tax
- Goodwill
- Intangible assets
- Investments
- Lease buyout
- Licenses
- Organisational costs
- Other noncurrent assets
- Other intangible assets
- Prepayments and accrued income
- Security Deposits

6 Creditors

- Creditors

7 Credit Card

- Credit Card

8 Current Liabilities

- Client trust accounts – liabilities
- Current liabilities
- Current tax liability
- Insurance payable
- Line of credit
- Loan payable
- Payroll clearing
- Prepaid expenses payable
- Rents in trust – liability
- Short term borrowings
- Tax and national insurance

9 Non-current liabilities

- Accruals and deferred income
- Long term borrowings
- Notes payable
- Other non-current liabilities

- Provision for liabilities
- Shareholder notes payable

10 Equity

- Accumulated adjustment
- Called up share capital
- Opening balance equity
- Ordinary shares
- Owners equity
- Paid-in capital or surplus
- Partner contributions
- Partner distributions
- Partners equity
- Preference shares
- Retained earnings
- Treasury shares

11 Income

- Discounts / refunds given
- Non-profit income
- Other primary income
- Sales of product income
- Service / fee income
- Unapplied cash payment income

12 Other income

- Dividend income
- Interest earned
- Other investment income
- Other misc income
- Tax-exempt interest

13 Cost of Sales

- Cost of labour – COS
- Cost of sales
- Equipment rental – COS
- Other costs of sales – COS
- Shipping, freight and delivery – COS

- Supplies and materials - COS

14 Expenses

- Advertising / promotional
- Auto
- Bad debts
- Bank charges
- Charitable contributions
- Cost of labour
- Distribution costs
- Dues and subscriptions
- Entertainment
- Equipment rental
- Finance costs
- Insurance
- Interest paid
- Legal and professional fees
- Meals and entertainment
- Office/general admin expenses
- Other misc service costs
- Payroll expenses
- Promotional meals
- Rent or lease of buildings
- Repair and maintenance
- Shipping, freight and delivery
- Supplies
- Taxes paid
- Travel
- Travel meals
- Unapplied cash bill payments
- Utilities

15 Other expenses

- Amortisation
- Depreciation
- Exchange gain or loss
- Other expenses
- Penalties and settlements

See the **Appendix** (end of the book) for an explanation of what each account type means / uses of the account.

Editing an account
If any of the accounts don't suit your needs, you can edit them.

To edit an account (rename):
1 In the chart of accounts, scroll down to the account that you want to edit e.g. *Office Supplies*, select *edit*
2 Rename the account *Office Stationary*.
3 *Save*

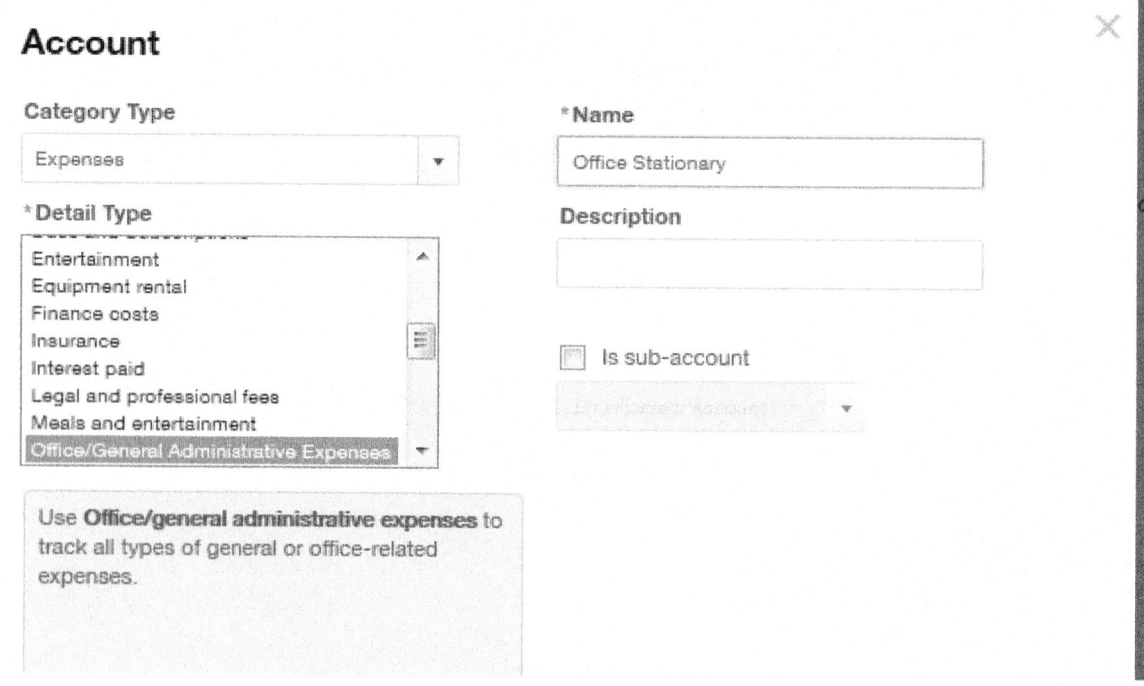

Adding subaccounts

Currently the insurance is listed as 4 separate lines of expenses – there's Insurance expenses, Insurance Expense-General Liability Insurance, Insurance Expense-Health Insurance and Insurance Expense-Life and Disability Insurance. You can make the last 3 a sub-account, of the first 'Insurance' account.

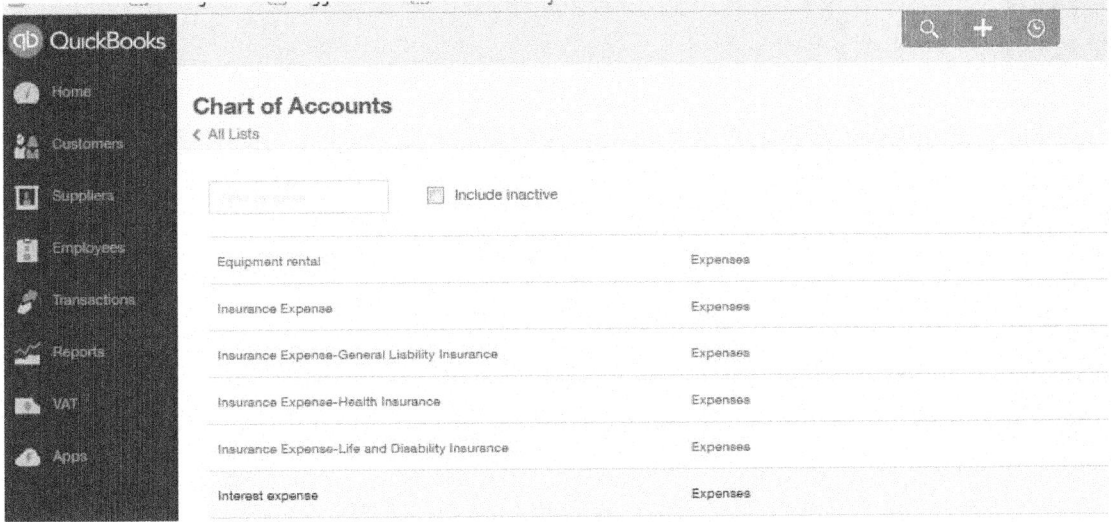

To add a subaccount:

1 In the chart of accounts, scroll down to the account that you want to edit e.g. *Insurance Expense* - General Liability Insurance, select *edit*.
2 Tick is sub-account, select *Insurance Expenses*.

3 *Save*

4 Repeat steps 1 & 2 for Insurance Expense-Health Insurance and Insurance Expense-Life

5 The Chart of accounts will then have Insurance, with three subaccounts. Note that subaccounts are indented in the Chart of Accounts.

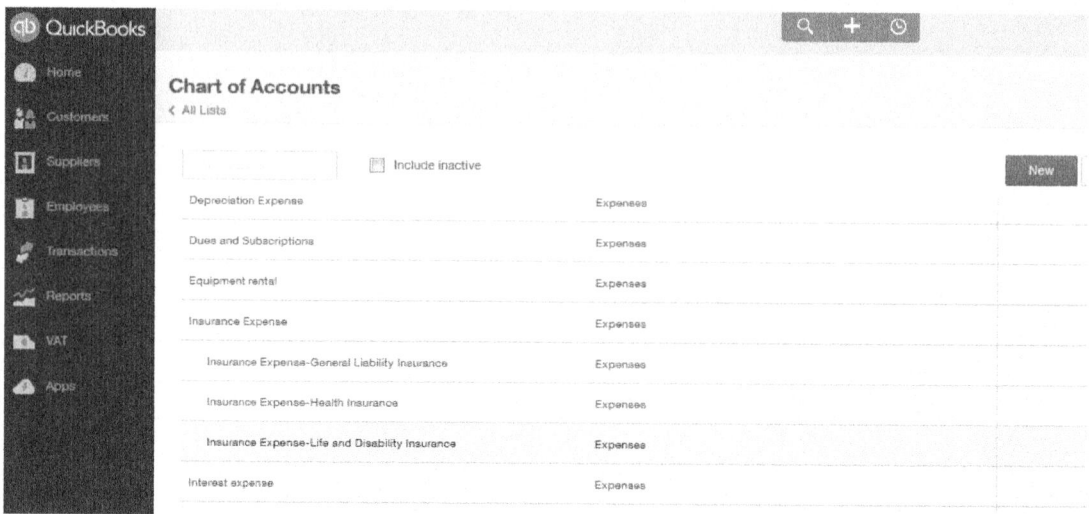

3.3 Working with the Customer: sub-customer list

The customer list stores names, addresses, and other information about your customers. To track jobs, we have to use Sub-customers. You'll have your parent customer - and each job will be a sub-customer of that parent.

Adding a new sub- customer:

1 Go to the *customers* and add *new customer*.

2 Leave the name blank, enter the name of the job in the Company box – e.g. *Repaint Wall.*

3 Tick 'Is a sub-customer' and choose Sally Jones (the customer we set up previously).

4 Choose *bill with parent.*

5 *Save.*

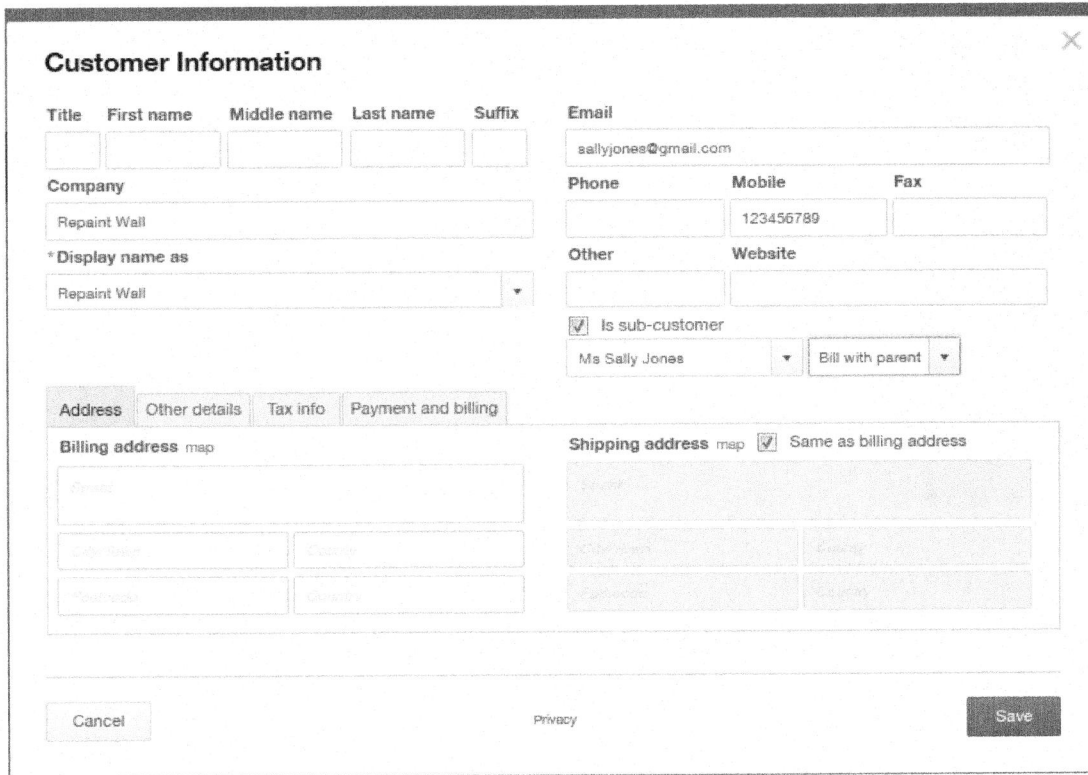

From the customer list, you can now see that Repaint Wall is now a sub account (or a customer job) or Sally Jones (our parent customer).

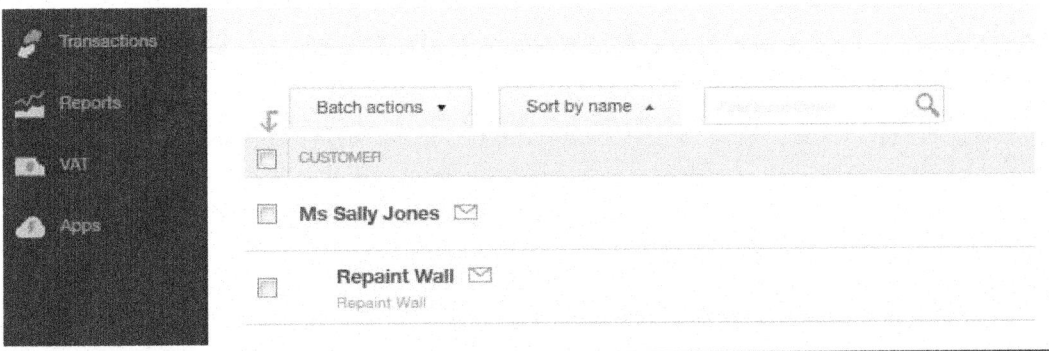

Editing customer Information

1 If we click on our customer (Ms Sally Jones) we can edit the information we have on the customer file of Sally.

2 On the next page, click *edit*.

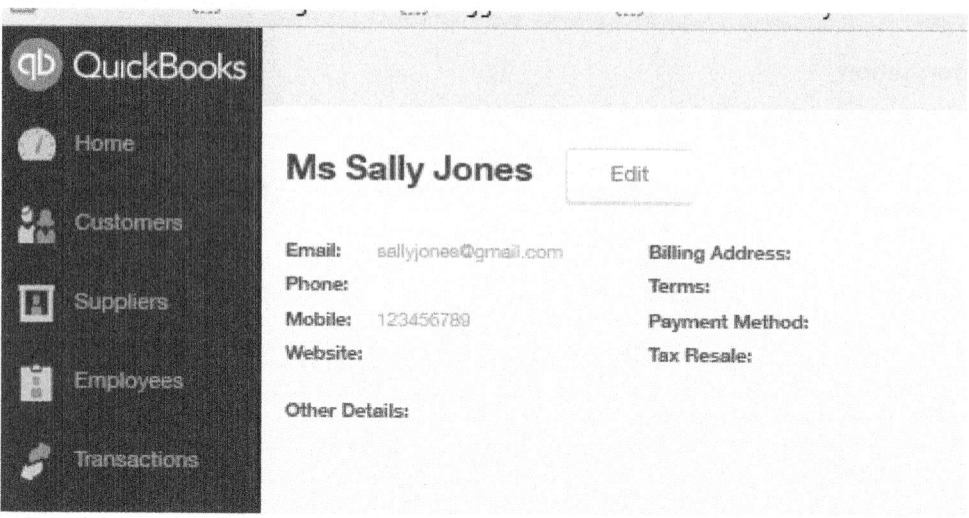

3 Add an address for Sally.

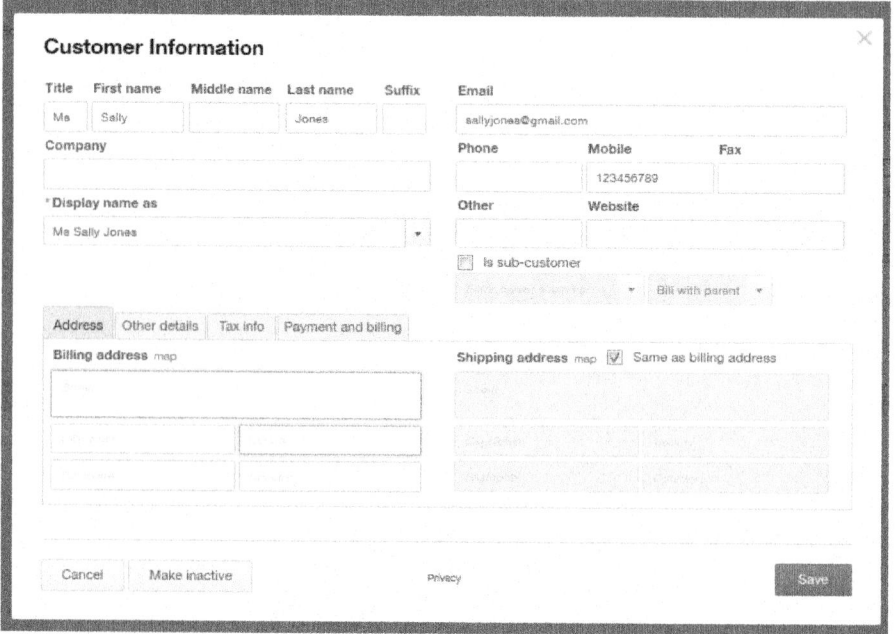

Providing additional customer information

4 In the other details, add details about Sally.

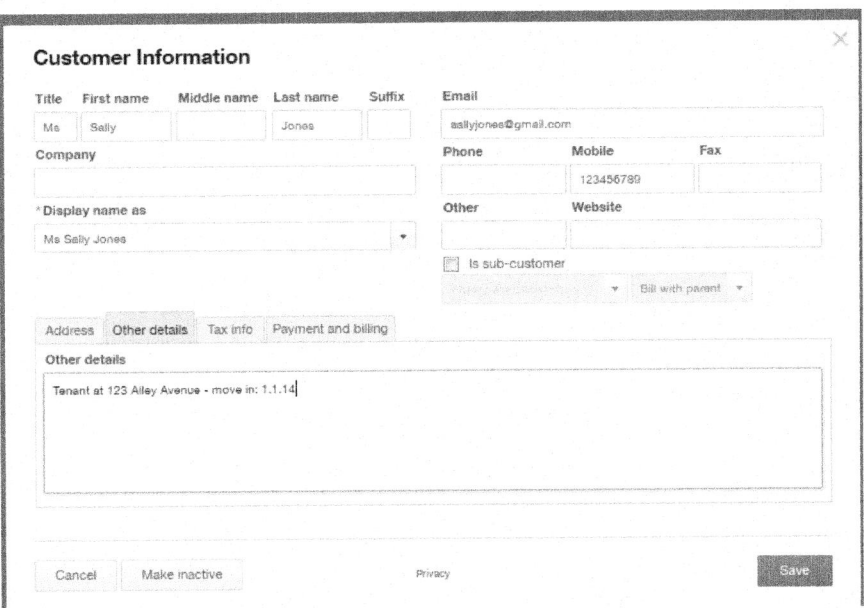

5 In the Tax Info, if Sally is VAT registered, enter her details here.

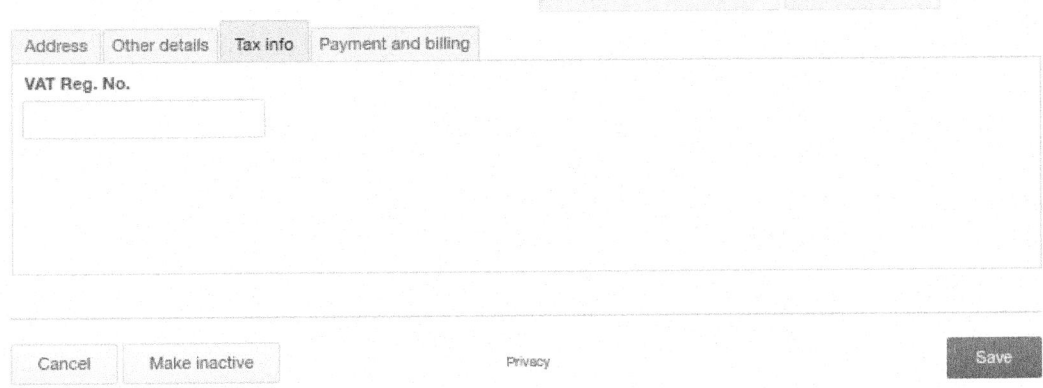

Providing customer payment information

6 In the Payment and billing, add Sally's payment preferences here. The preferred payment method could be American Express, Cash, Cheque, Direct Debit, Discover, MasterCard or Visa, or you can add one of your

own. The preferred delivery method (for invoices) has the options of print, email or none. The terms (or payment) has options of due on receipt, net 15, net 30 or net 60 or you can choose your own. For Sally, we opted for *Cheque, Print, Due on receipt*.

7 Save.

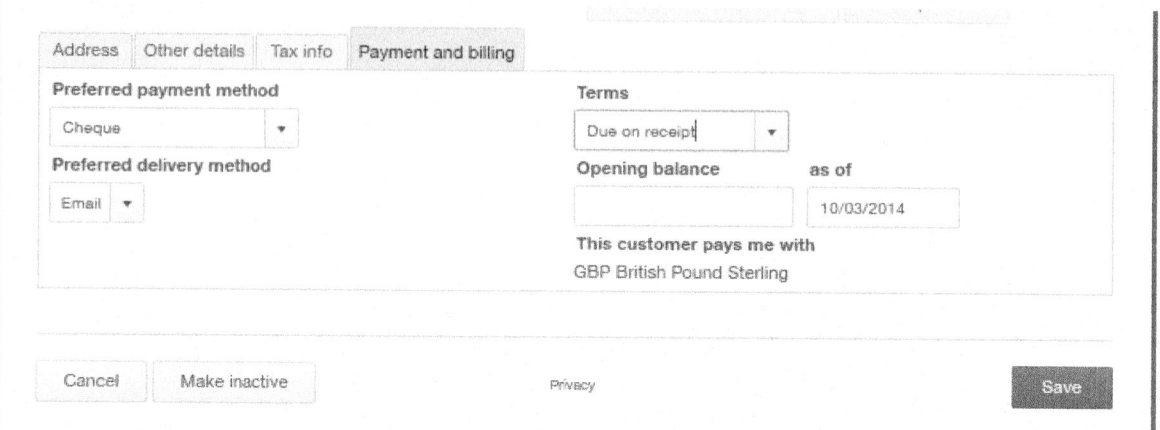

3.4 Working with the Employee list

The employee list stores information about your employees such as name, address, phone number and National Insurance Number.

Adding a new employee

1 Click *Employees* on the menu bar on the left hand side of the screen.

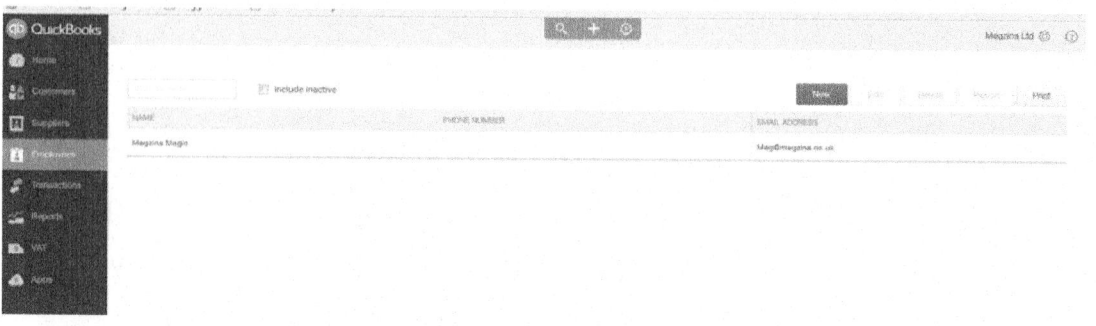

2 Click *New Employee* in the right hand corner of the screen.

3 Fill in the Employee Information form with your Employee details e.g. Megzina Magic – the more information you can fill in, the better.

4 *Save*

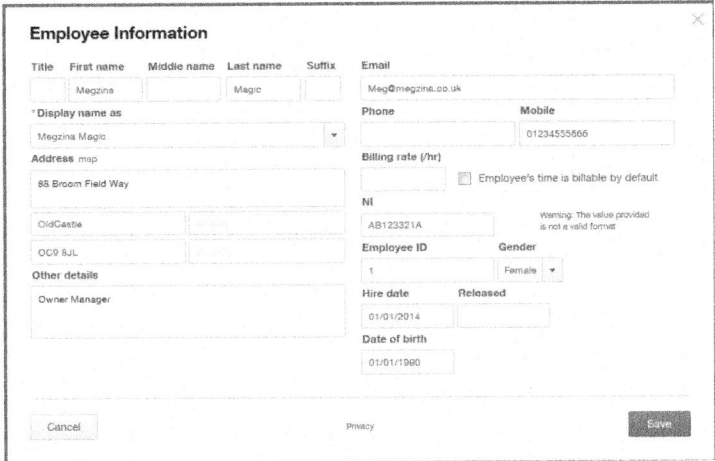

3.5 Working with the Supplier list

The Supplier list is where you record information about the companies or people from whom you buy goods or services. QuickBooks uses the data in the Supplier list to fill in purchase orders, receipts, bills and cheques as you receive and pay for goods and services.

To Edit supplier information

1 If we click on our supplier (Bob Browne) we can edit the information we have on the supplier file of Bob.

2 On the next page, click *edit*.

QuickBooks Online Help

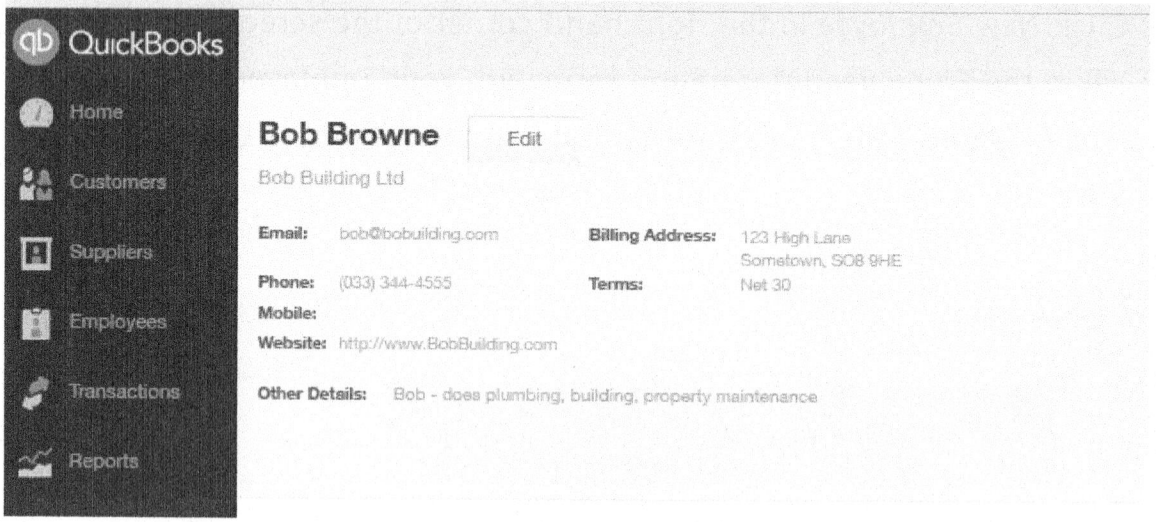

3 This screen comes up – and we can amend any information which is incorrect or incomplete.

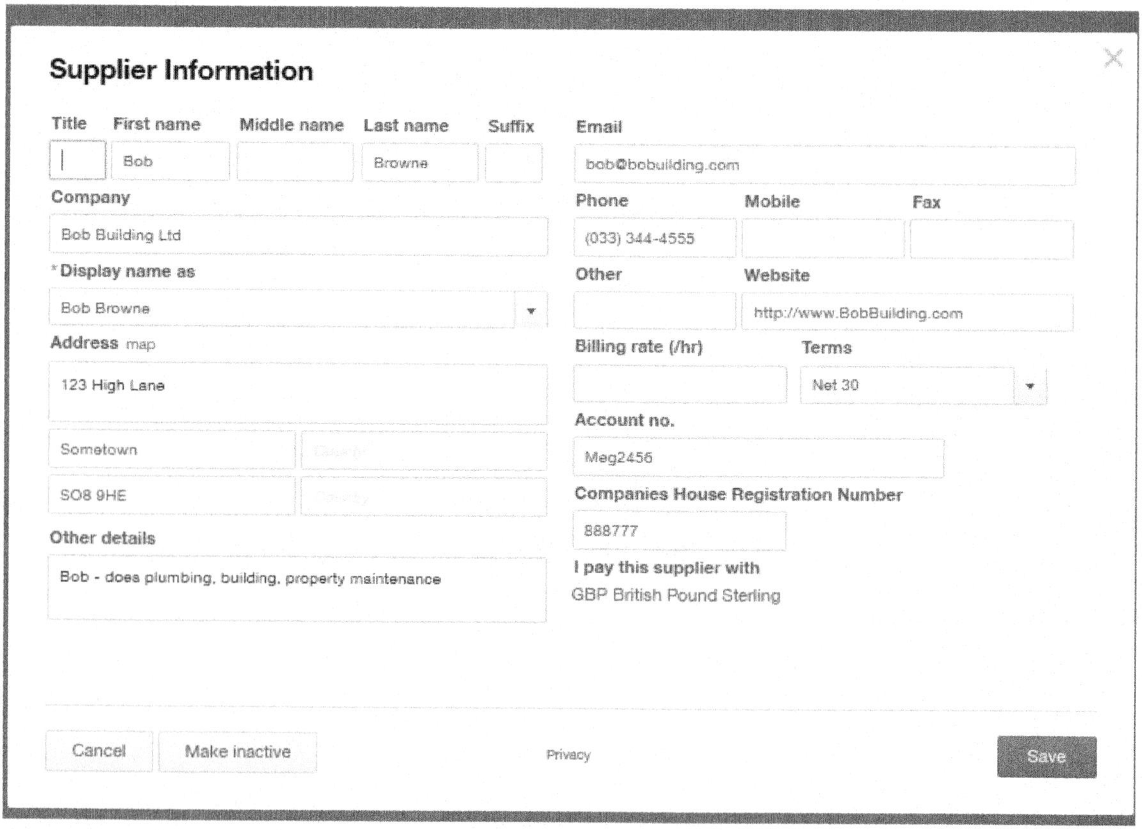

4 *Save*

3.6 Working with Other Lists (Terms, Payment, Classes)

There are several other lists available on QuickBooks.

1 Click the cog /wheel in the top right hand corner of the screen, and under Settings, choose *Chart of Accounts.*

2 Under the heading Chart of Accounts, click the link to *All Lists.*

The lists available are:
- Chart of Accounts
- Recurring Transactions
- Products and Services
- Locations
- Payment Methods
- Terms
- Classes
- Attachments

To amend the Recurring Transactions List

The recurring transactions list displays a list of transactions that have been saved for reuse. From here, you can schedule transactions to occur either automatically or with reminders. You can also save unscheduled transactions to use at any time.

1 Click *Recurring Transactions*, and click *New.*

2 Select the transaction type from the drop down menu – there's several to choose from e.g. Bill, Non-Posting charge, Cheque, Non-Posting Credit, Card Credit, Credit Note, Estimate, Deposit, Journal Entry, Invoice, Refund, Sales Receipt, Transfer, Supplier Credit, Purchase Order, Expense. In this example, we've chosen *Invoice*. Click *OK*.

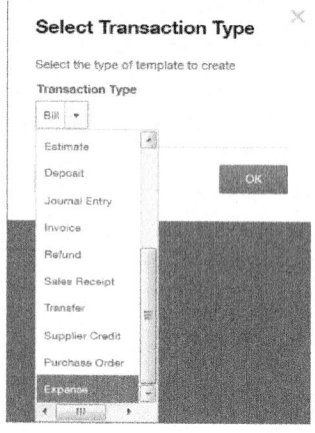

3 This will take you to a page called Recurring Invoice.
4 Give the Template a name. E.g. *Rental Invoice*.
5 Type – (scheduled, unscheduled, reminder) e.g. *scheduled*.
6 Tick automatically send emails.
7 Choose the customer from the drop down e.g. *Sally Jones*.
8 Choose interval (daily, weekly, monthly, yearly) e.g. *monthly*.
9 Choose specific dates e.g. 1st, 2nd, 3rd, last, Monday, Tuesday etc., every 1, 2, 3 months etc.,
10 Choose start date [Note: this must be in the future] and end date (if any).
11 If the invoice is to be sent a few days in advance – enter the number f days.
12 Tick to be alerted when the range has ended

13 If there is a location – enter it.

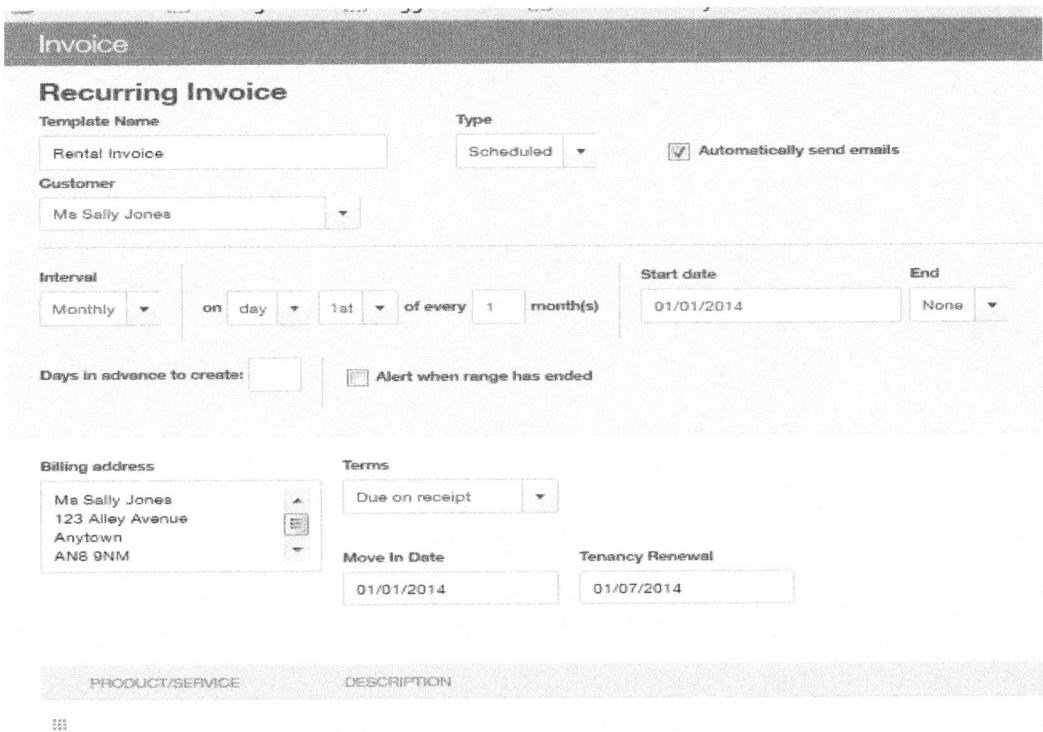

14 Next click under the fill in the product / service information and a drop down menu will be displayed. E.g. choose *rental income.*

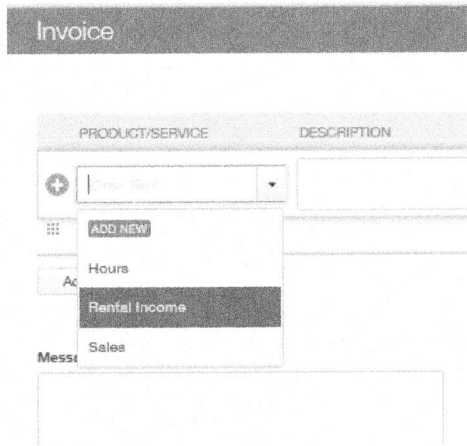

15 Click under class – and a drop down menu will be displayed.
16 Click the green ADD NEW button and type in 'Arcacia Avenue'.

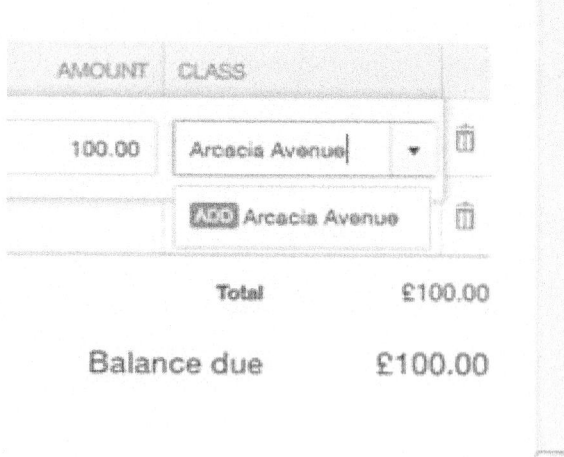

17 Click save.

18 To add a message to the invoice, type one in the box e.g. Thank you for staying with us.

19 If there's a memo for the statement – enter one in there.

20 If there's an attachment to include, drag it or upload it into the box.

21 Click Customise add further personality to your forms e.g. add a logo, change the font, add a header or footer or change the colour. *Save.*

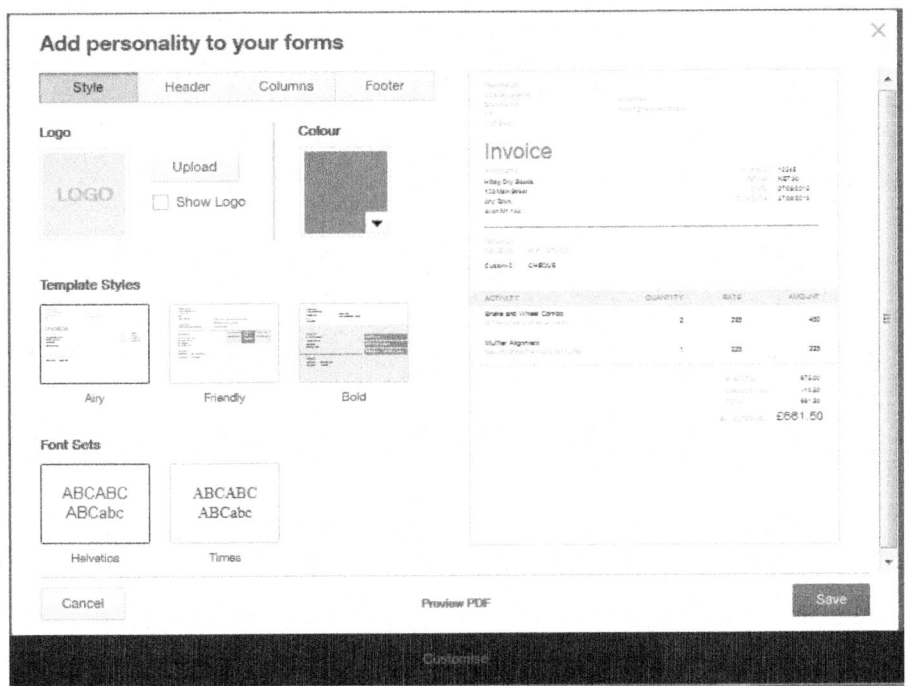

22 *Save* Template

To amend Products and Services List

The products and services list displays the products and services you sell. From here, you can edit information about a product or service, such its description, or the rate you charge.

1 Click *Products and Services* – and a list of the products and services available will be displayed.

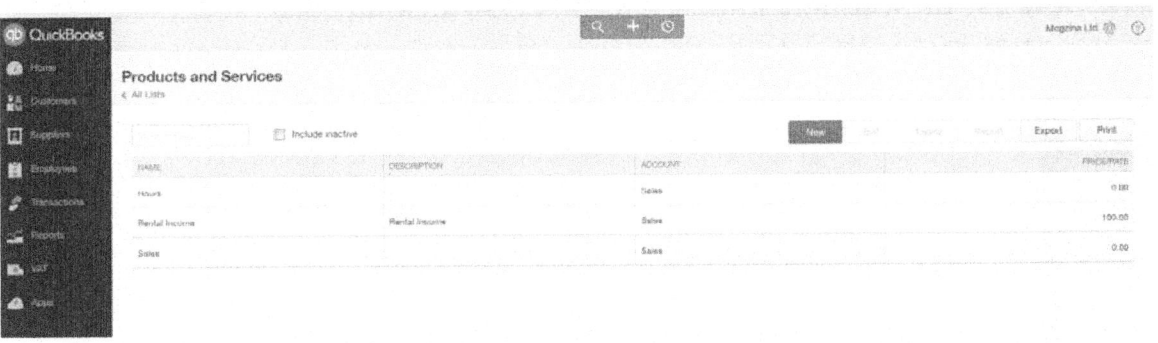

2 Click *New*.

3 Name – enter the name of the product / service e.g. *Initial Registration fee.*

4 Tick – if you sell this product / service to your customers.

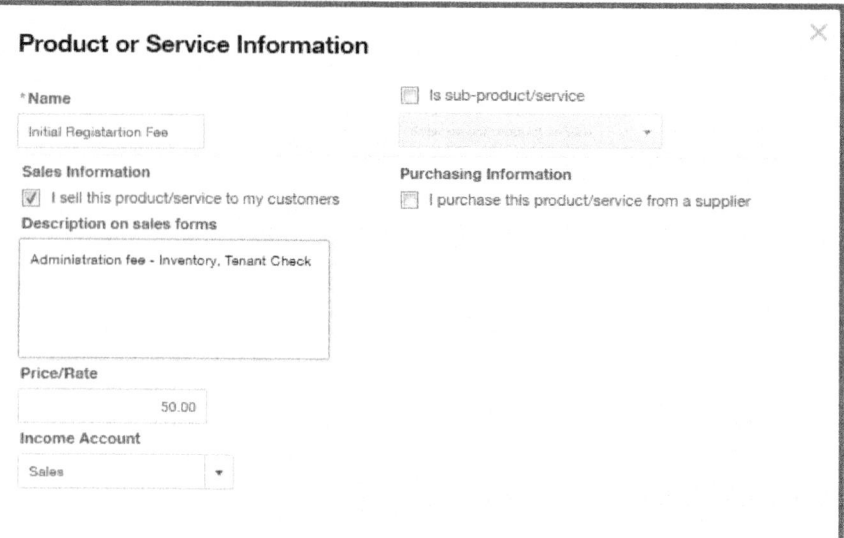

5 In the description box – enter a short description e.g. *Administration fee – Inventory, Tenant Check.*

6 Price / Rate – enter e.g. *50.00.*

7 From the dropbox, choose the account to associate this income with. E.g. *Sales.* Note – if the account isn't there. Cancel, go to the Chart of Accounts, add the account there and then return to this step.

8 *Save.*

The new list of products and services is now displayed.

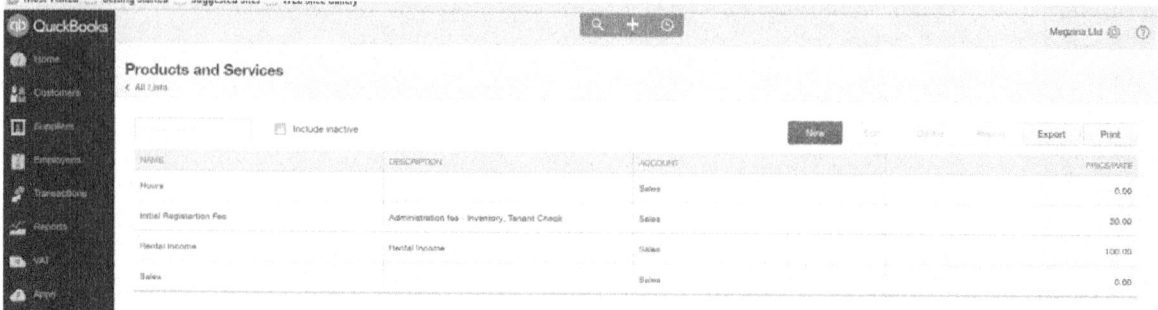

To amend Locations List

You can use locations to categorise your transactions by different parts of your company.

1 Click *Locations List* and click *New*. A list of options will pop up. Type in the location name e.g. *Anytown.*

2 Tick the relevant box(es) e.g. Is sub-location; This location has a different title for sales forms; This location has a different company name when communicating with customers; This location has a different address where customers contact me or send payments; This location has a different email address for communicating with customers; This location has a different phone number where customers phone me.

3 If any box is ticked, a further drop down will be displayed to fill in.

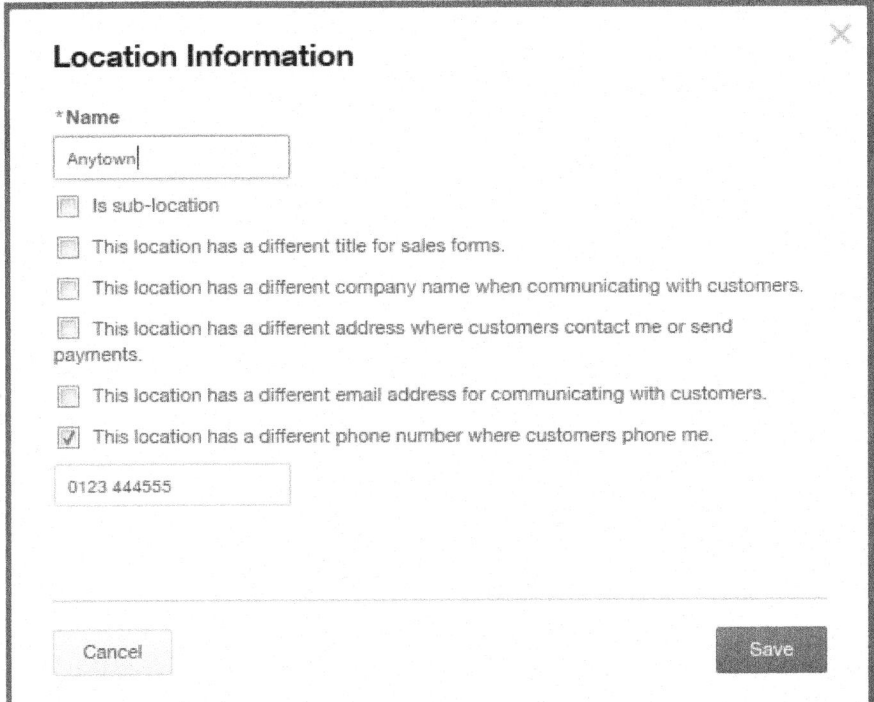

4 We ticked the box - this location has a different phone number where customers phone me. And typed in the new number e.g. *0123 444 555.*

5 *Save.*

To amend Payment Methods List

Displays Cash, Cheque, and any other ways you categorise payments you receive from customers. That way, you can print deposit slips when you deposit the payments you have received.

1 Click *Payment Methods* List.

2 A list of payment methods will be displayed.

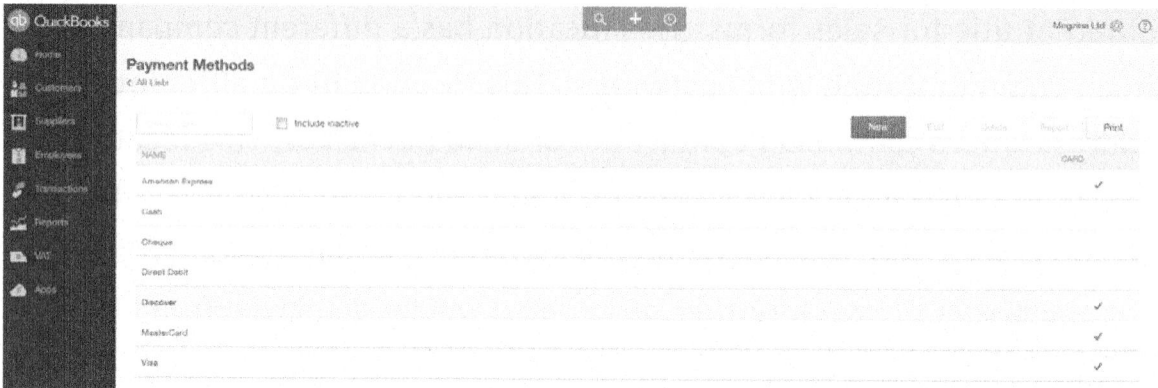

3 Click *New*.

4 A New Payment Method form will pop up – type in the name of the payment method e.g. BACS Online.

5 Tick if this is a credit or debit card.

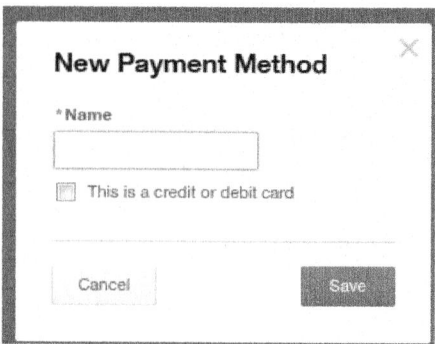

6 *Save*.

7 The revised list of payment methods will now be displayed – which now includes the new payment method that we've just added.

To amend Terms List

Displays the list of terms that determine the due dates for payments from customers, or payments to suppliers. Terms can also specify discounts for early payment. From here, you can add or edit terms.

1 Click *Terms List.*
2 A list of terms will be displayed.

3 Click *New.*

4 A New Term form will pop up – fill in e.g. Due by certain day of the month – 3 day of the month.

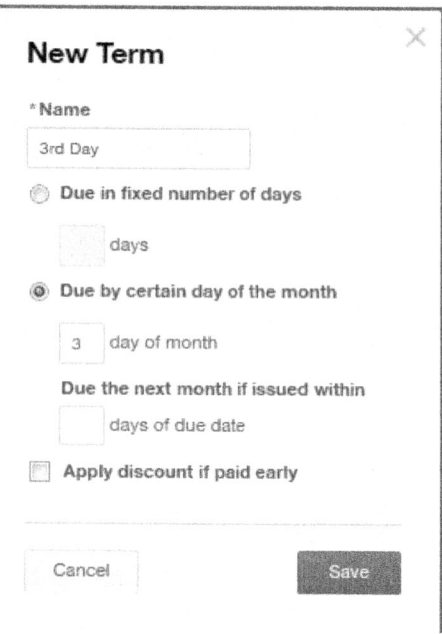

5 *Save*

6 The revised list of terms will now be displayed – which now includes the new term that we've just added.

To amend Classes List

Displays the classes you can use to categorise your accounting transactions. For example, if you ran a property company, you may want to give each property a class e.g. the name of the road – so that all income and expenses can be attributed to that class. Other companies may use classes (like departments) e.g. IT, Finance, Sales, Marketing.

1 Click *Classes List*.

2 A list of classes will be displayed.

3 Click *New*.

4 A New Class form will pop up – fill in e.g. Holloway Road.

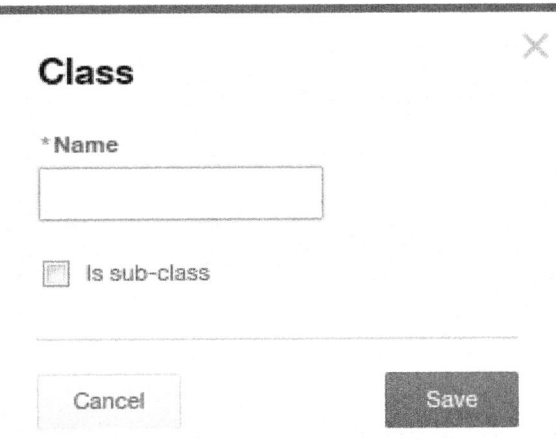

5 Save.

6 The revised list of classes will now be displayed – which now includes the new class that we've just added.

To amend Attachments List

Displays the list of all attachments uploaded. From here you can add, edit, download, and export your attachments. You can also see all transactions linked to a particular attachment.

1 Click Attachments List.
2 In the screen displayed, drag the attachment into the box.

3 When you do this, your attachment will be listed.

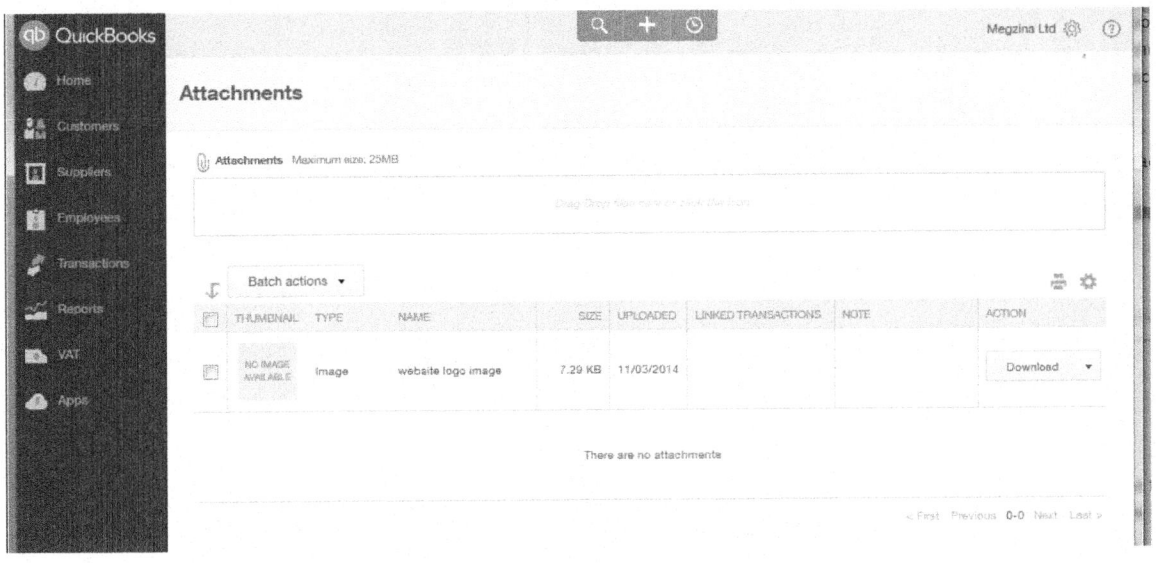

3.7 Adding custom fields

It's really handy that you can add extra fields to your forms in QuickBooks Online! The fields are even reportable, so you can create reports that use these fields on them.

To add a custom field for sales forms:
1 Click the **wheel / cog** in the upper right of your Home screen and choose *Company Settings* from the dropdown menu. From here, click *Sales Form Entry* on the left. You'll see the **Custom Fields** area.
2 Check the box (Internal and/or public). Select *Internal* to show the field in QuickBooks; select *Public* to show the field on customer forms.

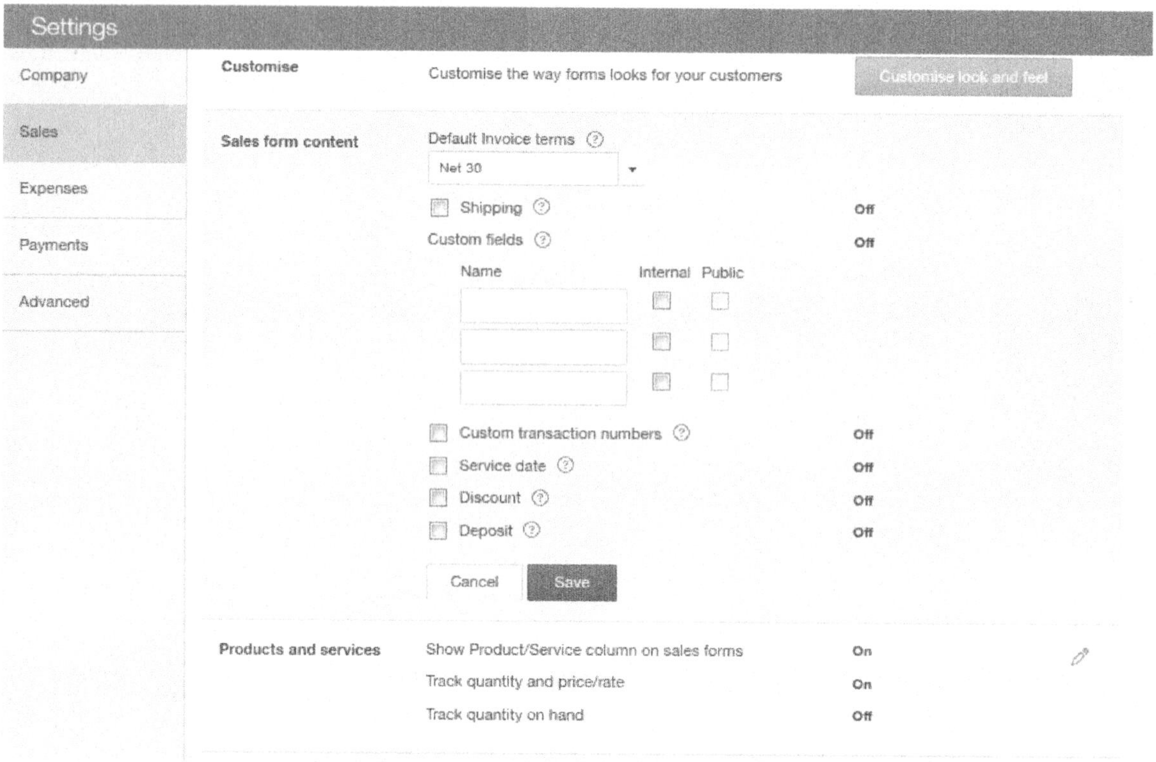

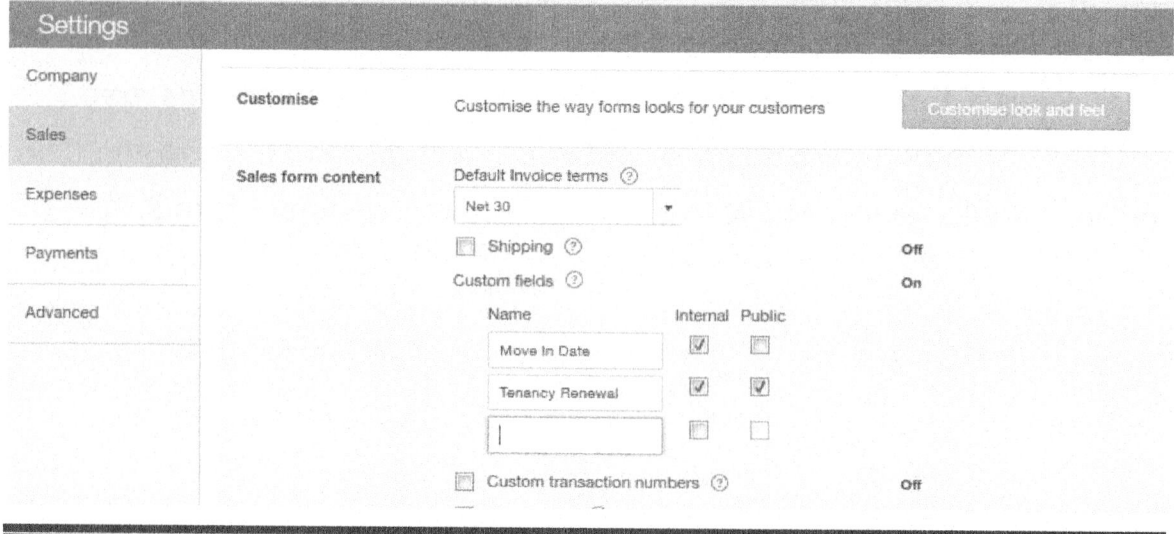

3 In this example, we've included Move In Date and Tenancy Renewal Date (as Megzina Ltd is a property management company and its customers are the tenants).

4 Click *Save*.

These options will now be available on our sales forms – which we'll see later.

To add a custom field for purchase orders:

1 Click the **wheel / cog** in the upper right of your Home screen and choose ***Company Settings*** from the dropdown menu. From here, click ***Expenses*** on the left. You'll see the ***Purchase orders*** option.

2 Click on the pen icon to *edit*.

3 Tick use purchase orders.

4 Type in the name of the custom field that you require e.g. *sales region*.

5 Tick the box to make the custom field live.

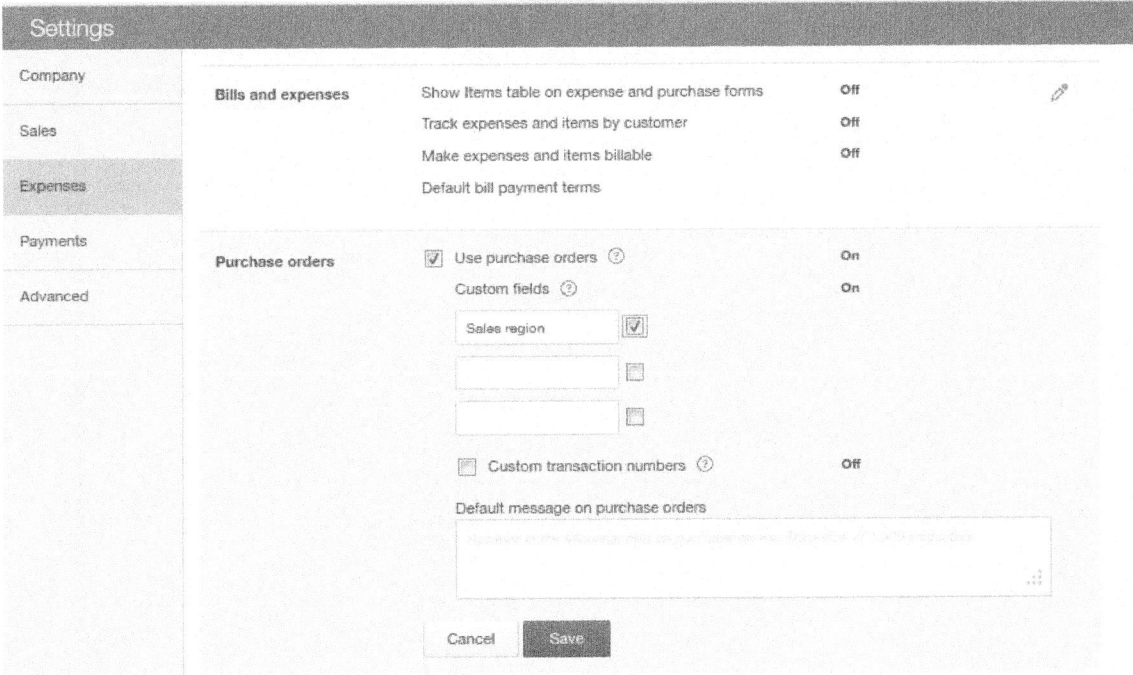

6 *Save*.

3.8 Managing lists

Lists are easy to manage in QuickBooks. You can sort lists, rename list items, delete list items, make list items inactive and print lists.

Renaming List Items

You can rename any list item. When you make the change, QuickBooks automatically modifies all existing transactions containing the item.

To rename a list item in the Chart of accounts:

1 From the *chart of accounts*, choose *Charitable Contributions* and click edit.
2 Rename the account *Donations – Charity.*

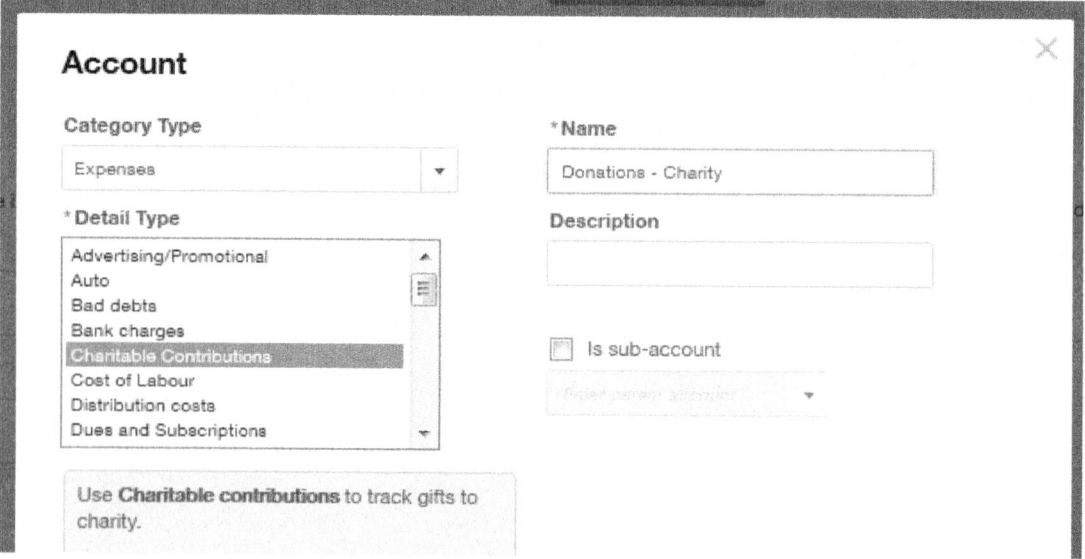

3 *Save.*
4 QuickBooks changes the name in the chart of accounts.

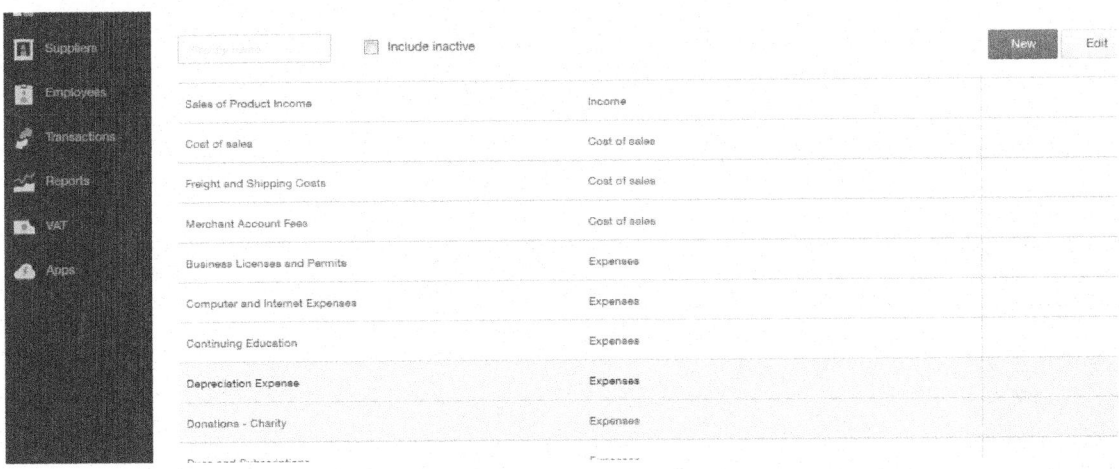

Deleting items and making list items inactive

You can only delete list items if you haven't used them in any transactions. If you try to delete a list item that is used in a transaction, or a recurring transaction - QuickBooks displays a warning that the item can't be deleted. If you don't want to use a list item but can't delete it, you can make it inactive.

To rename a list item inactive:

1 From the terms menu, choose *Net 60*.
2 Click *delete*.
3 A warning box will pop up, asking you if you are sure you want to delete this?

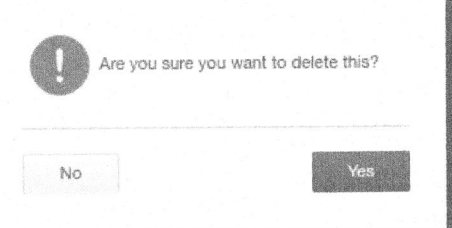

4 Click *Yes*.

5 Notice that Net 60 terms no longer appears in the terms list. The term is only removed from the list – transactions associated with this term will still appear in reports.

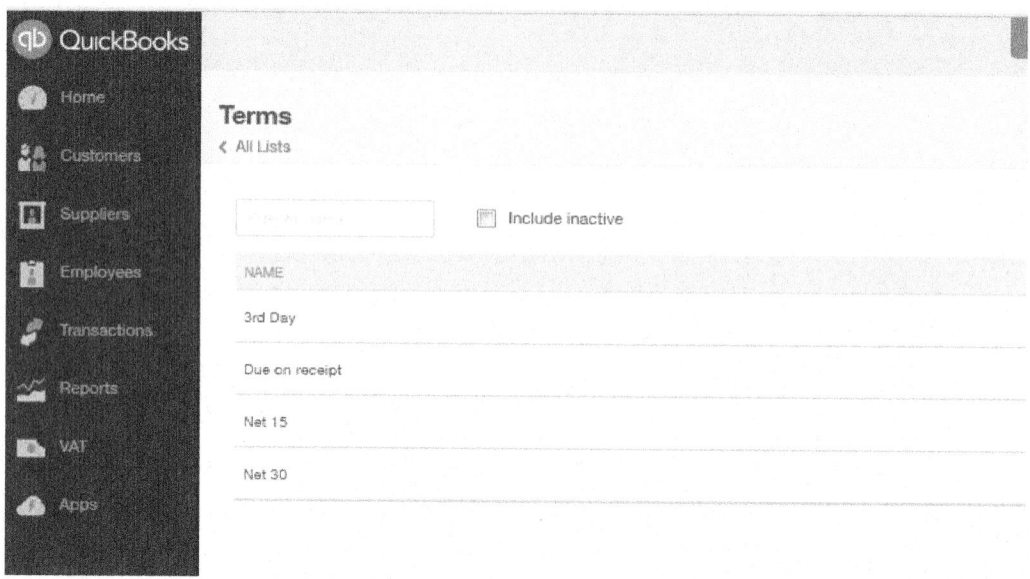

6 To see inactive list items, tick the *Include inactive b*ox. QuickBooks displays all the list items again, but word 'deleted' in brackets indicates that this term is inactive.

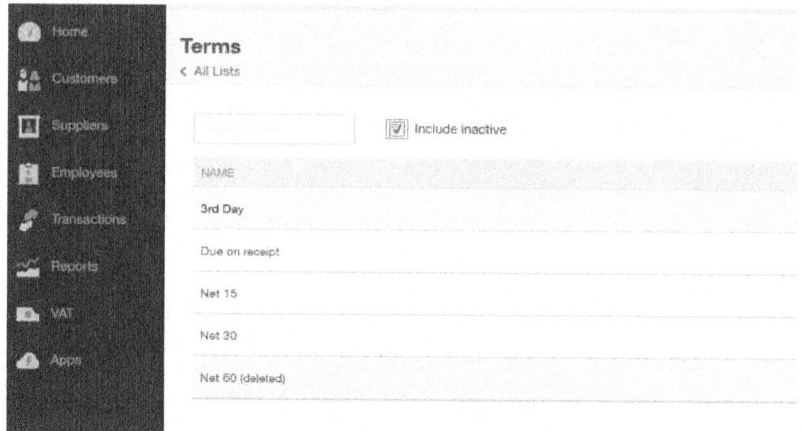

Printing a list

You can print a QuickBooks list for reference..

To print a list of customers:

1 Click *customers* on the left hand menu.

2 Click the *printer icon.*

3 A new screen will open - print the list.

4: Working with bank and credit card accounts

Summary of what is in this chapter:
- 4.1 Writing a QuickBooks cheque
- 4.2 Using bank account registers
- 4.3 Entering a handwritten cheque
- 4.4 Transferring money between accounts
- 4.5 Reconciling bank accounts
- 4.6 Tracking credit card transactions

4.1 Writing a QuickBooks cheque

You can enter cheques directly into the cheque register by using QuickBooks Write Cheques window. When you enter a cheque at the Write Cheques window, you can see the address information and easily allocate the cheque between multiple accounts.

Suppose that we need to write a cheque to pay Bob Browne (our supplier).

To write a Cheque:
1 From the Home menu, click the '+' plus icon in the middle of the screen.

2 From the dropdown options, choose *Suppliers* and then *Cheque*. QuickBooks displays the Write Cheques window.

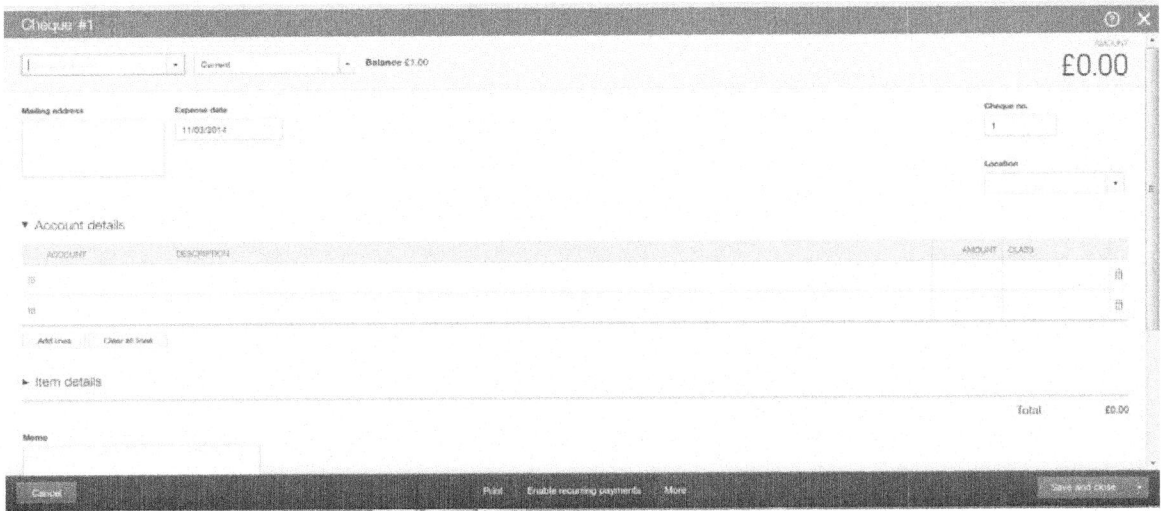

3 From the drop down choose a payee e.g. *Bob Browne.*

4 Next, choose which bank account to make the payment from e.g. *Current* – the balance of the account will also be shown on the screen.

5 The mailing address of the payee and today's date the 'expense date' will automatically be displayed. You can change the date if you wish by typing over it.

6 The cheque number will automatically be displayed. Overwrite it, if it is incorrect.

7 From the location box, (optional – only use if you want to track locations) choose from the dropdown menu the correct location e.g. *Anytown.*

QuickBooks Online Help

8 Move the mouse to under the *Account details* and under the word account, the mouse will change to a hand. Click here to enter *data.*

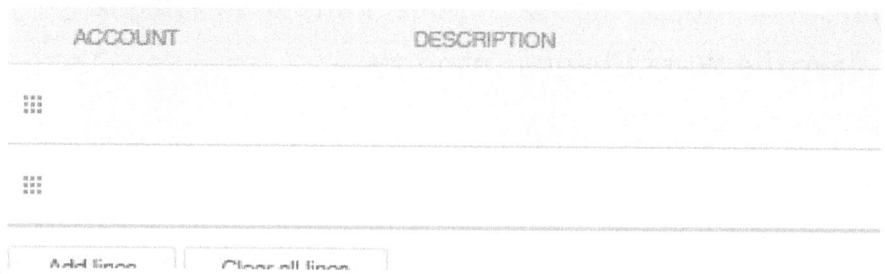

9 From the drop down menu, choose **repairs and maintenance** and in the DESCRIPTION box type: *Fixed leaky tap.*

10 In the AMOUNT type 20.00.

11 In the CLASS choose from the dropdown options – Arcacia Avenue.

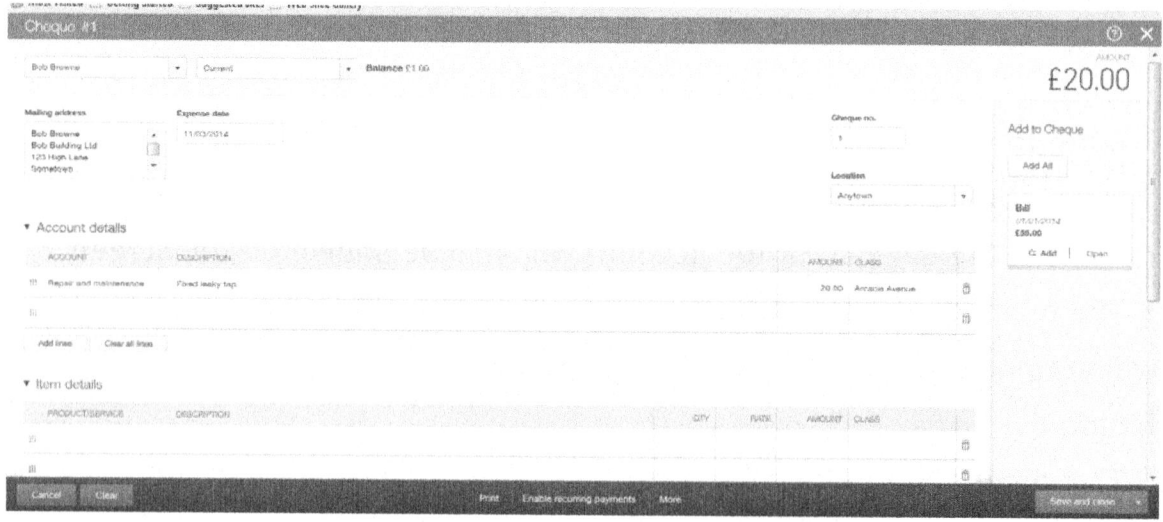

12 In the bottom middle of the screen, click **Print.**

13 You can print and/ or preview the expense voucher. If you were sending a cheque in the post, this is a useful remittance advice / expense

QuickBooks Online Help

voucher to include and enclose with the cheque, so that the recipient knows that the cheque was from you, and what it was for.

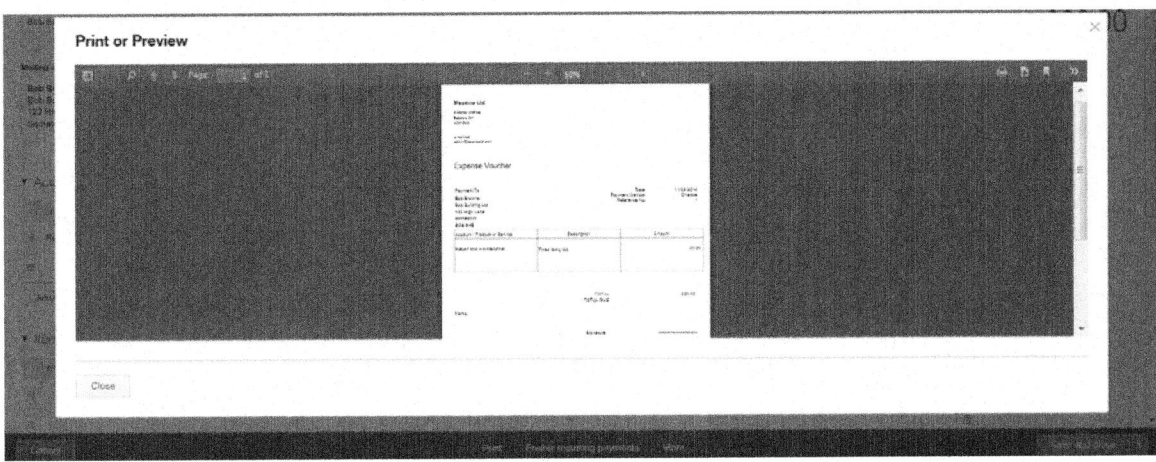

14 In the bottom middle of the screen, if you click 'enable recurring payments' – this would be appropriate if it's a cheque payments that you would make for the same amount regularly. The 'Recurring Cheque' payment screen would pop up, and you'd just specify the frequency of the cheque payment.

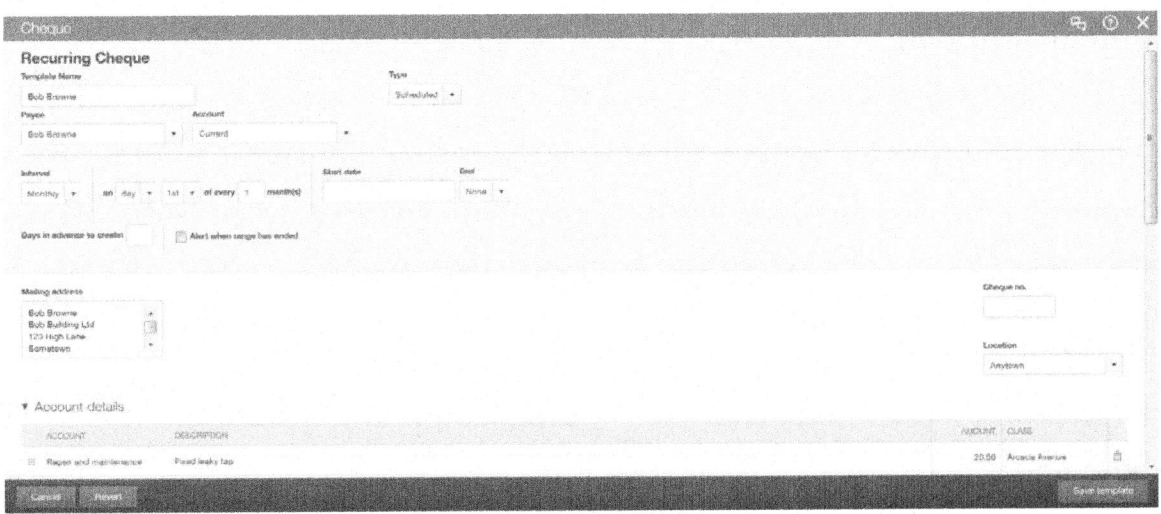

15 Click *Save and Close* – which saves and closes the window. (Note, this button has a drop down option, and if you chose the 'Save and New', the cheque would be saved, and you'd be taken to the next blank cheque screen, for you to repeat steps 3 onwards (above).

IMPORTANT NOTE

We currently owe Bob Browne £55. We see this displayed in the right hand side of the screen.

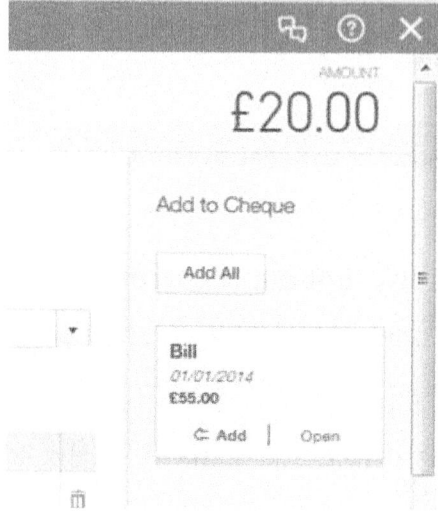

Note that paying a cheque in this way DOES NOT AFFECT ANY OUTSTANDING BILLS ALREADY ON THE SYSTEM!! This £20 cheque will not be applied to the £55 outstanding to Bob. It is a completely different and separate payment. If you wanted to use the pay cheque window to pay an existing amount (already on the system) – then follow the steps below.

To write a Cheque to pay an existing bill on the system:

1 From the Home menu, click the '+' plus icon in the middle of the screen.

2 From the dropdown options, choose *Suppliers* and then *Cheque.* QuickBooks displays the Write Cheques window.

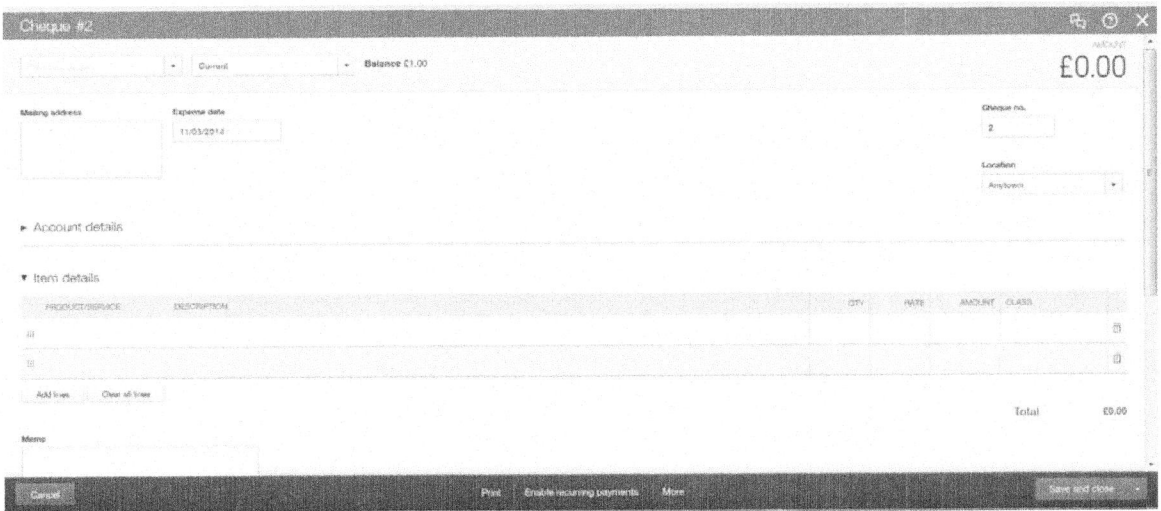

3 From the drop down choose a payee e.g. *Bob Browne.*

4 Next, choose which bank account to make the payment from e.g. *Current* – the balance of the account will also be shown on the screen.

5 The mailing address of the payee and today's date the 'expense date' will automatically be displayed. You can change the date if you wish by typing over it.

6 The cheque number will automatically be displayed. Overwrite it, if it is incorrect.

7 From the location box, (optional – only use if you want to track locations) choose from the dropdown menu the correct location e.g. *Anytown*.

8 Note: we currently owe Bob Browne £55. We see this displayed in the right hand side of the screen.

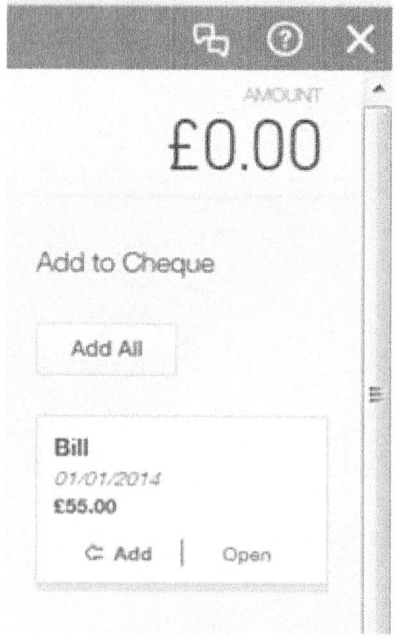

9 If we click on Open – it will take us to the bill outstanding.

10 Click **Add**

11 This then applies the cheque payment to the amount outstanding automatically.

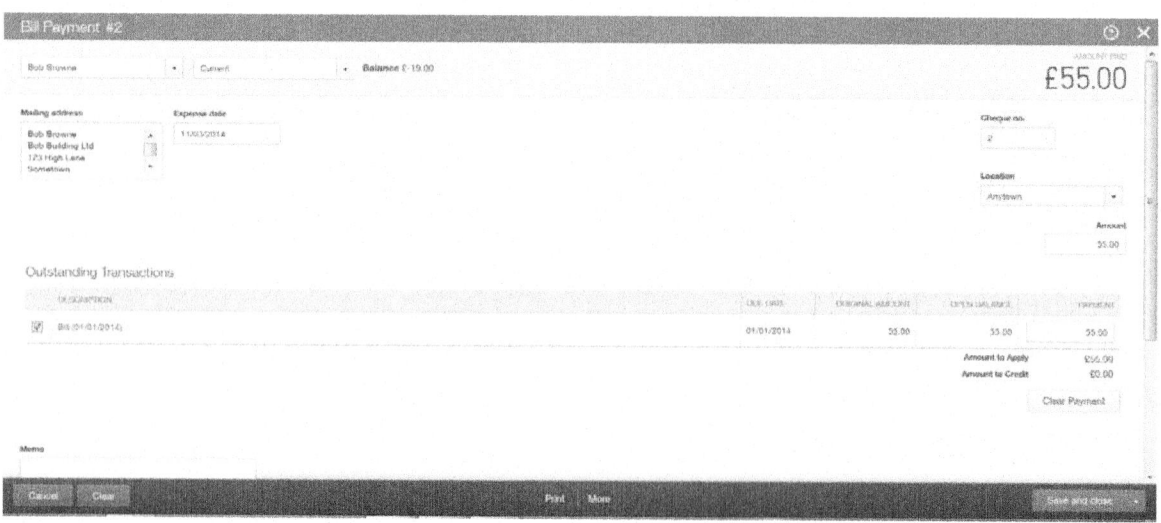

12 Click *save and Close*.

4.2 Using bank account registers

When you work in QuickBooks, you often use forms, such as cheque or an invoice, to enter information. Behind the scenes, QuickBooks records your entries in the appropriate account register. Each balance sheet account on the chart of accounts has a register (except for Retained Earnings).

Opening a register

You can view an account register by double-clicking the account name in the chart of accounts.

To open a register from the Chart of Accounts:

1 From the Home menu, click on the wheel / cog in the top right hand corner and choose *Chart of Accounts* from the drop down menu.
2 Click on the NAME of the account e.g. *Current* and the *Account History* button will become live.

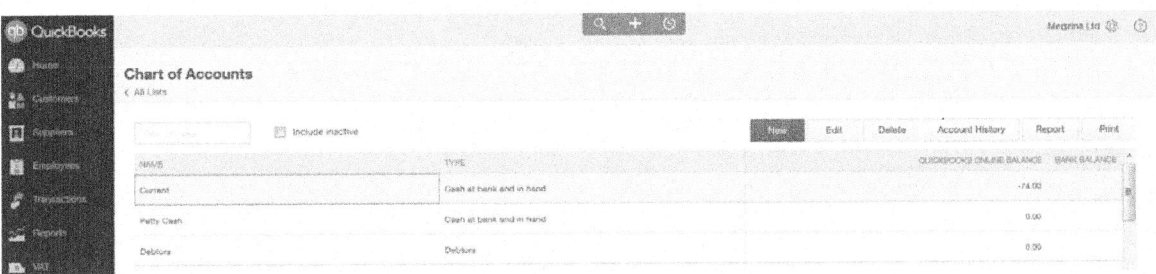

3 Click on **Account History** and the register will open.

QuickBooks Online Help

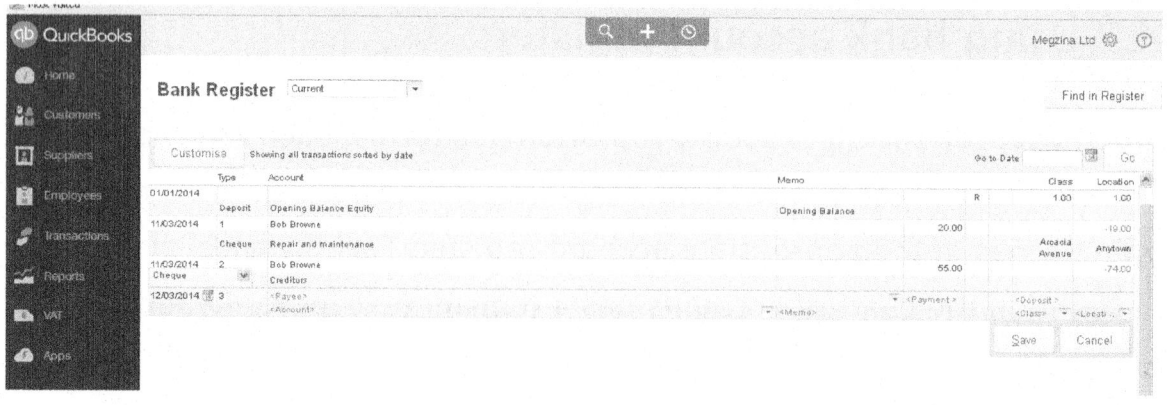

Common features of QuickBooks registers

All QuickBooks registers work in the same way, regardless of the accounts with which they're associated. Common features of all QuickBooks registers are:

- The register lists every transaction affecting the account balance in chronological order (although you can change the order by choosing clicking the 'Customise' button in the top right.
- A screen will pop up and you can choose your option. You can sort the register by Date, Ref No., Amount (ascending), Amount (descending), Reconcile Status or create date.

- Next, you select which transactions you want to show – the choice are All Transactions, Reconciled (R), Cleared (C) or Not Reconciled or Cleared.

- The last option is a tick box. Tick it if for each transaction you want to show on one line instead of two.
- Click OK.
- The columns in the register show information about the transaction. E.g. Columns.

Date	Ref No.	Payee	Payment	✓	Deposit	Balance
	Type	Account Memo			Class	Location

- The first column is the Date.
- The second column is for a Reference Number (e.g. a cheque number or a suppliers Purchase Order Number or payment method e.g. BACS) and Type (e.g. whether the transaction represents a cheque or a bill payment).
- The third column lists the Payee, the Account to which you've assigned the transaction, and any descriptive Memo.
- The final columns for the bank account show the transaction amount (either in the Payment or Deposit column) and whether the transaction cleared the bank (indicated with a tick in the column, or a R if it's reconciled).

- On every transaction line, QuickBooks shows the account's running balance.
- The bottom right-hand corner of the screen shows the accounts ending balance.
- IF the location and class options are turned on, these options will show too.
- Other registers available are found in the drop-down menu. Whilst you are in Bank Register – you can change, to select Petty Cash, Debtors, Finished Goods Stock, Prepaid Insurance, Raw Materials Stock, Stock Asset, Undeposited Funds, Work in Progress, Accumulated Depreciation, Vehicles, Creditors & Opening Balance Equity (amongst others).

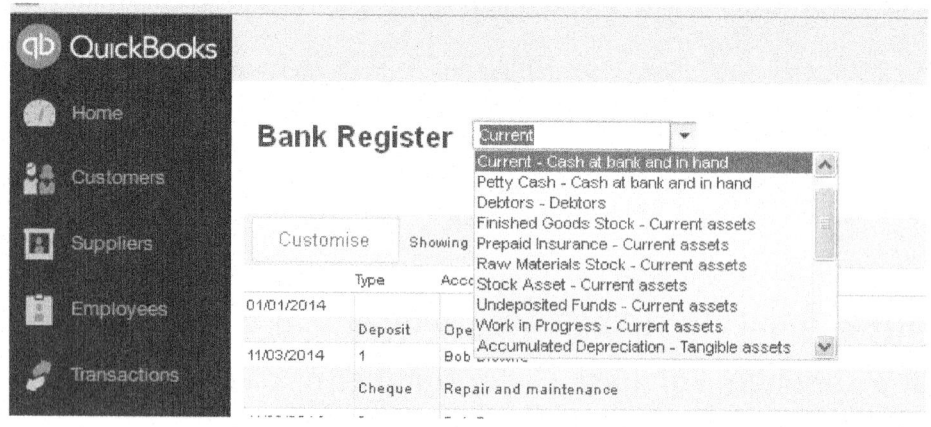

4.3 Entering a handwritten cheque

QuickBooks lets you write a cheque directly in the account register. For example, imagine you have to pay the water bill for the Holloway Road Property for £42.75 to Anytown Water Works and you send a cheque.

QuickBooks Online Help

To enter a handwritten cheque in the current account register:

1 From the Home menu, click on the wheel / cog in the top right hand corner and choose Chart of accounts from the drop down menu.

2 Click on the NAME of the account e.g. *Current* and the Account History button will become live.

3 Click on *Account History* and the bank register will open.

4 Click the Date field in the blank transaction at the bottom of the register.

5 Type *15/03* and then press Tab. [This will put in the date automatically, using this year that we're in]

6 In the next field, this will automatically put in the next cheque number [in our case 3], if this is correct, press Tab, otherwise type in the correct cheque number.

6 In the Payee field, type *Anytown Water Works*, then press Tab.

7 The 'Add Name' screen pops up because Anytown Water Works is a new supplier for us, and we've not used it before.

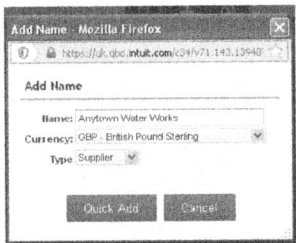

8 Click *Quick Add*.

9 Press Tab to get to the next field which is payment. Type *42.75*. Click Tab.

10. From the drop down menu choose the correct account. In this case, it's *Utilities*. Click Tab.

11. In the memo, (optional to use) you can add a note. E.g. *Bill to 28.2.14*. This tells you that the water bill is paid up to the 28th February. Press Tab.

12. In the class (optional) choose from the drop down box. E.g. *Holloway Road*, because this was the water bill for the property at Holloway Road. Press Tab.

13. In the location (optional) choose from the drop down box e.g. *Anytown* – because that's the location they are in.

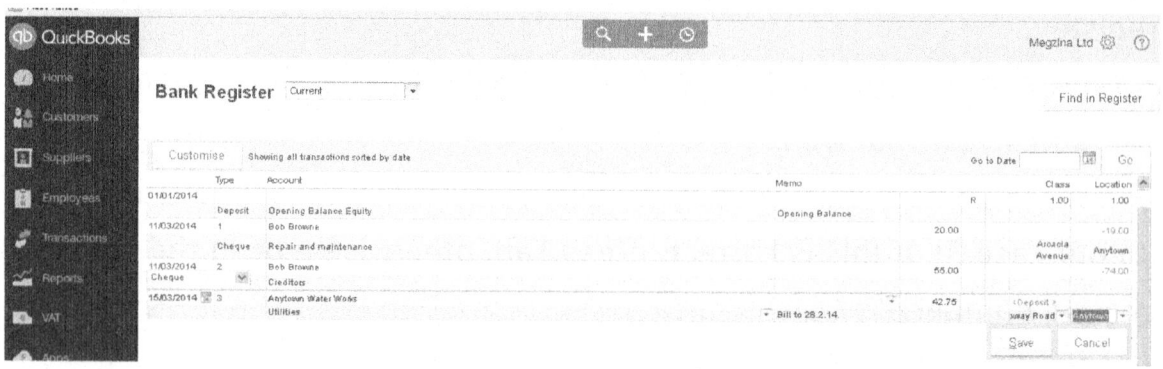

14. Click Save.

4.4 Transferring money between accounts

You can easily move money between accounts. Megzina Ltd withdrew £20 out at the cash point, and so (on the system) needs to transfer £20.00 from the Current Account to Petty Cash.

QuickBooks Online Help

To transfer money:

1 From the main menu click the blue '+' in the top middle of the screen.

2 Under Other, choose Transfer from the menu.

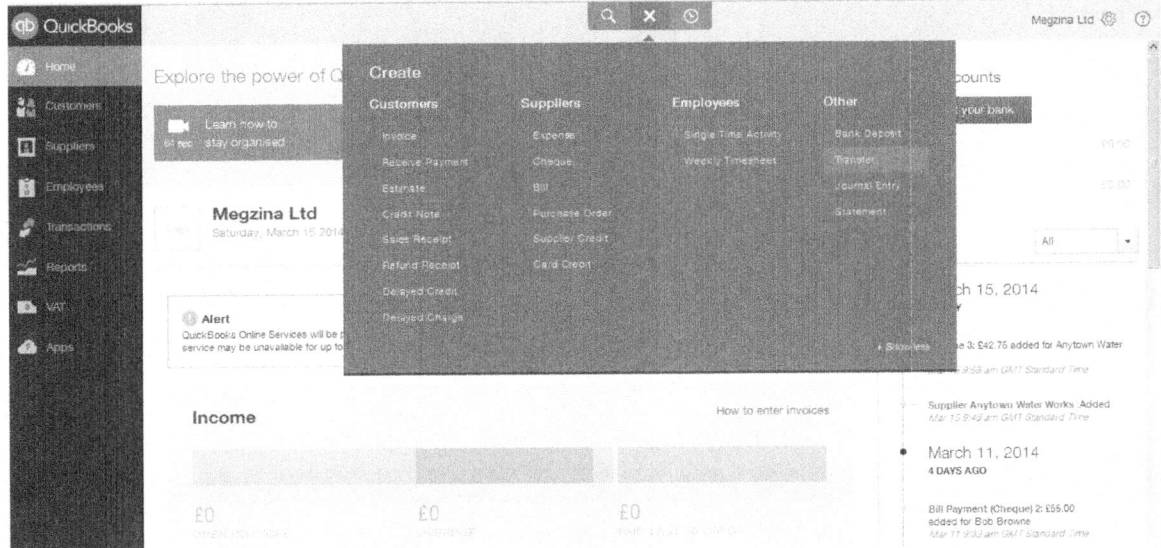

3 In the Transfer screen which pops up next, for: Transfer Funds From, select *Current* from the drop down menu.

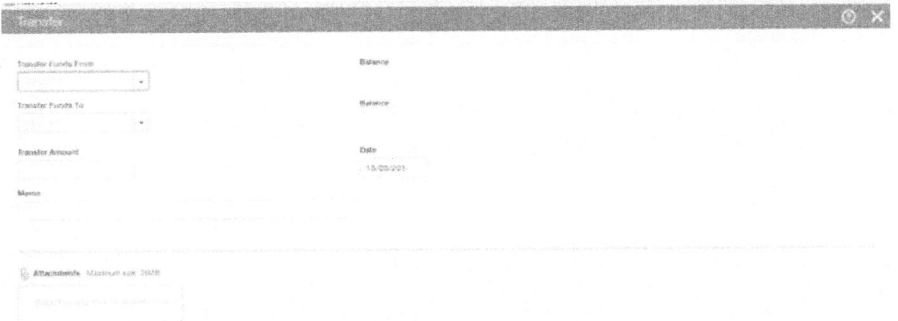

4 Transfer Funds To, select *Petty Cash* from the drop down menu.

5 For Transfer Amount, type in *20.00*.

6 The Memo box is option. In this cash, we just typed in *Cash Machine*.

7 Change the Date if necessary.

8 Note – you can also upload an attachment (optional). Your screen should now resemble this one:

9 Click Save and Close.

QuickBooks decreases the balance of the Current account by £20 and increases the Petty cash account by £20.

4.5 Reconciling bank accounts

Reconciling is the process of making sure that your bank account record matches the bank's record. Reconciling the bank account is a very important practise to carry out. It helps you to spot errors, avoid overdraft charges for bad cheques, spot possible bank errors and keep more accurate financial records.

Your bank sends you a statement for each of your accounts each month. The statement shows all the activity in your account since the previous statement:

- The opening balance (amount in your account as of the previous statement)
- The ending balance (amount in your account as of the closing date for the statement)
- The amount of interest (if any), that you've received for this statement period
- The amount of interest and charges (if any), that you've been charged for this statement period
- Cheques that have cleared in the bank
- Deposits which have been made to the account
- Any other transactions that affect the balance of your account (e.g. direct debits in or out, cash machine withdrawals or deposits).

When you receive a statement from your bank or from a credit card company, you need to reconcile the statement with your QuickBooks records. You can reconcile any QuickBooks bank account, including accounts for savings, money market funds and PayPal (online) accounts.

Note: If you have online internet banking set up, you can connect your bank account directly into QuickBooks which will speed up the reconciliation process.

Marking cleared transactions

To begin reconciling an account, you need you select which account you want to reconcile.

Then you can provide information from your bank statement.

To reconcile your account:

1 From the wheel / cog menu on the main page in the top right hand corner, click and choose *Reconcile* under the *Tools* option.

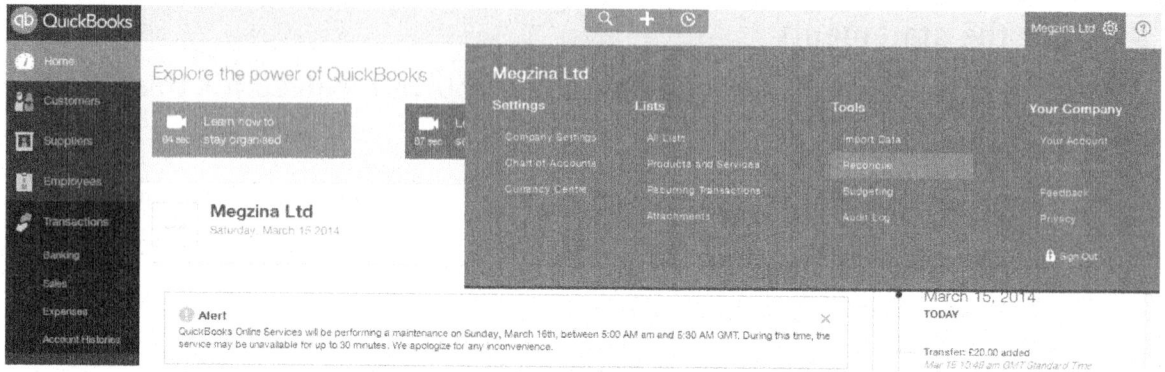

2 From the drop down menu, choose the account that you want to reconcile. In our case: *Current*. Click *Reconcile Now* button.

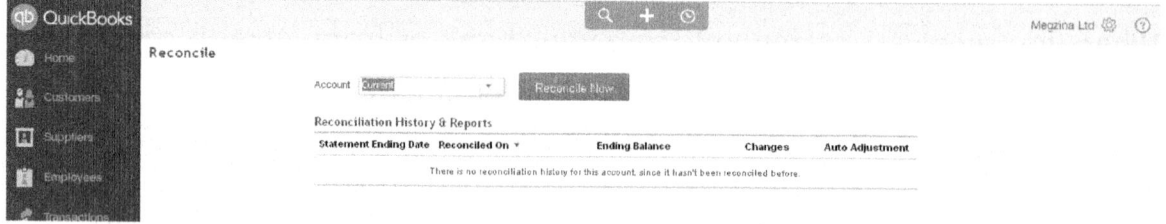

3 The start reconciling screen pops up. We have to fill out this Start Reconciling form in two steps.

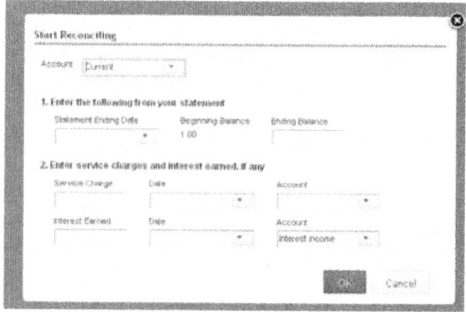

4 Choose *Current* from the drop down options. Then *Tab*.

111

Step 1 - Enter the following from your statement

5 From the drop down, choose the Statement Ending Date. This is the date of your bank statement. E.g. *15/03/2014.*

6 The bank balance will be there automatically. It's what you started the system with (in our case £1.00) or, the closing amount of the last reconciliation. In the Ending Balance, type in the statements closing balance. E.g. *-56.00* (in our case the bank is overdrawn). Then *Tab.*

Step 2 - Enter service charges and interest earned, if any

7 Service Charge – enter the bank charges here (if any). In our fictitious example, Megzina Ltd incurs a £2 bank charge on the 15th March. So, in the Service Charge field, type *2.00.* And Tab.

8 In the Date field, type in the date (according to the bank statement of the charge) e.g. *15/03/14.* Then *Tab.*

9 Choose the appropriate account from the drop down menu. E.g. *Interest Expense.*

10 Click *OK.*

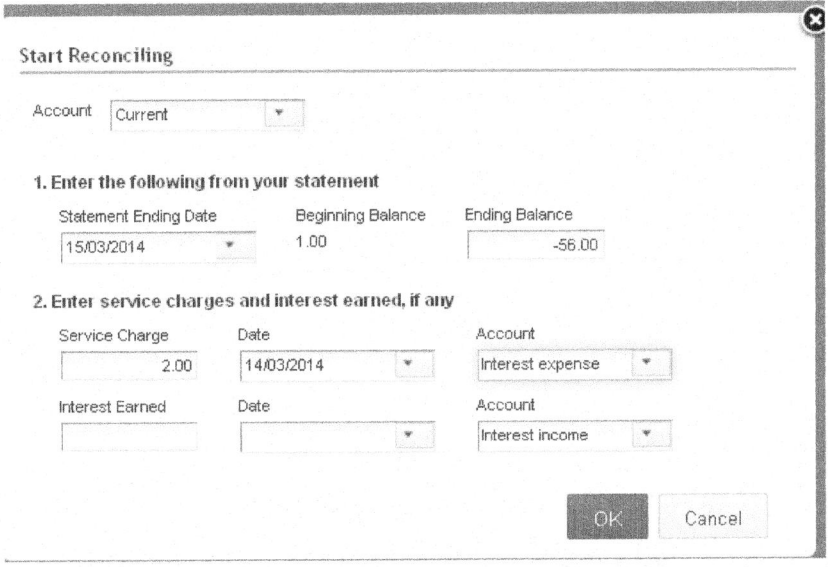

11 This then brings you to the next page – the reconciliation page, where we have to tick the items that are showing on our bank statement. Note, that the interest is already ticked for you.

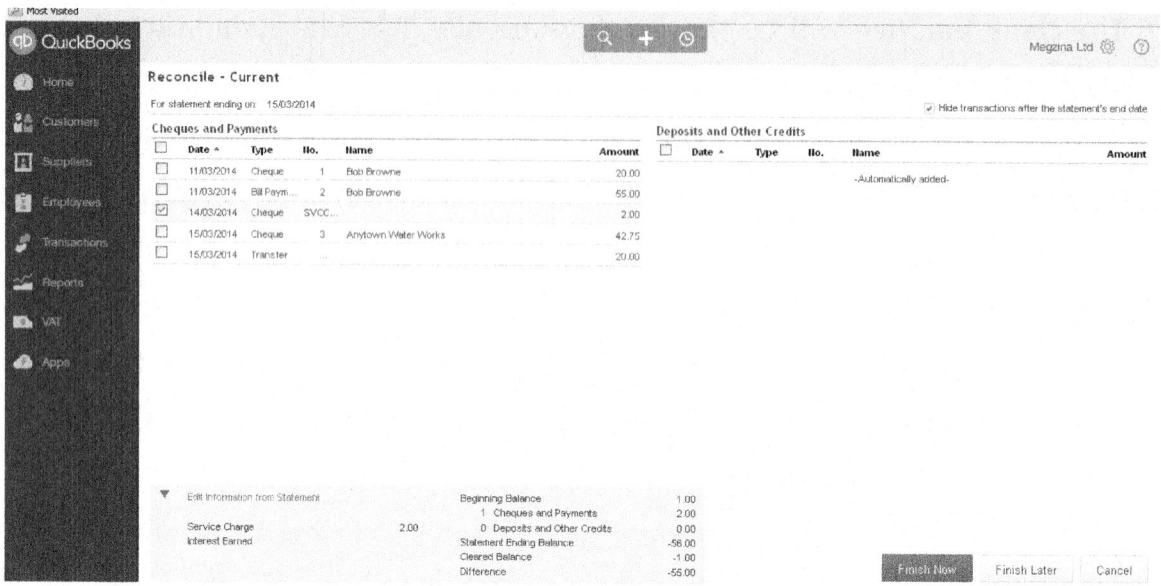

12 We then look at our physical bank statement – which is very short – with just 3 transactions: it opens with a balance of £1.00, there is a payment going out for £55.00 and there's bank interest charges of £2.00.

13 Pay attention to the grey box in the bottom left hand corner. The aim is to get the Difference to NIL.

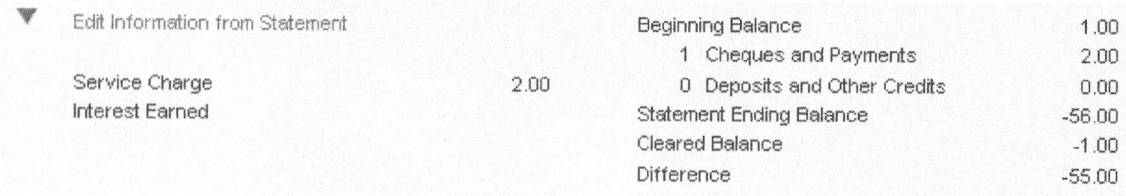

14 Tick the transactions that appear on the bank statement. In our case, it's just the £55.00 bill payment – cheque no. 2 to Bob Browne.

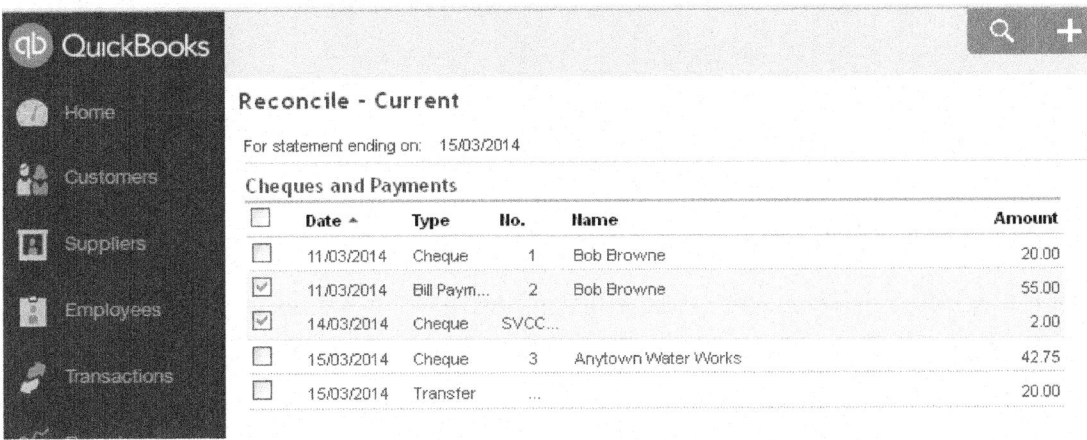

15 Once you've ticked all the cheques and payments that appear on the bank statement, you'd tick all the Deposits and Other Credits which appeared on the bank statement – in our case there haven't yet been any deposits.

16 Be aware that the selection currently ticked is Hide transactions after the statement's end date. If you have ever made an entry into the system, and when reconciling cannot find it... untick this box, because it could be that your entry has a later date.

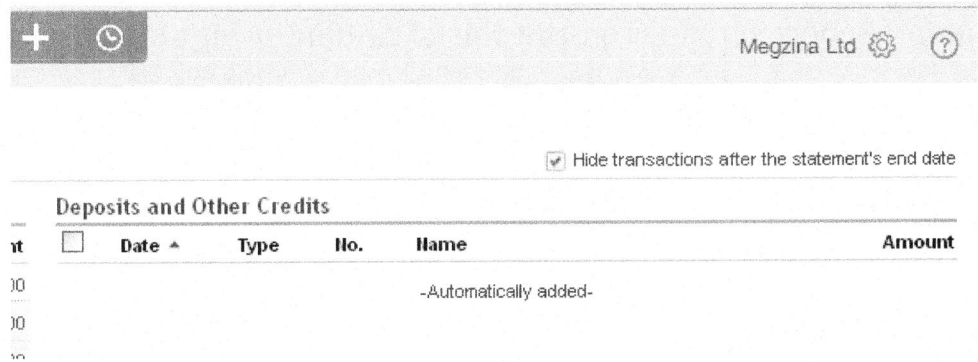

17 When we look at the Difference (bottom left hand corner of the screen, this is now at nil). So click the blue *Finish Now* button in the bottom right hand corner.

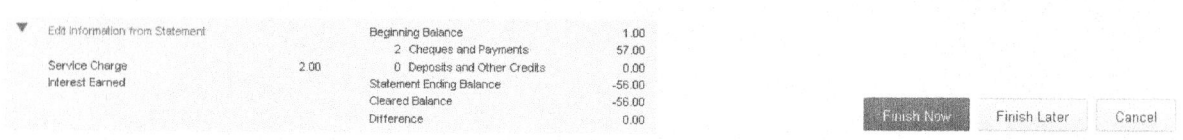

18 Note – NEVER EVER 'Finish Now' if there is a difference! If there is a difference, click *Finish Later*, and go and enter the missing transactions into the system from the bank statement OR if the amounts on the statement don't match the bank, investigate and amend the QuickBooks system, so that the amounts match the bank. If you click Finish Later, when you return to this page, it does remember what items were ticked.

19 You are then taken to a page which lists the Reconciliation Reports.

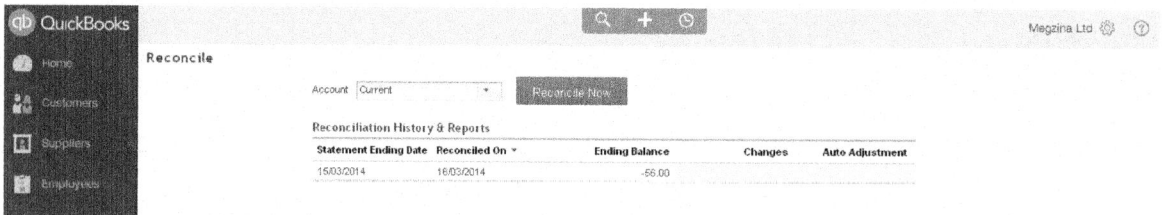

20 If you click on the line which you've just reconciled, it'll take you to the Reconciliation Report screen. To print this click blue *print* button.

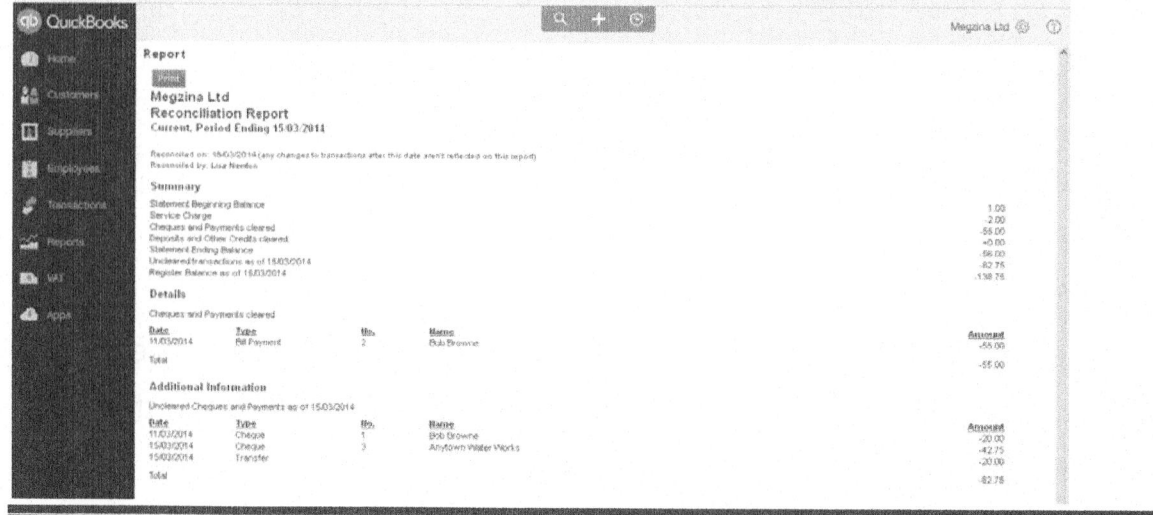

It is a good idea to print the reconciliation report and to save it with the physical bank statements in the same folder. You may (if you are a bookkeeper), ask the owner / manager to check, initial and sign the reconciliations so that they have acknowledged it.

Now you know that the balance in the QuickBooks Current account register is accurate as at the latest bank statement. The next time you look at the bank register you'll see an 'R' in the Cleared column next to each reconciled transaction. You'll see this column in certain reports too.

Viewing cleared transactions in the register
Open the Current Account Bank Register to see the cleared transactions.

To view the cleared transactions:
1 From the Home menu, click on the wheel / cog in the top right hand corner and choose *Chart of Accounts* from the drop down menu.
2 Click on the NAME of the account e.g. *Current* and the *Account History* button will become live. Click on *Account History*.

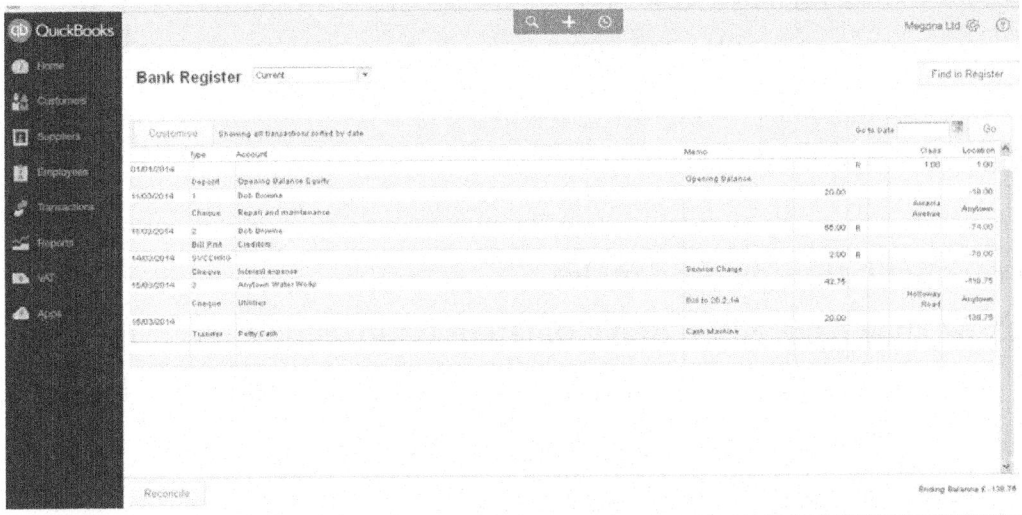

3 Notice that QuickBooks displays an R next to all cleared items.

Reconciliation discrepancies

In order to illustrate how QuickBooks makes it easy to find discrepancies, we are now going to make a change to one of the reconciled transactions.

4 Select the bank service charge transaction – and 4 options arise: Save, Edit, Cancel and Delete. Click *Delete*.

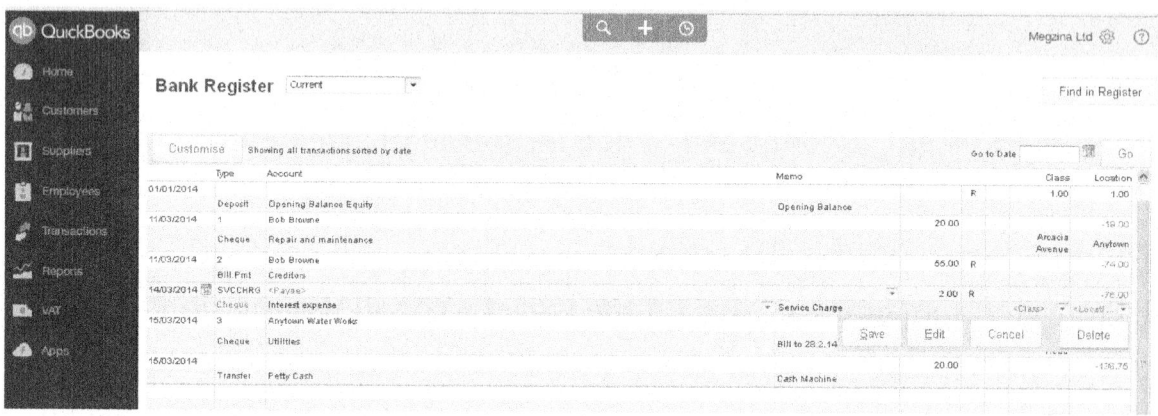

5 A message pops up on the screen: "The transaction you are editing has been reconciled. Saving your changes could put you out of balance the next time you try to reconcile. Are you sure you want to modify it?" Click *Yes*.

6 Close the Bank Register.

Locating reconciliation discrepancies

Sometimes we may have accidentally deleted a transaction, or (if the system is shared), another user could have deleted a transaction, but QuickBooks helps to find when the beginning balance is different from the ending balance from the bank statement.

QuickBooks Online Help

To find discrepancies in the last reconciliation:

1 To reconcile, go to the wheel / cog in the top right hand corner, click to reveal the menu, under *Tools*, click *Reconcile.*

2 Notice that there is an entry under the Changes column.

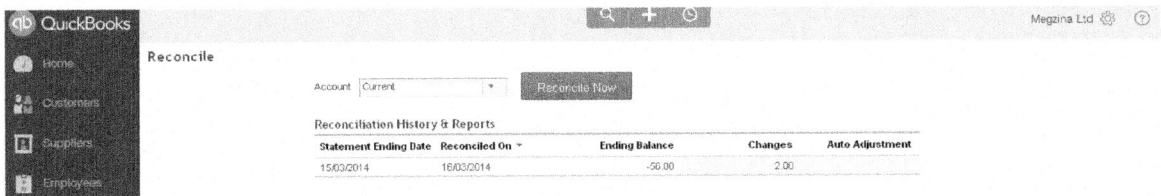

3 Click on the changes (where it says 2.00).

4 This screen then pops up – which explains how the change arose:

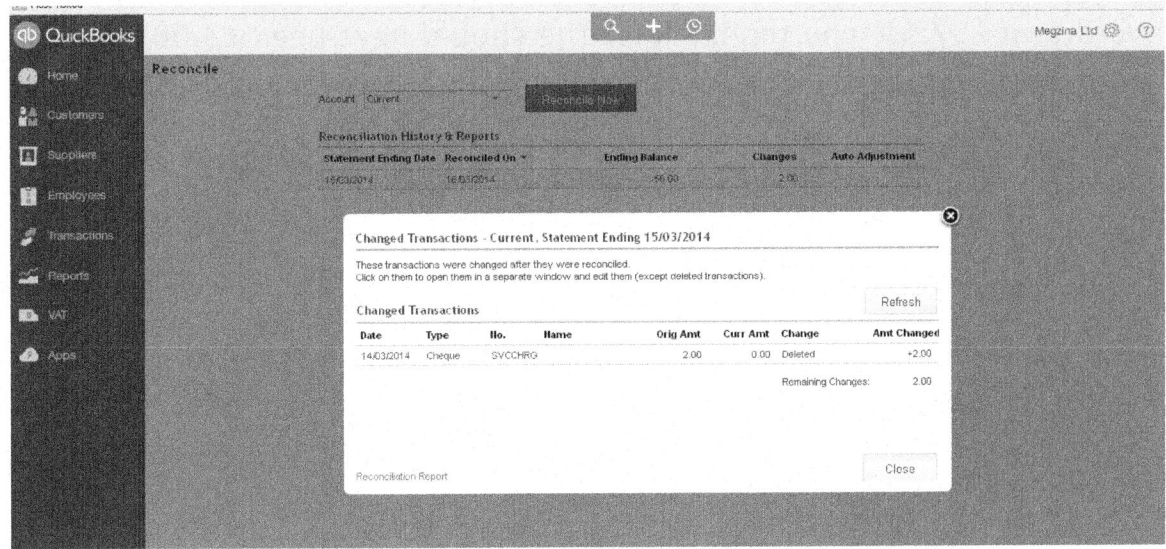

5 QuickBooks shows SVCCHRG (the Bank Service Charge) of £2.00 was deleted.

6 Close this report.

7 Click *Reconcile Now.*

8 The Start Reconciliation window appears. Note the Beginning Balance is now -£54.00 (and not the -£56.00 as before).

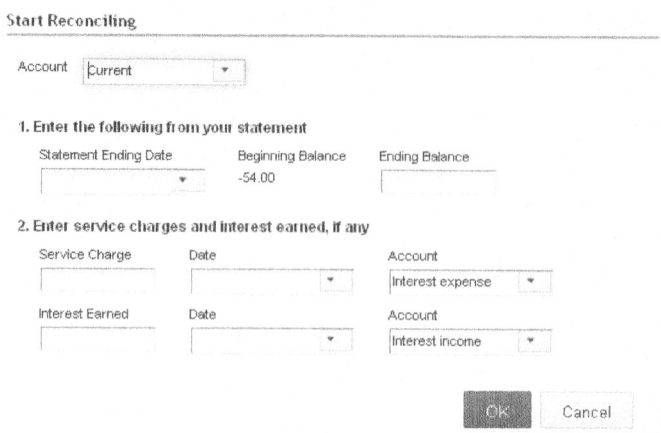

9 Imagine if our physical bank statement closing balance was actually overdrawn £57.00 (and the bank charge should have been £3.00), we would fill in this form as before, but putting *3.00* in the service charge field.

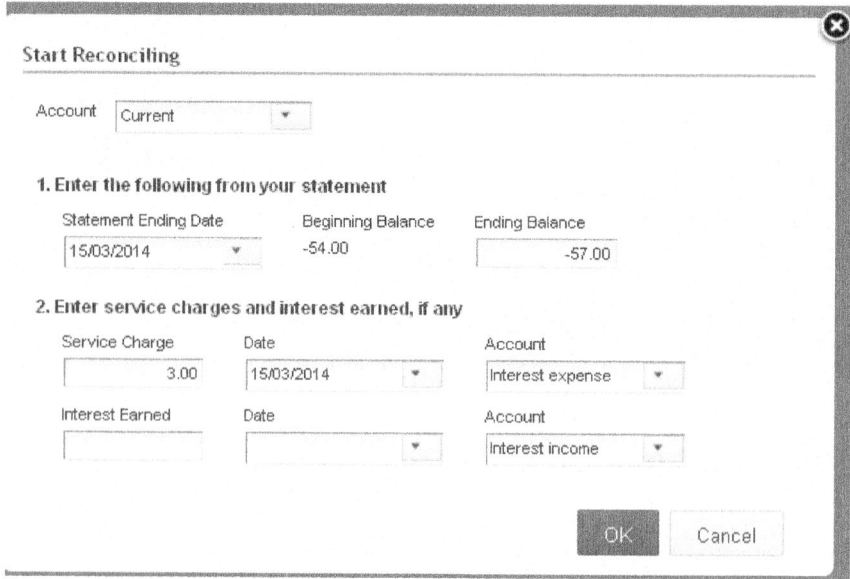

10 Click *OK*.

11 On the next screen – the reconciliation screen – the Interest transaction is ticked automatically. The Difference (grey box, bottom left) is at NIL. So we can click the blue *finish now* button in the bottom right.

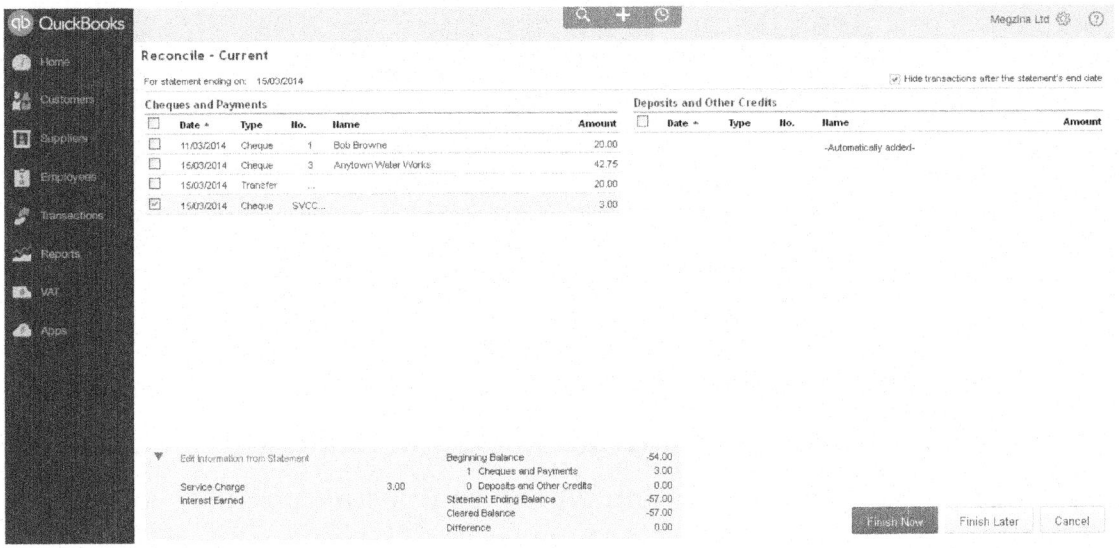

12 This takes you to the Reconciliation History and Reports screen. The most recent reconciliation is displayed at the top.

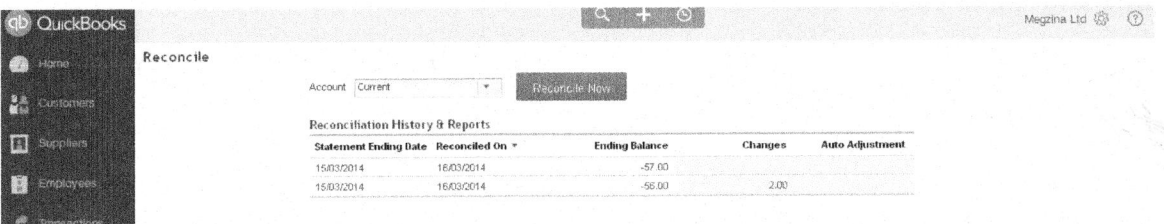

Therefore, if you are in a situation, where your bank reconciliation doesn't match your physical bank statements. Delete a previous reconciliation to get you to the point where the two do match, and then move forward. If you do still struggle, enlist the help of an accounting professional. Feel free to email us: admin@boogles.co.uk

4.6 Tracking credit card transactions

In your business, you sometimes pay for expenses with a credit card rather than a cheque. For convenience – a credit card is especially handy. Not only are you given 'interest free credit' but some cards come with rewards and bonus points or cash back for spending plus the monthly statement gives you a detailed list of exactly how and where you've spent your money that month. You can track your credit card transactions in QuickBooks just as easily as you track expenses you pay for by cheque.

You should set up a QuickBooks credit card account for each credit card you use in your business. Like any QuickBooks account, a credit card account has its own register, listing all the charges and credits you've recorded and payments you've made. The way you open and scroll through a credit card register is the same for any other QuickBooks account register.

Setting up a credit card account
To record the credit card transactions, you need to create the new credit card account itself.

To create the credit card account:
1 From the wheel / cog in the top right hand corner, choose *Chart of Accounts.*
2 Click *New.*
3 From the category type choose *Credit Card* from the drop down menu.
4 Type in the name of the card and the last four digits of the card number e.g. *ATBC Credit Card 7452.*

5 The Description field is optional.

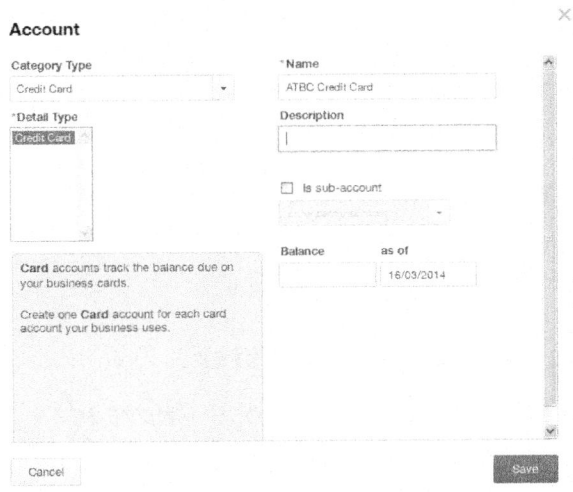

5 Click *Save*.

6 Scroll down the Chart of Accounts, and you'll see ATBC (AnyTown Banking Corporation) credit card now shows in the Chart of Accounts list.

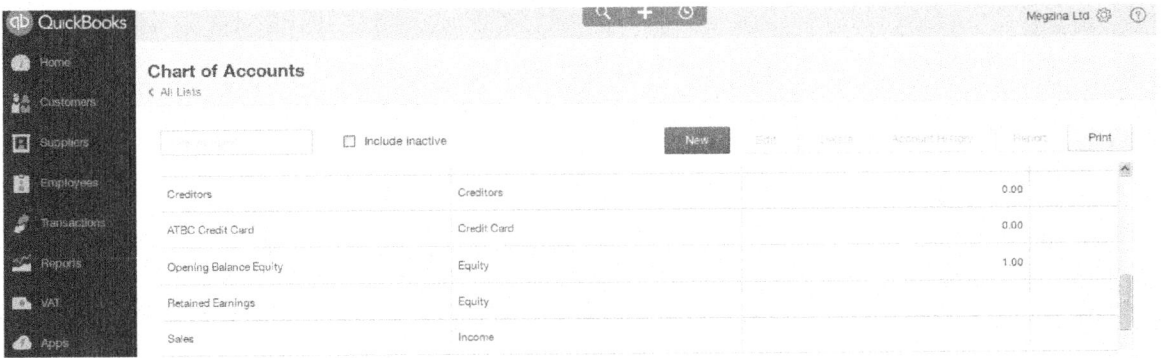

Entering credit card charges:

QuickBooks lets you choose when you enter your credit card charges – either when you charge an item or when you receive the bill. Your choice depends on whether you like to enter the information into QuickBooks incrementally or all at once. The advantage to entering charges when you charge an item is that you can keep close track of how much you owe. In addition, id the charge is for a particular job, you can keep track of how much you're spending on that job.

Imagine you have a £40 travel charge you want to enter into QuickBooks. We can enter it via the Credit Card register.

To enter a credit card charge via the Credit Card Register

1 From the wheel / cog in the top right hand corner, choose *Chart of Accounts.*
2 Scroll down and click *ATBC Credit Card* and then click *Account History.* The form below will be displayed. Note the option CC Expense from the drop down is already selected for us.

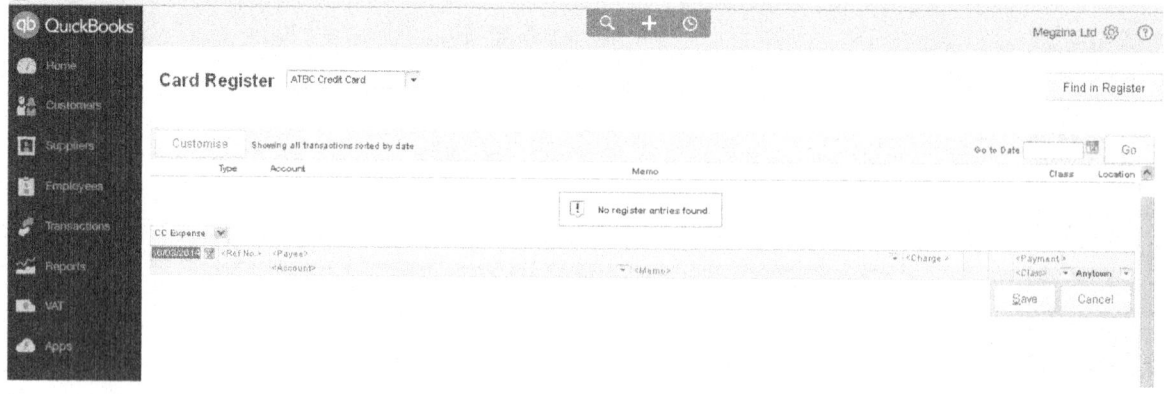

3 If you had the receipt, you can use the date of the receipt, or if you had the credit card statement to hand you could enter the date from the statement. Type in *06/03/14.* And press *Tab.*
4 This takes you to the reference number. We don't have one for this transaction, so press *Tab.*

QuickBooks Online Help

5 The Payee – is the next option. Choose from the dropdown menu. If your choice isn't there, then select << *Add New* >> from the menu (this is the first option). It will show all active Suppliers, Customers and Employees on the system.

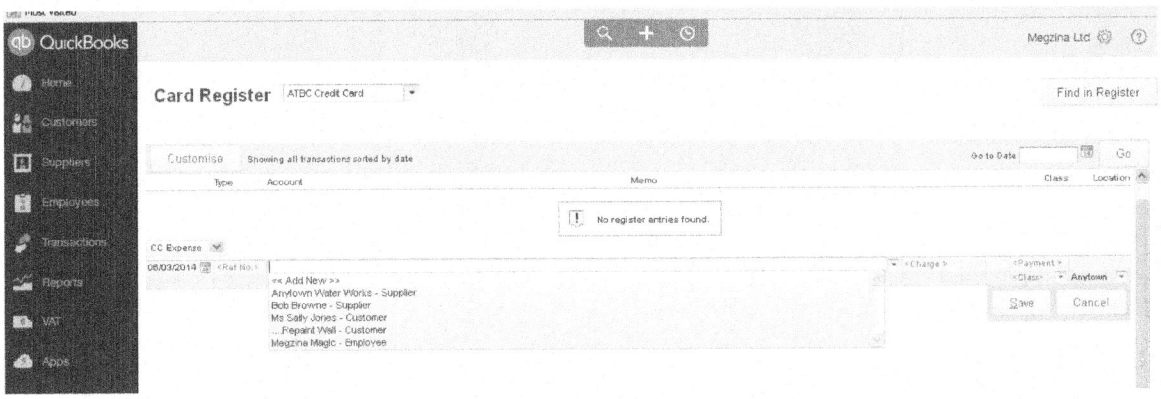

6 An Add Name screen pops up. Type in *AnyTown Train*. The Currency is GBP – British Pound Sterling and the Type is Supplier. Click *Quick Add*.

7 *Tab* to the next field, which is Charge. Type in *40.00*. Click *Tab*.

8 From the drop down list, choose *Travel Expense*. Click *Tab*.

9 Leave the memo blank and click *Tab*. (You could put a short note in there if you wanted e.g. purpose of that travel e.g. to view a property)

10 Class – for the purpose of this entry, just choose *Arcacia Avenue* from the drop down options. Click *Tab*.

11 Location – select *Anytown*. Click *Save*.

The Card register now looks like this.

To REVERSE a credit card charge – we can use the Credit Card Charges form

1 From the home page, click the + sign in the middle of the page, and choose *Card Credit*, under *Suppliers* in the drop down menu.

2 The Card Credit screen opens. Notice it opens with a Balance of £40.00 (this is the transaction we've just entered above).

3 To reverse the transaction above, we enter another travel expense of £40.00 by willing out the on screen form. From the drop down menu, choose a payee. Either click and scroll to find *AnyTown Trains*, or type '*a*' in the field and it'll automatically find all payees beginning with 'a'. Click *Tab*.

4 ATBC Credit Card is already selected, but if there were other credit cards on the system, we would select the correct one by either typing in the first letter of the name or scrolling through the drop down options. Click *Tab*.

5 Mailing address – if you want to complete it you can do. Otherwise, leave as it is and just click *Tab*.

6 Expense date – type in the date of the expense – use either the statement date or (if you're going by individual physical receipts), use the date on the receipt. E.g. *06/03/14*. Click *Tab*.

7 Reference number – if you have one, type this in the field. If you don't, just leave it blank. Click *Tab*.

8 Location – currently set by default to *AnyTown*. Click *Tab*.

9 Account – in this field use the drop down menu to scroll to the correct expense, or if you know the name of the expense start typing it in the field. Typing *tr* will bring up *travel expense*. Click *Tab*.

10 If there is a Description e.g. purpose of the travel, you can (optional) type this in here. Click *Tab*.

11 Amount – type in *40.00*. Click *Tab*.

12 Class – for the purpose of this reversing entry, choose *Arcacia Avenue* from the drop down options. By typing *a* – the Arcacia Avenue option will show. Click *Tab*.

13 If we wanted to scan and upload the receipt (to have a copy of it with the transaction within QuickBooks), then we'd go to the scanned receipt on our computer's hard drive. Find the receipt on the system and drag it onto the screen and drop it into the grey box to upload it.

QuickBooks Online Help

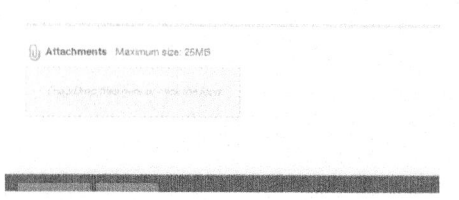

Once it's uploaded, a message then shows in the grey box – the name of the file and its size.

14 The form is now completely filled in. It should look like this:

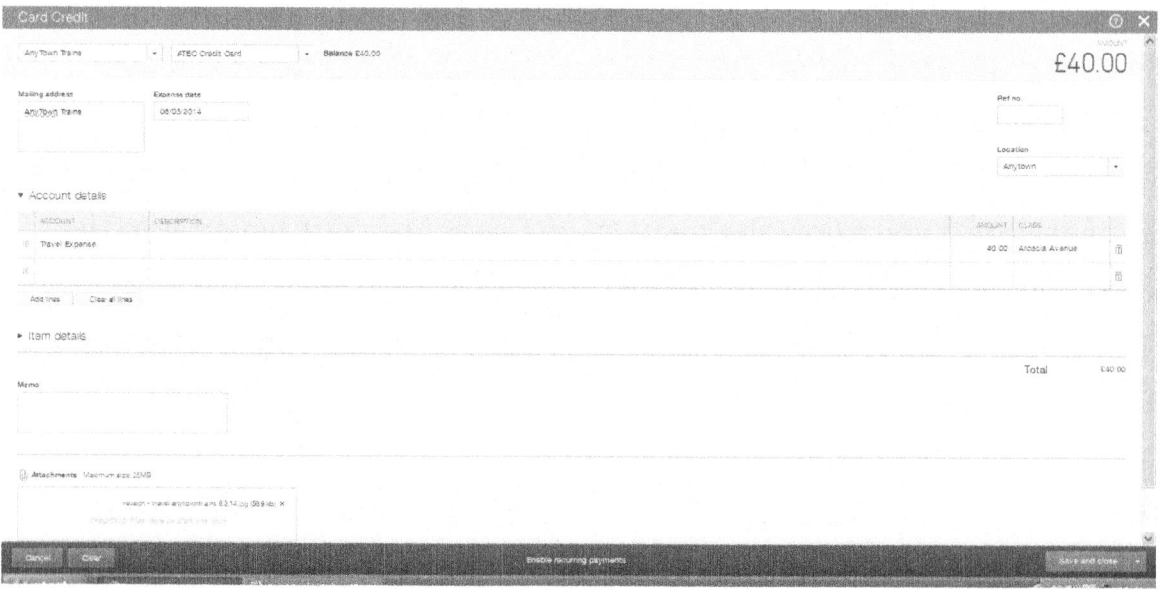

16 Click *Save and close.*

Reconciling and paying a credit card bill

As with the bank account, you should reconcile your credit card receipts with your credit card statement. Good practise is to staple your card receipts to your physical bank statement. Reconciling a credit card account is almost identical to reconciling a bank account (as seen earlier).

QuickBooks Online Help

To reconcile a credit card statement:

1 Open the Card Register (Wheel/cog in the top right corner, choose *Chart of Accounts*, click on the *Credit Card*, choose *Account History*).

2 In the bottom left hand corner, click the *Reconcile* button.

3 The Start Reconciling form pops up on the screen.

4 The account ATBC Credit Card is selected. Click *Tab*. The statement ending date is e.g. *10/3/2014*. Click *Tab*.

5 The Ending Balance is £1.25. Type in *1.25*. Click *Tab*.

6 Enter the Finance Charge (if any). Type in *1.25*. Click *Tab*.

7 Enter the Date as e.g. 7/3/2014. Click *Tab*.

8 Leave the Account as Interest Expense. Click *OK*.

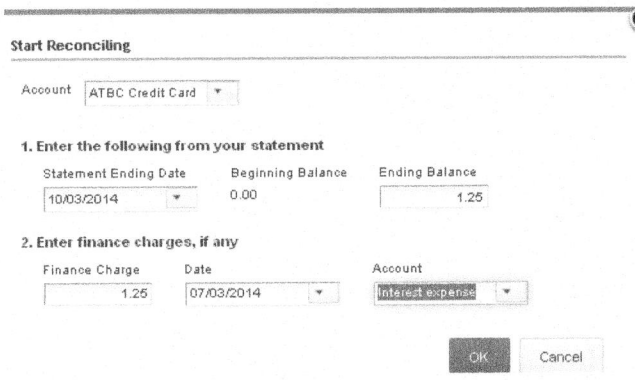

9 On the reconciliation page, tick the items which appear on the credit card statement. In this case, it's the £40 charges and £40 payments. The interest finance charge is automatically already ticked for us.

10 In the grey box in the bottom left corner, the difference is NIL.

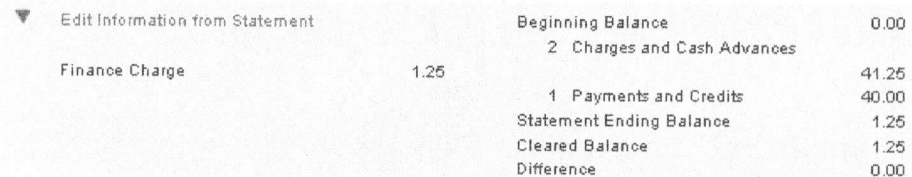

11 Click the blue button - *Finish Now*.

12 Three options appear on the screen: You can either:

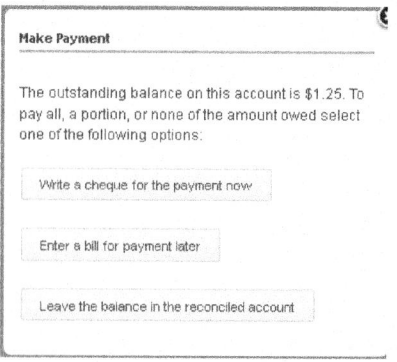

    i. Write a cheque for the payment now

    ii. Enter a bill for the payment later

    iii. Leave the balance in the reconciled report.

13 Click *Enter a bill for the payment later*.

14 The Bill payment screen appears. We can see the balance due is £1.25 – we just need to fill in the form, and (in order to pay the card), to set up the Credit Card ATBC as a Supplier too.

15 In the first field – we have to choose a supplier. If the credit card supplier name isn't there in the drop down, we click on ADD NEW.

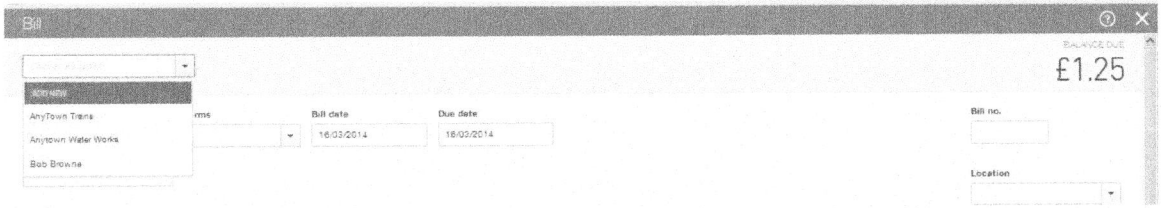

16 The New Supplier window pops up. In the Name field type in *ATBC Credit Card Company*.
17 Keep the currency as GBP.
18 Click *Save*.
19 Mailing address – if you have the address for the card company you can type it in, otherwise Click *Tab*.

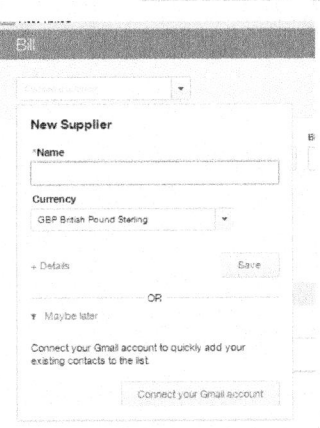

20 Terms – if known, enter the terms, otherwise leave blank. Click *Tab*.

21 Bill date - if known, enter the terms, otherwise leave blank. Click *Tab*.

22 Due date - if known, enter the terms, otherwise leave blank. Click *Tab*.

23 Bill number – leave blank. Click *Tab*.

24 Location – leave blank. Click *Tab*.

25 The account will already be chosen (*ATBC Credit Card*).

26 Description – enter a description e.g. *March bill*.

27 The amount is already filled in – *1.25*.

28 Class – choose from the dropdown e.g. *Arcacia Avenue*. Click *Tab*.

29 If you want to type a message in the Memo field, you can do so. Click *Tab*.

30 If you want to add an attachment, drag and drop it into the box. Click *Tab*.

31 Click *Save and close*.

This will take you back to the credit card reconciliation screen.

To pay your Credit Card Bill

32 On the left hand side of the screen, click *Suppliers*. This opens the suppliers' window. Here, we can see that ATBC Credit Card has an outstanding balance.

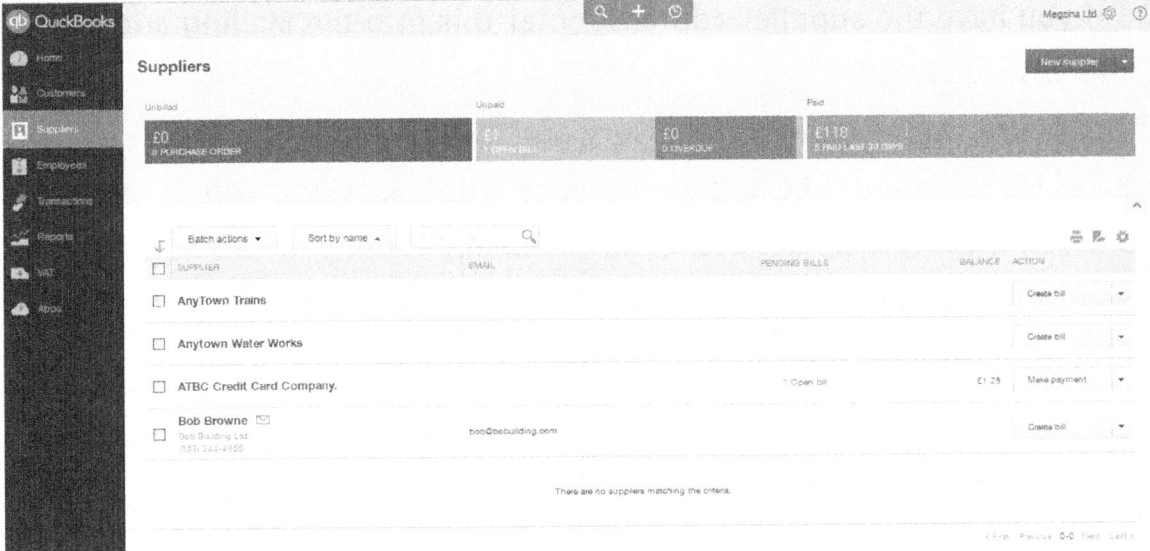

33 Click on *Make payment* on the ATBC Credit Card Company line. This screen then appears:

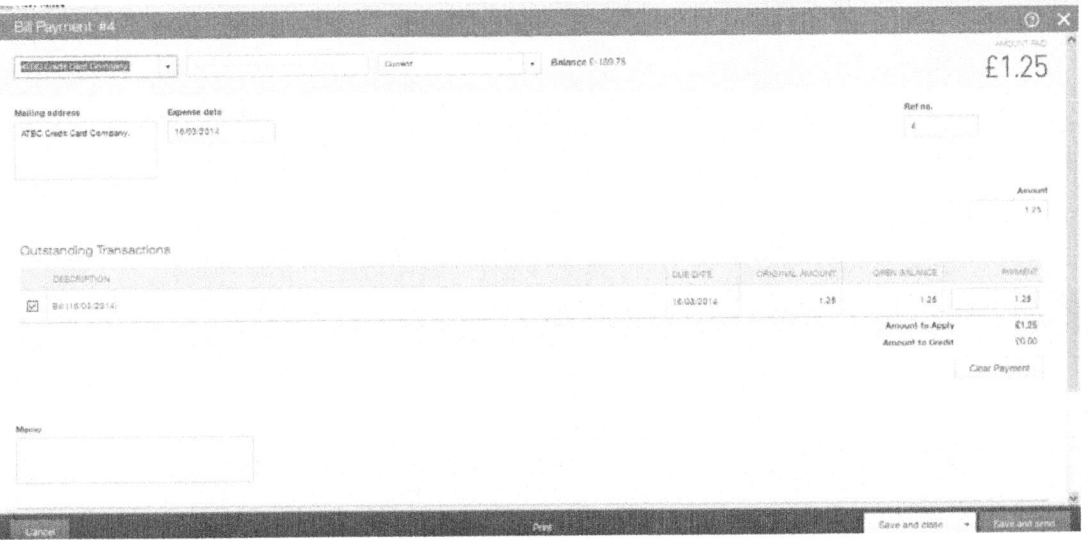

34 Click *Tab*. Enter an email address for the supplier e.g. *atbc@cc.com*. Click *Tab*.

35 The *Current Account* is already selected. This is the account which will pay this bill. Click *Tab*.

36 If you have the supplier address, enter this into the Mailing address. Otherwise click *Tab*.

37 Expense Date – input if necessary and click *Tab*.

38 Ref No – change if necessary, or leave it as it is. Click *Tab*.

39 If you want to type a message in the Memo field, you can do so. Note this is a message that appears on the remittance advice, and something which your supplier will see. Click *Tab*.

40 If you want to add an attachment, drag and drop it into the box. Click *Tab*.

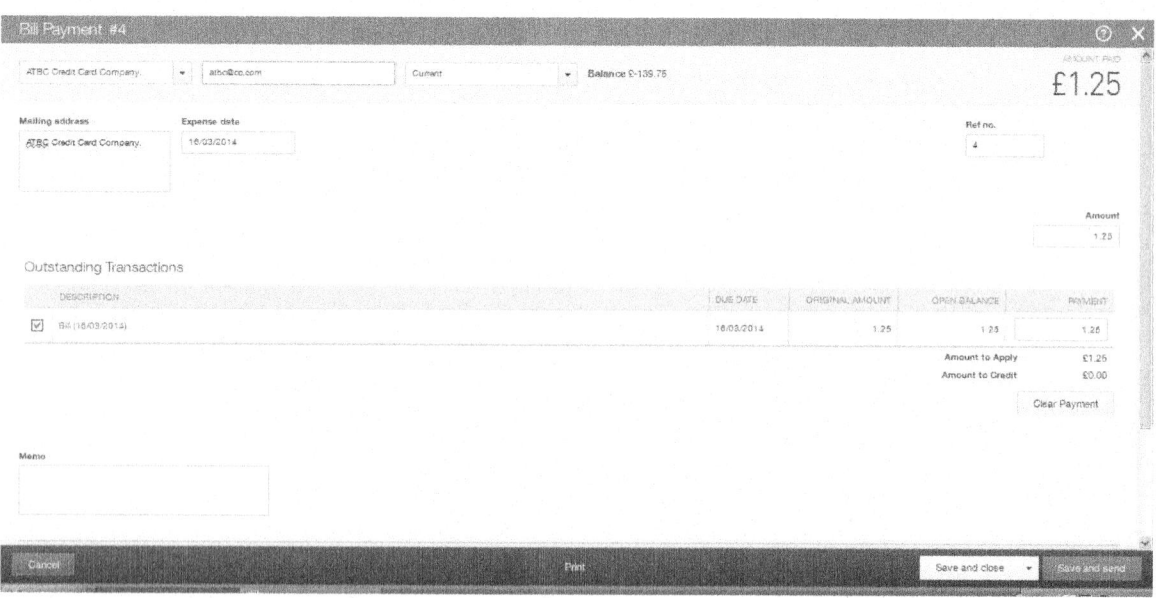

41 Click *Save and Send*.

42 Automatically, the PDF of the remittance advice appears. You can print this and post it you're your cheque payment, or just post it to let the supplier know that you've paid (if, you made an online payment).

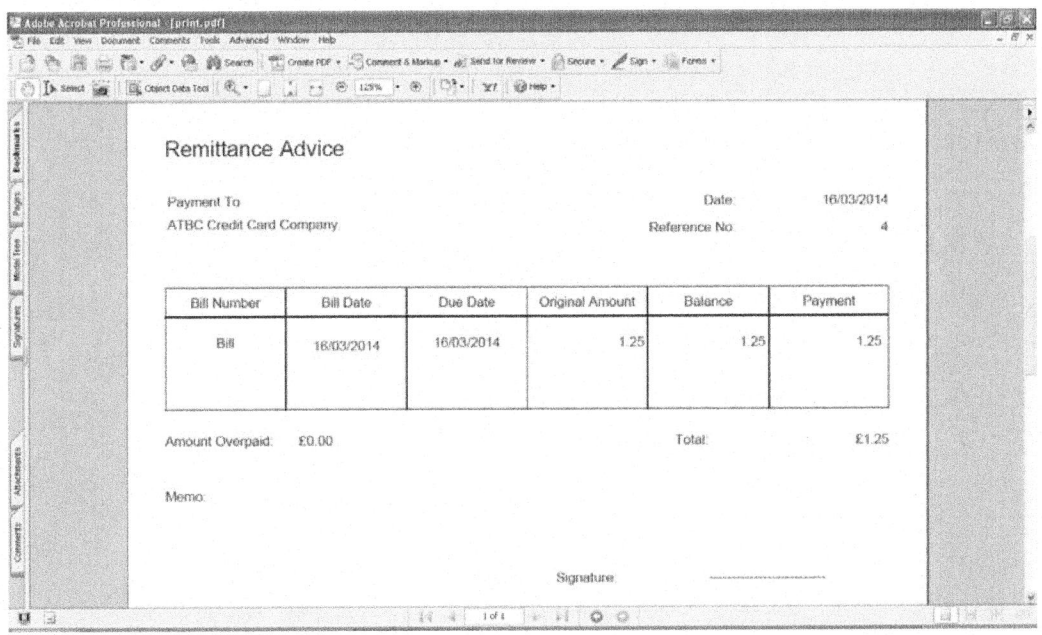

43 The following screen is the emailed remittance advice. You can amend the Subject and / or the Body. Once happy with the message composed, click *Send*.

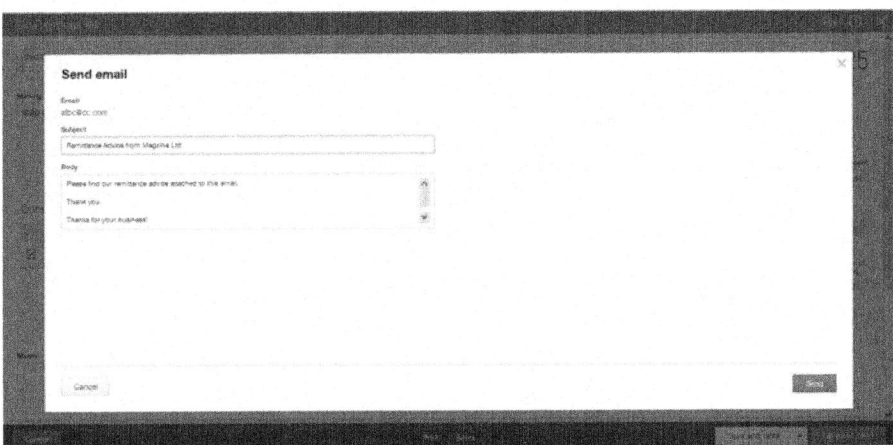

44 The Remittance advice has now been sent by email to the Supplier.

5: Using other accounts in QuickBooks

Summary of what is in this chapter:

5.1 Other account types in QuickBooks

5.2 Working with asset accounts

5.3 Working with liability accounts

5.4 Understanding equity accounts

5.5 Working with journal entries

5.1 Other account types in QuickBooks

This chapter will focus on asset accounts, liability accounts and equity accounts in QuickBooks.

Asset Accounts

These are used to track both current assets (those you're likely to convert to cash or use within one year e.g. stock) and fixed assets (long term items that aren't liquid, and generally are used to run the business e.g. equipment and vehicles).

Liability Accounts

These are used to track both current liabilities (items due to be paid within one year e.g. VAT, payroll taxes, short term loans) and long-term liabilities (those things due after more than one year e.g. bank loans, mortgages).

Equity Accounts

These are used to track the owners' equity, including capital investment, and retained earnings.

Note: A full explanation of all account types is given in the Appendix at the back of this book.

5.2 Working with asset accounts

QuickBooks has three account types for tracking the value of your assets:
- Current Assets
- Tangible Assets
- Non-Current Assets

Current Asset accounts track assets with a life of less than 1 year. It might include employee cash advances, loans to others, prepaid expenses, stock and undeposited funds.

Tangible Asset accounts track assets your business owns that are not likely to be realised within a year. It's usually something that is Fixed e.g. Buildings, Fixtures & Furniture, Leasehold improvements, Machinery and equipment, vehicles – but not always e.g. accumulated amortisation, accumulated depreciation, accumulated depletion.

Non- Current Asset accounts track assets with a life of more than one year. It might include deferred tax, goodwill, licenses, security deposits, intangible assets.

Setting up a Current Asset account

Suppose you need a Current Asset account to track a prepaid expense for rent. (Our landlord requires a six-month advance payment.)

1 Go to the Chart of Accounts (wheel/cog in the top right hand corner, click *Chart of Accounts*). Click *New*.
2 QuickBooks displays the New Account window.
3 For Category Type choose *Current assets*. For Detail type choose *Prepaid Expenses*. Leave the name field as Prepaid Expenses. In the Description, type in *Prepaid Rent*.
4 In Balance, type in *3000.00* as of (date) e.g. *01/03/2014*
5 Click *Save*.

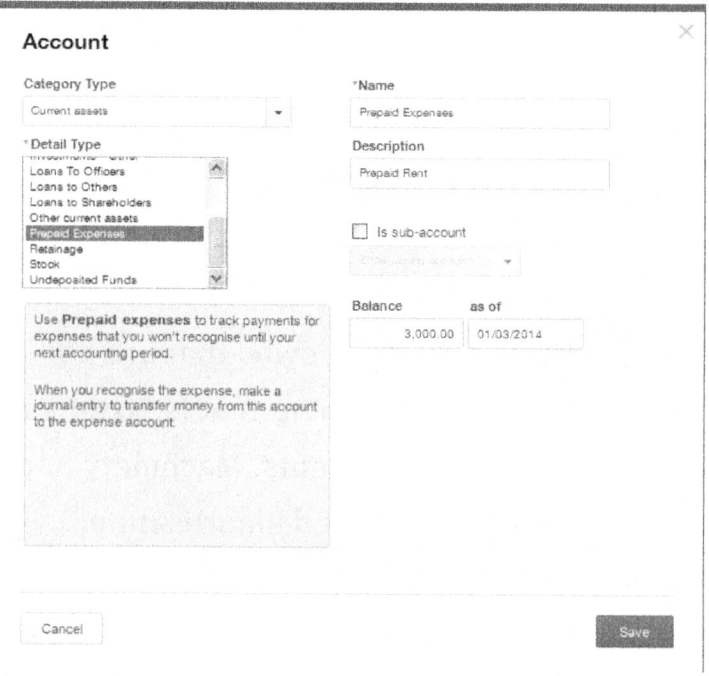

QuickBooks displays the new account in the Chart of Accounts.

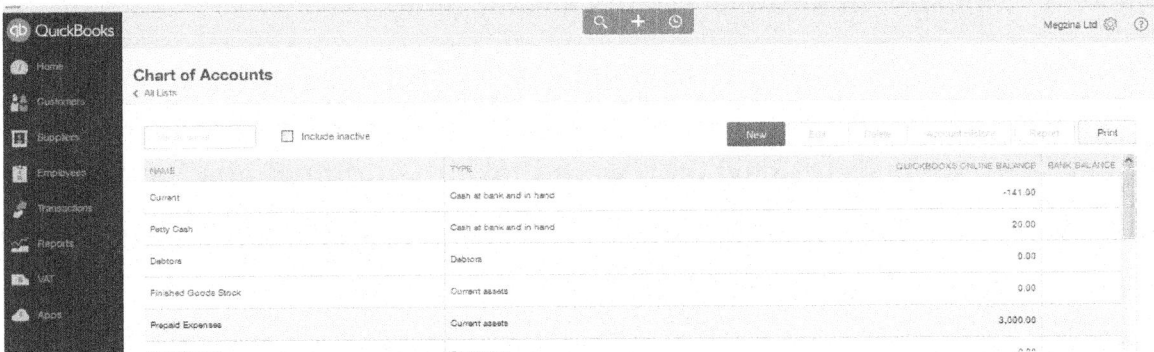

As each month goes by you use up part of this prepaid expense. £500 is the monthly rent, and this is used to decrease the current asset and assign it to the rent expense account. You'd enter these transactions directly in the register for the Prepaid Expenses rent asset account.

Setting up asset accounts to track depreciation

Fixed assets are equipment or property your business owns that are not for sale and are used within the business e.g. vehicles, equipment, furniture. However, due to wear and tear fixed assets will wear out and/or become obsolete, thus their value declines from the day you purchase them. This decline for the wear and tear is called Depreciation, and is normally determined by the accountant and entered annually.

One straightforward method for calculating the depreciation is on the 'straight line' method. You decide on the 'economical useful life' of the asset. For example, say we buy a computer for £600. We decide that it'll likely to last 3 years. So we charge depreciation at £200 for 3 years (£600 divide by 3 years). After 3 years, we can write the asset down to a value of £1, and if we're still using it in our business – that's fine. If doesn't last as long as 3 years, when we come to sell it or throw it away, we'll make an adjustment in the accounts at that time.

To determine the Net Book Value (price you could hope to get if you were to sell the fixed asset today), you would take the original purchase price, minus the accumulated depreciation (total amount of depreciation since the asset was purchased).

Usually, you'll want your balance sheet to show the original cost of an asset (plus any subsequent improvements) on one line, with the accumulated depreciation subtracted from the original cost on a second line, and the current value (net book value) on a third line.

In this chapter, we'll see an asset's cost and its accumulated depreciation on the balance sheet. We'll see how to set up a fixed asset account and to track its depreciation.

To set up asset accounts to track depreciation:
1 In the Chart of Accounts (wheel/cog in the top right hand corner, select *Chart of Accounts*), the choose *New*. The New Account window will open.
2 From the Category Type choose *Tangible assets.*
3 From the Detail Type choose *Machinery and depreciation.*
4 In the Name field type *Laptop – Office.*
5 In the Description you could put the make / model name.
6 Tick the box which says *Track depreciation of this asset.*
7 In the Original Cost type in what you paid for the laptop e.g. *600.00* as of (the date) you bought it. E.g. *01/01/2013*
8 Put in the Depreciation charged to date e.g. *200.00* as of *01/01/2014.*

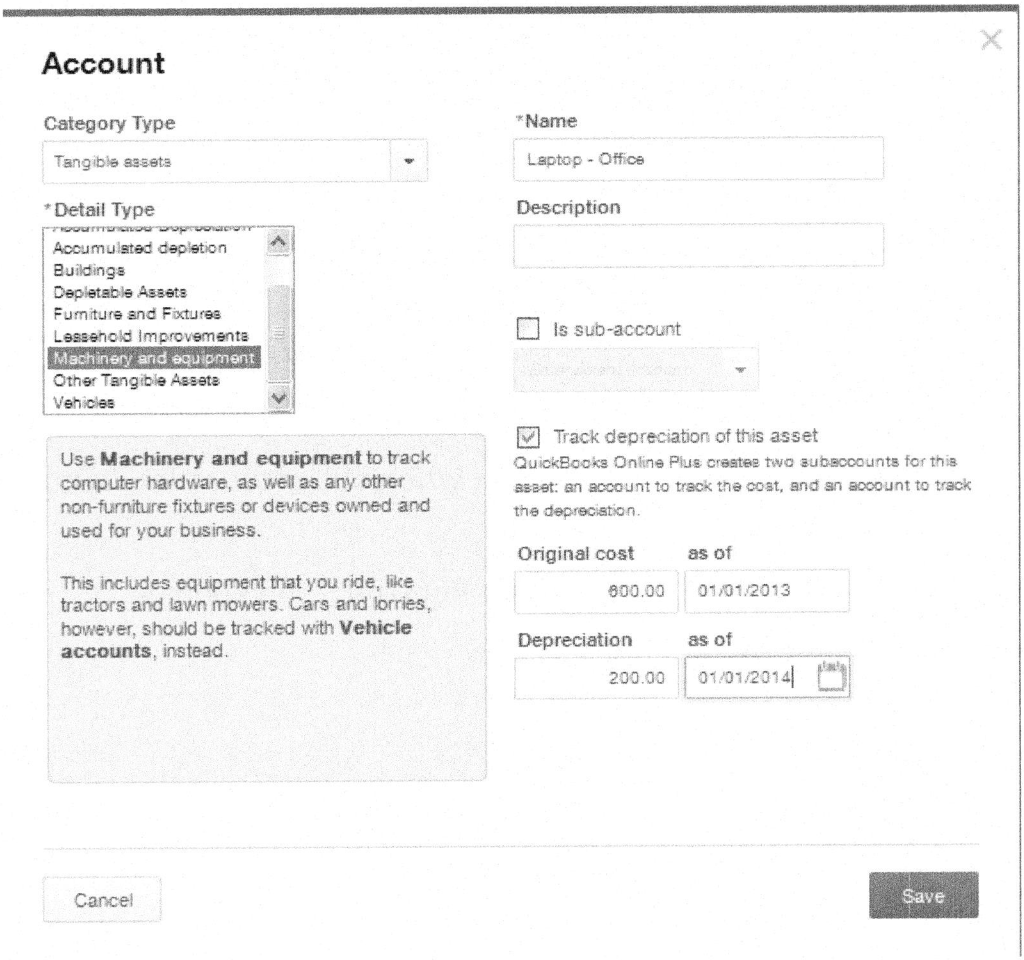

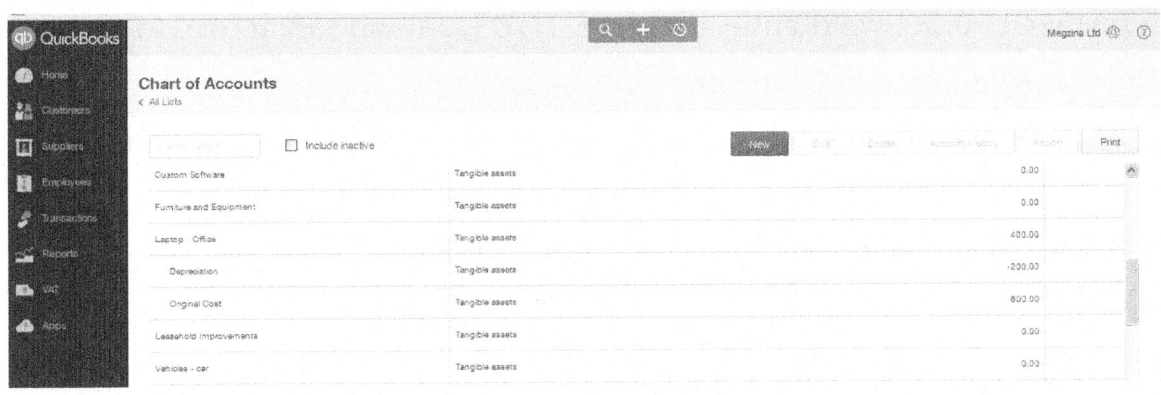

9 Click *Save*.

The Chart of Accounts now shows the laptop account (its net value of £400), plus the original cost of £600, and the depreciation of £200.

Tip: The opening balance is the ORIGINAL cost of the asset, if you purchased the asset before your QuickBooks start date.

Entering a depreciation transaction

When it's time to enter depreciation for an asset, you can use the register for the assets accumulated depreciation account.

To enter a transaction for depreciation:

1 In the chart of accounts, select the *Depreciation* subaccount for *laptop – office*.

2 Select *Account History* to get to the Asset Register. QuickBooks displays the Register for the Laptop – Office.

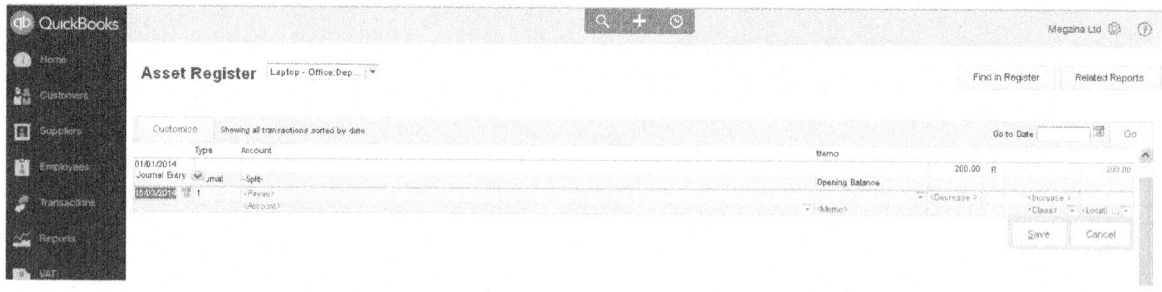

3 Say we wanted to put in a depreciation amount each quarter (instead of annually)... and so 31 March 2014, we wanted to depreciate the laptop by a further £50.00, we'd enter the date *31/03/14* and tab across to Decrease and type in *50.00* and press *Tab*.

4 In the Account drop down, choose *Depreciation Expense*. Remember if you start typing *dep* the account should appear. Click *Tab*.

5 If there is a Memo type this in, otherwise leave blank. Click *Tab*.

6 From the class choose from the dropdown or << *add new*>>. In this case, we're adding a new class called *Office*. A pop up box comes on the screen. Type in *Office* and click *Quick Add*.

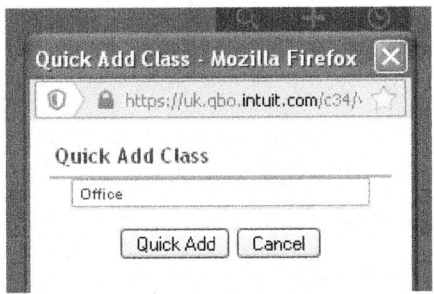

7 Press *Tab*. For the location choose *Anytown* from the dropdown.

8 Click *Save*.

The Asset Register now shows the accumulated depreciation is £250.00

And if we take another look at the Chart of Accounts, we'd see that the net book value of the laptop is now showing £350.00. The original cost of £600.00 remains unchanged & the Depreciation now shows £250.00.

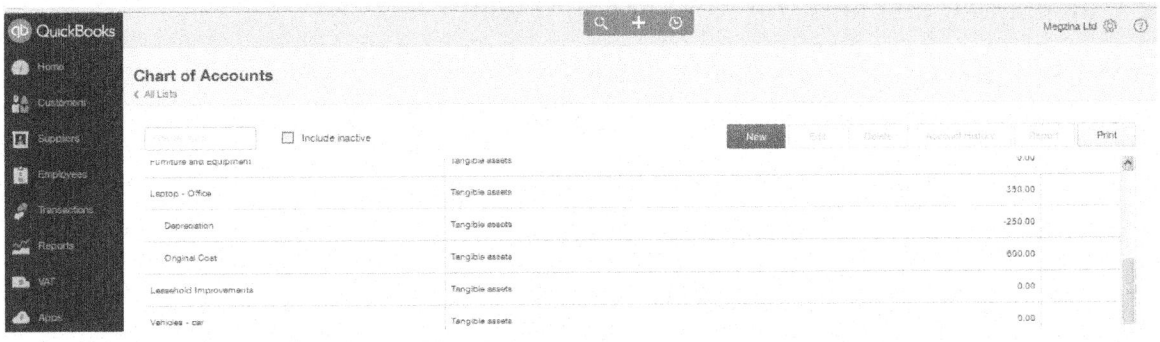

5.3 Working with liability accounts

QuickBooks has two account types for tracking the value of liabilities:
- Current Liabilities
- Non-Current Liabilities

Current Liability accounts track debts that your business is likely to pay off within the year. It might include client trust accounts, insurance payable, payroll clearing, short term borrowings, tax and national insurance.

Non- Current Liability accounts track debts that your business is NOT likely to pay off within a year. Non-current is also known as long-term. The most common are borrowings. But it could also include accruals and deferred income, notes payable and shareholder notes payable.

Tracking a loan with a long- term liability account
Imagine we've taken out a 5 year business loan with our bank.

To add a long- term liability account (a non- current liability):
1 Go to the Chart of Accounts (wheel/cog in the top right hand corner, click *Chart of Accounts*). Click *New*.
2 QuickBooks displays the New Account window.
3 For Category Type, choose *Non-Current liabilities*. For Detail type choose *Long Term Borrowings*.
4 Type in the name field *ATBC Bank Loan*.
5 In the Description, type in *5 yr Loan ends 15.3.2019*
6 In the Balance, type in the amount outstanding – leave NIL.

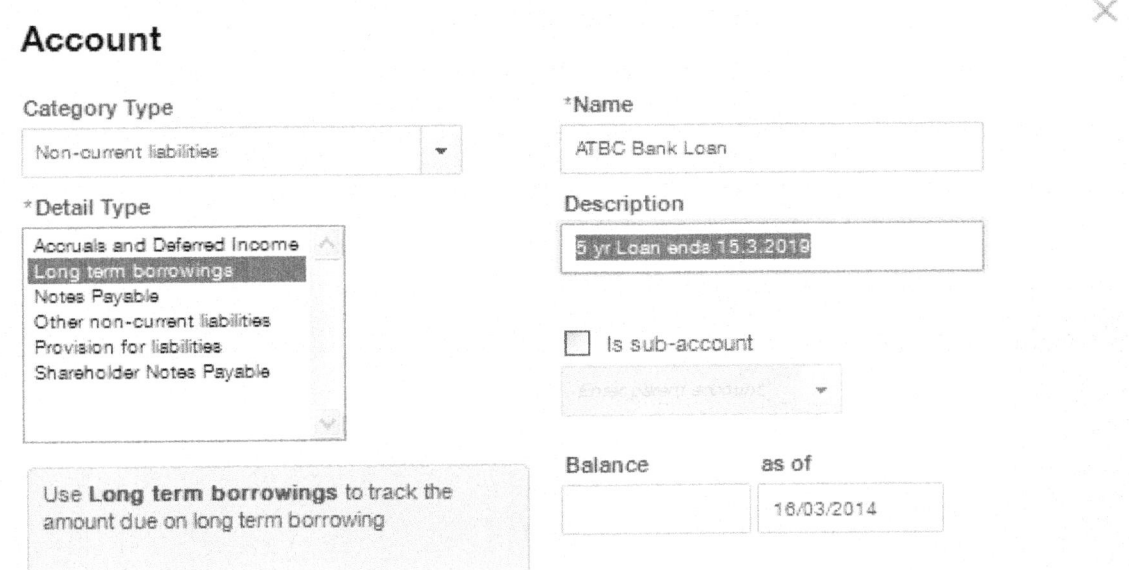

7 Click *Save*.

QuickBooks now shows the new liability in the Chart of Accounts.

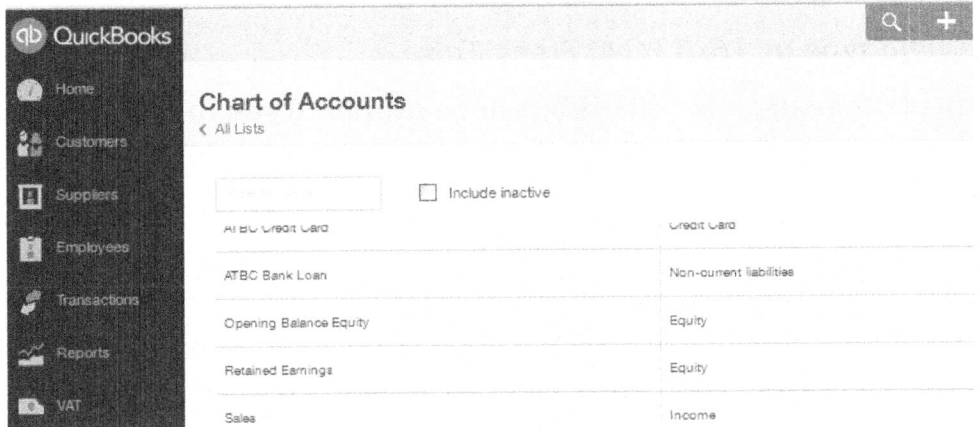

Since this is a new loan, you are either receiving money to deposit into your bank account or receiving a new asset. In this example, you received money (cash), so you need to show an increase in the bank account.

QuickBooks Online Help

To record an increase in the bank account:

1 Go to the Chart of Accounts (wheel/cog in the top right hand corner, click *Chart of Accounts*). Click *Current* and *Account History* to get to the Current account Bank Register.

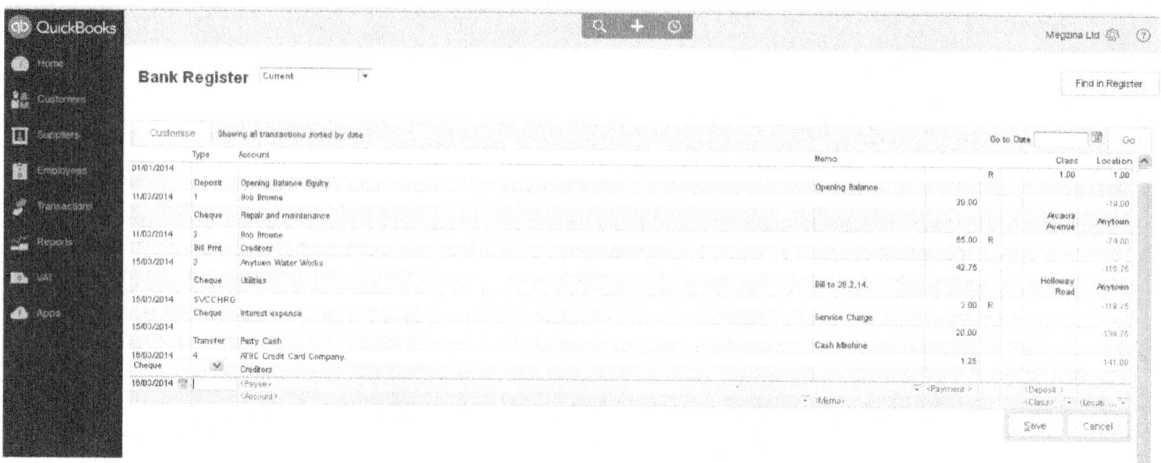

2 In the Date field type in *16/03/14*. Press *Tab*.

3 In Type – this is the space for the reference number. Type in *TRF*. Press *Tab*.

4 In the Payee field, leave blank. Press *Tab*.

5 In the payment field, leave blank. Press *Tab*.

6 In the Deposit field, type in *10000.00*. Press *Tab*.

7 For the Account, choose *ATBC Bank Loan* from the drop down. Press *Tab*.

8 In the Memo type in *5 years to 15.3.19*. (This is just the loan terms) Press *Tab*.

9 From the class choose from the dropdown *Office*. Press *Tab*.

10 For the location choose *Anytown* from the dropdown.

11 Click *Save*.

When you complete these steps, QuickBooks increases the value of the bank balance by £10,000 and it also enters the liability to the ATBC loan account to track the loan.

The Chart of Accounts now shows the 10,000 in the ATBC Bank Loan.

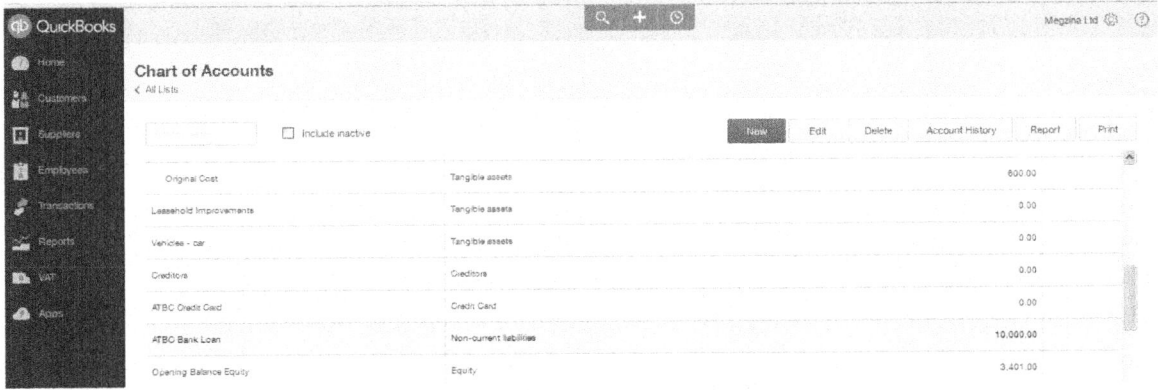

Recording a payment on a loan

When it's time to make a payment on a loan, use the Write Cheques window to record a cheque to your lender. You'll want to assign part of the payment to loan interest expense and the remainder to loan principal.

QuickBooks Online Help

To record a payment on a loan:

1 From the home menu click the + in the top middle of the screen, choose *Cheque* under the *Suppliers* headings. This displays the Write Cheque form.

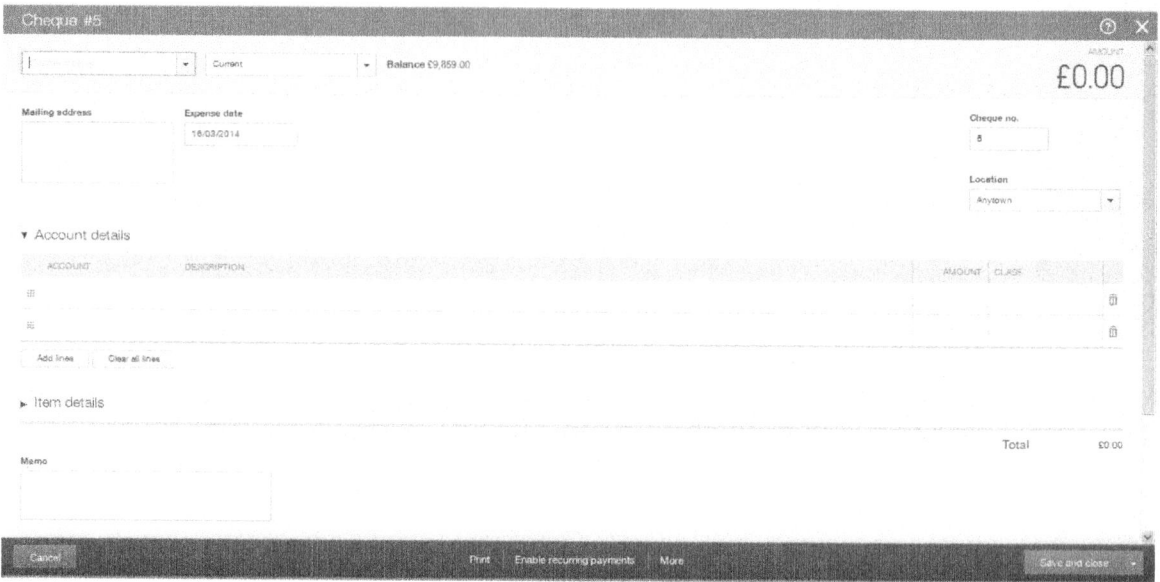

2 In the Choose a Payee field, type *AT Banking Corporation* and press *Tab*. QuickBooks will prompt you to add this Supplier. Click *Save*. Press *Tab*.

3 We're paying from the current account. Press Tab and move to the Expense Date. Type in *15/04/14*. Press *Tab*.

4 In the Cheque No. type in DD (for Direct Debit). Press *Tab*.

5 For the location, from the dropdown choose Anytown. Press *Tab*.

6 In the account, (first line) choose *interest expense* from the drop down menu. Press *Tab*. Leave the memo blank. Press *Tab*. Amount, type in *13.33* and for class choose *Office* from the drop down. Press *Tab*.

QuickBooks Online Help

7 In the account, (second line) choose *ATBC Bank Loan* from the drop down menu. Press *Tab*. Leave the memo blank. Press *Tab*. Amount, type in *166.67* and for class choose *Office* from the drop down. Press *Tab*. The screen should look like this:

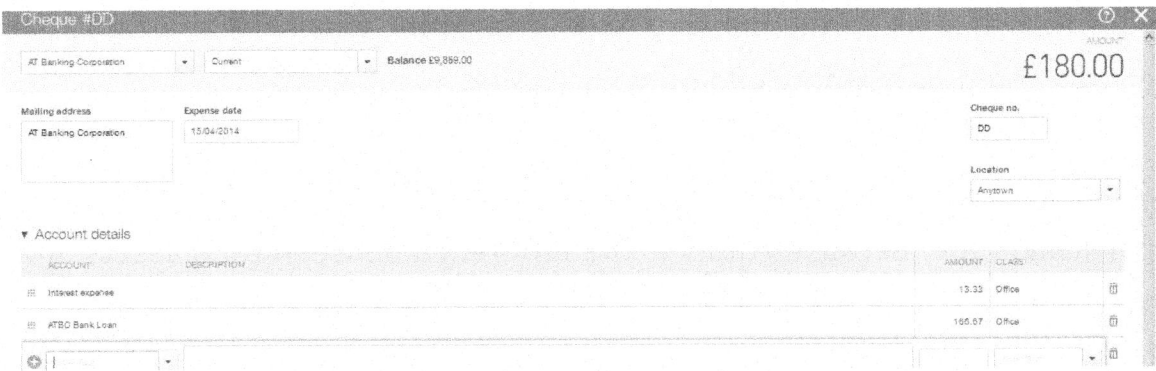

8 Click *Save and close* to record the payment.

When you record the transaction, QuickBooks automatically updates the accounts affected by this transaction:

- In the current account, QuickBooks subtracts the £180.00 (the amount of the direct debit) from your balance.
- In the expense account the tracks interest, QuickBooks enters the interest amount as an increase to your businesses company's interest expense.
- In the ATBC Bank Loan account, QuickBooks subtracts the principal amount from the current value of the liability (reducing the amount of the debt).

5.4 Understanding equity accounts

Equity is the difference between what you have (your assets) and what you owe (your liabilities). If you sold all your assets today and paid off your liabilities using the money received from the sale of your assets, the money you'd have left would be your equity.

A balance sheet shows your company assets, liabilities and equity on a particular date. Because equity is the difference between total assets and total liabilities, it's also true that total assets equal the sum of total liabilities and equity. The accounting equation is assets + liabilities = capital. Capital is another name for equity.

As you enter the opening balances of your assets and liabilities, QuickBooks calculates the amount of equity and records it in an equity account called Opening Bal Equity.

In addition to the Opening Bal Equity account, QuickBooks sets up another type of equity account for you called Retained Earnings. This account tracks your company's net income from previous financial years. QuickBooks automatically transfers your profit (or loss) to Retained Earnings at the end of each financial year.

If you are operating as a sole trader, you don't have to add any more equity accounts to your chart of accounts. All equity belongs to the company's sole owner.

You can get as involved in tracking equity as you wish. Some people like to track owner investments, owner's drawings, and retained earnings prior to their QuickBooks start date by putting them in separate equity accounts. If your business is a partnership, you'll probably want to set up separate equity accounts for each partner.

To learn more about equity and to learn how to set up equity accounts for your business, search the onscreen Help index for equity or contact your Accountant.

5.5 Working with journal entries

QuickBooks helps you to make Journal entries by:
- Automatically numbering journals
- Having a Description on every line of the journal for your notes
- Producing reports which can break down every transaction by date

Journals can be used to enter transactions, to amend or correct a transaction, to reverse an entry (when it can't be deleted from the system) and for putting in entries such as opening balances, accruals, prepayments and payroll figures.

For this exercise, we use a journal entry to record an income payment (£260) we received from our insurance company for a break-in, at Holloway Road.

Making journal entries

1 From the home menu, in the top middle of the screen, click + and under *Other*, choose *Journal Entry*.

The journal form is then displayed:

2 Enter the journal date e.g. *17/3/14* and click *Tab*.

3 Type in the journal number and click *Tab*.

4 Account – choose from the drop down *Insurance Proceeds Received*.

5 Credit £260 – in the credit field type in 260. In the Description field, type *Break in*.

6 Tab across to the Location, choose *Anytown* and class *Holloway Road*.

7 On the second line, choose account *Current*. The 260 will automatically appear in the debit field. The location will automatically be *Anytown*. Your form should look like this:

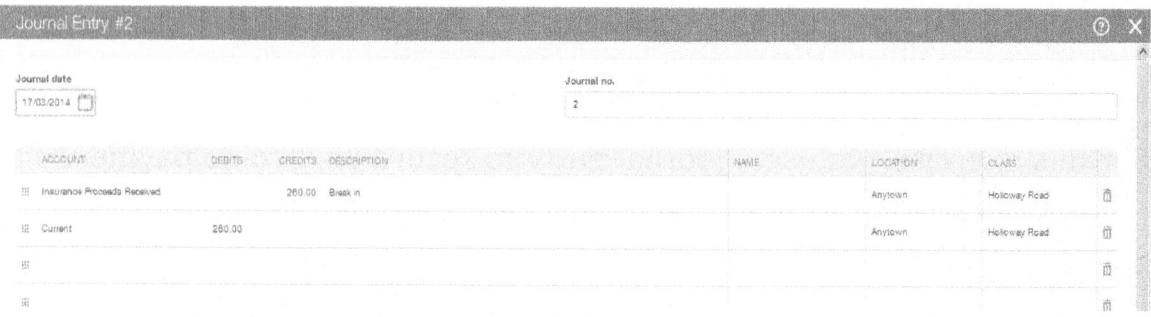

8 Click *save and new*.

QuickBooks Online Help

Producing a journal entries report

When you have made a number of journal entries in a session, it can be helpful to produce a report listing them.

To produce the report:

1 Click *Reports* on the menu on the far left hand side of the screen. Then click *All Reports*.

2 Choose *Journal*.

3 On the transaction date, choose *custom* from the drop down. And in the date field type in *17/3/14*.

4 Click *Run Report*.

The report shows all the entries you've made on this date.

5 Close the report.

6: Entering sales and invoices

Summary of what is in this chapter:

6.1 Using sales forms in QuickBooks

6.2 Filling in a sales form

6.3 Memorising a sale

6.4 Entering a new service item

6.1 Using sales forms in QuickBooks

Anytime your business makes a sale, you need to record it in QuickBooks on a sales form. A sales form can be an invoice (when you expect payment later), a cash sale (when you've received the payment at the time of the sale), or a credit memo.

To create an invoice: (and expect payment later)
1 Click *Customers* on the menu on the far left hand side of the screen.
2 Find the customer name on the list and under the ACTION menu (far right) choose *Create invoice* from the dropdown list

The alternative way is:
1 Click *Customers* on the menu on the far left hand side of the screen.
2 In the middle of the screen click '+' then *Customers* and *invoice*.

Assuming we created the invoice using the first method, and we'd chosen Sally Jones (customer) – this page would show.

To create a cash receipt: (and receive payment immediately)
1 Click *Customers* on the menu on the far left hand side of the screen.
2 Find the customer name on the list and under the ACTION menu (far right) choose *Create sales receipts* from the dropdown list

The alternative way is:
1 Click *Customers* on the menu on the far left hand side of the screen.
2 In the middle of the screen click '+' then *Customers* and *sales receipt*.

Note, from the form, that because payment is made at the time of the sale, the sales receipt lets you enter the payment method and the 'Deposit to' account.

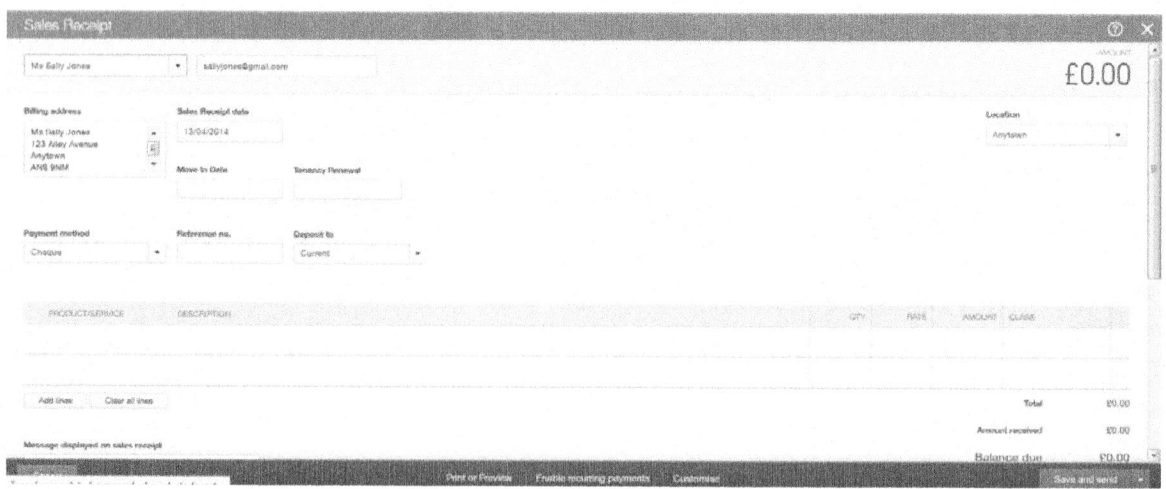

6.2 Filling in a sales form

Filling in the sales form (whether it's an invoice or sales receipt) is just like filling in a paper form. The customer information is entered first, and then the description of the products / services and the costs.

To enter customer information on an invoice:
1 Click *Customers* on the menu on the far left hand side of the screen.
2 In the middle of the screen click '+' then *Customers* and *invoice*.
3 In the first field click the arrow and a drop down list will appear with existing customers and jobs (sub-customers).
4 Choose the name of the customer e.g. Sally Jones. The customer's details will then populate the other fields i.e. the billing address, terms, location and invoice date. Note - today's date is automatically the invoice date.

The product / service description:

Each line of the invoice lists the product/item sold, and the price for that item. To add a new product/service, click on the drop down arrow, and choose the relevant product/service. Note that whenever you're in a field where you'll use a list item, you can start typing the first few letters of the list item you want, and QuickBooks fills in the field with the item that matches the letters you're typing.

5 In this example, we choose 'Rental Income' – the description automatically appears. You can overwrite this, or add further details to the description by clicking in the box and typing.

6 The quantity, rate and amount are already displayed. In this case, the rate is £100 and the quantity is 1. Press Tab to go through the fields. And overwrite any entry.

7 Select the class e.g. Arcacia Avenue.

8 If there are further items to add to the invoice, click 'add lines' and add other products/services to the invoice.

9 Press Tab until you reach the box 'Message displayed on Invoice'. In here, you may put the companies' bank details e.g. 'Please pay by BACS to Sort: 00-00-00 Account: 12345678 using your name as the reference'.

10 Press Tab to go to the Statement memo. Enter a summary of this transaction. This will appear on the customers' statement.

11 Press Tab to go to attachments. Here, you can upload an attachment to go with the invoice when it's sent. It could be a contract or terms of business. The maximum size of an attachment is 25MB.

Once the form is complete, at the bottom, middle of the page, there are various options – you can print or preview, enable recurring payments or customise.

To print or preview the invoice:

1 At the bottom, middle of the screen click *Print or Preview*.
2 The invoice appears on the screen.
3 Click Print.

INVOICE			
INVOICE TO Ms Sally Jones 123 Alley Avenue Anytown AN8 9NM		INVOICE NO. 1002 TERMS Due on receipt DATE 13/04/2014 DUE DATE 13/04/2014	
ACTIVITY	QUANTITY	RATE	AMOUNT
Rental Income Rental Income	1.00	100.00	100.00
		BALANCE DUE	£100.00

If you wish to change the way the invoice looks, you are able to customise it.

To change the look / feel of the invoice:

1 At the bottom, middle of the screen click *Customise*.
2 The options to add a logo, change the colour and font and invoice template appear. From the footer – you can also customise a message to the customer. Choose your selection and preview it.
3 Once you're happy with your selection, click *save*.

Sending the invoice:

12 The final step – once you've created the invoice and are happy with the way it looks – you click *save and send*.

13 A send email screen pops up. You can amend this email which is just the message that will be sent with the invoice to the customer. Note – it's only possible to have the save and send option, if an email address is entered for the customer. The invoice is sent as a PDF attachment.

14 Click *Send and Close*. This email is then sent to the customer and a confirmation pops up on the screen.

QuickBooks records the invoice in your Accounts Receivable register. If this had been a cash sales receipt, the amount recorded in the sale would be deposited to the account specified on the 'Deposit to' field e.g. Current Account or Petty Cash etc.,

The Accounts Receivable register keeps track of the money your customers owe you.

To see the Accounts Receivable Register:

1 From the COG (top right hand corner of the screen), click once to display further options.

2 Under 'Settings' choose *Chart of Accounts*, and click once.

3 The Chart of Accounts is displayed. Click once on *Debtors*. And then click on *Account History*. QuickBooks displays the Accounts receivable register.

4 Select the sale you just recorded in the register.

5 Double click the entry. This will display the original invoice 1002 for Sally Jones.

6 Leave the invoice open – as this is what we'll use to memorise a sale (below).

6.3 Memorising a sale

Lots of the sales you make in your business are likely to be repeated again. Depending on your industry e.g. property – you may have a repeated sale (e.g. monthly rent) – whereby it's literally the same sale each time to the same client. QuickBooks lets you memorise the sales form so that you don't have to retype or post the information each time.

To memorise the invoice:

1 Open the invoice that you want to repeat displayed on the screen (see above)

2 In the bottom middle of the screen, click *Enable Recurring Payments*. The recurring Invoice template screen pops up.

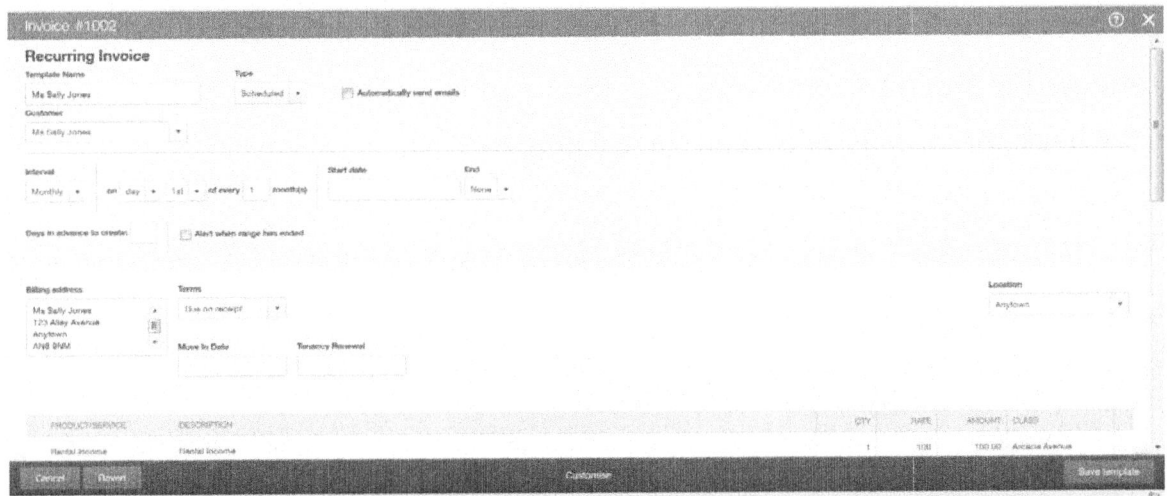

3 The template name is the name of the customer (this can be changed), the billing address and terms are pre-populated. Select the type – scheduled, unscheduled or reminder. An unscheduled template will simply be saved in the list of Recurring Transactions where it is always available for you to use. But a scheduled template will post the transaction for you. Choose *scheduled*. Press Tab.

4 Tick automatically send emails – so that the customer receives the invoice. Press Tab.

5 The interval choice is daily, weekly, monthly or yearly. Choose *monthly*. Press Tab.

6 Select: On *day* 1st of every *1* months – and this will invoice the customer on the first day of the month.

7 Type in the start date e.g. *01/05/2014* and the end date (if any). It's useful to put in an end date if, for example, it's just a '6 month' tenancy agreement, then the end date would be *end by 31/10/2014.*

8 Tab to Days in advance to create – type in *2.* This means invoices will be raised 2 days before the 1st of the month (the invoice date). Press Tab.

9 Tick – to alert when the range has ended, so that if the tenant does renew, (or the rental amount changes), then these changes can be reflected in the new template.

10 Check the details and then Save Template.

A warning box will pop up: "Every time you save an invoice, your customer will see it updated on the online invoice page."

To recall a memorised sale:

1 From the COG (top right hand corner of the screen), click once to display further options.

2 Under 'Lists' choose *Recurring Transactions*, and click once.

3 All Recurring Transactions are listed. If you want to amend any – click on it once and click *edit*. Or to delete it, click *delete*.

6.4 Entering a new service item

When you create an invoice, you have to enter items on each line, in the products / description.

To create a new service item:

1 From the COG (top right hand corner of the screen), click once to display further options.

2 Under 'Lists' choose *Products and services*, and click once. The list of all the service items is displayed.

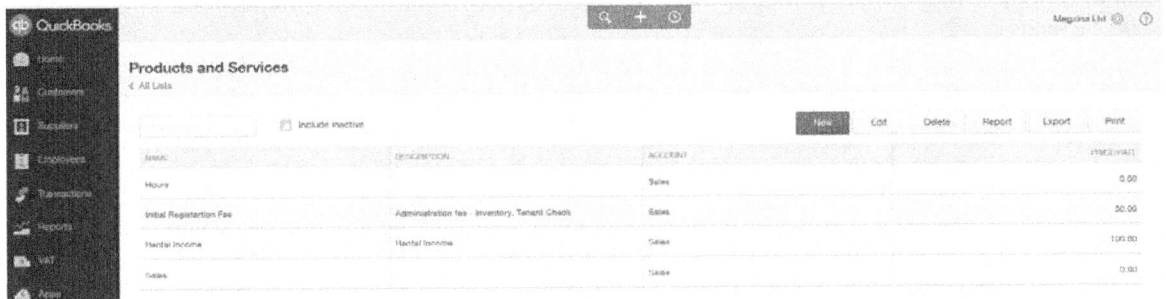

3 Click *New*.

4 The name, description and price has to be entered. Alongside the income account that this income should be attributed to. Then *save*.

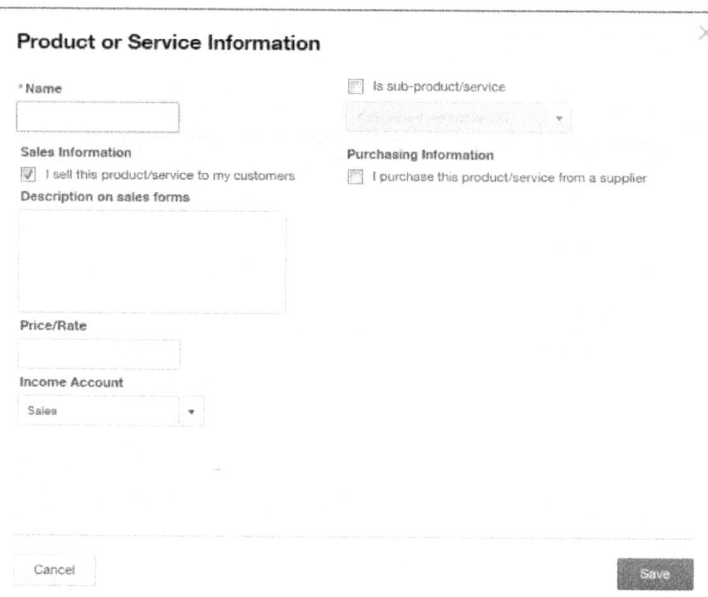

Once the items are listed, the company can invoice for each item separately, plus, they can also create sales reports that show sales for each item separately.

7: Receiving payments and making deposits

> *Summary of what is in this chapter:*
> 7.1 Recording customer payments
> 7.2 Making deposits

7.1 Recording customer payments

If you are receiving payment at the time of a sale, then use the cash sales receipt and QuickBooks records a customer payment. When you invoice a customer, but receive a payment later then you enter the payment on the receive payments form.

To record a payment in full:
1 From the Customers menu on the far left of the screen, click on the customer name e.g. *Sally Jones.*
2 Choose on the invoice to be paid e.g. 1001 and select from the drop down click *Receive Payment.*

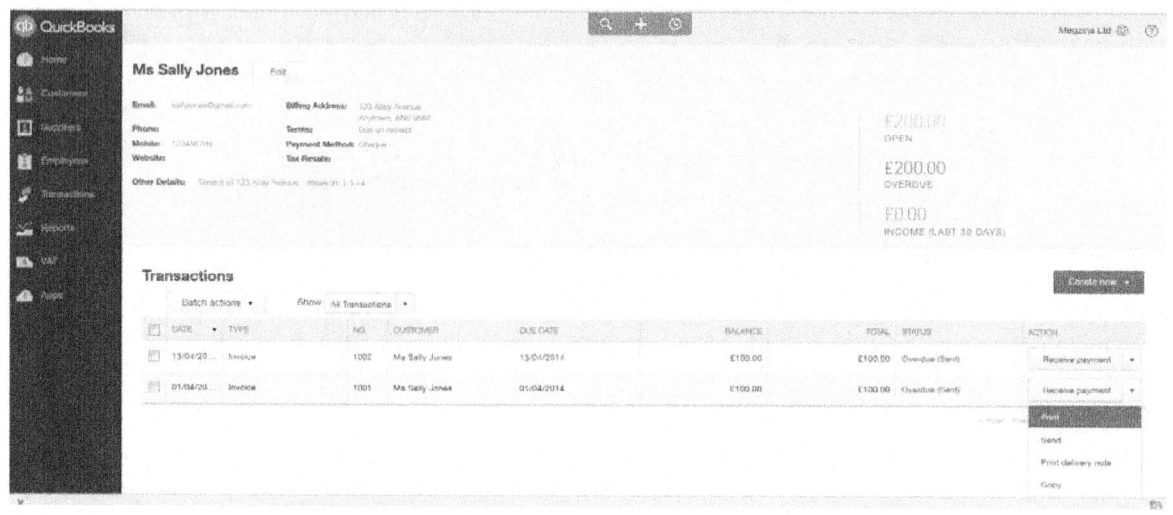

3 From the receive payments form – some fields will already be populated. Tab through each field to enter the correct information e.g. date, payment method and amount (*13 April 2014, Cheque, £100*). Tab to Reference Number and type in: *100856* (to represent the cheque number).

4 Deposit to: *Current account*.

5 Click Save and New.

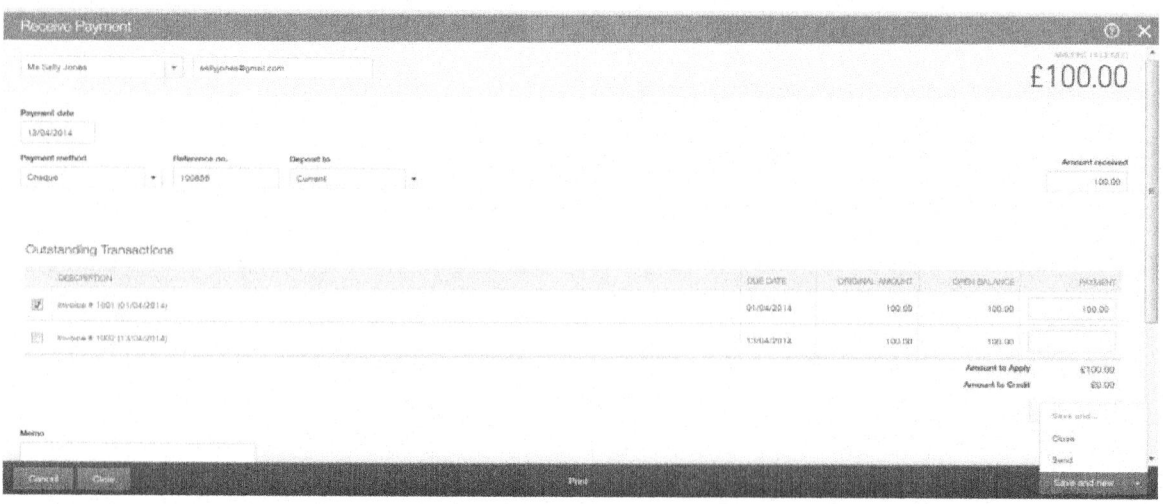

This records the payment and clears the window to move to the next screen to receive a payment. This invoice is now marked as paid.

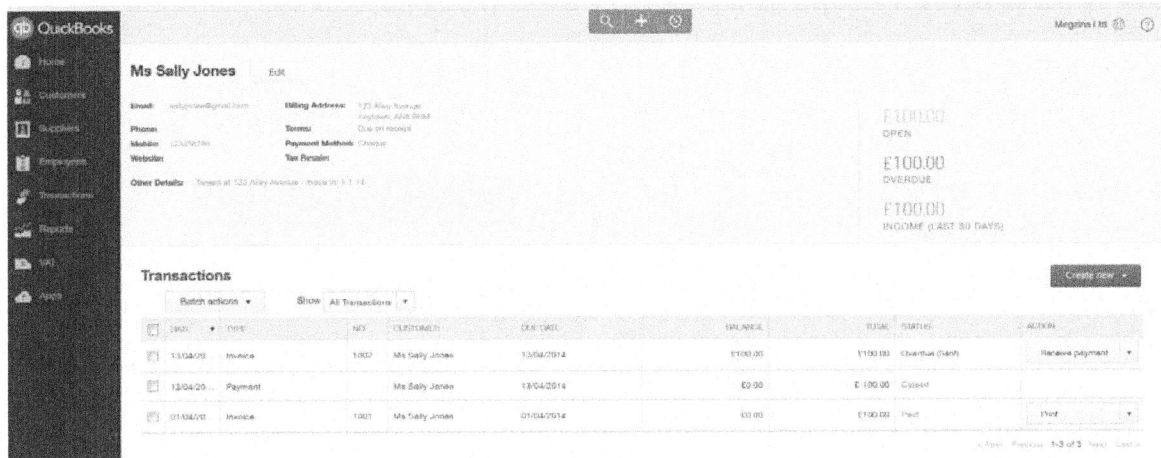

Sometimes customer do not pay the full amount of the invoice in one go, so you have to record what they do pay you.

To record a part- payment:
1 From the Customers menu on the far left of the screen, click on the customer name e.g. *Sally Jones.*
2 Choose on the invoice to be paid e.g. 1002 and select from the drop down click *Receive Payment.*
3 From the receive payments form – some fields will already be populated. Tab through each field to enter the correct information.
4 Tab to date type in: *13 April 2014.*
5 Tab to payment method type in: *Cash.*
6 Tab to amount type in: *£20.* And in the payment, type in: £20

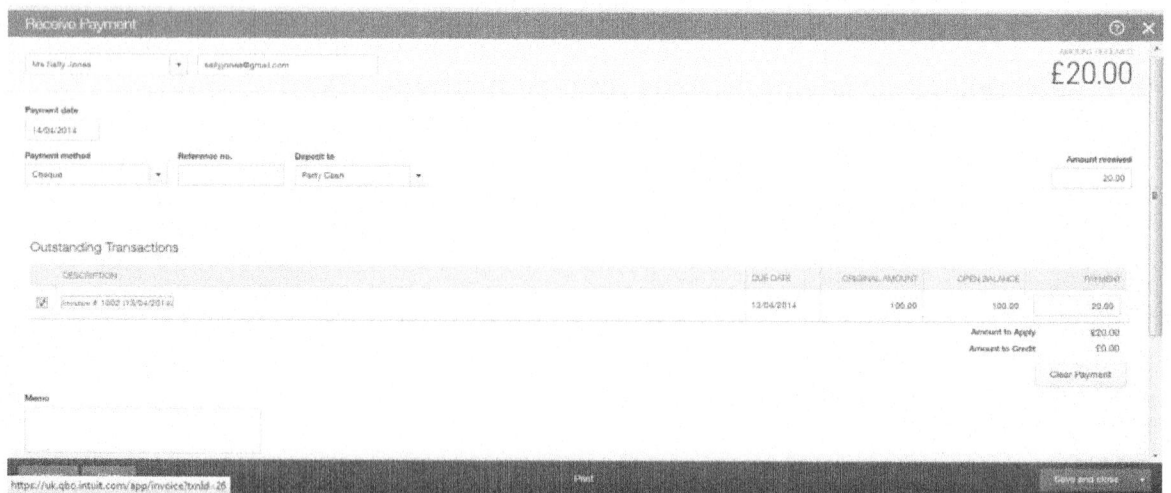

5 Click Save and Close.

6 On the next screen, you'll see the list of outstanding invoices for that customer.

Sometimes customer pay more than the invoice amount outstanding. In these cases, enter the amount that you receive, and the overpayment is tracked by QuickBooks. The next time that customer is sent an invoice, this overpayment will be on the system for them to use. In the following example, Sally Jones owes £80.00, but pays £130.00.

QuickBooks Online Help

Entering over- payments:

1 From the Customers menu on the far left of the screen, click on the customer name e.g. *Sally Jones*.

2 Choose on the invoice to be paid e.g. 1002 and select from the drop down click *Receive Payment*.

3 From the receive payments form – some fields will already be populated. Tab through each field to enter the correct information.

4 Tab to date type in: *13 April 2014*.

5 Tab to payment method type in: *Direct Debit*.

6 Tab to Deposit to, and in the drop down choose: *Current Account*.

7 Tab to Amount received, and type in: *130.00*. The payment amount will automatically change to the amount outstanding (in this case 80.00). The Amount to Apply is 130.00 and the Amount to Credit is 50.00.

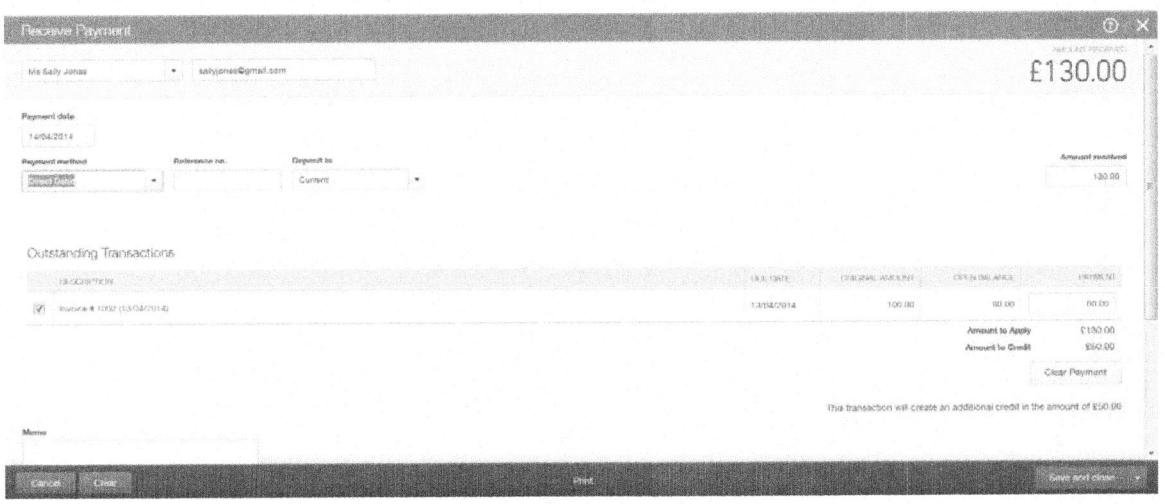

8 Save and close.

On the next screen you'll see that Sally Jones now has an outstanding balance of -£50.00. This means she has overpaid by £50.00. This unused payment can be applied to future invoices for the customer.

Using Over-payments

The next time you invoice this customer, if it's for less than the balance e.g. £10.00, then as soon as you enter the invoice, it will automatically show up as paid. Example – we enter invoice 1003 for £10.00 and immediately, this PDF pops up – and it's ALREADY PAID.

The next screen then shows that Sally has overpaid by £40.00.

QuickBooks Online Help

Receiving a pre-payment:

If a customer makes a payment before you've invoiced them for services – e.g. it could be a down payment or a retainer fee, you can still record the payment using the receive payments form. QuickBooks holds the unapplied amount in the customer's name, and displays the amount as an unapplied payment.

For example Sally Jones, our customer paid £200 as a payment on account – and we've not invoiced her yet.

To enter the down payment:

1 From the Customers menu on the far left of the screen – the list of customers will appear. Sally Jones has a -40.00 balance. Under action click *Receive Payment*.

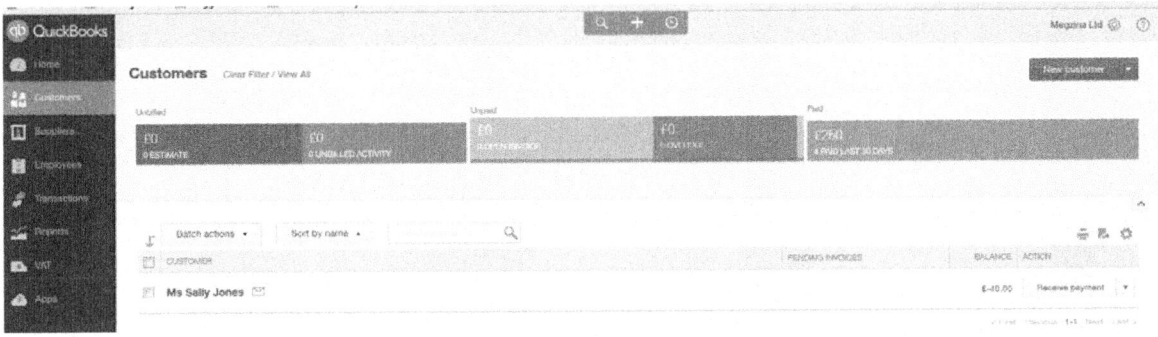

2 It shows the existing unapplied credit amount of 40.00 which Sally has already.

3 Tab to date type in: *14 April 2014.*

5 Tab to payment method type in: *Cash*

6 Tab to Deposit to, and in the drop down choose: *Current Account.*

7 Tab to Amount received, and type in: *200.00.*

The screen will look like this:

8 Save and close.

Sally Jones now has a balance of -240.00.

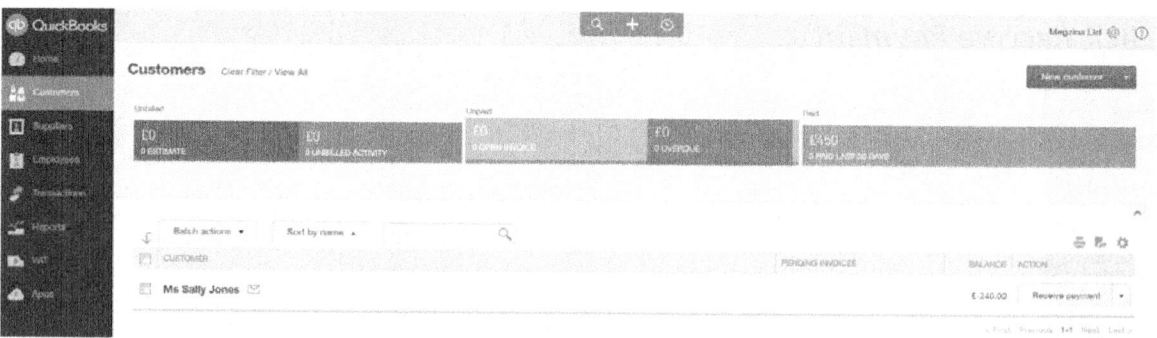

This balance will sit on the customer's account.

Entering and applying credit memos

If a customer has returned goods or cancels their order, you'll need to enter a credit memo and then apply it to the original invoice to reduce the balance owing. If a customer cancels, you need to create a credit memo, write a refund cheque and apply the credit memo to the invoice.

To enter a credit memo:

1 Click the Customers menu on the far left of the screen, then click '+' in the middle of the screen and choose *Credit Note* under customers.

2 The form appears. Choose the customer name from the drop down menu *Sally Jones*.

3 Tab to the Product/Service description and choose the item which is being refunded e.g. *Rental Income*.

4 Tab to the rate and type in 15*0.00* (the amount to be returned).

5 Choose the class: *Arcacia Avenue*.

The screen should look like this:

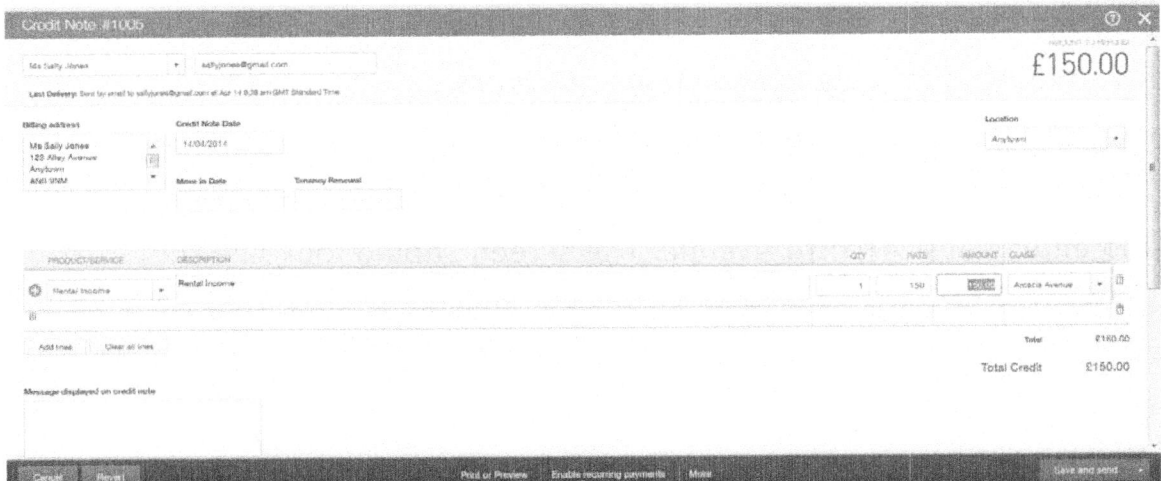

6 Save and close.

Sally had an existing balance of -£240.00. With this credit memo, the balance outstanding is now -£390.00.

If Sally will never order from us again e.g. she's a tenant who has moved out of our property, then we'd need to refund this overpayment balance sitting on her account to her.

Repaying a customer over-payment:

1 From the home screen '+' in the middle of the screen and choose *Cheque* under suppliers.

2 The form appears. Choose the customer name from the drop down menu *Sally Jones*.

3 Choose the account you're refunding the customer from e.g. *Current*.

4 Tab to the date, and enter e.g. *14/04/2014*.

5 Tab to Account details and choose *Debtors*.

6 In the Description, type: R*efund*

7 Tab to the amount that you're giving back to the customer e.g. 390.00 and enter class: *Arcacia Avenue*. The screen should look like this:

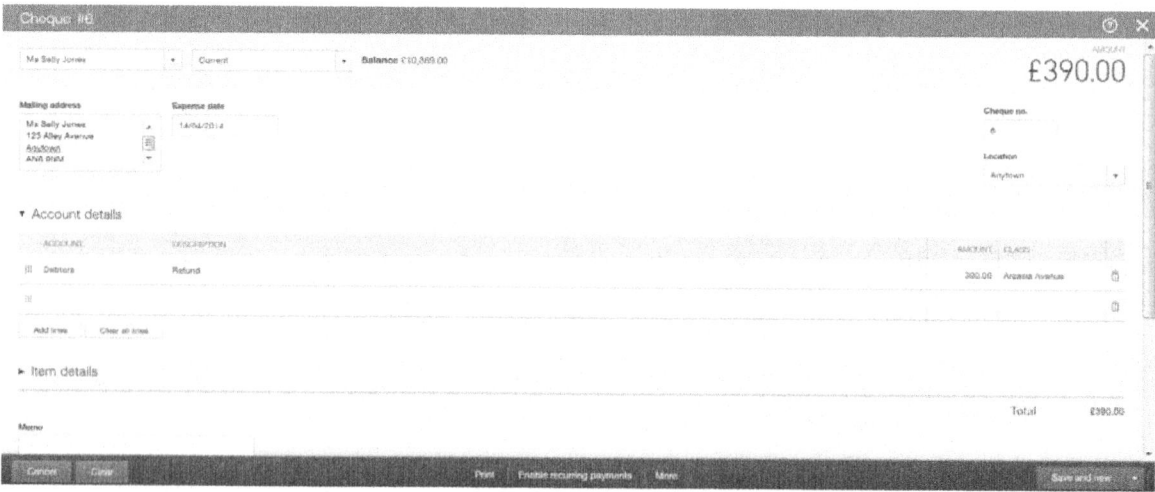

8 Save and Close.

Next, we have to apply this cheque to the Customer's account.

QuickBooks Online Help

1 From the home screen '+' in the middle of the screen and choose *Receive payment under* customers.

2 The form appears. Choose the customer name from the drop down menu *Sally Jones.*

3 Tick both the cheque, and the credit memo and unapplied credits.

4 Save and close.

Now, Sally's account balance is now NIL.

Applying Credits to specific invoices:

If the customer has more than one invoice which is outstanding, QuickBooks will apply the credit to the oldest invoice first. But, you can choose to apply any credit memo payment to any invoice or distribute across multiple invoices using the same steps as above.

7.2 Making deposits

When you use the Enter Sales Receipts window (cash sales), the payments received are deposited to the place which you select. This could be straight to the Petty Cash or Current Account – or it could be to the 'Undeposited Funds' account.

Receiving money into the undeposited funds account:

1 From the home screen '+' in the middle of the screen and choose *Receive payment under* customers.

2 The form appears. Choose the customer name from the drop down menu *Sally Jones*.

3 Payment method – choose: *Cash*.

4 Deposit to – choose: *Undeposited Funds*.

5 Tab to the product/service - choose *rental income*. The amount is automatically 100.00.

6 Tab to class and choose *Arcacia Avenue* from the drop down. The screen will look like this:

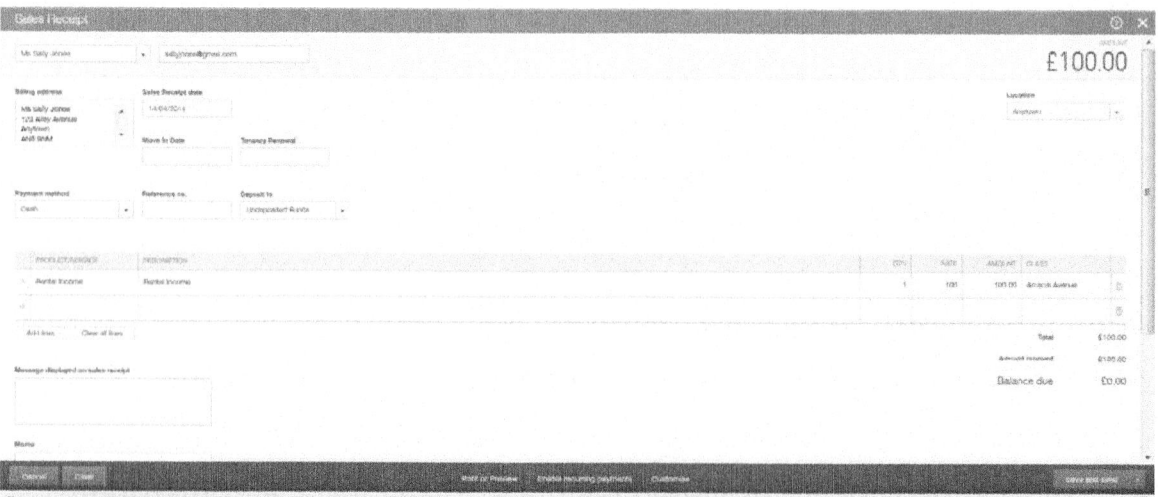

7 Save and send.

The undeposited funds is a useful account if several people pay you all at once. You can put cash or cheques to bank, into this account until you are ready to physically bank them all. Enter all of these payments into this account, and then make ONE deposit into your bank account on the system. When it comes to reconciling the bank – this will make the process easier.

To select payments to deposit:

1 From the home screen '+' in the middle of the screen and choose *Bank Deposit under* Other.

2 The first field in the top left hand corner is the account into which this deposit is being made e.g. *Current*.

3 Tick the existing payments that you want to include in this deposit e.g. *Sally Jones - £100.00*. The screen should look like this:

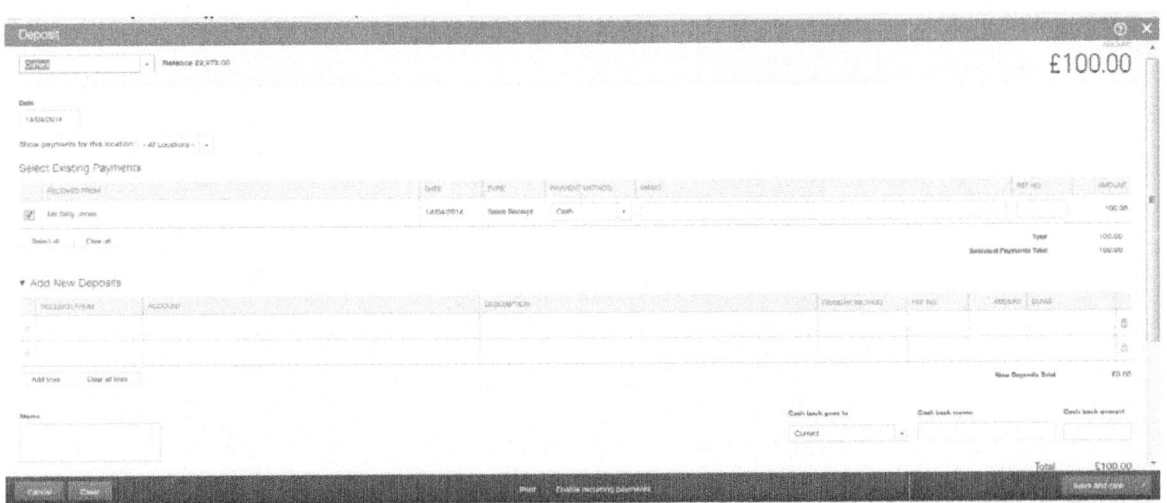

4 Click Save and close to record the deposit.

How QuickBooks handles the deposit

QuickBooks updates your undeposited funds account to show that you've made a deposit, and it also adds the deposit to your bank account register.

To view the Undeposited Funds account:

1 From COG (top right hand corner of the screen), click once to display further options
2 Under 'Settings' click *Chart of Accounts*.
3 Scroll down and find *Undeposited Funds*. Click once.
4 Click *Account History*.

QuickBooks displays your deposits and reduces the balance in the account by the amount of the deposits made.

You can also look at the deposit in the Current Account.

5 From the Asset Register drop down, choose Current Account.
You will see that QuickBooks has entered the deposit as a transaction in the Current Account and has updated the balance:

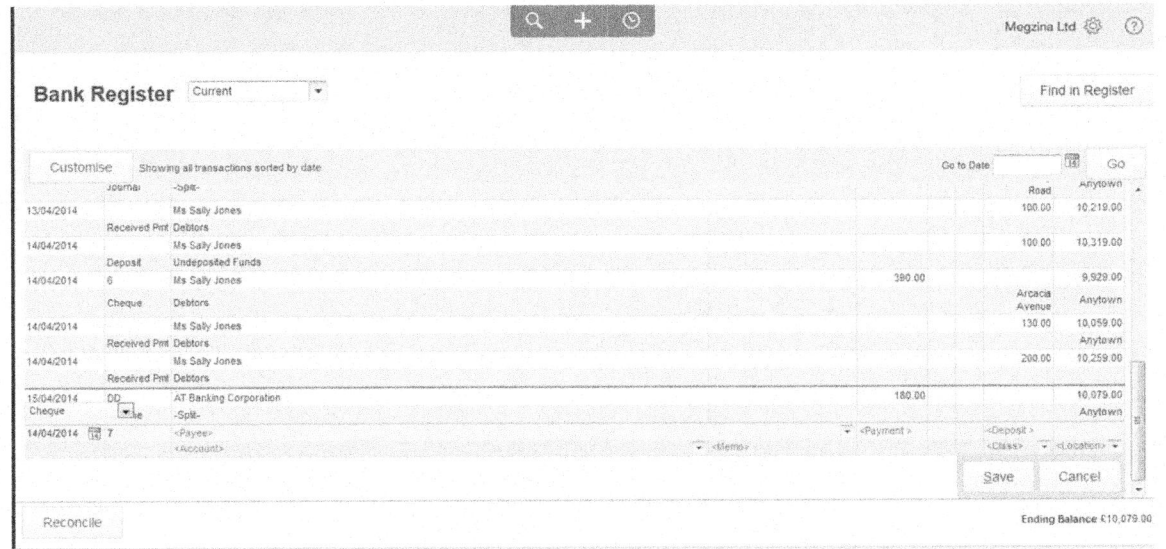

Getting cash back from a deposit

When you are recording the deposit in the Make Deposits window, you can enter information about any cash you took out of the deposit.

To record cash back from a deposit:

1 From the home screen '+' in the middle of the screen and choose *Bank Deposit* under Other.

2 The first field in the top left hand corner is the account into which this deposit is being made e.g. *Current*.

3 Tick the existing payments that you want to include in this deposit e.g. *Sally Jones - £50.00*. The screen should look like this:

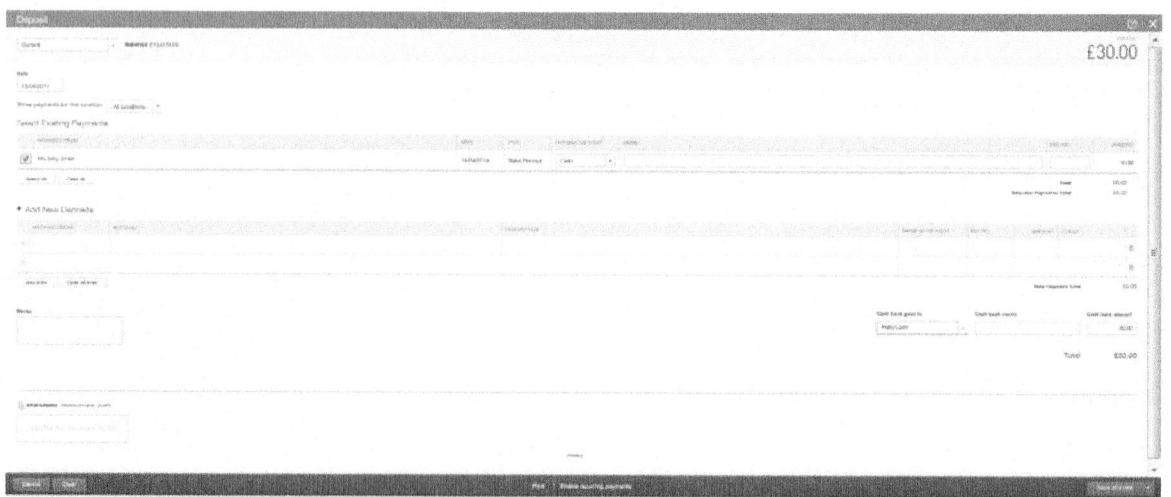

4 The Cash goes back to: Petty Cash. And the cash back amount: £20.00.

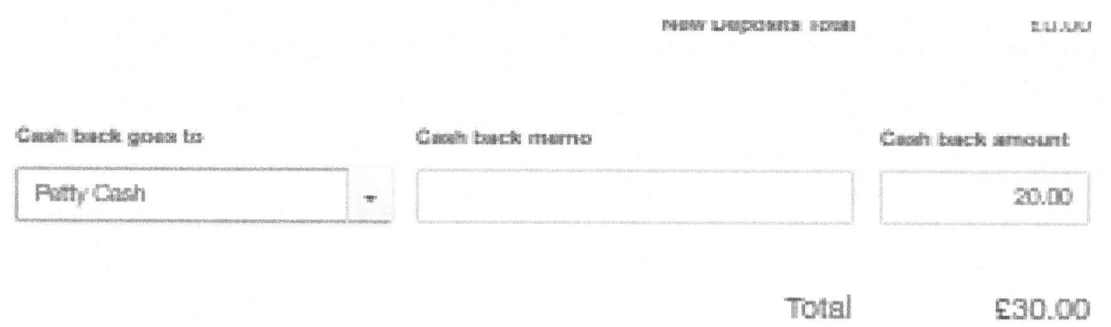

5 Click save and close.

The end result of the £50 sales receipt which Sally Jones made – it has now been deposited: £20 into petty cash and £30 into the bank account.

8: Entering and paying bills

> *Summary of what is in this chapter:*
> 8.1 Handling bills in QuickBooks
> 8.2 Using QuickBooks for accounts payable
> 8.3 Entering bills
> 8.4 Memorising bills
> 8.5 Paying bills

8.1 Handling bills in QuickBooks

When you have a business expense, you can handle it in several ways:
- Enter the bill and pay it on QuickBooks.
- Enter a cheque directly from the bank account.
- Enter a credit card receipt into QuickBooks.

In chapter 4, we looked at how to enter handwritten cheques and credit card payments. In this chapter, we'll look at the two-step process – entering the bill and paying the bill.

8.2 Using QuickBooks for accounts payable

Some business owners pay their bills as soon as they receive them. However, if you don't pay your bills right away, you can enter the bill into

QuickBooks to pay later. QuickBooks will keep a track of how much you owe to others. It is useful when you're running a business to know your exact liability position. It gives you a truer reflection. The money you owe for unpaid bills is called your accounts payable, and the total is shown as a liability on your Balance Sheet. The Accounts Payable has a register where you can view all your bills at once.

To see the Accounts Payable register:
1 From COG (top right hand corner of the screen), click once to display further options
2 Under 'Settings' click *Chart of Accounts*.
3 Scroll down and find *Creditors*. Click once.
4 Click *Account History*. The register is displayed:

The register keeps track of every bill entered. It shows the due date (and whether the bill is paid or not), and a running balance of the total bills due. This will help you to plan your cashflow.

8.3 Entering bills

When you receive a bill from a supplier, you should enter it into QuickBooks as soon as you can. The more up-to-date the information is in the system, the more accurate and useful your accounts will be. It's important to be aware of your liabilities at all times.

To enter a bill:

1 From the Home menu, click '+' in the top middle of the screen, and under Suppliers, click 'bill'. The bill form is displayed:

The top part of the form is where you enter the bill details. The bottom half is where you choose the expense account.

2 In the first field (supplier name) type *AnyTown Gas* and then press Tab.

3 The New Supplier screen pops up. Click Save.

4 Tab through to the bill date field, type *14/04/2014.*

5 Tab across to Bill No. And enter *5984.*

6 Tab to location, and choose *Anytown* from the dropdown menu.

7 Tab to Account Details. Choose *Utilities* – sub account: *Gas* and tab.

8 In the description type: April *2014 supply.*

9 Tab to amount, type in *78.00.*

10 Tab to Class, choose *Office* from the drop down.

The screen will look like this:

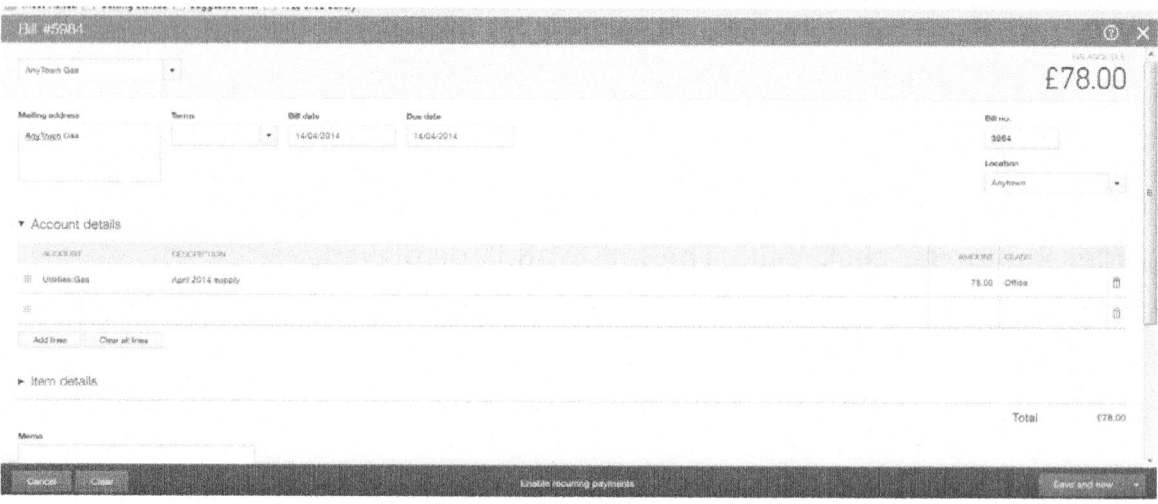

11 It is optional – put if you tab down to '*attachments*' you could upload the physical copy of the bill (so that you have it saved in your system). Some people (who dream of having the paperless office) may like this idea. You may be on paperless billing, and receive a bill by email. This can be saved on the system. It will save you having to print the bill and store it, or keep a separate electronic folder for all bills. To upload the bill, find it on your computer, and drag the icon to the box. As long as it's fewer than 25MB it will upload. The name of the file e.g. Tulipa will show in the box. Note – you can drag and drop more than one file into the box.

12 Click save and close to record the bill.

You can view a list of all attachments saved on the system by going to the COG / wheel in the top right hand corner, click List and then Attachments to list all attachments on the system.

8.4 Memorising bills

If you have regular bills for the same amount from a supplier, QuickBooks lets you set up a bill so you don't have to keep entering the same information.

The company Megzina Ltd have a direct debit with the bank to pay for a subscription to a property magazine which they receive every other month (bi-monthly).

To enter a memorised bill:
1 From the Home menu, click '+' in the top middle of the screen, and under Suppliers, click 'bill'. The bill form is displayed:
2 In the first field (supplier name) type *Property Today Magazine and* then press Tab.
3 The New Supplier screen pops up. Click Save.
4 Tab through to the bill date field, type *30/04/2014.*
5 Tab to location, and choose *Anytown* from the dropdown menu.
7 Tab to Account Details. Choose *Dues and Subscriptions.*
8 Tab to amount, type in *17.99.*
10 Tab to Class, choose *Office* from the drop down.
11 On the bottom, middle of the screen click *enable recurring payments.* The top half of the screen is to select the frequency of the transaction. The bottom half of the screen is to choose the account details.

12 Fill in the recurring bill form. The type: scheduled. Interval: *Monthly* on *Last Sunday* every *2* months.

13 Start date: *30/04/2014*. End date: *None.* Days in advance to create – leave blank. Alert when range has ended – leave.

14 The account details will already be filled in from the information above. The screen will look like this:

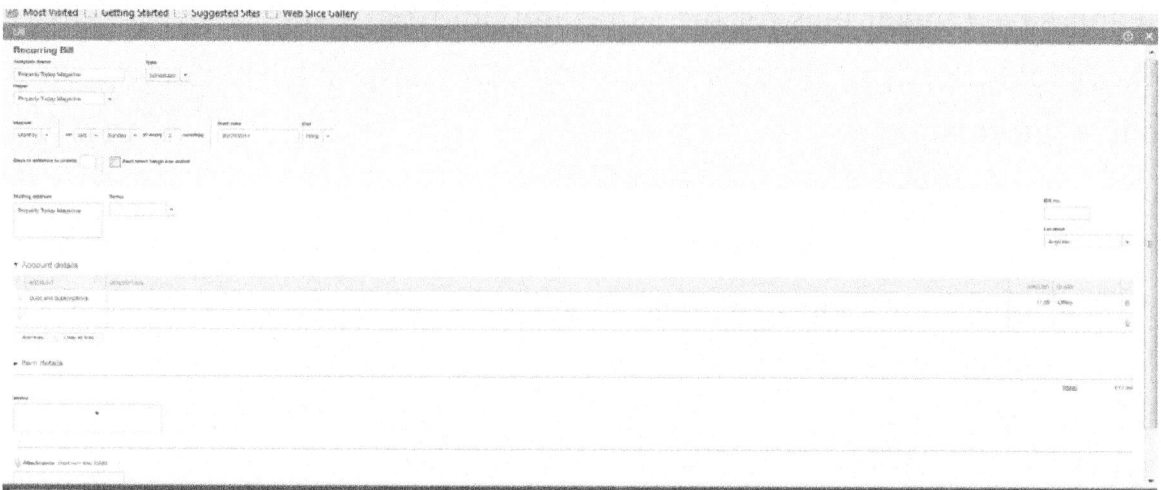

15 Click *Save Template.*

This will save your memorised bill. You can amend or delete your memorised transaction at any time.

To view your memorised transactions list:

1 From the COG (top right hand corner of the screen), click once to display further options.

2 Under 'Lists' choose *Recurring Transactions,* and click once.

3 All Recurring Transactions are listed. If you want to amend any – click on it once and click *edit.* Or to delete it, click *delete.*

8.5 Paying bills

To pay a bill:

1 From the Supplier menu (on the far left hand side), click once to view a list of the Suppliers. The summary at the top will list the amount of unpaid bills. And number of open bills. Click on this to display what bills remain open and unpaid. See the screen shot:

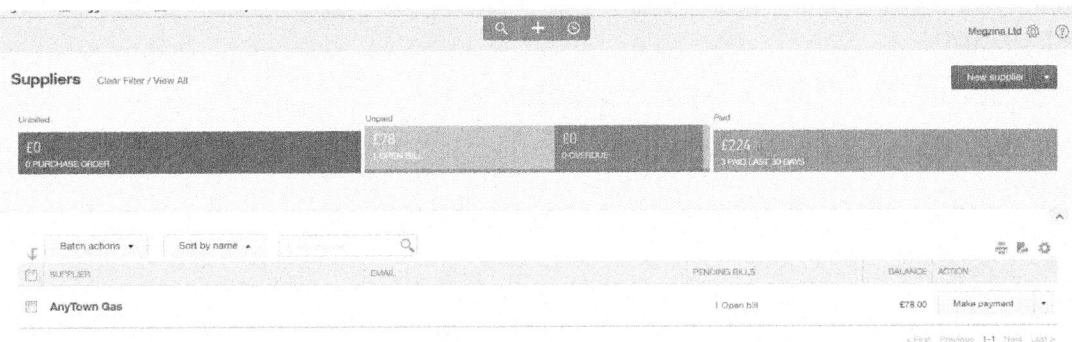

2 In this example, only Anytown Gas is outstanding for £78. Under Action, click *Make Payment*.

3 Under payment method, choose Current Account.

4 The outstanding transaction (bill no. 5984) should be ticked. The entire amount of 78.00 should be ticked. The screen should look like this:

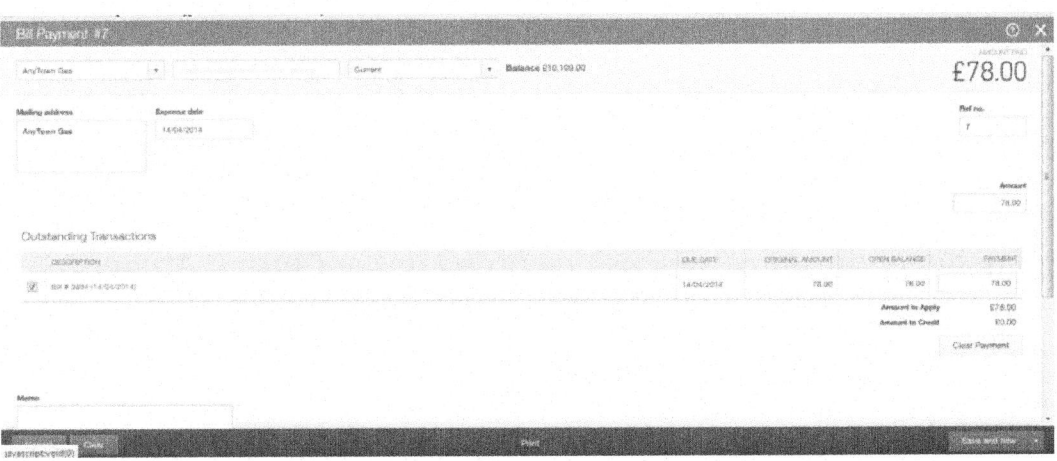

5 Click save and close.

When the bill is paid using this method, QuickBooks makes an entry into the Accounts Payable register – showing a decrease of £78 in the total outstanding. It also create a cheque from your current account to pay the bill.

To see the entry in the Accounts Payable register:

1 From COG (top right hand corner of the screen), click once to display further options
2 Under 'Settings' click *Chart of Accounts.*
3 Scroll down and find *Creditors.* Click once.
4 Click *Account History*. The register is displayed:

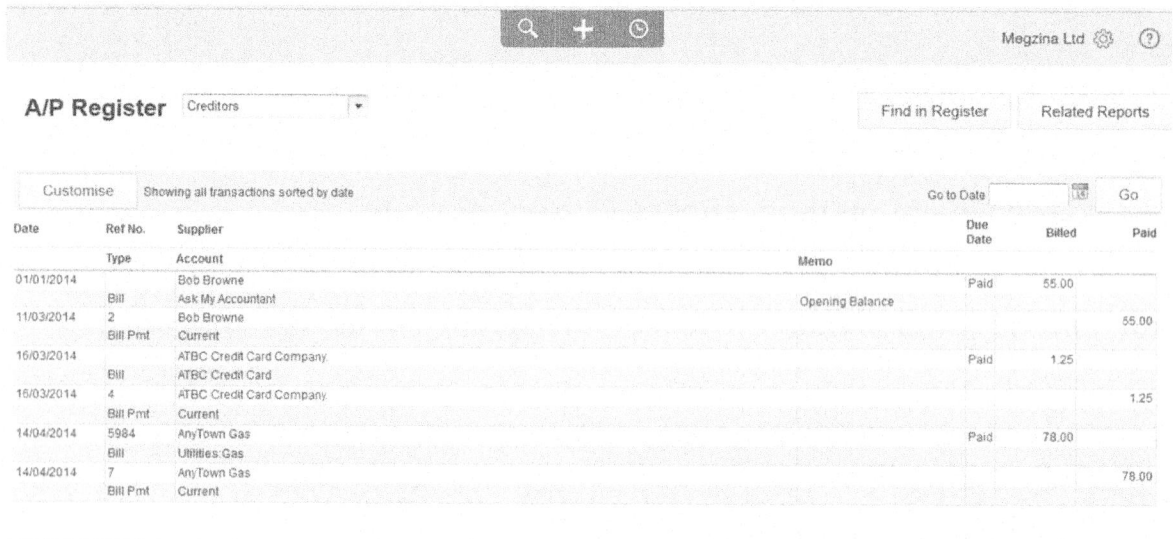

At the same time, the entry was also recorded in the Current Account.

To see the entry in the Current Account:

5 From the A/P Register drop down, choose Current Account.

You will see that QuickBooks has entered the payment as a transaction in the Current Account and has updated the balance:

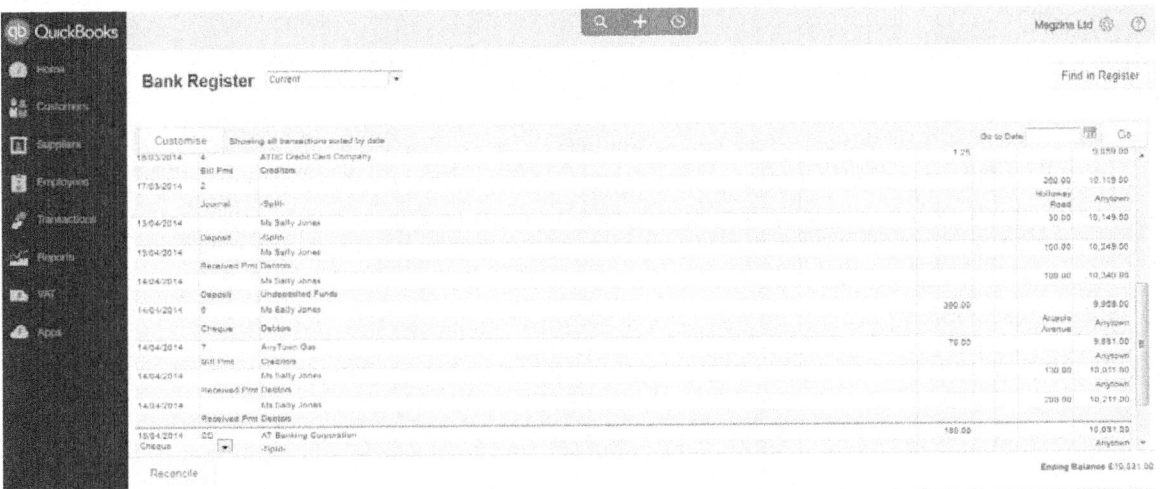

6 Select the Anytown Gas transaction. It will turn yellow to show it is selected. Click edit. And the Bill payment menu will be displayed again. From here you could edit the date, or amend the amount.

Printing Remittances

7 In the bottom, middle of the screen click Print – the Remittance Advice PDF would pop up. You can email this to the supplier to inform them that you'd made a payment or one was on its way. Or, print the remittance advice and enclose it with a cheque and post it to the supplier. This saves time, and looks professional when the supplier receives your payment.

Remittance Advice

Payment To: AnyTown Gas

Date: 14/04/2014
Reference No: 7

Bill Number	Bill Date	Due Date	Original Amount	Balance	Payment
5984	14/04/2014	14/04/2014	78.00	78.00	78.00

Amount Overpaid: £0.00

Total: £78.00

Memo:

Signature: ---------------------------

To List of Expenses paid:

1 From far left click *Transactions* and then *Expenses*. You can filter by transaction type (e.g. cheque, bill), Status (e.g. paid, overdue), the dates and payee name. Click apply – and this will filter the transactions.

2 Then click on printer icon. A list will be displayed:

Megzina Ltd

All transactions from All dates

Date	Type	No.	Payee	Category	Total
15/04/2014	Cheque	DD	AT Banking Corporation	-Split-	£180.00
14/04/2014	Cheque	6	Ms Sally Jones	Debtors	£390.00
14/04/2014	Bill Payment (Cheque)	7	AnyTown Gas		£78.00
14/04/2014	Bill	5984	AnyTown Gas	Gas	£78.00
16/03/2014	Bill		ATBC Credit Card Company	ATBC Credit Card	£1.25
16/03/2014	Bill Payment (Cheque)	4	ATBC Credit Card Company		£1.25
15/03/2014	Cheque	3	Anytown Water Works	Utilities	£42.75
15/03/2014	Cheque	SVCCHRG		Interest expense	£3.00
11/03/2014	Cheque	1	Bob Browne	Repair and maintenance	£20.00
11/03/2014	Bill Payment (Cheque)	2	Bob Browne		£55.00
07/03/2014	Card Expense	FINCHRG		Interest expense	£1.25
06/03/2014	Card Expense		AnyTown Trains	Travel Expense	£40.00
06/03/2014	Card Credit		AnyTown Trains	Travel Expense	£40.00
01/01/2014	Bill		Bob Browne	Ask My Accountant	£55.00

To Print a Remittance advice or expense voucher:

1 From far left click Transactions and then Expenses and click on the one transaction type: (cheque or bill payment) that you want to print.

2 Bottom middle of the screen, click Print

3 If it's a cheque – the remittance advice will display. If it's an expense, the expense voucher will display.

Expense Voucher

Payment To
Ms Sally Jones
123 Alley Avenue
Anytown
AN8 9NM

Date: 14/04/2014
Payment Method: Cheque
Reference No: 6

Account / Product or Service	Description	Amount
Debtors	Refund	390.00

TOTAL £390.00
TOTAL DUE

Memo:

9: Analysing Financial Data

Summary of what is in this chapter:

9.1 Reports and graphs help you to understand your business

9.2 Creating QuickReports

9.3 Creating and customising preset reports

9.4 Saving report settings

9.5 Printing reports

9.6 Exporting reports to Microsoft Excel or CSV file

9.7 Creating QuickInsight graphs

9.1 Reports and graphs help you to understand your business

Some people like figures, others like numbers. Graphs are a useful way to pictorially illustrate what the numbers are saying. Reporting is extremely important in business. Bookkeeping isn't just about data entry and inputting figures. It's useful to take the time to run reports and to analyse the information. This will give you a clearer picture of what is happening in your business. Are you meeting your targets? How can the business be improved?

QuickBooks Online has plenty of reports to help you see the performance of your business. There are lots of pre-set reports, plus you can customise them to show the exact details that you want.

9.2 Creating QuickReports

A quick way to create a report in QuickBooks is to use a QuickReport. These are pre-designed reports which present the information being shows on the screen. Whenever you have a list, a register or a form displayed – you can create a QuickReport.

For example – if you want to see a history of all transactions for a certain customer, select the customer's name from the Customers ledger. Ensure 'all transactions' is clicked, and then click the printer icon and print the list.

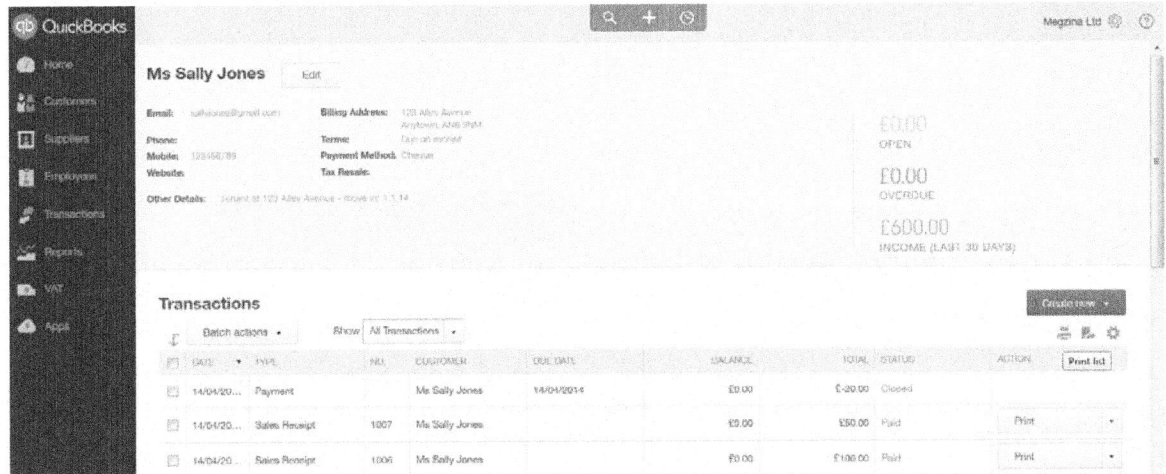

A list of all the transactions will be displayed on the screen.

Megzina Ltd

All transactions from All dates for Ms Sally Jones

Date	Type	No.	Customer	Due date	Balance	Total	Status
14/04/2014	Payment		Ms Sally Jones	14/04/2014	£0.00	£-20.00	Closed
14/04/2014	Sales Receipt	1007	Ms Sally Jones		£0.00	£50.00	Paid
14/04/2014	Sales Receipt	1006	Ms Sally Jones		£0.00	£100.00	Paid
14/04/2014	Payment		Ms Sally Jones	14/04/2014	£0.00	£0.00	Closed
14/04/2014	Cheque	6	Ms Sally Jones	14/04/2014	£0.00	£390.00	Paid
14/04/2014	Credit Note	1005	Ms Sally Jones	14/04/2014	£0.00	£-150.00	Closed
14/04/2014	Payment		Ms Sally Jones	14/04/2014	£0.00	£-200.00	Closed
14/04/2014	Invoice	1003	Ms Sally Jones	14/04/2014	£0.00	£10.00	Paid
14/04/2014	Payment		Ms Sally Jones	14/04/2014	£0.00	£-130.00	Closed
13/04/2014	Invoice	1002	Ms Sally Jones	13/04/2014	£0.00	£100.00	Paid
13/04/2014	Payment		Ms Sally Jones	13/04/2014	£0.00	£0.00	Closed
13/04/2014	Payment		Ms Sally Jones	13/04/2014	£0.00	£-100.00	Closed
01/04/2014	Invoice	1001	Ms Sally Jones	01/04/2014	£0.00	£100.00	Paid

To see what you owe your suppliers:

1 Click suppliers (on the far left)

2 Click sort by open balance

3 Click print list

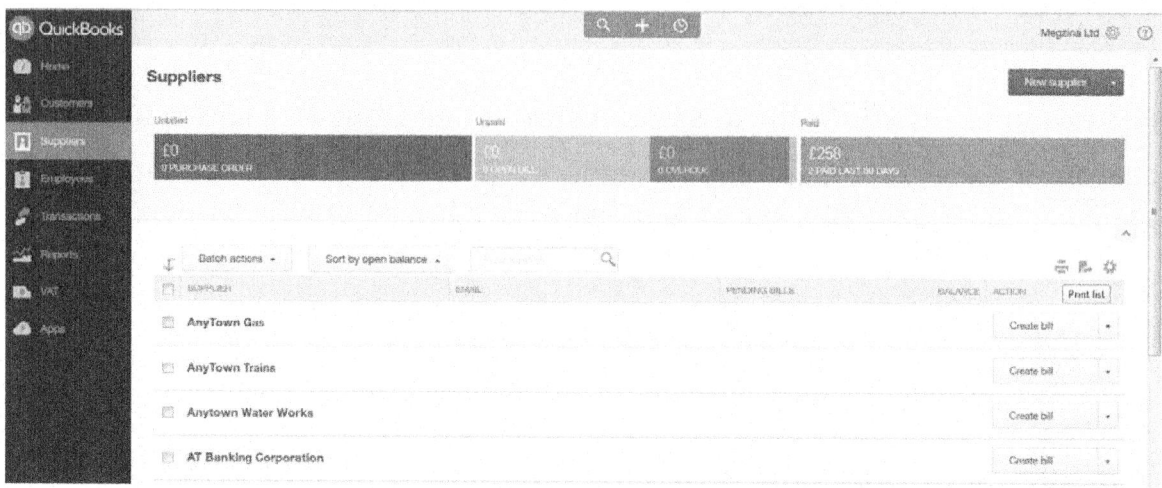

The list of suppliers, and the balance outstanding to each one will pop up. (In this case it's NIL).

Supplier	Email	Pending Bills	Balance
AnyTown Gas			
AnyTown Trains			
Anytown Water Works			
AT Banking Corporation			
ATBC Credit Card Company	atbc@cc.com		
Bob Browne			
Bob Building Ltd (033) 344-4555	bob@bobuilding.com		
Property Today Magazine			

To find out more information on any one supplier, from the supplier list, double click on the supplier that you want to focus on e.g. AnyTown Water Works.

1 Click on show all transactions.

2 Print list.

QuickBooks Online Help

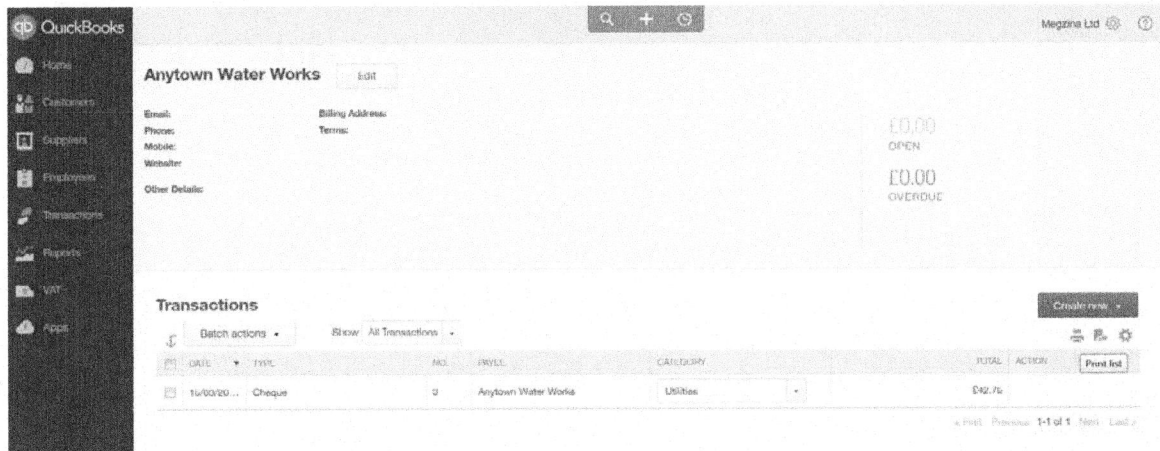

The report of all the transactions for that one supplier will be displayed:

9.3 Creating and customising preset reports

QuickBooks has many reports which are pre-set. These are the typical, most popular reports which are requested. To run any pre-set / QuickReports:

1 Click on Reports in the far left hand side of the screen.
2 You'll see a profit and loss graph at the top of the screen. And below this are the options to run a report.
3 Click on All Reports and familiarise yourself with the various types of report that are available (there's 7 pre-set, but if VAT is switched on, there'll be 8).

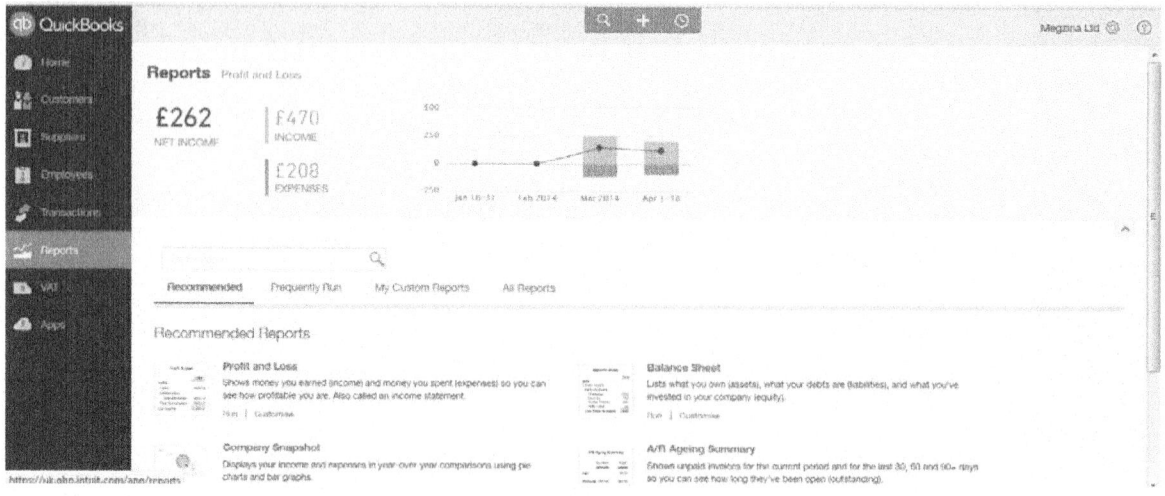

Seven Types of Reports available: (see the appendix for full explanation of each report type):

i. **Business overview** - These reports show different perspectives of how your business is doing:

    Profit and Loss

    Profit and Loss Detail

    Profit and Loss by Class

    Profit and Loss by Location

    Statement of Cash Flows

    Balance Sheet

    Balance Sheet Summary

    Audit Log

    Company Snapshot

ii. **Manage Accounts Receivable** - These reports let you see who owes you money and how much they owe you so you can get paid:

    Customer Balance Summary

Customer Balance Detail
Collections Report
Statement List
A/R Ageing Summary
A/R Ageing Detail
Invoice List

iii. **Manage Accounts Payable** - These reports show what you owe and when payments are due so you can take advantage of the time you have to pay bills but still make payments on time:
A/P Ageing Summary
A/P Ageing Detail
Bill Payment List
Unpaid Bills
Supplier Balance Detail
Supplier Balance Summary

iv. **Manage Employees** - These reports help you manage employee activities and payroll:
Time Activities by Employee Detail
Recent / Edited Time Activities

v. **Review Sales** - These reports group and total sales in different ways to help analyse your sales to see how you're doing and where you make your money:
Sales by Customer Summary
Sales by Customer Detail
Sales by Product/Service Summary

Sales by Product/Service Detail
Income by Customer Summary
Customer Contact List
Transaction List by Customer
Sales by Location Summary
Sales by Location Detail
Sales by Class Summary
Sales by Class Detail
Time Activities by Customer Detail
Estimates by Customer
Unbilled Charges
Unbilled Time
Deposit Detail

vi. **Review Expenses and Purchases** - These reports total your expenses and purchases and group them in different ways to help you understand what you spend:
Expenses by Supplier Summary
Supplier Contact List
Purchases by Supplier Detail
Purchases by Product/Service Detail
Cheque Detail
Transaction List by Supplier
Open Purchases Order List
Purchases by Class Detail
Purchases by Location Detail

vii. **Accountants Reports** - These are reports accountants typically use to drill down into your business details and prepare your tax returns:
- Account Listing
- Trial Balance
- Profit and Loss
- Transaction Detail by Account
- Reconciliation Reports
- Journal
- Balance Sheet
- General Ledger
- Recent Automatic Transactions
- Transaction List with Splits
- Statement of Cash Flows
- Transaction List by Date
- Recent Transactions

IF the VAT option is switched on, the VAT report options will also be displayed:

viii. **Manage VAT** - These reports help manage the VAT you collect and then pay to the HM Revenue and Customs (HMRC):
- VAT Liability Report
- VAT Detail Report
- VAT 100 Report
- VAT Exemption Report

To run a report on what your customers owe you – choose:

    1 Reports.

    2 Manage Accounts Receivable.

    3 Customer Balance Summary.

QuickBooks will ask you whether you want to create a report on a 'cash basis' or 'accrual basis'. **Cash basis** means that you count income or expenses only when you actually receive or pay money. Accrual **basis** means that you count income or expenses when you send an invoice or receive a bill, *before* you actually receive or pay money.

The Customer Balance Summary shows each customer's total open balances. Whereas the Customer Balance Detail lists unpaid invoices for each customer, including invoice date and number, due date, total, and amount owed to you (open balance), so some reports go into more detail than others.

To run a report on what you owe your suppliers – choose:

    1 Reports.

    2 Manage Accounts Payable.

    3 Supplier Balance Summary.

Recommended Reports

Under 'Recommended Reports' is the report: Company Snapshot. This displays your income and expenses in year-over-year comparisons using pie charts and bar graphs.

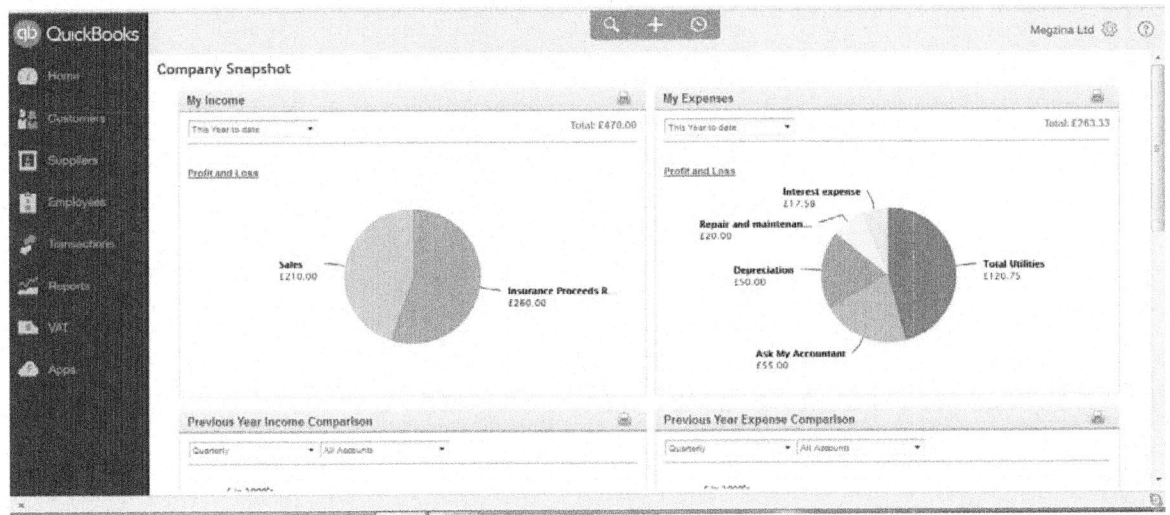

Another recommended report is Expenses by Supplier Summary. This report shows your total expenses for each supplier. Run this report.

Zooming in

To get a better understanding of the information presented in the report, you can trace the data in the individual transaction back to the original transaction level by zooming in. Hover over the total column where the number / amount is, and the figure will become underlined. Click on Anytown Water Works to drill down into that transaction.

AnyTown Gas	70.00
AnyTown Trains	0.00
Anytown Water Works	42.75
AT Banking Corporation	13.33
Bob Browne	75.00

The next report tells you that it was for Utilities.

Gross Profit	£0.00
Expenses	
Utilities	42.75
Total Expenses	£42.75

Once again, hover your mouse over the figure '42.75' and click once to drill down further into the transaction.

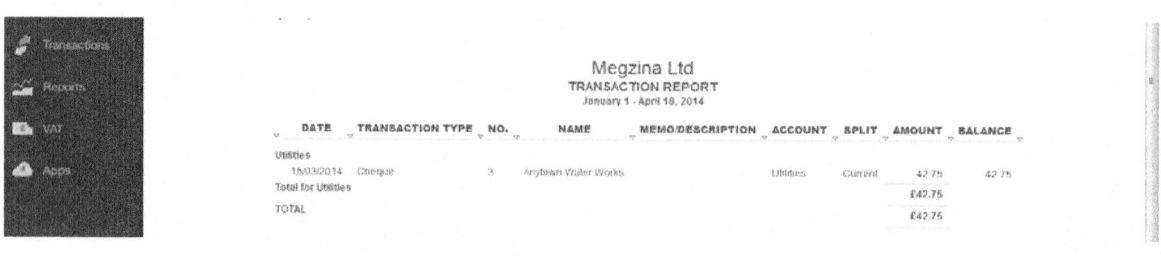

This report shows you the date, the transaction type, number, any description, account, amount etc., We can drill down further. Click on this line, and QuickBooks takes you to the actual cheque, which was written.

QuickBooks Online Help

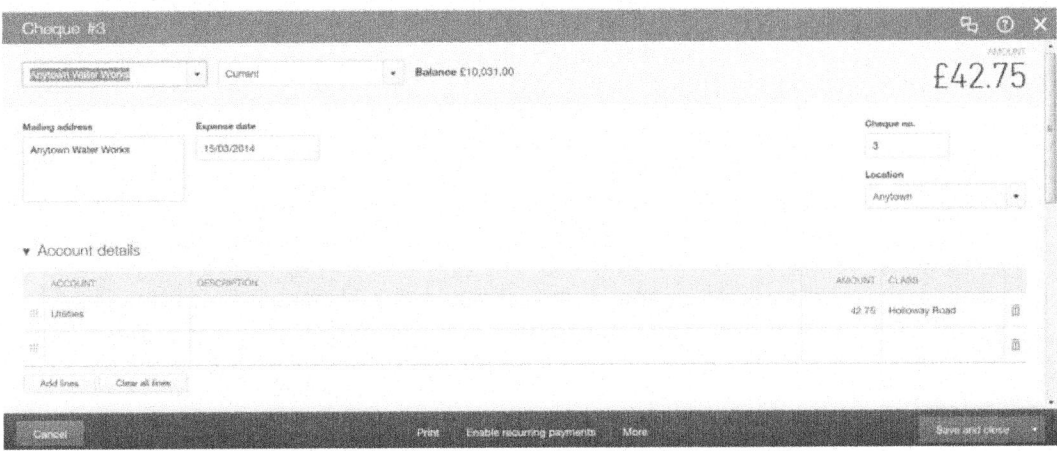

Customising QuickReports

Each QuickReport has a 'Customise' option at the top of the page.

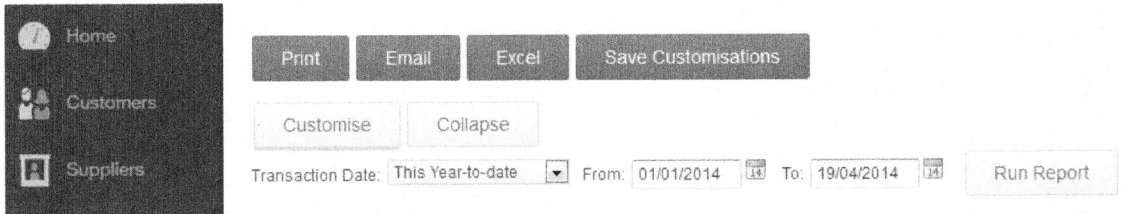

1 On the far left hand side, click Reports
2 Choose (under Recommended Reports) Profit and Loss
3 Click Customise
4 A Menu of the custom settings pops up

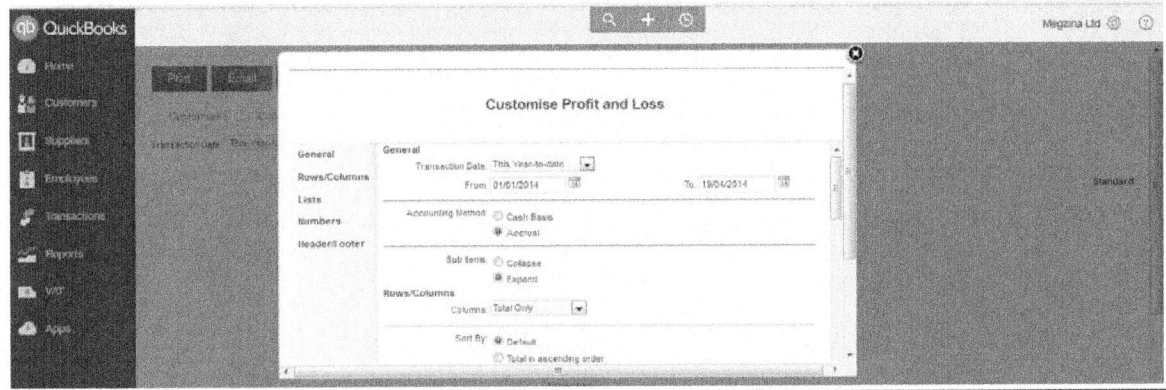

5 Under Rows/Columns tick '% of Income' and '% of Expense'
6 Scroll to the bottom and click Run Report

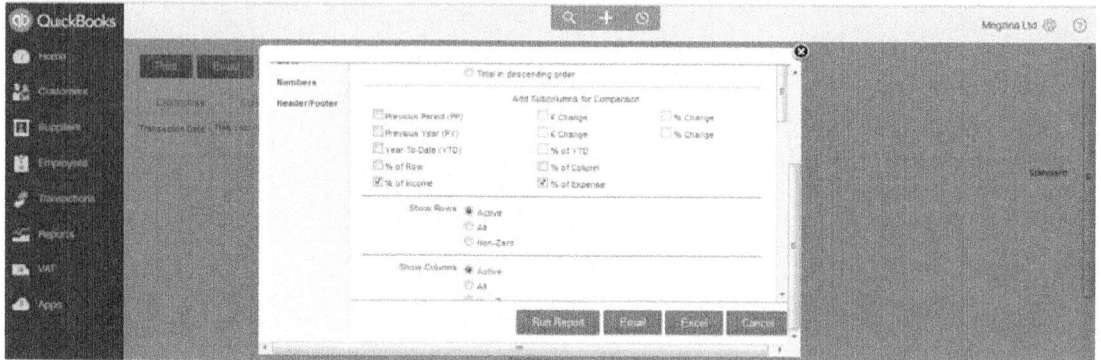

The report will look like this:

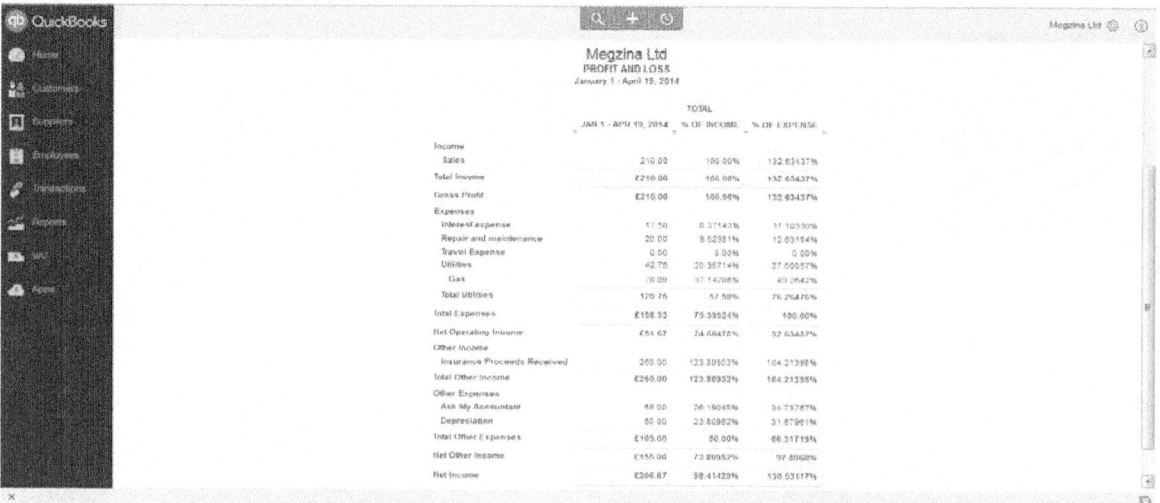

Some users find percentages easier to analyse, others prefer pictures, other just want the bottom line figures. Think about who the end user of the report will be, and what will be most useful to them.

To change information in the report heading:
1 On the far left hand side, click Reports
2 Choose (under Recommended Reports) Profit and Loss

3 Click Customise

4 A Menu of the custom settings pops up

5 Click Header/Footer

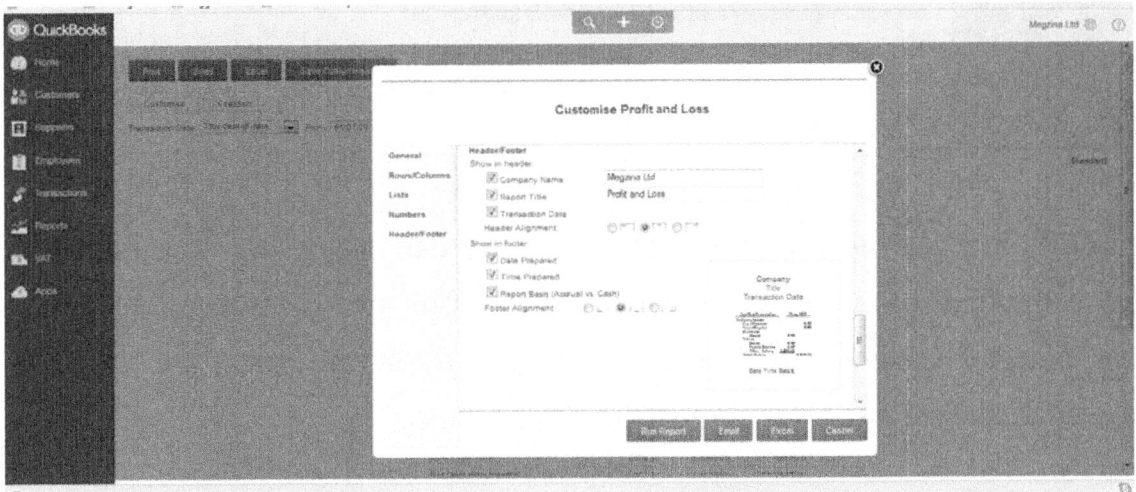

This screen gives you the option to change the header details - the Company Name, Report Title and whether or not to show the transaction date. The header can be aligned in the middle, or left or right justified. In the footer, the options are whether or not to show the date prepared, the time prepared, and the basis upon which the report was prepared (cash or accrual). The footer can be aligned in the middle, or left or right justified. Choose the setting that you want, then click 'Run Report'.

9.4 Saving report settings

After you have customised a report to provide the information you want, you can memorise the settings, by clicking "Save Customisations" so you can quickly produce the same report in the future. QuickBooks will remember the report's settings, but not the actual data.

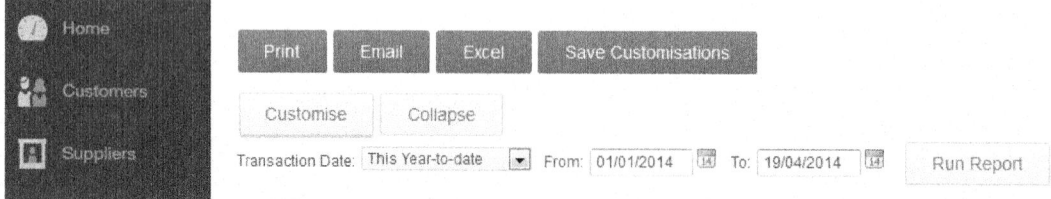

In addition to saving the report settings, you can create memorised report groups that you can use to organise your memorised reports in a way that makes sense for your business and to enable you to be able to access and run a group of reports quickly.

To create a memorised report group:

1 When you click on 'Save Customisations' the following screen appears:

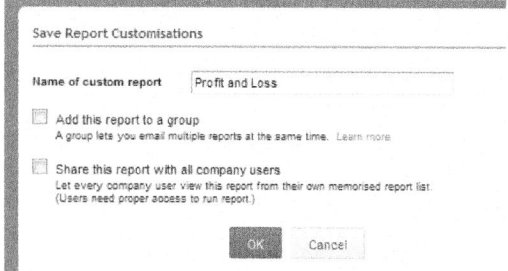

2 You have the option to add the report and to share the report with all company users.

3 Tick: add the report to a group.

4 The drop down option appears – add the group to add the report to.

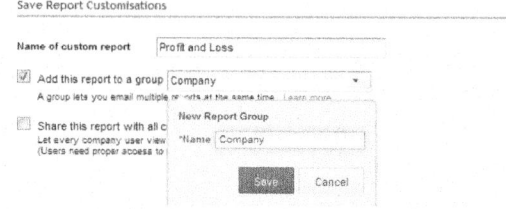

QuickBooks Online Help

5 Click Save. Click OK.

Viewing Memorised Reports

1 Click: Reports (far left hand side menu bar).

2 Click: My Custom Reports.

3 The list of memorised reports is displayed.

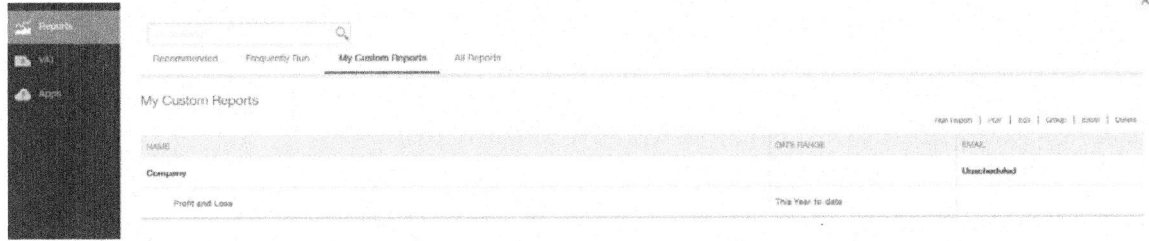

Sending Memorised Reports

1 Click: Reports (far left hand side menu bar).

2 Click: My Custom Reports.

3 The list of memorised reports is displayed.

4 Click on the bold line 'Company' (name of the group) – and then click Edit.

5 Click 'set the email schedule for this group'.

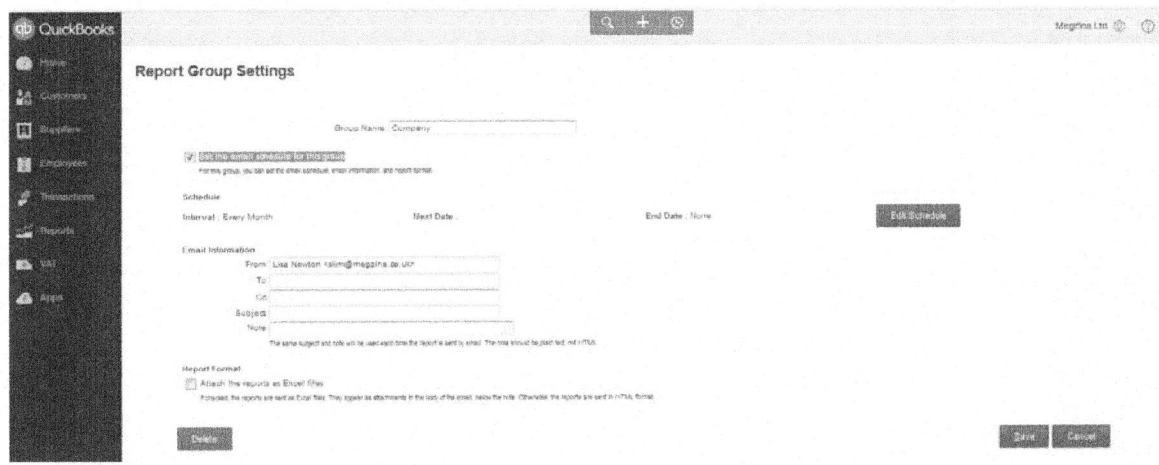

6 In the 'To' box - enter email addresses of the people who need to receive this report

7 In the 'Subject' line - type in: Profit & Loss Weekly Report

8 In the 'Note' - type in: Please find attached the end of week profit and loss report.

9 Report Format - tick if you want the recipient(s) to receive the report in excel format (if unticked, they'll receive an HMTL file).

10 Click 'Edit Schedule' and an option screen pops up.

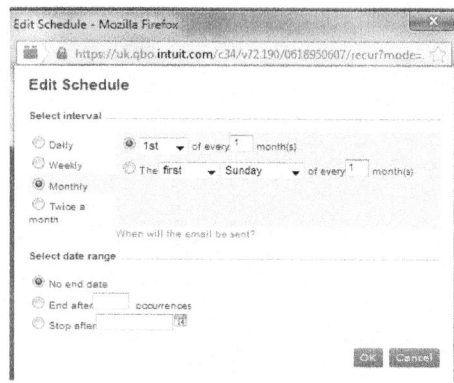

11 Click Weekly on a Saturday. Click OK.

12 The screen will then have changed the scheduled interval.

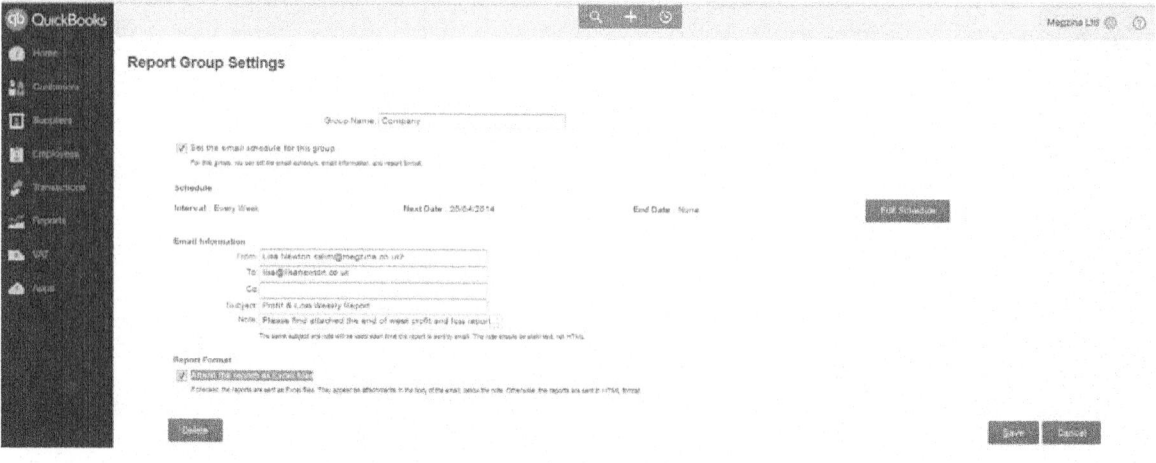

13 Click Save. And the memorised reports list now displays the emailed scheduled date. Automating the reporting is very handy whereby there are partners or people who have a vested interest on the business, who want regular reports on how the business is doing. This mechanism saves the bookkeeper (or whoever is responsible for the data entry) from having to remember to produce and send agreed reports.

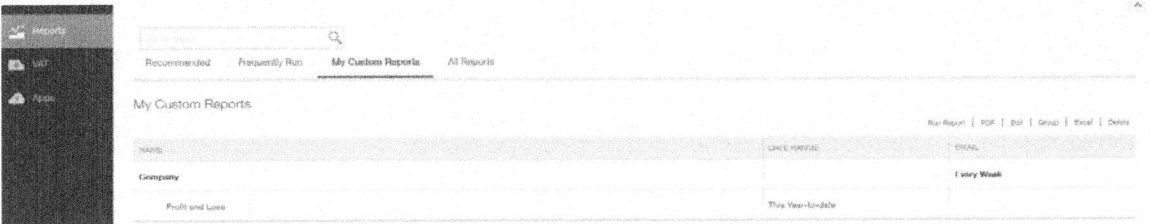

9.5 Printing reports

Any time you have a report displayed on the screen, you can print it.

1. Click the Print button.

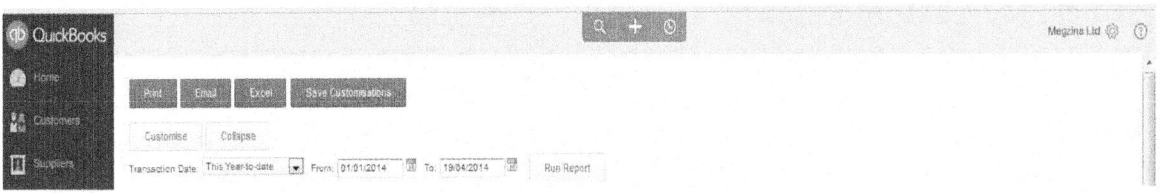

2 The print screen will pop up on screen. Click OK.

QuickBooks Online Help

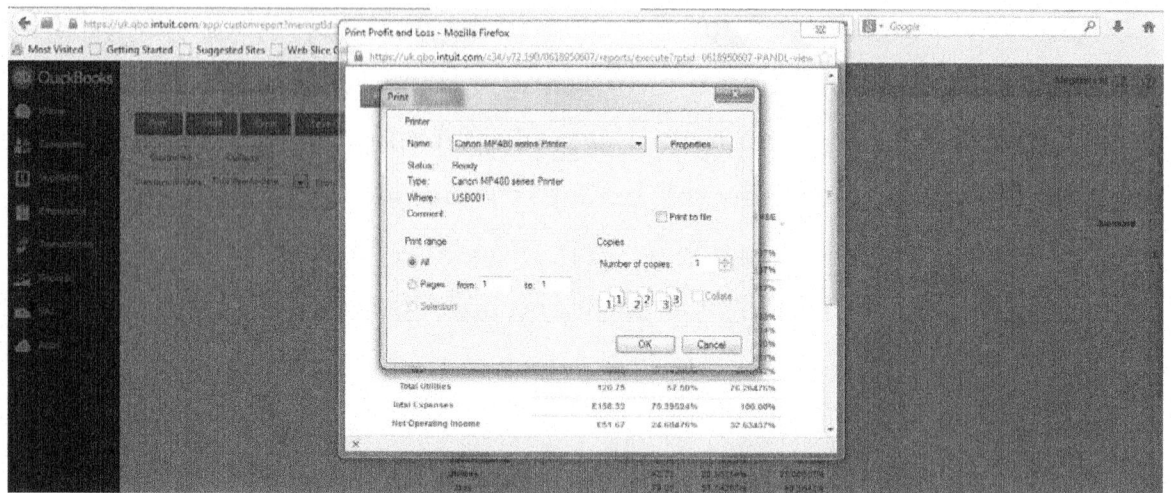

3 Click 'Close' to close the screen.

Printing a Group of Reports

If there is more than one memorised report in the group, you can run a report once, to include everything. This save time, as there's no need to run a report individually.

1 Click: Reports (far left hand side menu bar).
2 Click: My Custom Reports.
3 The list of memorised reports is displayed.

4 Click on the **bold** line 'Company' (name of the group) – and then click PDF.

5 The reports listed (e.g. Balance Sheet and Profit & Loss) will be downloaded in one document as a PDF.

9.6 Exporting reports to Microsoft Excel

You may prefer to view your reports as an Excel document, and not a PDF.

1 Click: Reports (far left hand side menu bar).
2 Click: My Custom Reports.
3 The list of memorised reports is displayed.

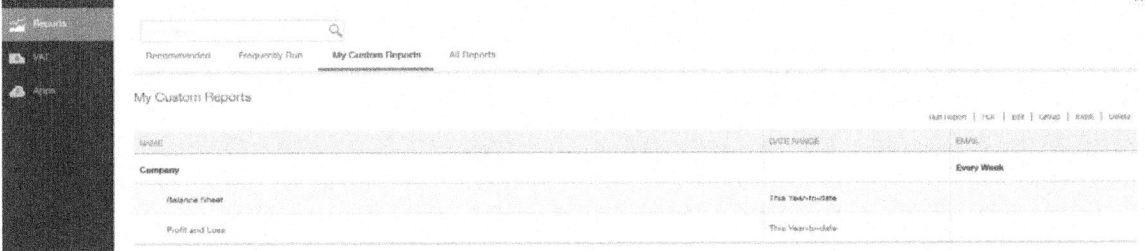

4 Click on the one report that you wish to view e.g. Balance Sheet – and then click Excel.
5 The option – 'open with' will be displayed on screen. Choose Excel. Click 'OK'.

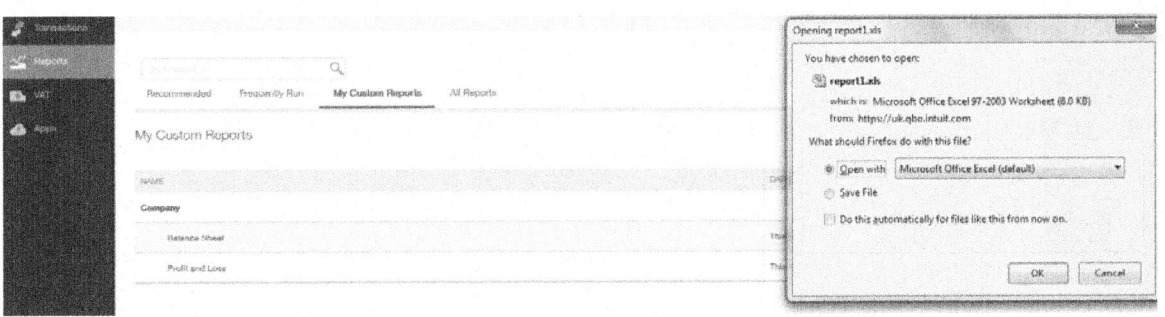

QuickBooks Online Help

6 The report will open in excel.

Running a report in excel

1 Click: Reports (far left hand side menu bar).

2 Choose the report: Expenses by Supplier Summary.

3 In the top left hand corner, click the blue button 'Excel' to run the report in excel. And the 'open with' option will pop up. Click 'OK'.

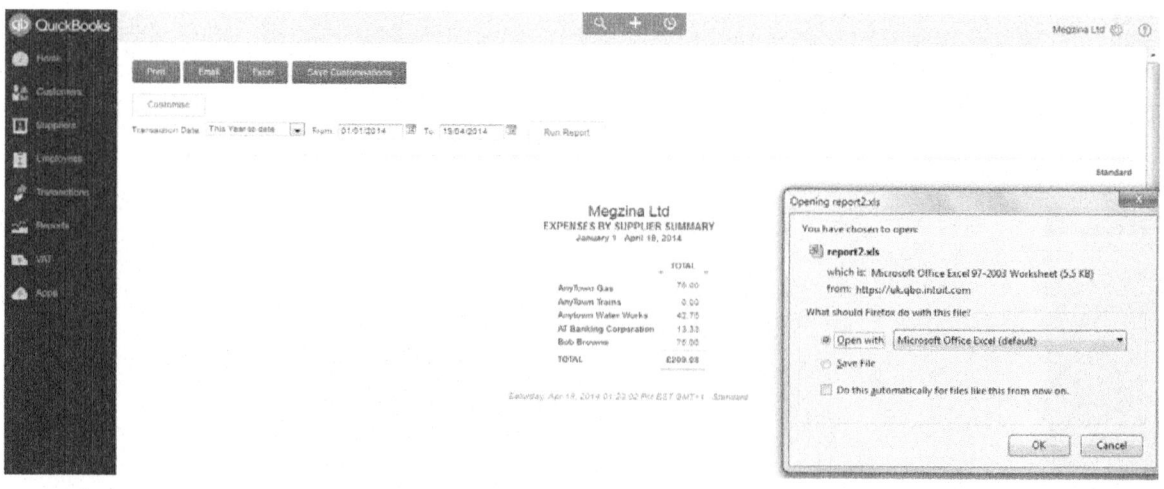

The information is then displayed in an excel spreadsheet.

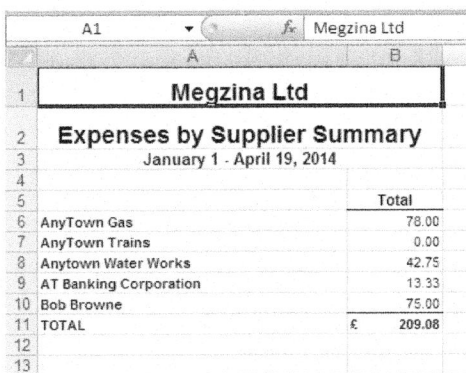

9.7 Creating QuickInsight graphs

If you want a visual picture of the performance of the business, under 'Recommended Reports' click: Company Snapshot.

There are six reports that are available (four of which are graphs):
- Income and expenses (graphs)
- Previous year income and expenses (graphs)
- Debtors and Creditors

This report shows the income by percentage and amount.

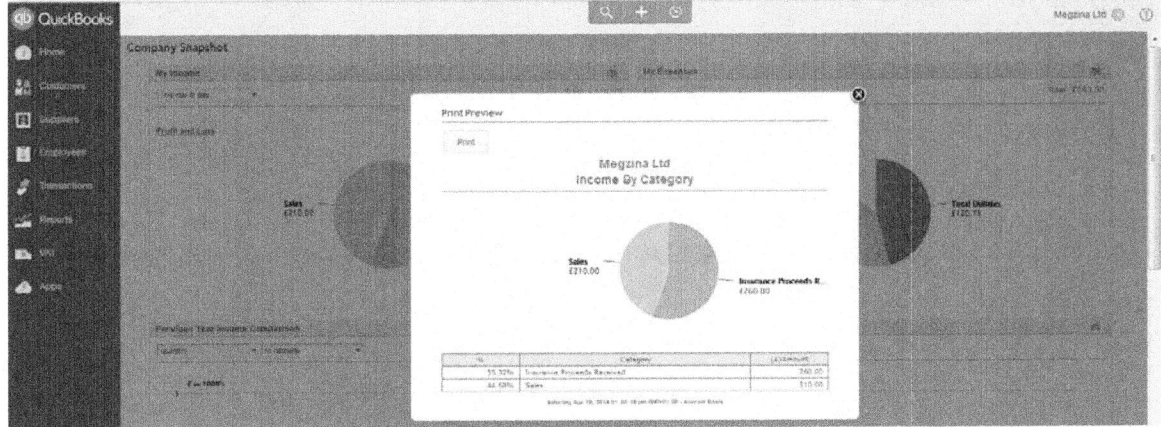

This report shows the expenses by percentage and amount.

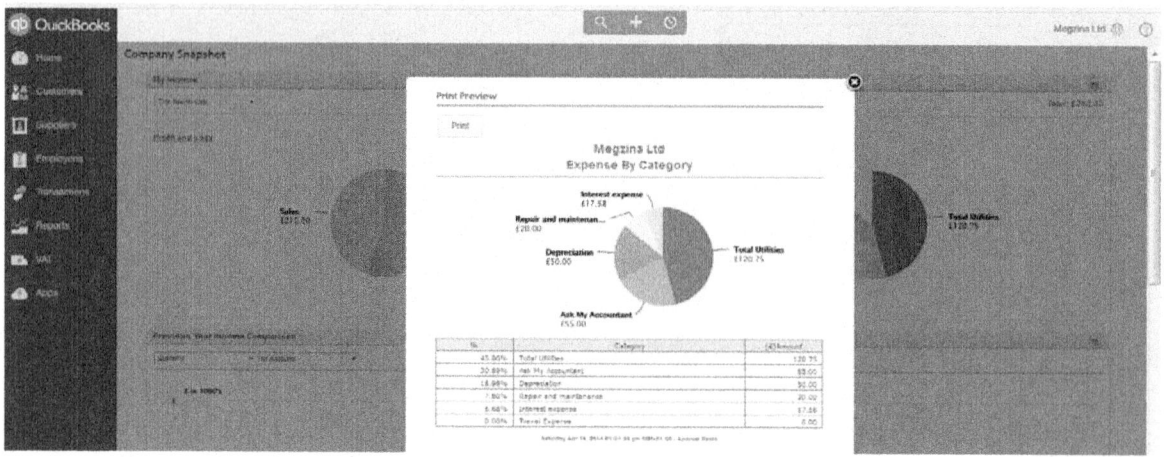

This report shows the previous year's income, compared against this current year.

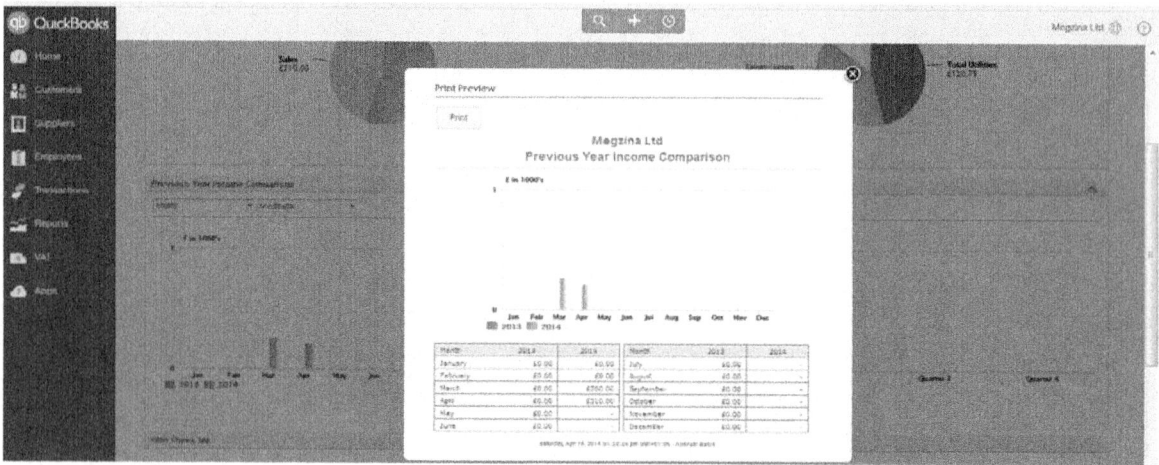

This report shows the previous year's expenses, compared against this current year.

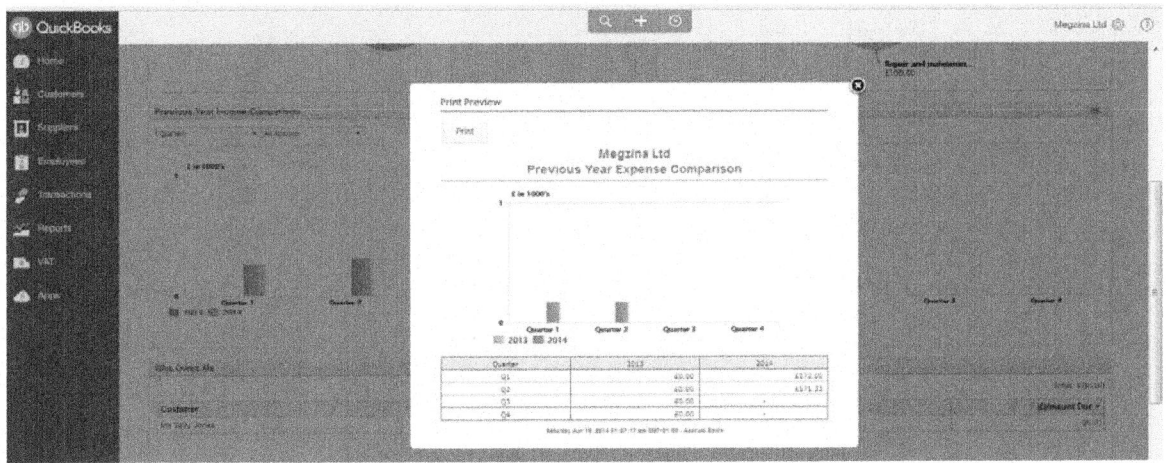

To customise the graph chart

1 Click the drop down menu under the name of the graph e.g. Under Previous Year Expense Comparison is the option of time (choose from Quarterly or Monthly)

2 Next to this option, is the option to choose 'all accounts' or just one account specifically.

3 Then click the printer icon, and this will run the report.

QuickBooks Online Help

10: Setting up stock

> *Summary of what is in this chapter:*
>
> 10.1 Turning on the stock feature
>
> 10.2 Entering products into stock
>
> 10.3 Ordering products
>
> 10.4 Receiving stock and entering the bill
>
> 10.5 Manually adjusting stock

10.1 Turning on the stock control feature

To enable stock control:

1 Click your company name (top right hand corner) and select Company Settings.

2 Click Sales. And then edit: Products and services section.

3 Click Track Quantity on Hand to "On".

4 Click Save. And Done.

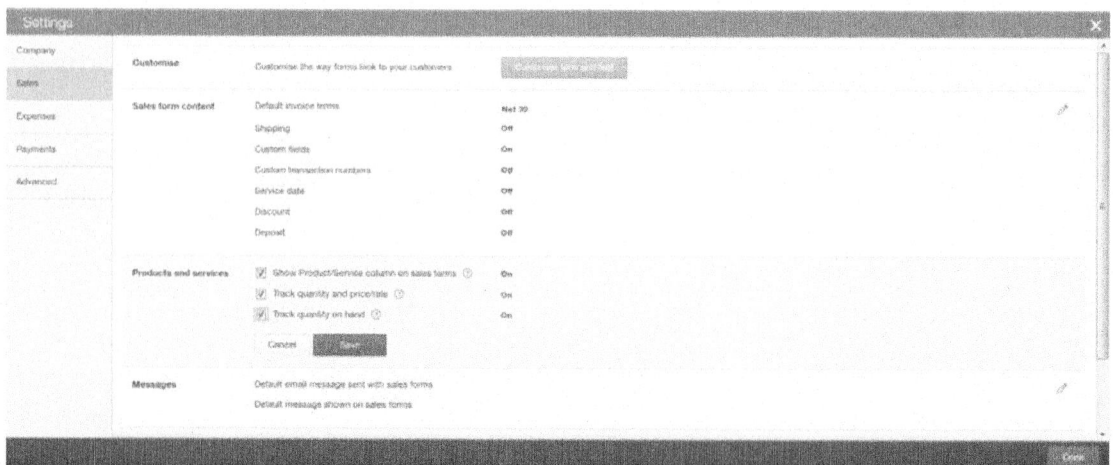

10.2 Entering products into stock

You can use QuickBooks to manage your stock. It can track the number of items in stock and the value of your stock after every purchase and sale. Once each product is entered into the Item list as a stock part, QuickBooks tracks each stock-related transaction – as you sell and reorder the product.

To enter a product into stock:

1 Click on the COG by your company name in the top right hand corner, and select Products and Services under lists. The lists are displayed.
2 Click 'New' and a new window will pop up.
3 Tick 'Track Quantity on Hand (for stock items)' and further options will pop up.

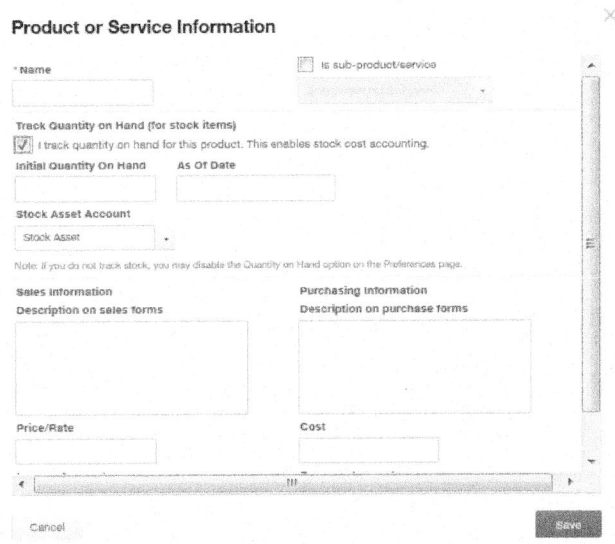

4 Fill in the form. Name: *Beds*. Initial Quantity On Hand: *5*. As Of Date: *01/01/2014*. Stock Asset Account: *Stock Asset*. Description on sales forms: *Single Beds*. Price/Rate: *100.00*. Description on purchase forms:

Single Beds. Price/Rate: *35.00*. Income Account: *Sales of Product Income*. Expense Account: *Cost of sales*.

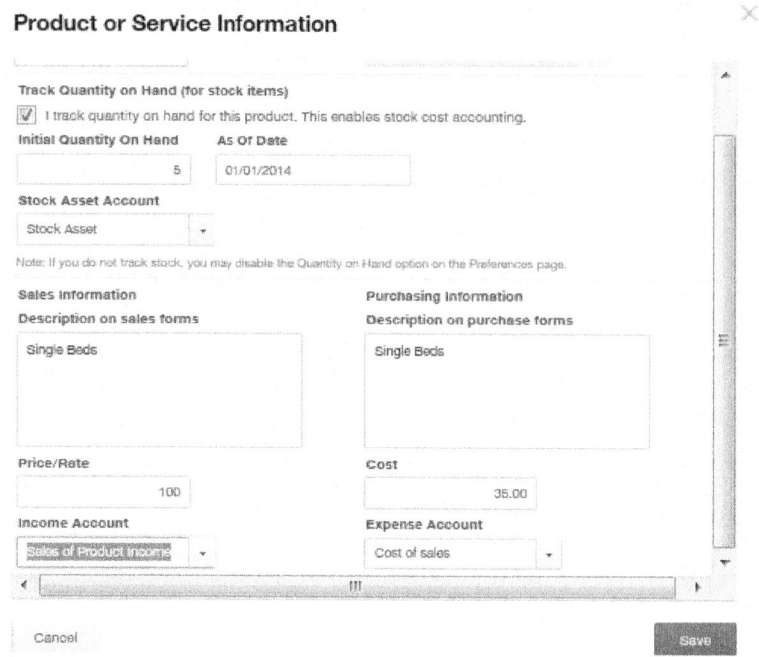

5 Click Save.

10.3 Ordering products

You need to order products to maintain your stock levels.

Creating purchase orders

To order a product using a purchase order:
1 From the Company Name in the top right hand corner, choose 'Purchase Order' from Suppliers, in the menu from the middle of the screen

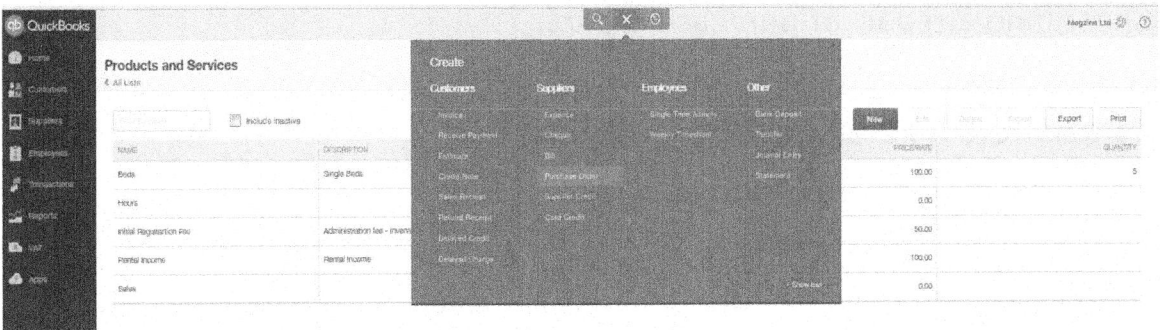

2 The Purchase Order screen will pop up.

3 Create New Supplier: Beds R Us.

4 Item Details – click beds.

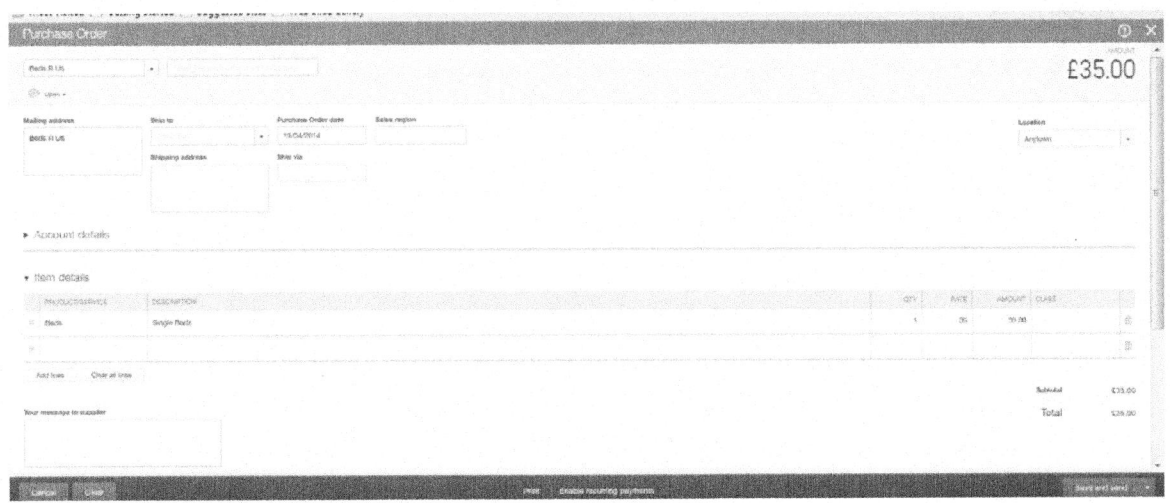

5 Save and close.

After you have created a purchase order, QuickBooks adds the purchase orders account to the chart of accounts. This is a non-posting account and doesn't actually affect your profit and loss or balance sheet. The purchase orders account is used to produce a QuickReport showing current purchase orders so you always know what is on order.

Generating a report of purchase orders.

To generate a Purchase Orders report:

1 Click on Reports (left hand side bar).

2 Click on all reports.

3 Click: 'Review Expenses and Purchases'. And click 'Open Purchase Orders List'. QuickBooks displays a report of all the purchase orders:

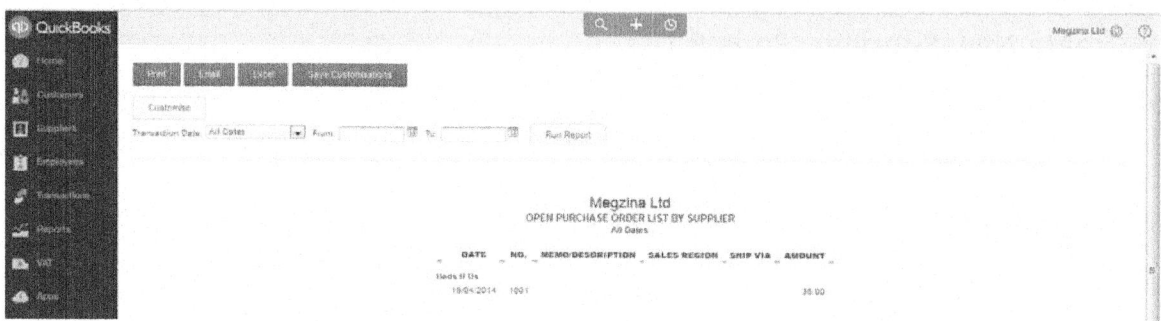

4 Close the report.

10.4 Receiving stock and entering the bill

When you receive the items on your purchase order, you have to enter them into stock. You can receive items with or without a bill.

To receive stock and enter a bill:

1 From Suppliers (left hand side menu), click on the supplier (Beds R Us)

2 From the drop down, choose Create Bill and this screen will pop up:

QuickBooks Online Help

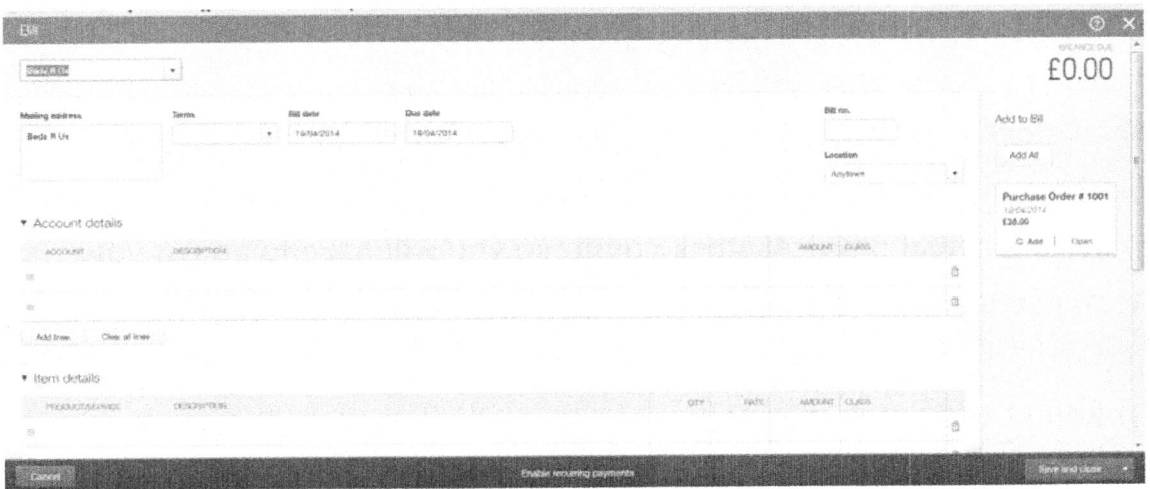

3 On the right hand side, QuickBooks tells you that there are open purchase orders for this supplier and asks if you want to add this to the bill.

4 Click add.

5 Enter the Bill No. 156.

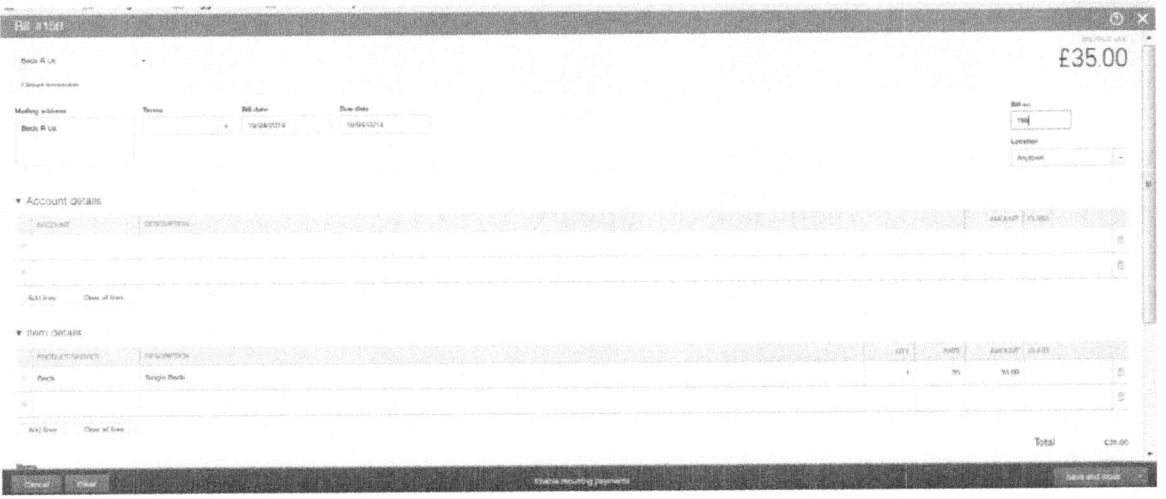

6. Click Save and close.

10.5 Manually adjusting stock

When stock is pilfered, stolen, spoiled or you do a stock take – the numbers in stock (as per the system) won't match the numbers in stock as per the actual physical stock count, so you will have to adjust your stock manually.

To adjust the stock manually:

1 Click the COG by the company name in the top right hand corner of the screen.
2 Choose 'Products and Services' from under the 'Lists' section.

3 The quantity of beds in stock currently shows as 6. Click on the line which needs to be adjusted, and click 'Edit'.
4 On the pop up screen click on 'update'

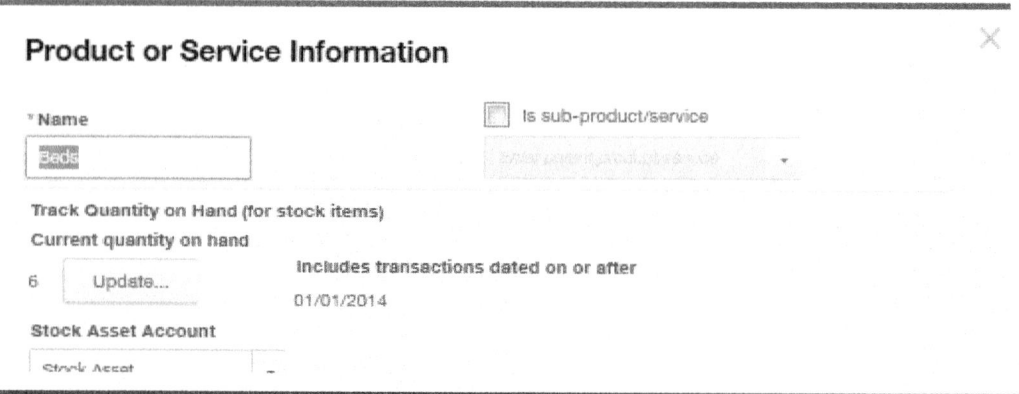

5 In the box 'New Quantity on Hand' type in *4*. Press *Tab*. A new figure in the Difference box e.g. *-2*.

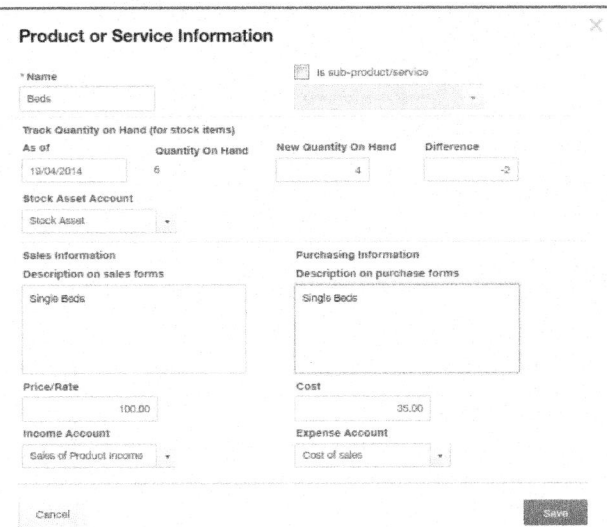

6 Click Save.

10.6 Stock Valuation

To create a report on the value of the stock:

1 Click 'Reports' on far left hand side.

2 Click *All Reports*, then *Manage Products and Stock*. Choose: Stock Valuation Detail. The Stock Valuation Detail Report will be displayed.

3 Close.

11: Tracking, reporting and paying VAT

> *Summary of what is in this chapter:*
> 11.1 Overview of VAT in QuickBooks
> 11.2 Setting up VAT
> 11.3 Viewing the VAT Control Account
> 11.4 Paying VAT to HM Revenue and Customs
> 11.5 VAT Reports

11.1 Overview of VAT in QuickBooks

VAT stands for Value Added Tax. If you are registered for VAT, you must account for VAT on all goods and services you buy and sell in your business. There are specific rules which govern VAT in the UK. See www.hmrc.gov.uk for the most up-to-date rules. You become liable to register for VAT once your income passes a certain level in any 12 month period. If you don't meet this threshold, but wish to register anyway, you may do so. But once registered, you have to charge VAT to your customers as part of your invoice to them. This is known as output tax.

When you buy in goods and services for your business, your suppliers may charge you VAT if they are VAT registered. This is input tax. You can recover this input tax only if you too are VAT registered.

If you are VAT registered – the VAT which you charge your customers is paid over the HMRC, and the VAT which you incur (pay to your suppliers) is recoverable from the HMRC. If you have suffered (paid out more VAT) than you have received (from your customers), then HMRC will refund you the difference.

QuickBooks keeps track of all the input and output VAT. It tracks:

- Invoices to Customers – QuickBooks deals with the VAT element on invoices sent to customers, including part payments, credit notes and sales receipts.
- Bills from Suppliers - QuickBooks deals with the VAT element on bills from suppliers, including the VAT on part payments, credit notes and expenses.
- QuickBooks produces VAT reports needed for your VAT return.
- You can file the VAT Return online, via your QuickBooks system.

11.2 Setting up VAT

It is important to always refer to the supplier bills when inputting them onto the system and deciding on the VAT code. If your business makes exempt products, you may find that the amount of input tax that you recover in your VAT return is restricted by partial exemption rules. If in doubt, always check with your local tax office: www.hmrc.gov.uk.

Who your customers are and where they are located can affect whether you charge VAT on a particular product. You can normally zero-rate the goods you supply to customer in another member state of the EC if you have a record of their VAT registration number and print it on your invoice to them. If your EC customer does not provide you with a VAT number, you must treat the sale in the same way as you treat a sale to a UK customer.

Setting up VAT on QuickBooks
1 Click on 'VAT' on the left hand side of the menu.

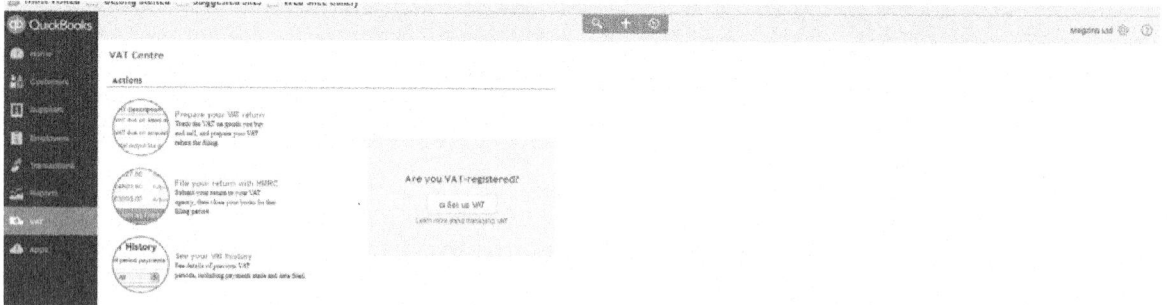

2 Click on 'Set up VAT'. Fill in the form which appears on the screen:

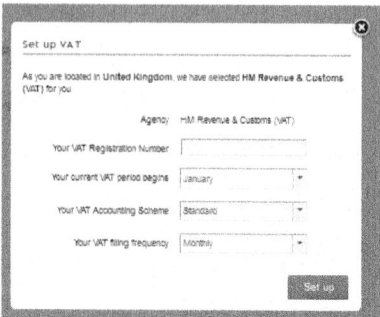

3 Enter your VAT Registration Number (found on communication from HMRC – i.e. Vat Registration Certificate) e.g. *GB123456789*. Current VAT period begins *January.* VAT Accounting Scheme: *Cash.* VAT filing frequency: *Quarterly.* Click Set up.

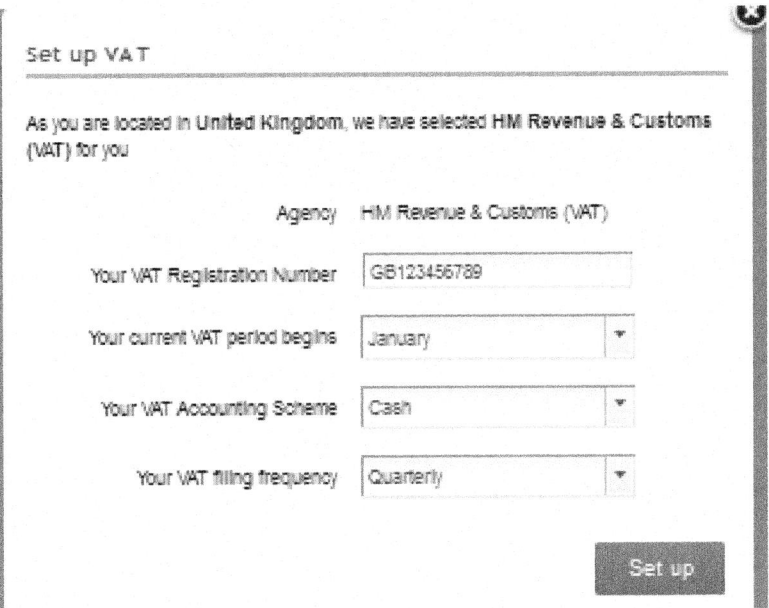

4 The screen which appears is the VAT Centre.

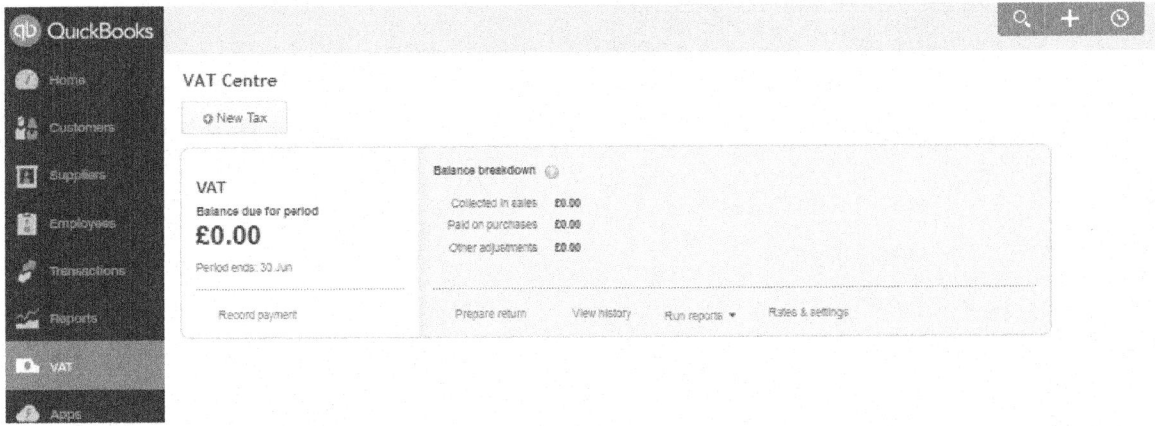

VAT Codes

There are different VAT rates in existence – standard, reduced, exempt and zero rated.

To create the VAT codes:

1 Click on 'VAT' on the left hand side of the menu.
2 Click on 'New Tax' and then 'Additional Tax Code' and click 'Next'. This screen appears:

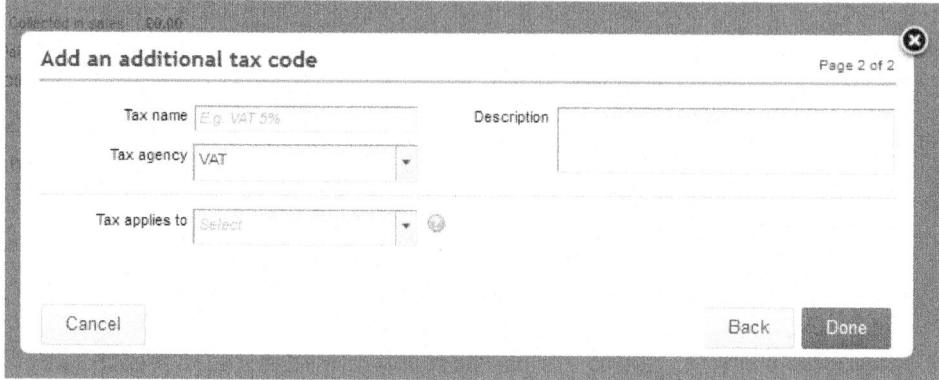

3 Fill in the form. Tax name: *Standard VAT*. Tax agency – leave as VAT. Tax applies to: from dropdown select *Sales*. The form then expands.

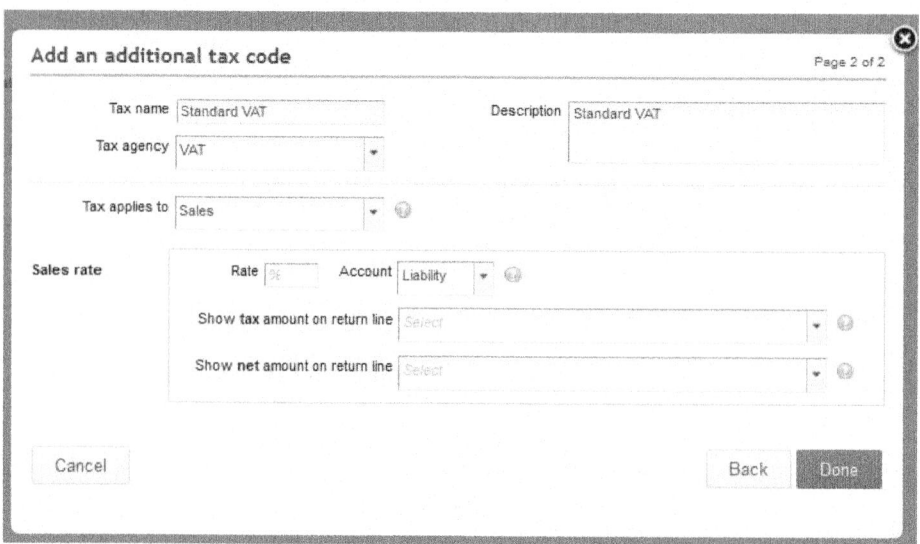

4 In the Rate box, type in *20*. Leave the account as Liability. Show the tax amount on the return line (from the drop down choose): *VAT due on sales and other outputs*. Show net amount on return line (from the drop down choose): *Net value of sales*.

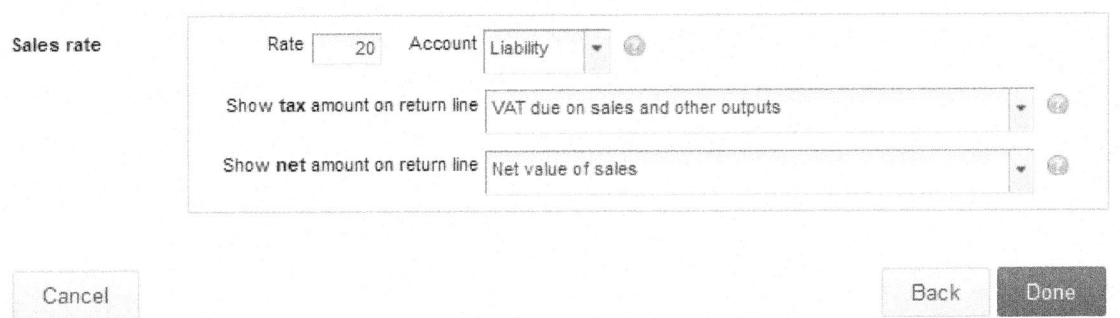

5 Click Done. QuickBooks will confirm that you've successfully added a new code.

VAT Rates

There are different VAT rates.

To see the list of VAT Rates:

1 Click on 'VAT' on the left hand side of the menu.

2 Click on 'Rates & settings'. This screen appears:

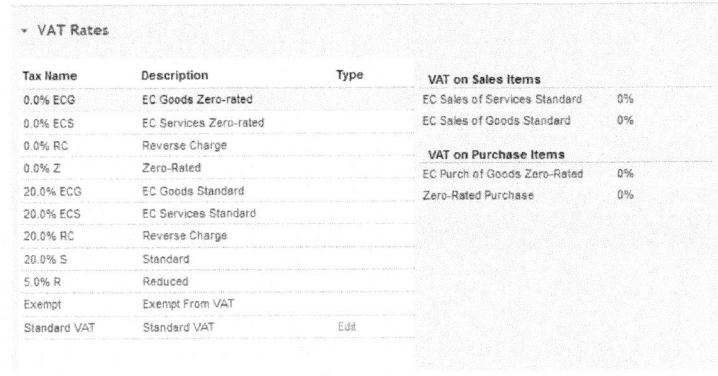

Trading with European member states

ECG & ECS - 0%   EC Goods and Services Zero- rated

Used for all zero-rated sales to EC member states and all purchases from EC member states that would be exempt acquisitions in the UK.

ECG & ECS - 20% EC Goods and Services Standard

Used for all standard-rated sales to customers in EC member states who are not registered for VAT and all purchases from EC members states that are not registered for VAT.

To invoice a European Customer:

1 Click 'Customers' from the left hand menu bar.
2 Click: New Customer. The customer's name is: *Maria Lopez*.
3 The address is: *88 Calle Sanchez, Madrid, Spain, 12345*.
4 Click save. Create invoice.
5 Product service: *Beds*.
6 VAT: *0.0% ECG.* Notice that the VAT amount column is NIL.

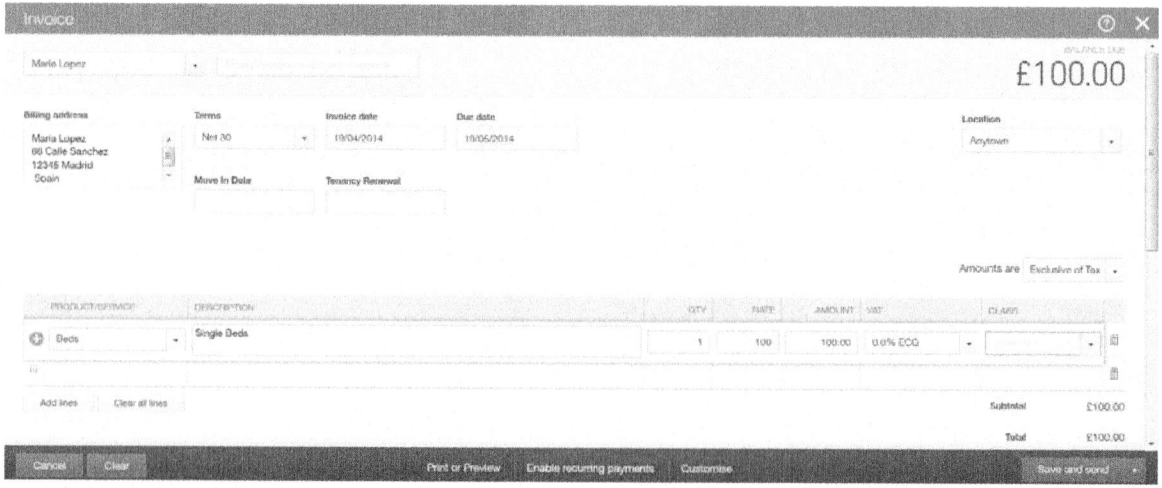

6 Save and close.

QuickBooks Online Help

Handling import VAT from non- EC countries

When you import a shipment from outside the EC, it must be cleared through HMRC before being imported into the UK. Customs clearance usually invoices paying import VAT.

Imagine Megzina has a new supplier from Canada called Canada Beds, from whom they buy 10 beds. As Canada Beds are outside the EC, it doesn't charge any VAT.

To enter an import bill:

1 From suppliers menu on the left hand menu, click New Supplier.
2 The address: *195 Nightingale Way, Toronto, Canada, T01 7HJ*. Click save.
3 Create bill.
4 Tab to 'Amounts are' and from the dropdown, choose: *Outside the scope of VAT.*
5 Ignore 'Account details' and tab down to 'Item Details' and in 'product/service' choose: *beds*. Tab across to quantity, and type in: *10*.

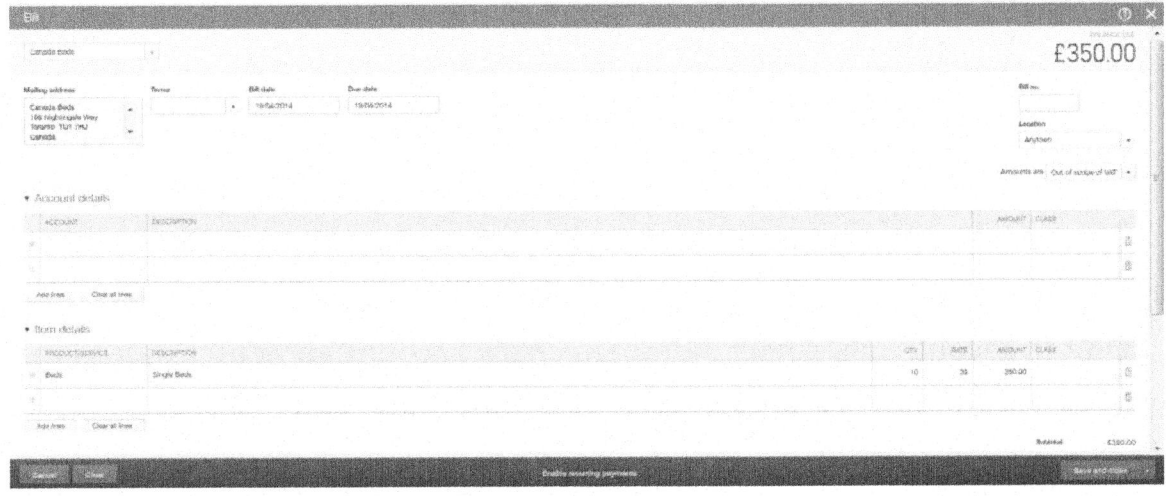

6 Click save and close.

Handling fuel scale charges

QuickBooks can handle the VAT owing if you provide fuel to employees for business and private use. For each VAT period you should calculate the VAT due using the HMRC fuel scale charge table. Refer to HMRC.gov.uk.

To enter fuel scale charges:

1 From the home menu screen, click '+' in the top middle of the screen and choose 'Journal Entry' under Other.

2 Under Account, type in Motor Expenses. Create this new account, as an expense, under the type of travel and save.

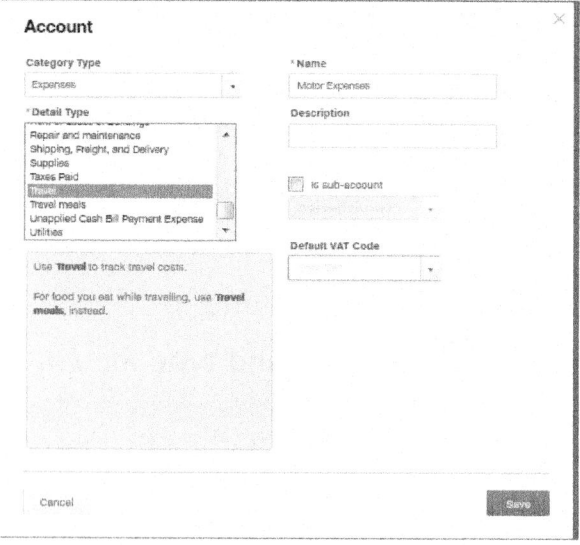

3 Debit *150.00* for the VAT-inclusive amount of fuel benefit. Choose the location: *Anytown*.

4 On the second line, select *Motor Expenses* account and enter a Credit of *125.00* for the VAT exclusive amount. On the same line, choose *20.0% S* for VAT. Tick 'sale'. Choose the location: *Anytown*.

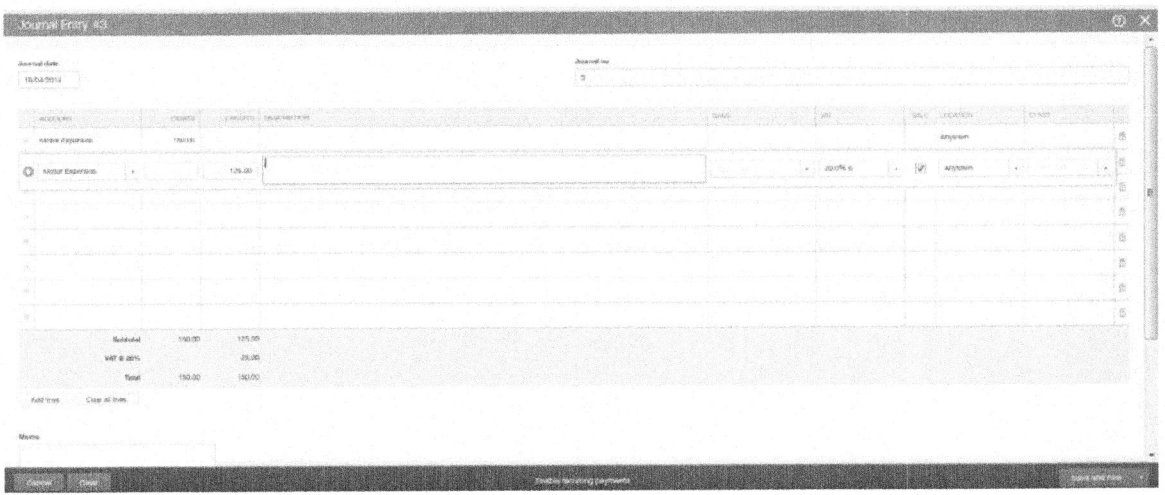

5 Click save and close.

11.3 Viewing the VAT Control Account

Each time you record an invoice or sales receipt or purchase that includes VAT, QuickBooks enters the information in the VAT Control account register. The register displays all the transactions that are recorded in the VAT Control account, and provides a running balance of the account.

To view the VAT Control account:
1 From the left hand menu bar, click *Transactions* and *Account Histories*. Scroll down and click once on *VAT Control*.
2 Click on *Go To Account History*.

QuickBooks Online Help

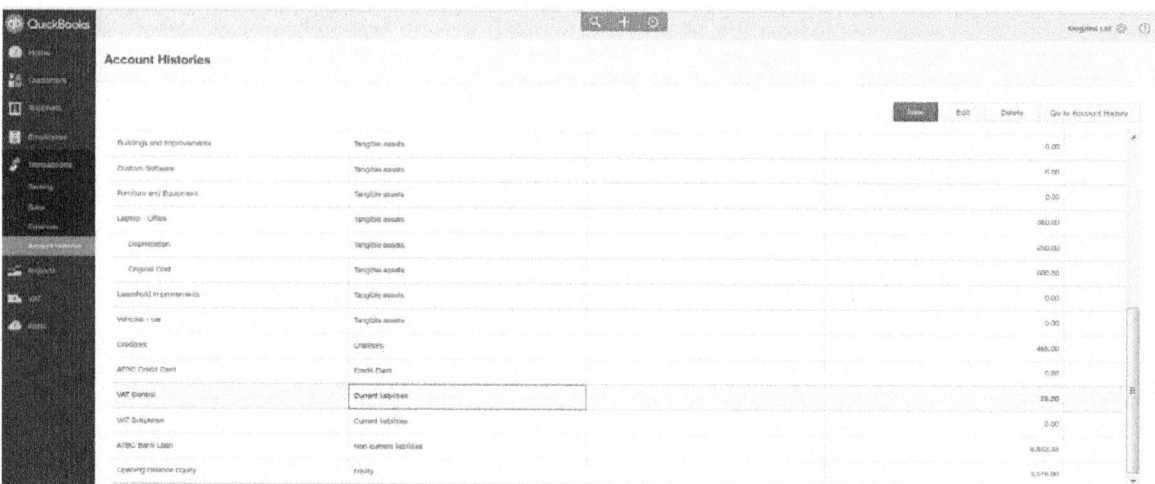

3 The Liability Register is displayed:

4 Close the window.

Adjusting the VAT Return

1 Click *VAT* from the left hand side menu bar. Click *Prepare Return*.

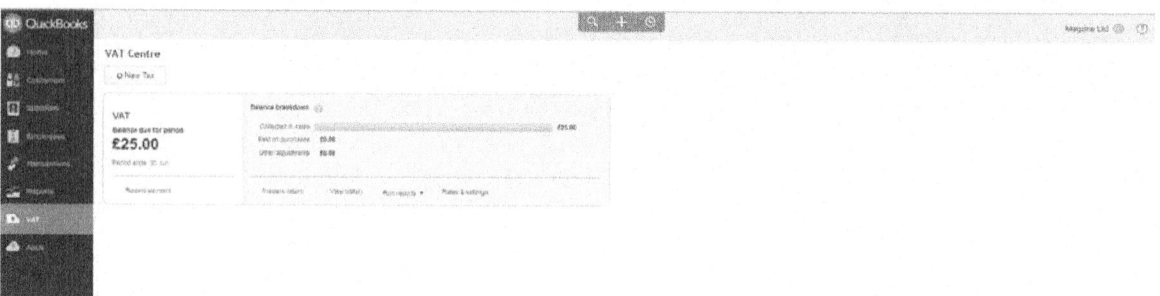

2 You can choose the dates which apply. And *refresh* the report.

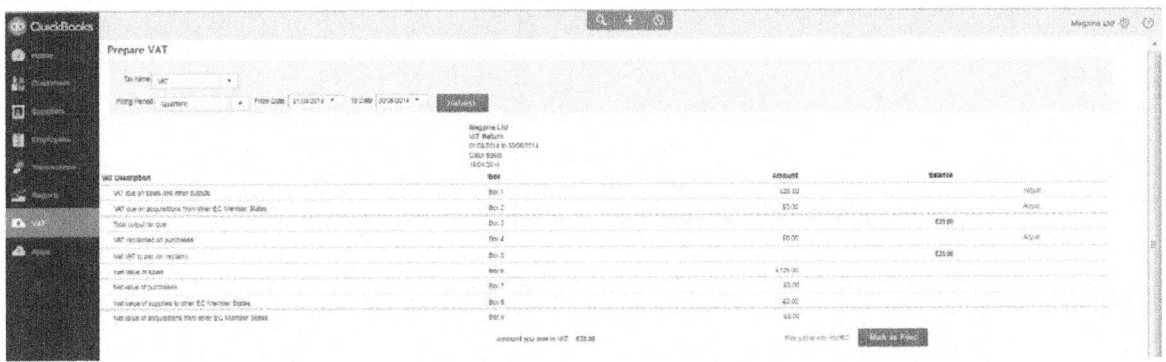

3 If you wish to Adjust box 1 or 2 or 4, then click the blue 'Adjust' word. Box 1 is for VAT due on sales and other outputs. Box 2 is for VAT due on acquisitions from other EC Member States. Box 4 is VAT reclaimed on purchases.

4 For example, if the VAT due on sales and other output were too low, you'd click the word 'adjust' on the same line as Box 1. A screen would pop up. On VAT Rate – select the VAT Rate from the drop down menu. For 'The Adjustment Account' – choose VAT adjustment. This account may need to be added. Set up the new account. Category type: Other Expense. Click *save.*

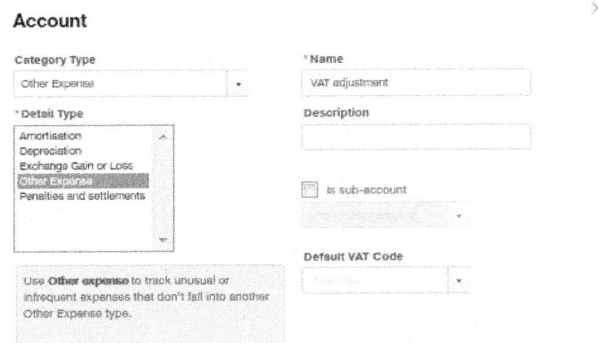

5 Choose the amount: *10.00.*

QuickBooks Online Help

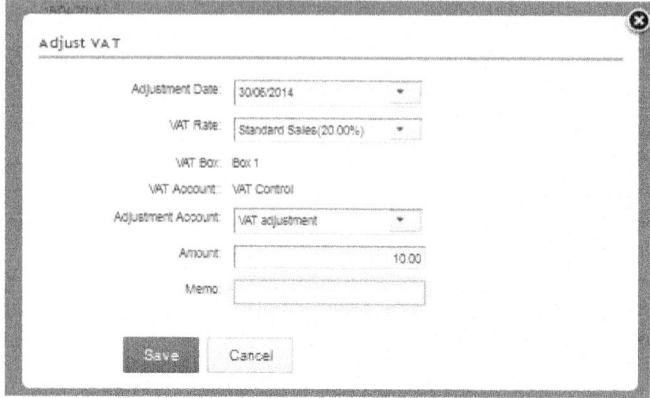

6 Click save.

7 The VAT return is now adjusted.

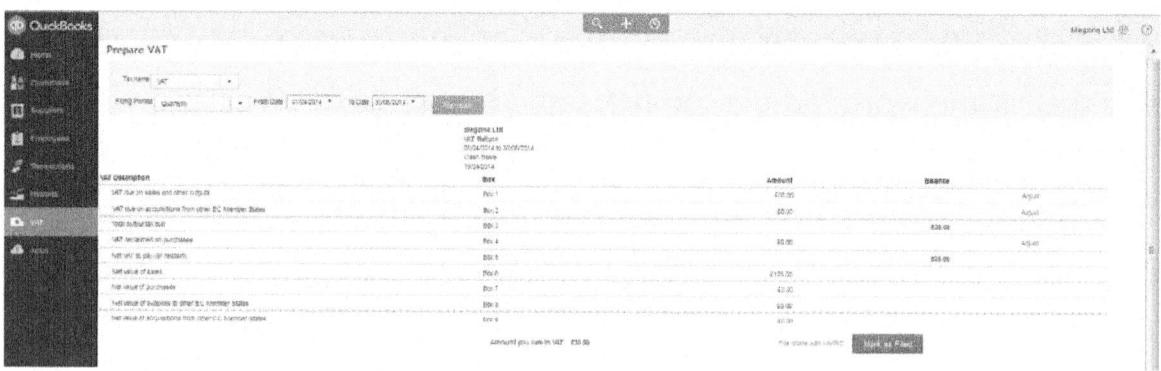

11.4 Paying VAT to HM Revenue and Customs

QuickBooks gives you a single procedure for producing the figures you need for your VAT return along with a QuickBooks cheque to pay your VAT liability.

To pay VAT Liability:

1 Click *VAT* from the left hand side menu bar. Click *Prepare Return*.

2 You can choose the dates which apply. And *refresh* the report.

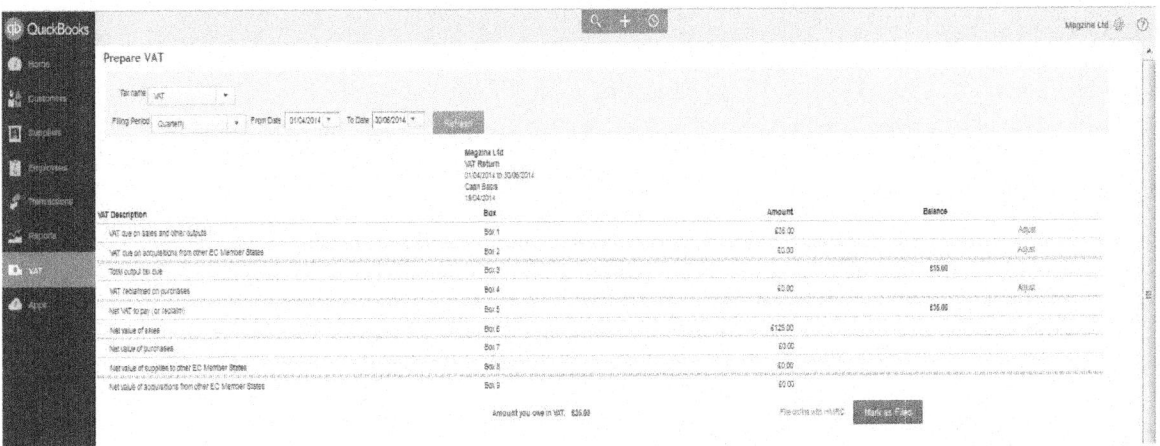

File the return.

Click File Online with HMRC and the HMRC screen pops up. You then need to log into HMRC's website (with a user ID and password). The exact figures which are on the VAT report (box 1 to box 9) are what you need to use when filing the return with HMRC.

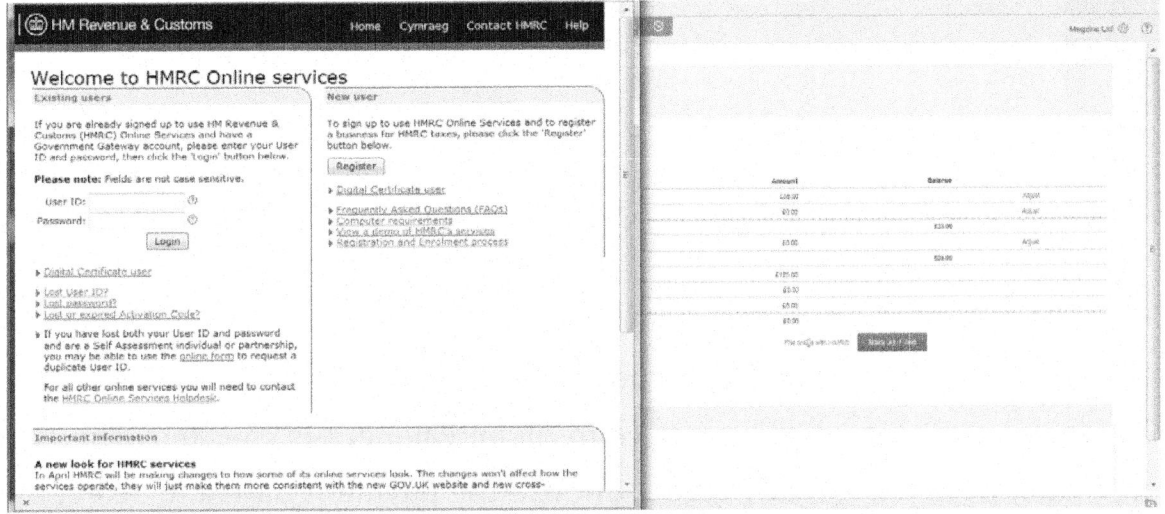

Copy the amounts from your QBO return and paste them into your VAT return in the HMRC window.

After you have filed, click **Mark as Filed**. This lets QuickBooks Online know that you have filed your VAT return and saves a snapshot of your return.

Transactions from this period that are changed later will be shown in the VAT exception report.

You can view the VAT History.
1 Click *VAT* from the left hand side menu bar. Click *View History*.
2 You can view the reports with *VAT 100*.

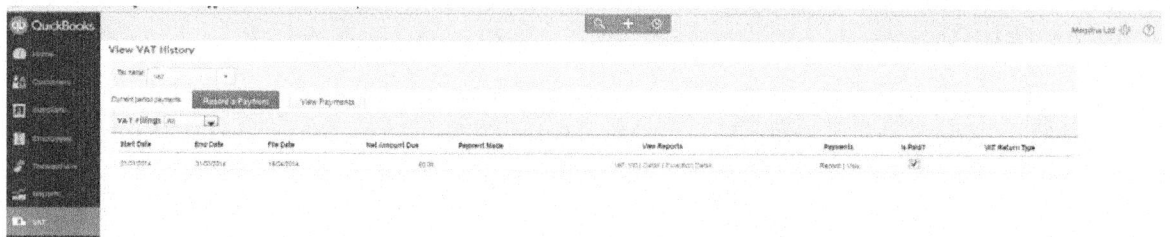

3 You can view your payments made by clicking Reports: View.

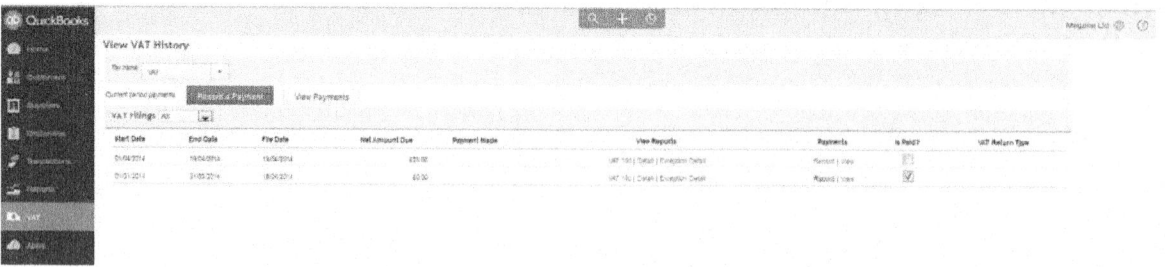

To make a VAT payment:
1 Click *VAT* from the left hand side menu bar. Click *Record Payment*.
2 A screen pops up which you have to fill in. Payment is checked. The VAT amount due is already given. Choose the payment date and select the Account from which the payment will be made. Type in: Payment Amount(£25.00).

3 Click Save.

11.5 VAT Reports

QuickBooks can create reports to show your VAT position at any time, whether cash or accrual based. There are 4 reports to choose from. The reports available are:

- **Vat 100** – This report, also called VAT Agency Report, shows you the summary information for each box of the VAT return. This will help you as you file your return in QuickBooks Online Plus and then complete and submit your return to HMRC.
- **Vat Detail** – This report lists the transactions that are included in each box on the VAT return.
- **VAT Exemption Report** – This report lists the transactions containing VAT that have been added, modified or deleted in prior filed VAT periods and have changed the company's VAT liability.
- **VAT Liability Report** - This report lists the transactions that are included in each box on the VAT return. The report is based on

standard VAT accounting (accrual accounting) unless you changed your VAT reporting preference to cash basis.

The reports are available from the Reports menu. Once the VAT has been switched on – there will be VAT reports available.

VAT Reports:
1 Click on Reports from the left hand side of the menu.
2 Choose *All Reports*. Click: *Manage VAT*.
3 There are four reports to choose from.

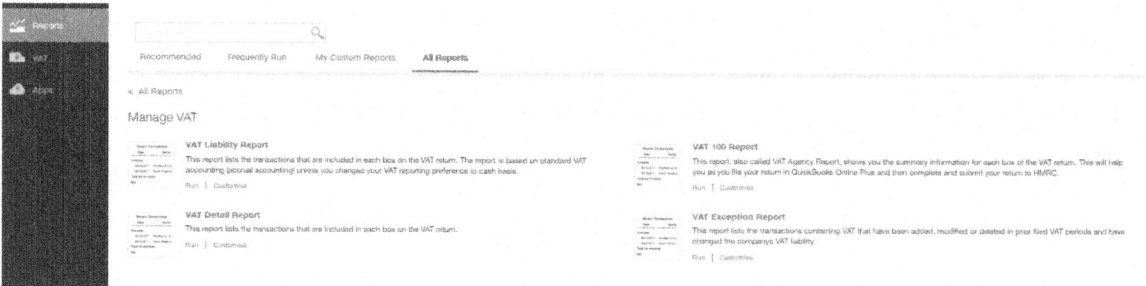

You should print and save all these reports when you are preparing your VAT return. QuickBooks automatically creates each report for the last full VAT quarter using the dates and accounting method (accrual or cash basis) you chose in VAT Preferences.

12: Doing payroll

Summary of what is in this chapter:
- 12.1 Overview of payroll tracking
- 12.2 Setting up the payroll
- 12.3 Setting up employee payroll information
- 12.4 Paying employees
- 12.5 Tracking your tax liabilities
- 12.6 Paying employees
- 12.7 Paying payroll taxes
- 12.8 Paying over payroll deductions
- 12.9 Leavers – p45
- 12.10 Processing payroll at year end

12.1 Overview of payroll tracking

You need to turn on Payroll within QuickBooks in order for QuickBooks to calculate the payroll. QuickBooks calculates each employee's gross pay, and the calculates taxes and deductions including SSP, SMP, SPP or SAP if applicable, to arrive at the net pay. With the software you can write the pay cheque, record the transaction and keep track of your tax liabilities.

As an employer, you must subtract income tax (PAYE) and National Insurance contributions (NICs) before issuing the employee's pay cheque.

You may also deduct for benefits such as contributions to health insurance or pensions.

12.2 Setting up the payroll

To turn on Payroll:
1 Click *Employees* on the far left hand menu.
2 Click on the button: *Turn on Payroll*.

3 PaySuite Payroll screen pops up, detailing the pricing structure. At the time of writing, payroll is free for up to 5 employees.

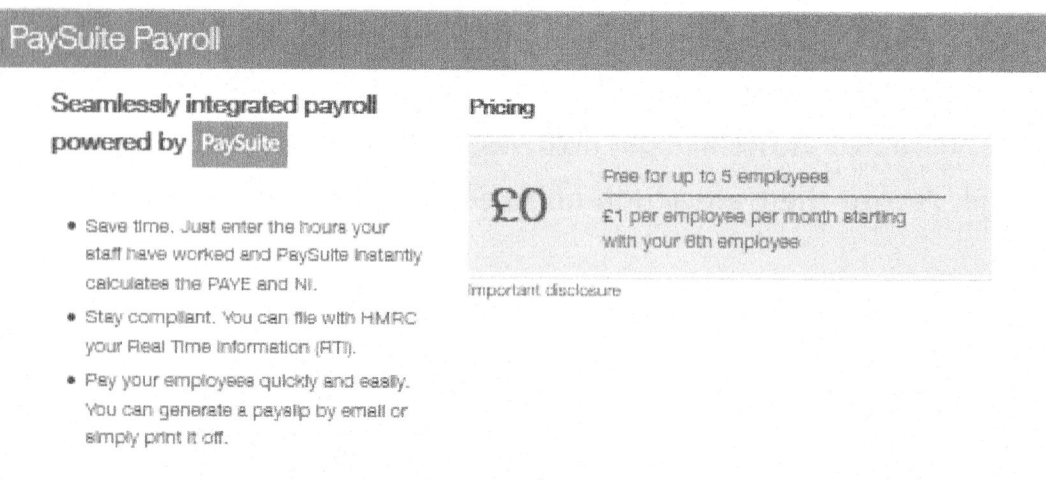

QuickBooks Online Help

4 Click continue.

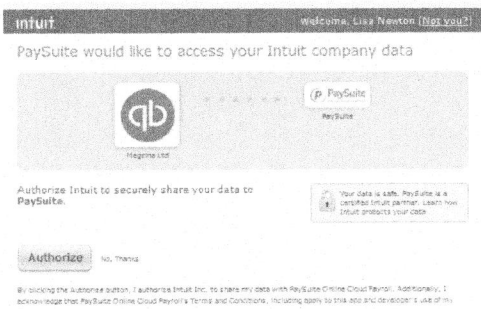

5 Click the yellow button *Authorize* to connect QuickBooks to PaySuite.

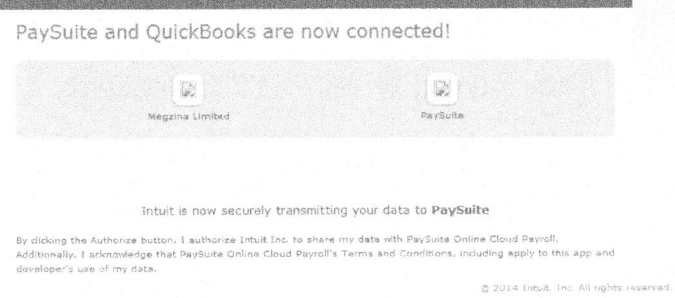

6 Fill out the *New Company Setup* form. And click save.

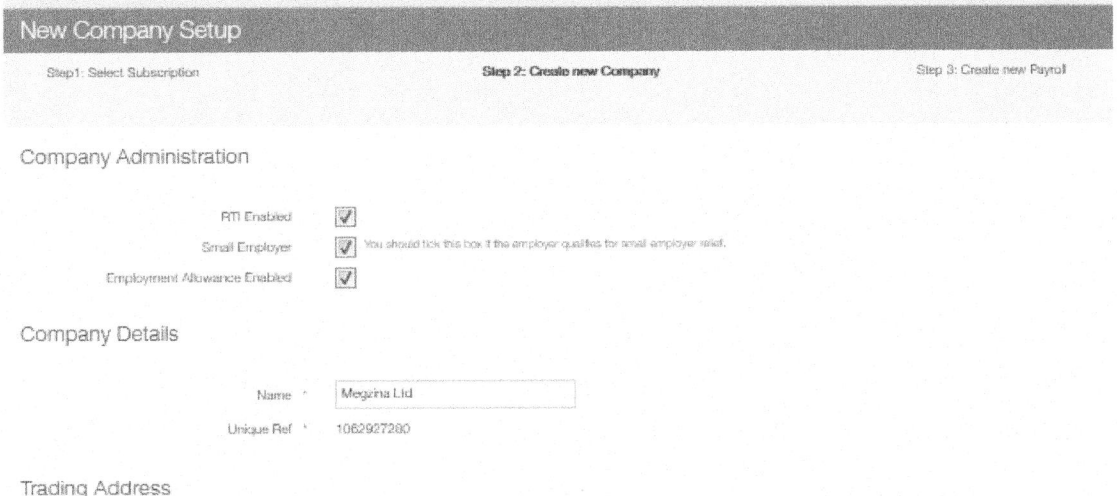

7 The next screen is the New Payroll Setup form.

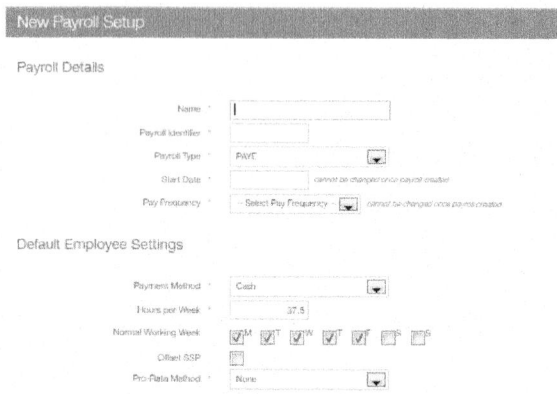

The payroll Identifier will already be allocated by paysuite e.g. *P1-1211945860*. Fill in the rest of the form with the company Payroll Details – (Company) Name: *Megzina*. Press Tab. Payroll type: *PAYE*. Start Date: *01/04/2014*. Pay frequency – choose from the dropdown: *Monthly*. Pay day mode – choose from the dropdown: *Specific day each month*. Normal pay day – choose *20*.

8 Default employee settings – Payment method - choose from the dropdown: *Bank*. Hours per week: 37.5. Tick: *M, T, W, T, F*. Prorata method: Choose from the dropdown: *None*.

9 Create New payroll.

12.3 Setting up employee payroll information

1 Click *Employees* on the far left hand menu.
2 Click on the button: *New employee*. Fill out the New Employee form for Miss Samantha Jones. Female:

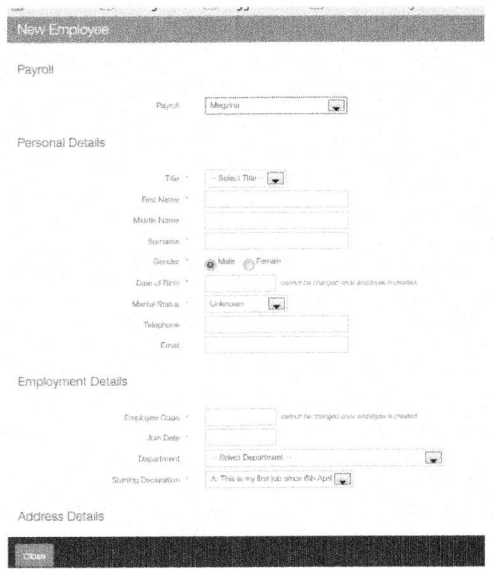

Miss Samantha Jones. Female. Date of birth: 1st July 1970. Marital status: unknown. Employee Code: JONES01. Join date: 1st April 2013. Starting Declaration: B This is my only job. Address: 454 Gaspoint Road, Anytown, Anyshire, AN8 9FG.

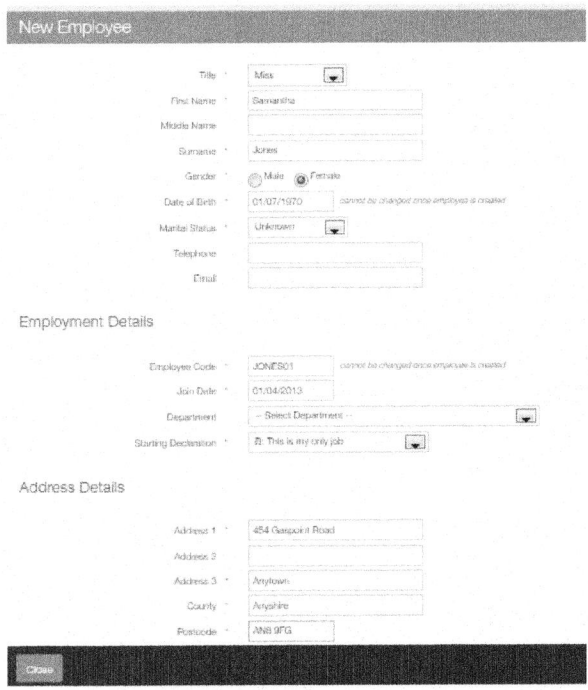

3 Click continue.

4 Fill in the New Employee form. Tax Details - The Tax Code and Tax Basis can be changed if necessary. NI Number: *JW000000A*. NI Code letter – choose from the dropdown: A - Not contracted out. Payment Details – the Pay Basis: choose from the dropdown: Salaried. Payment Method: choose from the dropdown: Bank. Salary – type in *12000.00*. Total per Month – type in *1000.00*. Normal Hours per week: *22.5*. Pro Rate Method: *None*. Normal Working Week: *M, W, F*.

5 Click save.

Editing Employee Information

1 Click *Employees* on the far left hand menu.

2 Click once on the employee: Samantha Jones.

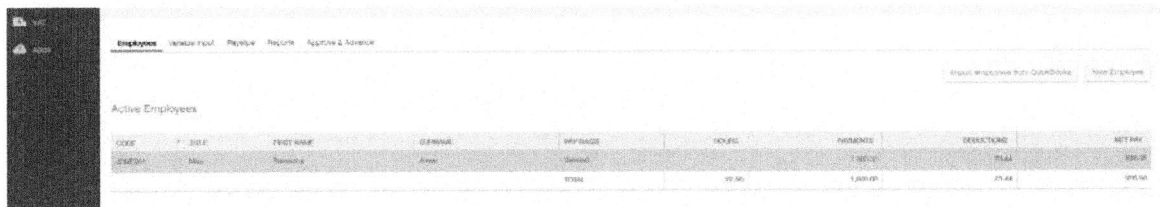

3 The Edit Employee screen appears:

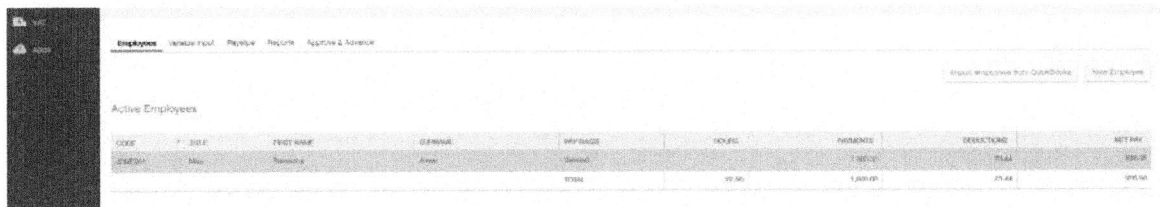

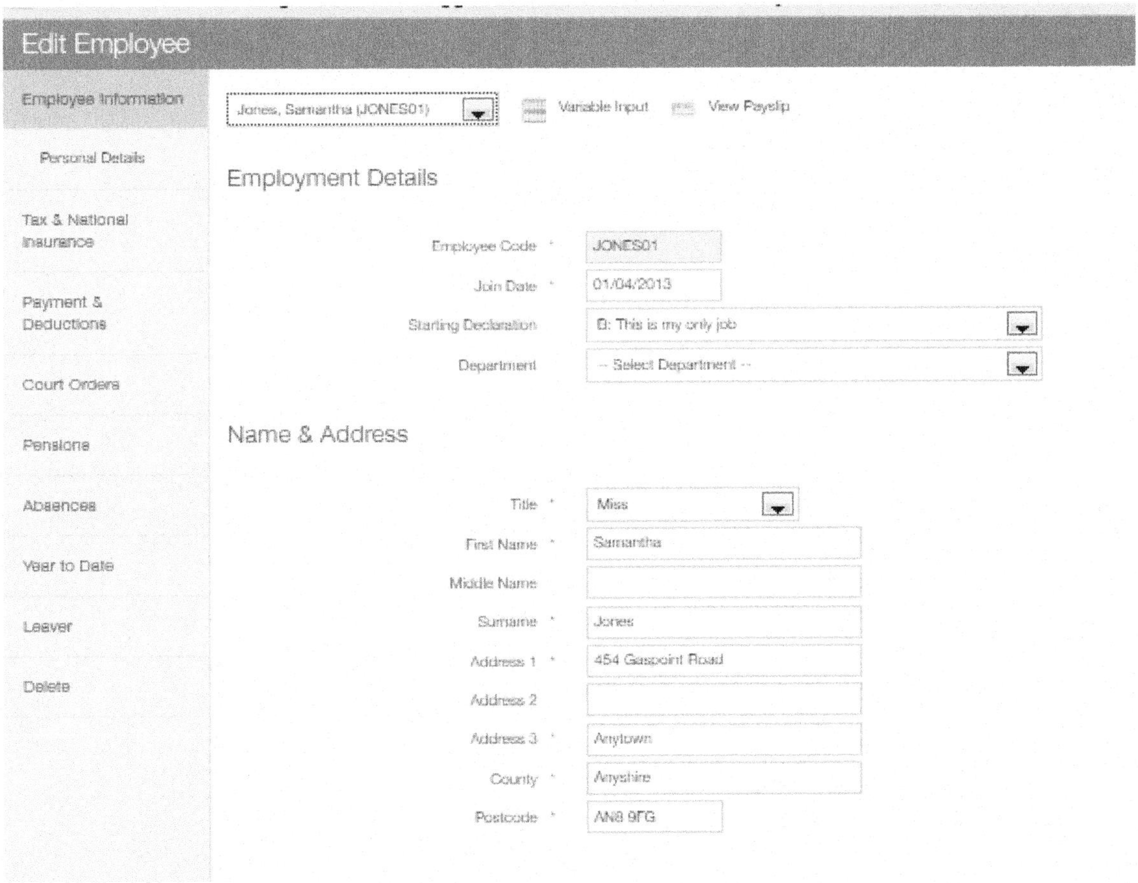

4 In the grey box, click Personal Details. QuickBooks gives you the option to enter additional information such as passport number and Partner details.

5 If a new employee joins you and they give you a p45, you can add the details under the p45 tab. Or if you are given p6 or p9 details, click on the P6P9 tab.

6 Court Orders. If the employee has court orders, enter the details on this form.

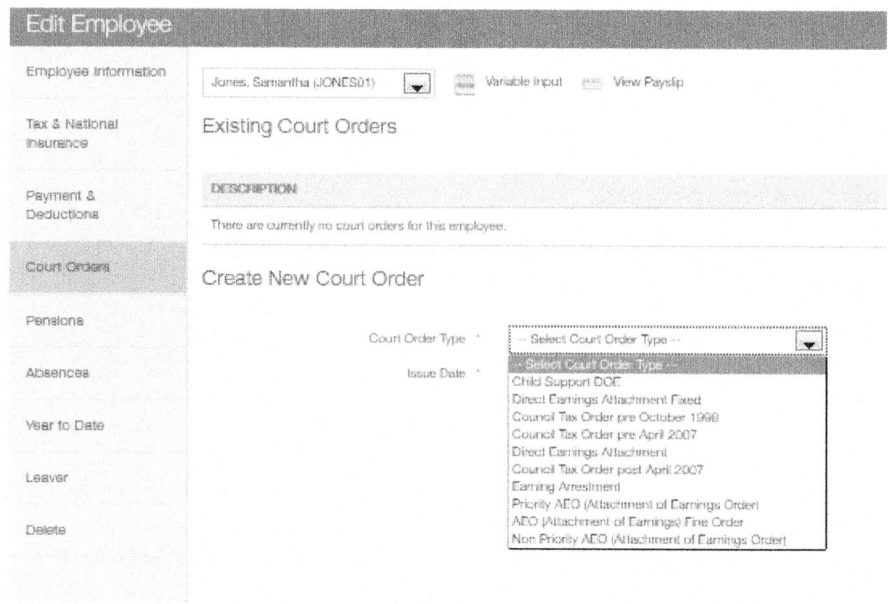

7 Pensions. If the employee is registered for a pension – fill in the form.

8 Absences. If the employee is absent (due to Maternity, Paternity or sickness) – fill in the form.

QuickBooks Online Help

QuickBooks enables you to record time that employees take off due to sickness or maternity leave and automatically calculates the amount of any Statutory Sick Pay (SSP), Statutory Maternity Pay (SMP) or (SPP) that applies.

SSP is payable after the first three waiting days. When entering sick leave for an employee, you also need to record their normal working pattern so that QuickBooks can recognise which days qualify for SSP. For example, if (as in our fictitious employee Samantha) works Mondays, Wednesday and Fridays, and she is sick from Monday of one week until Friday of the following week, this would count as SIX qualifying days: 3 waiting days in the first week, followed by THREE days in the second week for which SSP would be payable. The working patterns all start on a Sunday, and you can record as many patterns as you need for the same employee to reflect their schedule.

For SMP, you need to record the Sunday of the week maternity leave starts, the date on which the employee finishes work, the date the birth is expected, and the actual birth date. SMP is payable for 26 weeks from the date the employee finished work.

The details you enter for SPP depend on whether the absence is taken for a birth or an adoption. SPP is payable for one or two full weeks within 8 weeks of the birth or adoption.

To enter SSP:

1 Click *Employees* on the far left hand menu.
2 Click once on the employee: Samantha Jones.
3 Click once on absences (grey menu bar on the left)
4 Choose *Statutory Sick Pay (SSP)* from the drop down. Start date *07 April 2014*. Click: *Create New Absence*
5 A new form called 'Absence Details' appears.
6 Enter the end date: 16 April 2014.
7 Override average weekly earnings: £230.76 (Samantha's annual wages is £12,000, divide by 52 weeks = £230.76)
8 If SSP1 is required, tick the box and enter the date. If evidence is required, tick the box and enter the date it was seen e.g. Doctors sick note... in this case. We leave these fields blank. Our form looks like this:

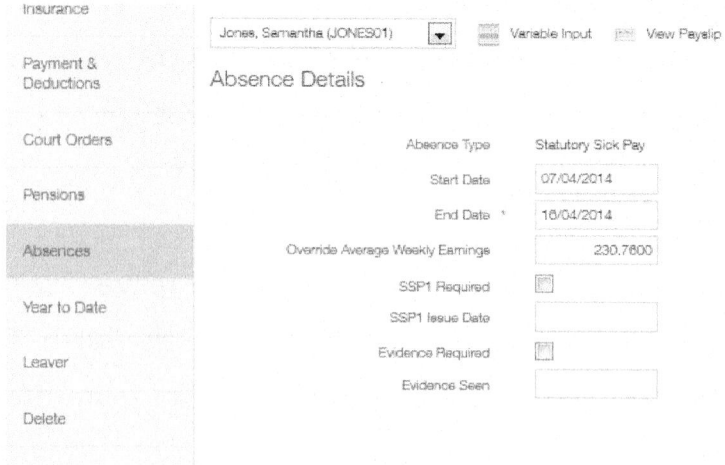

9 Click save. The absence will be recorded.

QuickBooks Online Help

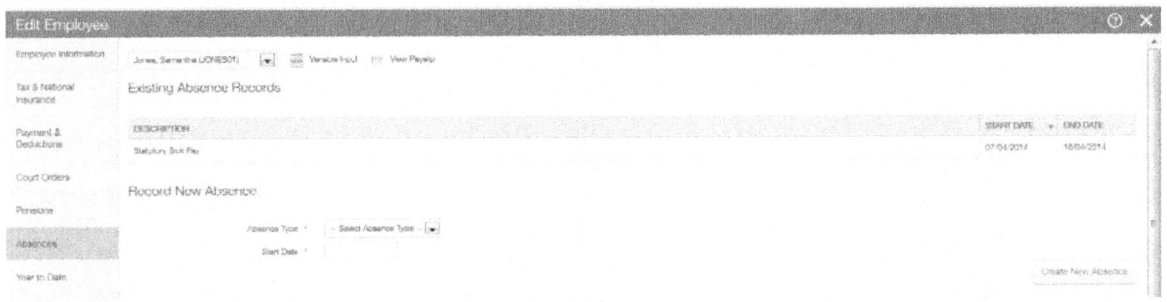

10 If the employee had further absences, then you can also add them here.

To record SMP:

1 Click *Employees* on the far left hand menu.

2 Click once on the employee: Samantha Jones.

3 Click once on absences (grey menu bar on the left)

4 Choose *SMP* from the drop down. Start date *18 April 2014*. Click: *Create New Absence*

5 A new form called 'Maternity Leave Details' appears:

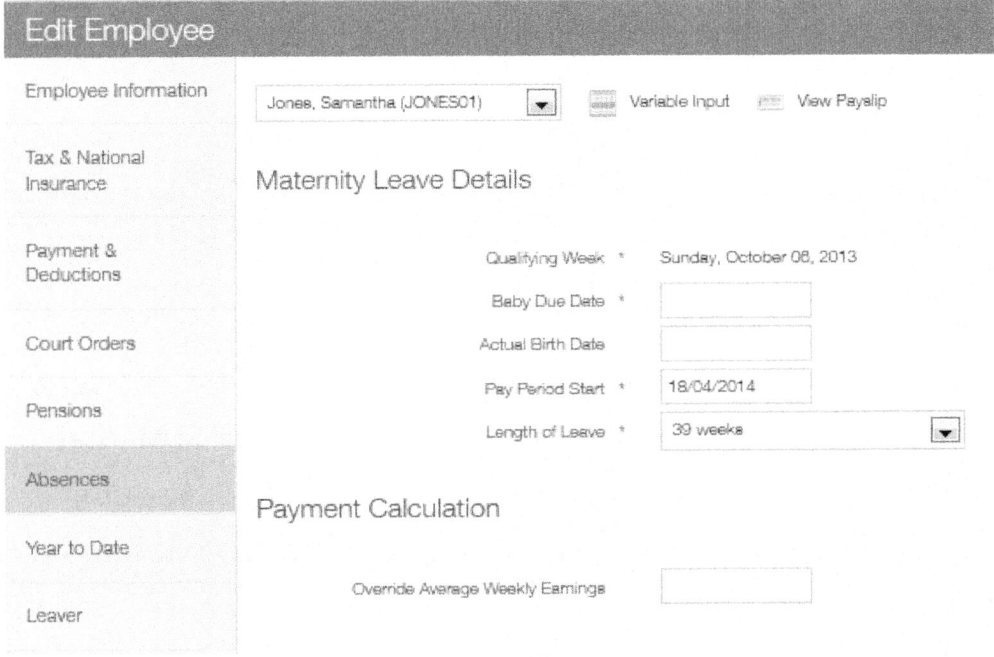

6 The Qualifying Week will display automatically (this is the last week of maternity pay). Type in the baby due date: *20 May 2014.* Click Tab.

7 The Pay Period Start is automatically displayed. For the Length of leave 39 weeks is automatically chosen. Leave this as is, unless the expectant mother has stated otherwise.

8 Once the Actual Birth Date is known, come back to this page to fill in that information

9 Your form will look like this:

10 Click save.

To record SPP:

1 Click *Employees* on the far left hand menu.

2 Click new employee: Joseph Smith. Date of birth: 1 Jan 1965. Marital status: Married. Employee code: 1000L. Joined: 14 Feb 2013. Starting Declaration: B: This is my only job. Address: 17 Magnus Way, Burlington, Anyshire, BU7 8HL. Click: Continue.

3 Tax Details: NI Number AB000000A. Payment Details – Pay Basis: Hourly. Payment Method: Cheque. Hourly Rate: 10.00. Total per week: 375.00. Normal Hours per Week: 37.5. Pro-Rate Method: None. Normal Working Week: M, T, W, T, F. The form will look like this:

Click save.

4 Mr Smith is now showing as an active employee. Click on the name once.

5 Click *Absences*.

STATUTORY ADOPTION PATERNITY PAY:

6 Absence Type – from the drop down list, choose: *Statutory Paternity Adoption Pay*. Start Date: *04 April 2014*. Click: *Create New Absence*.

7 A new form called 'Absence Details' appears:

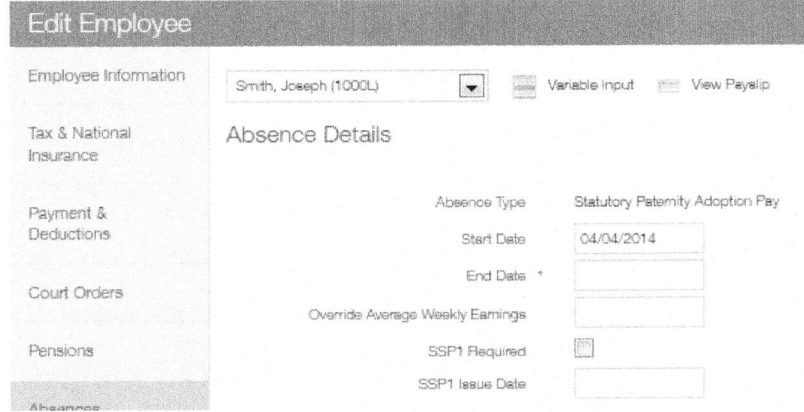

8 Fill in the relevant dates as given by the employee. Click Cancel.

STATUTORY ADOPTION PATERNITY PAY:

9 Absence Type – from the drop down list, choose: *Statutory Paternity Pay*. Start Date: *03 April 2014*. Click: *Create New Absence*.

7 A new form called 'Paternity Leave Details' appears:

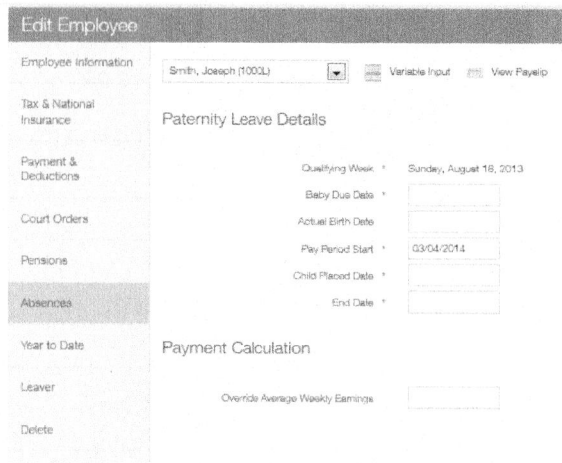

This is very much like the Maternity Leave details. Fill in the relevant dates as given by the employee. Click Cancel.

12.4 Paying employees

We select one employee at a time to run the payroll. In this example, we're paying Month 1, which is paid out on 20th April 2014. Lets first start with Employee – Samantha Jones. Her payslip preview is seen on the left-hand side of the screen. The system recalls the Absence data which we entered previously in 12.3 and the employee salary data we'd entered when we first created Samantha Jones as an employee.

To run the payroll:
1 Click Variable Input. This screen appears.

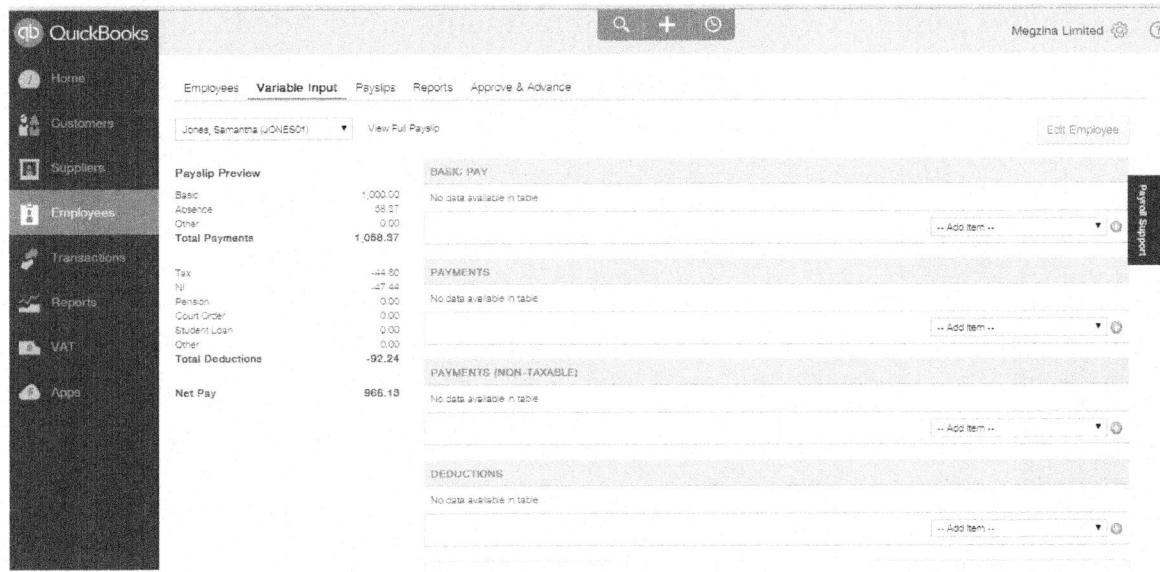

2 From this page, we can add any variables that might have happened in the month. E.g. Basic Pay – we can add items such as: pay adjustment, variable pay or overtime. From Payments, there's various items in the drop down menu – for example: Share award, bonus payment, salary sacrifice, commission, miscellaneous payment, service charge, holiday pay, allowance. These are all payments which are taxable that may be added to an employees basic pay.

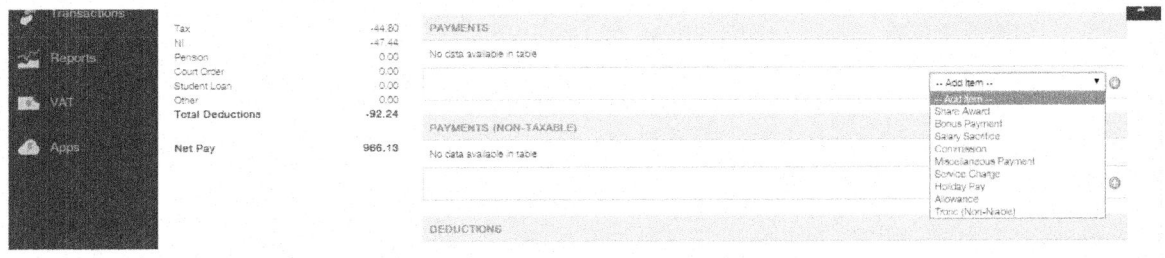

3 Non-Taxable payments which the employee may have received in the pay run include: redundancy, mileage, expenses.
4 Deductions – which the employee may incur include: Give As You Earn, Save As You Earn, Advance, Miscellaneous Deduction.

5 For our example, the following 3 adjustments are needed: Samantha received payments of £18.50 for expenses, and had £10.00 deducted for Give As You Earn. We also add Holiday pay for her at a rate of *x2*, for *3.00* hours at *10.00*. To enter these amounts, click on the green '+' plus symbol, and the option will open up to type in the figures. The form should resemble this:

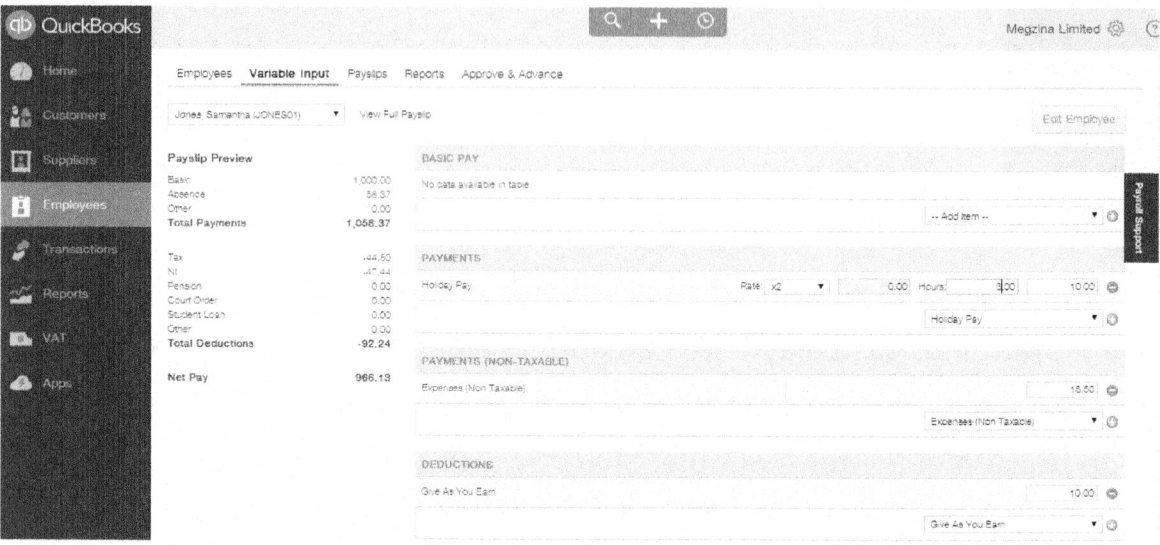

6 Scroll to the bottom of the screen and click *save changes*.

7 The payslip preview then changes. It's now showing:

8 Click view full payslip, and the full (draft) payslip will be displayed on the screen.

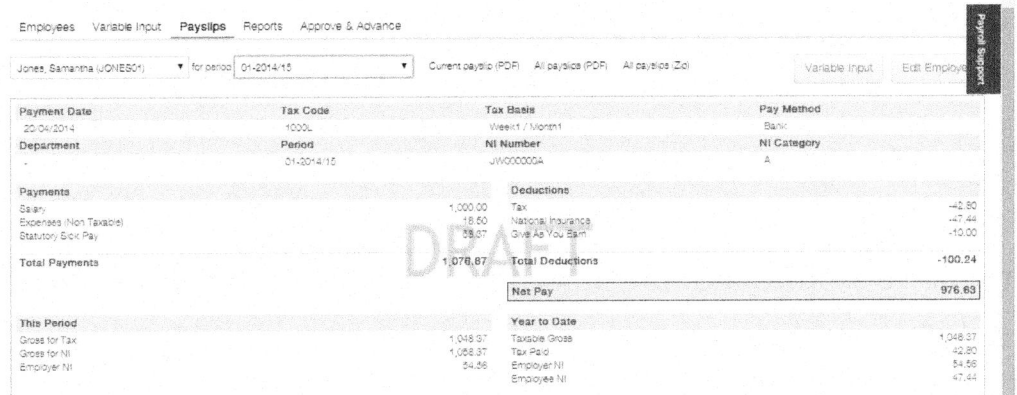

9 Click on Employees, the list of active employees is displayed.

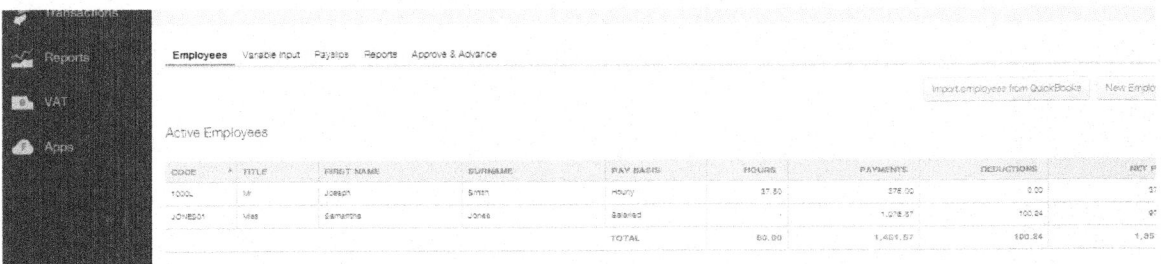

10 Click *Variable Input.* And choose our second employee from the dropdown list – *Joseph Smith.*

11 Joseph did 4 hours of overtime, and overtime is paid at double rate (x2). Click on the '+' plus sign and enter this information. The screen should resemble this:

12 Scroll to the very bottom of the screen and click *save changes*.

13 The payslip review now shows:

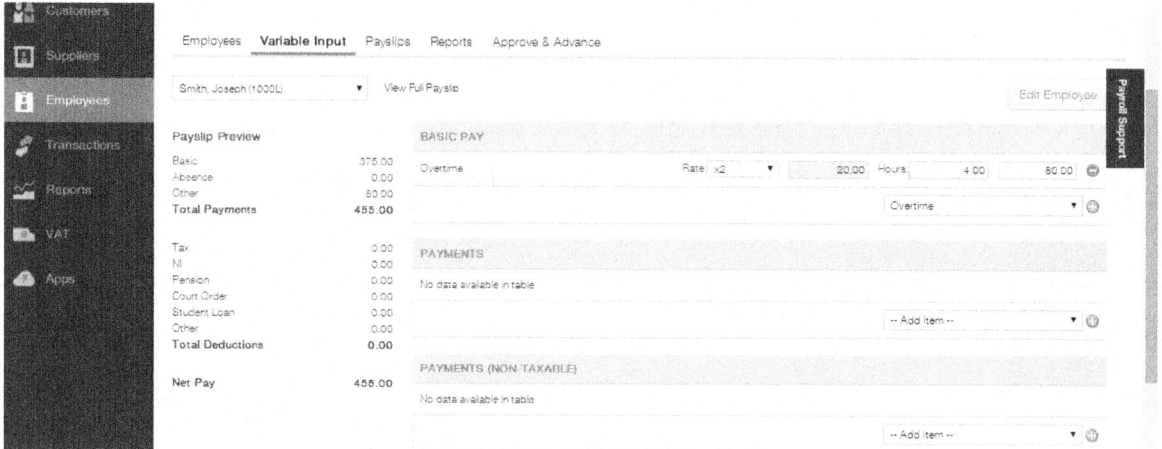

14 Once you've input all payroll data adjustments, then click *Approve & Advance tab*.

15 You'll have a list of all the employees, the paydate and what they're about to be paid:

16 If you're happy with this click *Approve Payrun*.

QuickBooks Online Help

17 The next page gives you your summary:

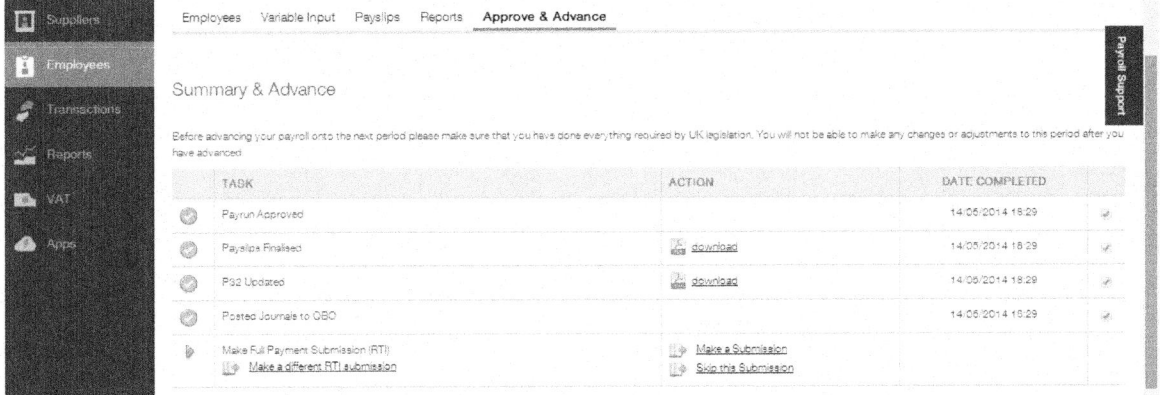

18 You can click on *download*, on the payslips finalised line, and your payslips will be downloaded as a PDF. (You can then distribute these to the relevant employees). Here is an example of a downloaded payslip:

19 You can click on *download*, on the p32 updated line, and your p32 form will be downloaded as a PDF. It shows how much is due to Inland Revenue each month for Tax and NI and other deductions. Here is an example of a downloaded p32:

QuickBooks Online Help

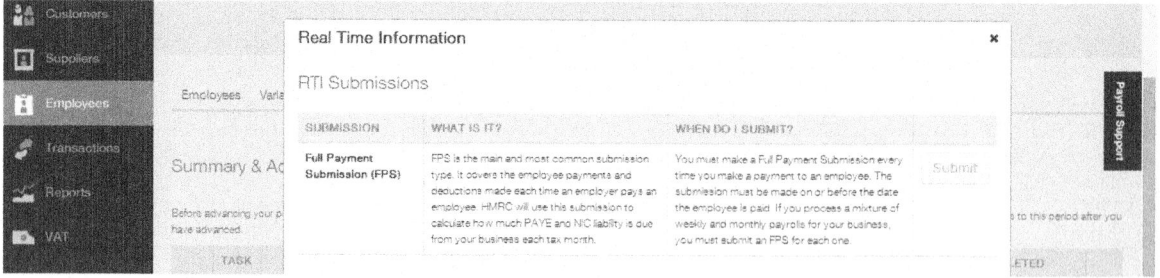

20 You can make a RTI submission directly to HMRC from this page by clicking *Make Submission*. This screen will pop up.

21 Click *Submit*.

Note – if you don't submit a Full Payment Submission (FPS) to HMRC you should submit an Employer Payment Submission (EPS) for your PAYE scheme.

22 For the purpose of this exercise, we skip the submission, and our page now looks like this:

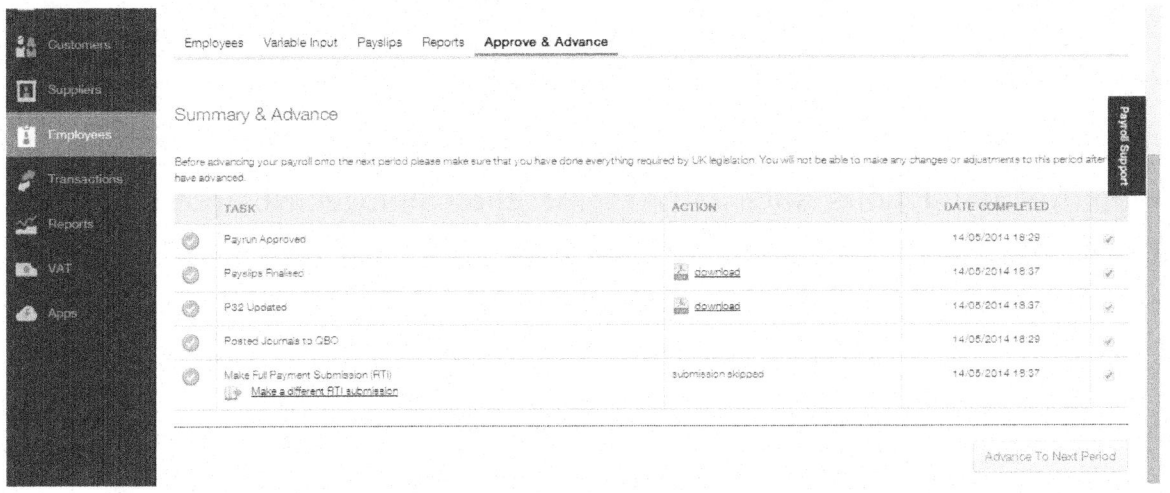

23 Click *Advance To Next Period*. You cannot go back and change anything, so always be sure that you're completely finished. You'll be taken back to the Employees home page.

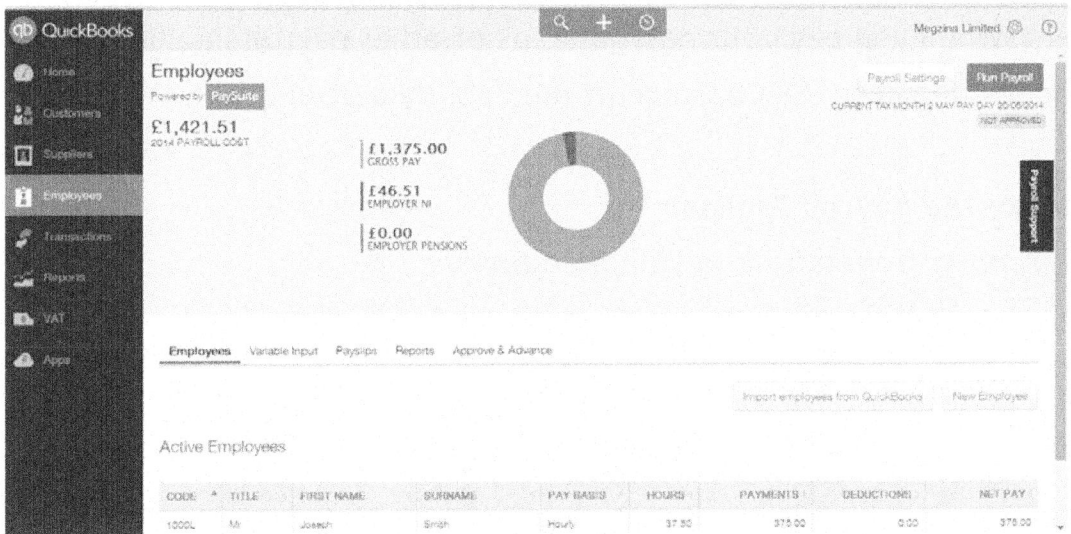

12.5 Tracking your tax liabilities

As an employer, you need to track both payroll expenses (Gross pay and Net pay) and payroll liabilities (taxes such as PAYE and NICs).

QuickBooks Online Help

When quickbooks runs your payroll, it enters the relevant journals for the transaction. Quickbooks uses the payroll expenses account to track these actual costs to your company (Employers NI and Gross Wages). Note that employee deductions (such as PAYE Tax and Employee NI) aren't considered an actual cost to you, because this is monies you are holding for the government – and they don't come directly from your pocket.

Quickbooks uses the Tax and National Insurance account to track what you owe to the government. When you do your payroll, quickbooks calculates how much you owe for each tax, deduction, or employer contribution payroll item and records that information as a transaction in the liability account via a journal. This produces a record of how much tax you owe at any time, so you can plan to have the cash available for payment. When you pay your payroll taxes or other payroll liabilities, quickbooks decreases the balance of the liability account.

To display the payroll journal:
1 Click *reports* from left hand side menu bar.
2 In the search bar type in *Journal*.

Megzina Limited
JOURNAL
May 1-14, 2014

DATE	TRANSACTION TYPE	NO.	NAME	MEMO/DESCRIPTION	ACCOUNT	DEBIT	CREDIT
14/05/2014	Journal Entry	2014-1		Gross Wages	Payroll Expenses	£1,531.87	
				Employers NI	Payroll Expenses	£54.56	
				Net Wages Due	Payroll Clearing		£1,431.63
				PAYE (Tax)	Tax and National Insurance		£42.80
				EE + ER NI	Tax and National Insurance		£102.00
				Other Deductions	Other Payroll Deductions		£10.00
						£1,586.43	£1,586.43
TOTAL						£1,586.43	£1,586.43

Note that the journal number refers to the year (2014) and the payroll period (1) - the first run - April 2014.

Other payroll reports available:
1 From the employees screen, click *reports*.

2 The *p32 summary report* tells you amount due each month for Tax, NI deductions etc., The entire year will be displayed, which is useful.

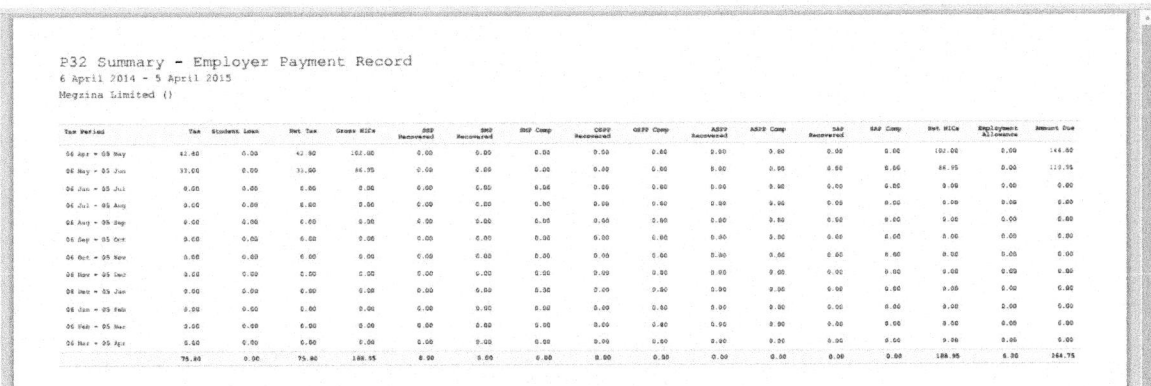

Alternatively, another way to find these payroll reports can be found:
1 Click *reports* from left hand side menu bar.
2 Click *All Reports.*
3 Choose *Payroll Reports.*

12.6 Paying employees

First of all, print the *Net Pay Report*.

1 From the employees screen, click *reports*.

2 The *Net Pay Report* tells you how much each employee should be paid. In our example, the report looks like this:

3 To make the payment, we enter a journal. We can see from the payroll journal (2014-1), that payroll clearing is the account that is holding the net wages due.

QuickBooks Online Help

Megzina Limited
JOURNAL
May 1-14, 2014

DATE	TRANSACTION TYPE	NO.	NAME	MEMO/DESCRIPTION	ACCOUNT	DEBIT	CREDIT
14/05/2014	Journal Entry	2014-1		Gross Wages	Payroll Expenses	£1,531.87	
				Employers NI	Payroll Expenses	£54.56	
				Net Wages Due	Payroll Clearing		£1,431.63
				PAYE (Tax)	Tax and National Insurance		£42.80
				EE + ER NI	Tax and National Insurance		£102.00
				Other Deductions	Other Payroll Deductions		£10.00
						£1,586.43	£1,586.43
TOTAL						£1,586.43	£1,586.43

4 So to pay the net wages, we'll debit: Payroll Clearing and credit: Bank

5 Go to the top middle of the screen and click on the plus sign '+' and under Other, click *Journal Entry*.

6 Make the Journal Number *2014-1-netpay*. The date should be the payday date *(20 April 2014)*. Account Debit: *Payroll Clearing £1431.63*. In the description type in: *April 2014 Wages*. On the following line Account Credit: *Anytown Bank £455.00*. In the description type in: *April 2014 Wages*. For the name, click in the box. On the dropdown arrow, click *+ Add New*. Type in the name: *John Smith*. Add: *Employee. Click Save.*

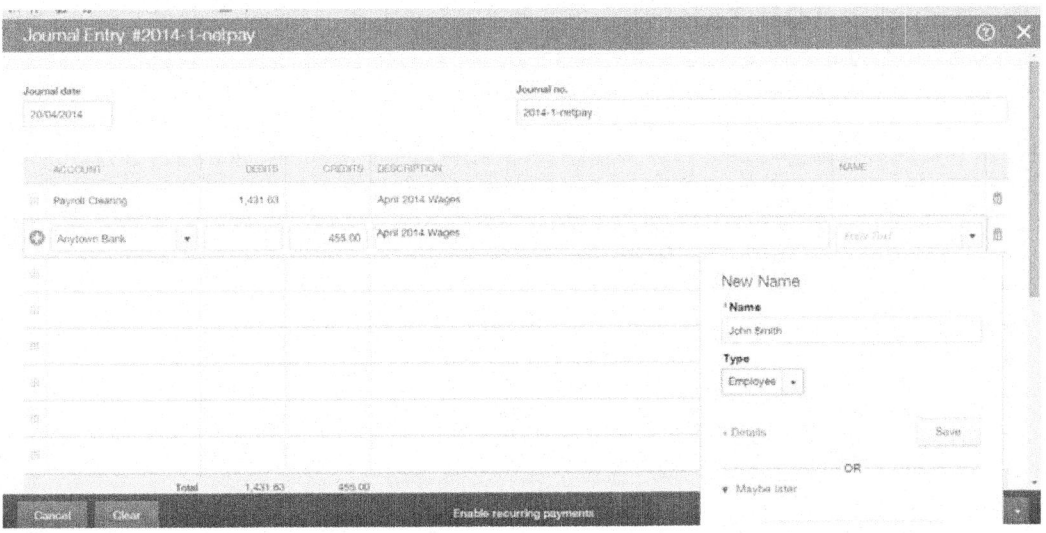

264

7 On the third line Account Credit: *Anytown Bank £976.63*. In the description type in: *April 2014 Wages*. For the name, click in the box. On the dropdown arrow, click *+ Add New*. Type in the name: *Samantha Jones*. Add: *Employee*. Click *Save*.

8 Your screen will resemble this.

ACCOUNT	DEBITS	CREDITS	DESCRIPTION	NAME
Payroll Clearing	1,431.63		April 2014 Wages	
Anytown Bank		455.00	April 2014 Wages	John Smith
Anytown Bank		976.63	April 2014 Wages	Samantha Jones

Journal date: 20/04/2014
Journal no.: 2014-1-netpay

9 Click *Save and New*.

10 These payments will now show on the bank statement. If you go to the Chart of Accounts, and look at the bank account, you'll see the two payments leaving the account. Also, look at the payroll Clearing – which will be at NIL.

12.7 Paying payroll taxes

First of all, you want to find out what you owe. We can see from the payroll journal (2014-1), that the account called 'Tax and National Insurance' is £42.80 + £102 = £144.80.

Megzina Limited
JOURNAL
May 1-14, 2014

DATE	TRANSACTION TYPE	NO.	NAME	MEMO/DESCRIPTION	ACCOUNT	DEBIT	CREDIT
14/05/2014	Journal Entry	2014-1		Gross Wages	Payroll Expenses	£1,531.87	
				Employers NI	Payroll Expenses	£54.56	
				Net Wages Due	Payroll Clearing		£1,431.63
				PAYE (Tax)	Tax and National Insurance		£42.80
				EE + ER NI	Tax and National Insurance		£102.00
				Other Deductions	Other Payroll Deductions		£10.00
						£1,586.43	£1,586.43
TOTAL						£1,586.43	£1,586.43

QuickBooks Online Help

1 To make the payment, we enter a journal. Go to the top middle of the screen and click on the plus sign '+' and under Other, click *Journal Entry*.

2 Make the Journal Number *2014-1-PayHMRC*. The date should be the date which we'll pay HMRC *(19 May 2014)*. Account Debit: *Tax and National Insurance £144.80.* In the description type in: *April 2014 HMRC*. On the following line Account Credit: *Anytown Bank £144.80.* In the description type in: *April 2014 HMRC*. Your screen will resemble this.

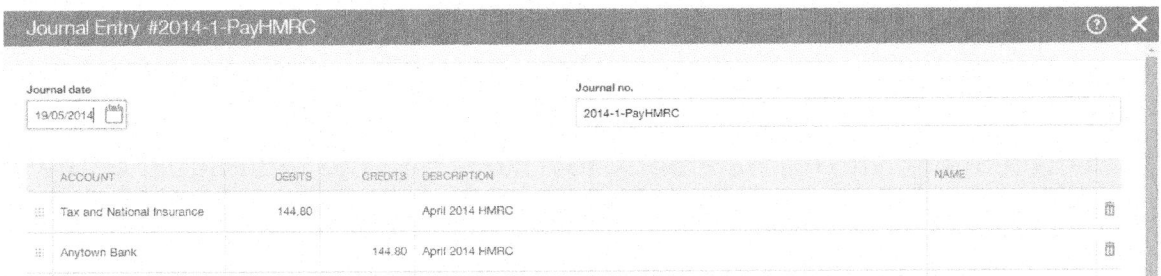

NB If you wanted to add HMRC as a supplier under the name you can do. In this case, we haven't.

3 Click save and new.

4 To double check, go to the chart of accounts, and look at the Tax and National Insurance liability account. It will be at NIL. Example:

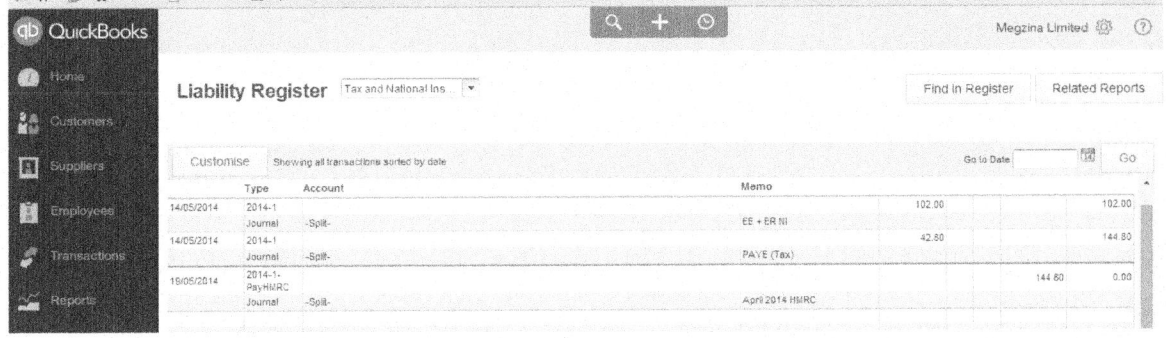

12.8 Paying over payroll deductions

First of all, you want to find out what you owe. We can see from the payroll journal (2014-1), that the account called 'Other Payroll

Deductions' is £10.00. If you recall from the payroll run, this was for 'Give As You Earn'.

Megzina Limited
JOURNAL
May 1-14, 2014

DATE	TRANSACTION TYPE	NO.	NAME	MEMO/DESCRIPTION	ACCOUNT	DEBIT	CREDIT
14/05/2014	Journal Entry	2014-1		Gross Wages	Payroll Expenses	£1,531.87	
				Employers NI	Payroll Expenses	£54.56	
				Net Wages Due	Payroll Clearing		£1,431.63
				PAYE (Tax)	Tax and National Insurance		£42.80
				EE + ER NI	Tax and National Insurance		£102.00
				Other Deductions	Other Payroll Deductions		£10.00
						£1,586.43	£1,586.43
TOTAL						£1,586.43	£1,586.43

1 To make the payment, we enter a journal. Go to the top middle of the screen and click on the plus sign '+' and under Other, click *Journal Entry*.

2 Make the Journal Number *2014-1-PayGIVE*. The date should be the date which we'll pay *(19 May 2014)*. Account Debit: *Other Payroll Deduction £10.00*. In the description type in: *April 2014 GIVE*. On the following line Account Credit: *Anytown Bank £10.00*. In the description type in: *April 2014 GIVE*. Your screen will resemble this.

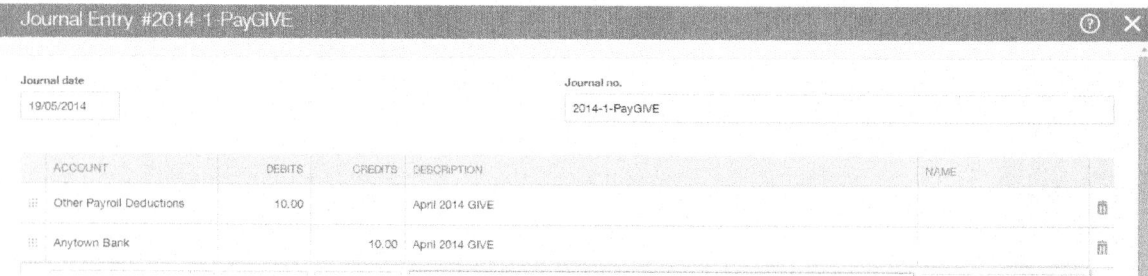

NB If you wanted to add GIVE as a supplier under the name you can do. In this case, we haven't.

3 Click save and new.

4 To double check, go to the chart of accounts, and look at the Other Payroll Deductions liability account. It will be at NIL. Example:

QuickBooks Online Help

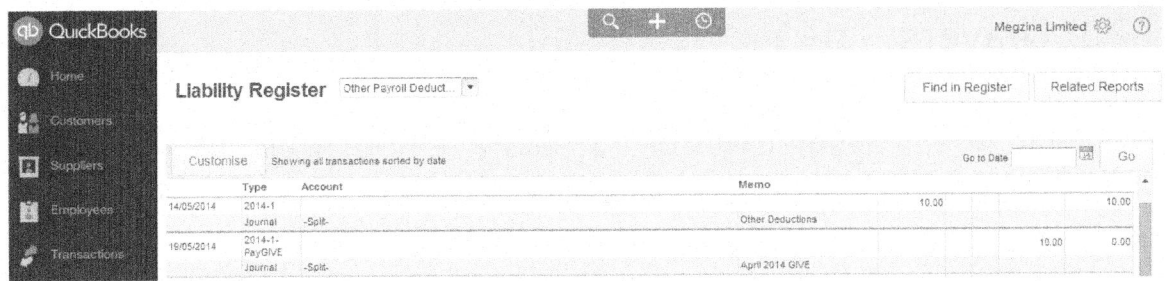

Remember, to get to the Chart of Accounts to look at your liability accounts, click on the wheel/cog icon in the top right hand corner next to the company name. Then click on Chart of Accounts. Click on Account History to see the transactions that have taken place within that account.

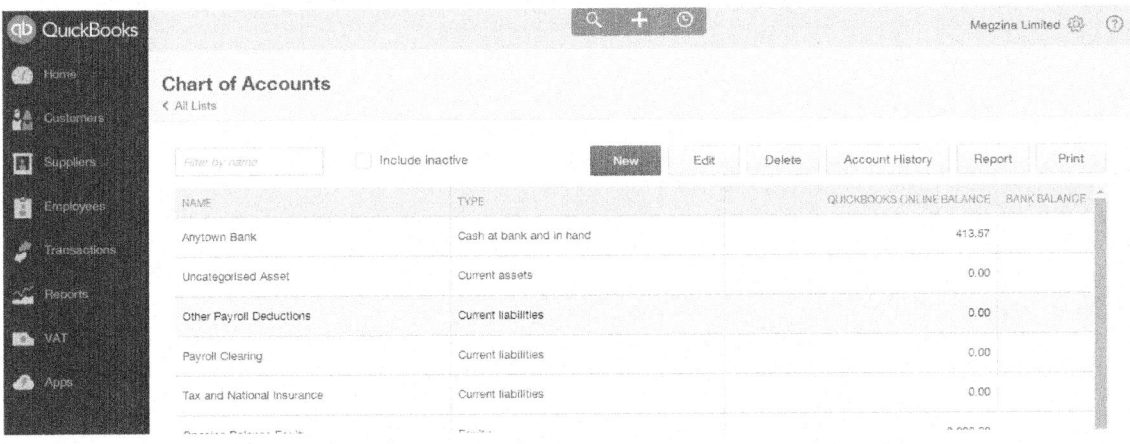

Recent Transactions

If you want to look back over the last transactions just entered, click on the 'clock' icon in the top middle of the page, and the last few transactions just entered into the system are shown.

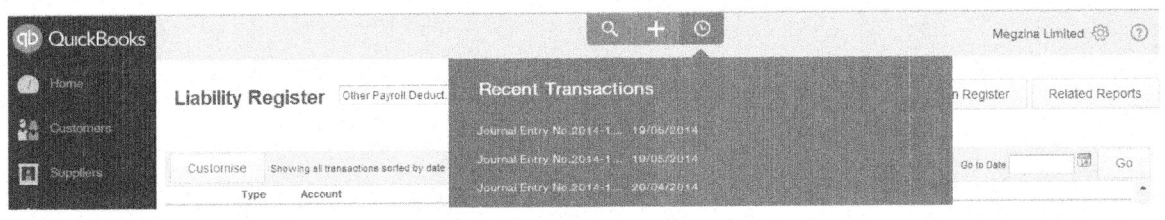

12.9 Leavers – p45

Assuming Joseph Smith leaves on 15th May 2014, we would need to enter his leaving date, and give him his p45.

Employees leaving:

1 Go to *employees*.
2 Click *Leaver*.
3 Choose the reason for leaving i.e. *Resigned*. And the leaving date: *15/05/2014*.

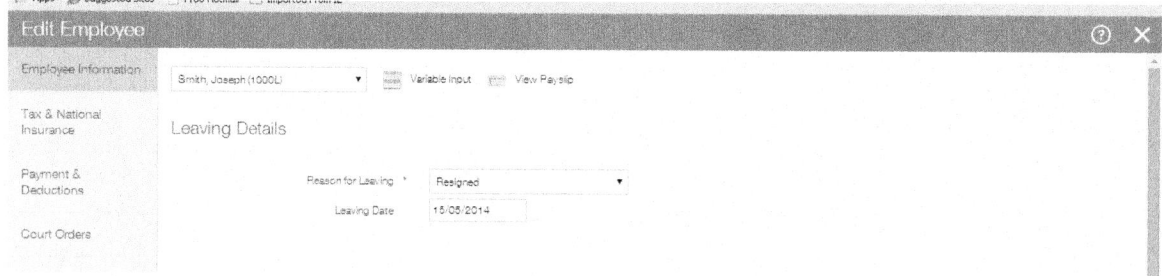

4 Click *Save*.
5 The icon to Download the p45 is now available. Click *Download p45*.

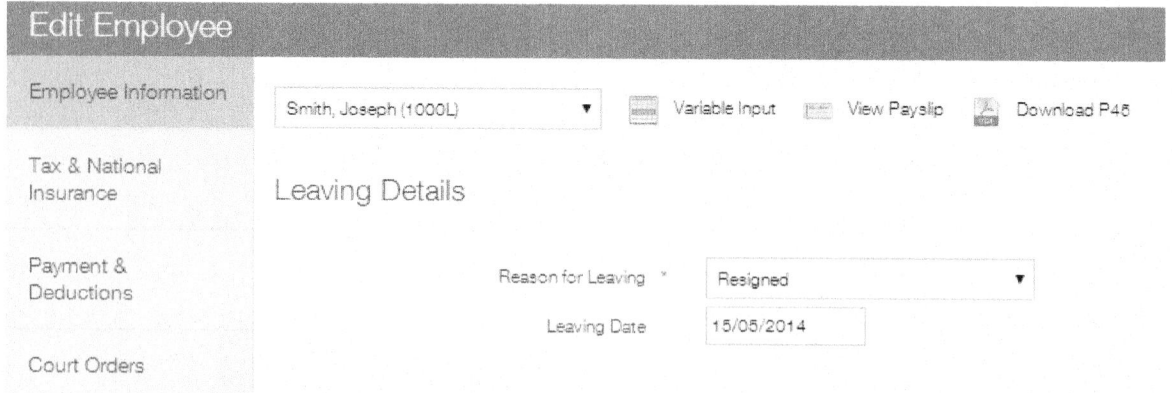

6 Part 1, 2 and 3 is then downloaded. The 4 pages are, example:

QuickBooks Online Help

12.10 Processing payroll at year end

Quickbooks can process your P60 end-of-year forms for employees. You can file your end-of-year (final submission for the year) electronically directly from quickbooks. The system does guide you through the stages.

Note that under settings > payroll settings you can enter HMRC Details. You can get a user ID and activate your account with HMRC by registering in advance with www.gateway.gov.uk Please consult the HMRC website for all the latest news, information, deadlines dates and submission arrangements.

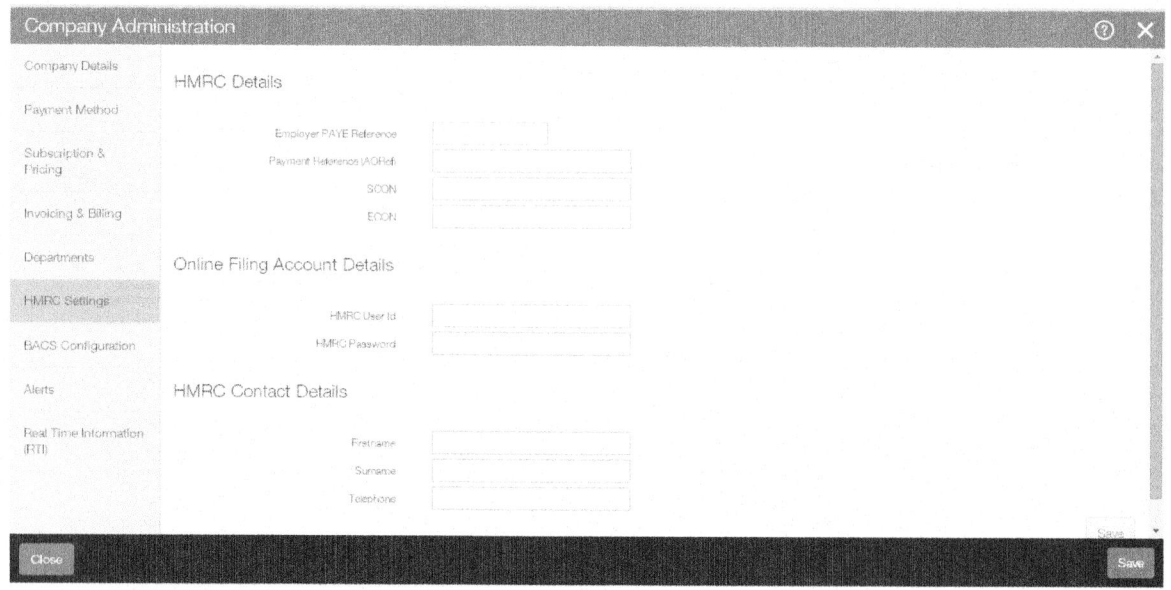

Employees p60 report

At the end of every financial year (5th April) – the deadline normally being 19th May each year, every employee should receive a p60 from you. This is simply an annual summary of their earnings for the previous year. To find this information:

1 Click *Employees. Reports.*

QuickBooks Online Help

2 Under Reports for tax year, click *p60*. The p60s for all employees will be displayed. Example:

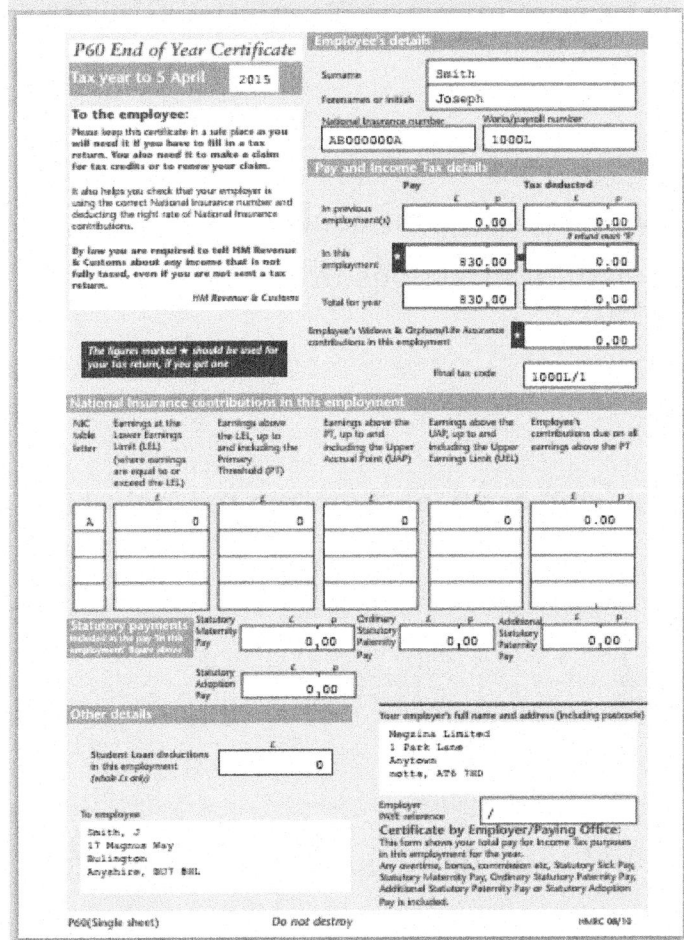

13: Banking

Summary of what is in this chapter:
- 13.1 Banking
- 13.2 Bank Deposit
- 13.3 Transfer
- 13.4 Bank Reconciliation
- 13.5 Credit Cards

13.1 Banking

QuickBooks online has the facility to connect your bank account to the system and then automatically 'pull in' transactions from your bank account.

To set up internet banking

1 Click on the home page. Click on connect bank from the top right hand corner.

2 Type in the name of your bank and click 'find'. QuickBooks online is connected to many banking institutions.

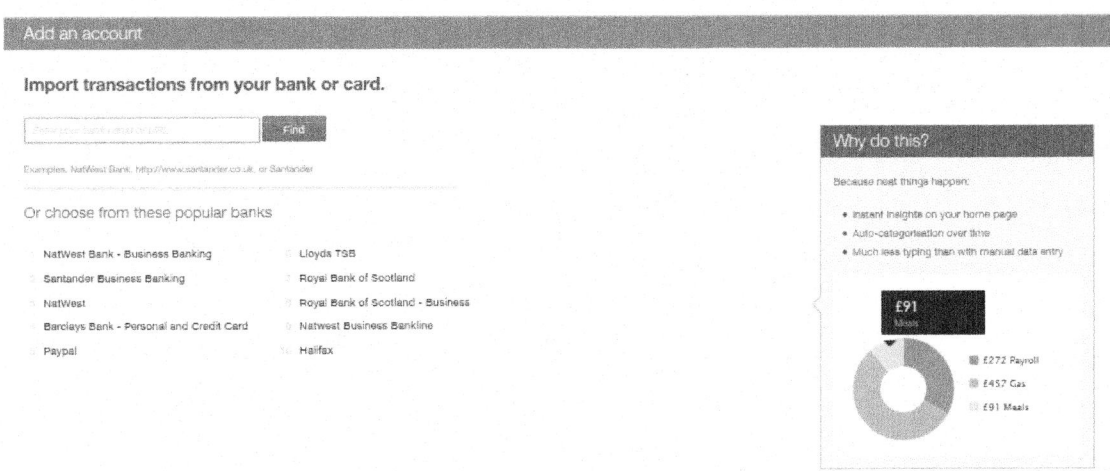

3 Type in the name of your bank, and QuickBooks will come up with its best match.

4 Click Manually import a CSV statement. The instructions are:

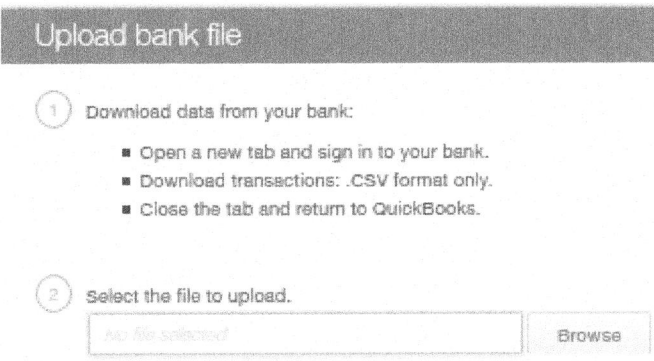

QuickBooks Online Help

5 We logged into our bank and downloaded the transactions in .CSV format.

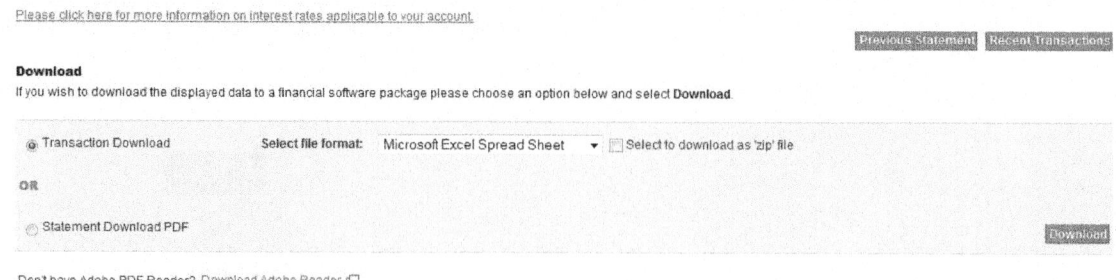

6 We saved the file onto the computer and called it transactions.

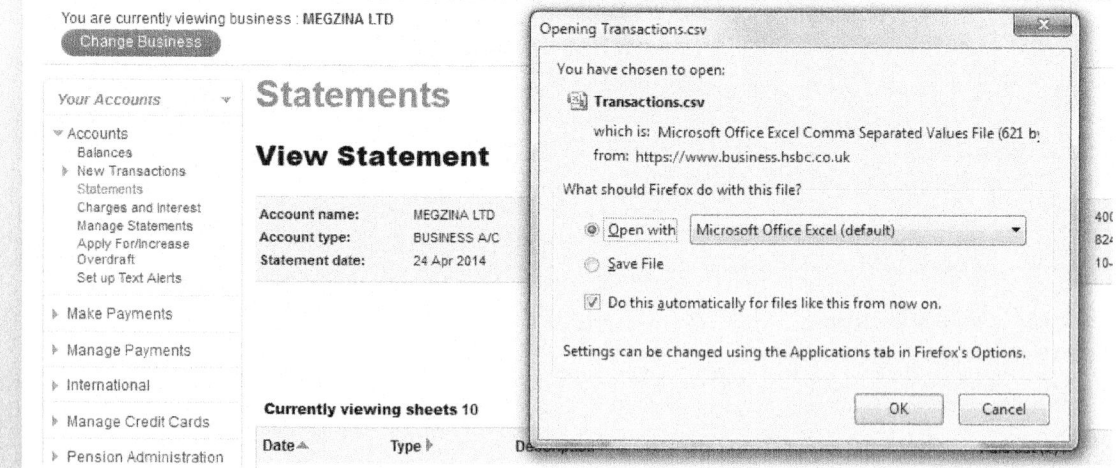

7 When the file opened, it looked like this.

	A	B	C	D	E	F
1	Date	Type	Description	Paid out	Paid in	Balance
2	15-Mar-14		CASH BARCLAY MAR15 ANYTOWN@16:20	20		-77
3	16-Mar-14	TRF	ANYTOWN BANK LOAN		10000	9923
4	20-Mar-14	VIS	INT'L 0002140203 QUICKBOOKS ONLINE LONDON EC4V 6	15		9908
5	29-Mar-14	2	CHEQUE	42.75		9865.25
6	02-Apr-14	1	CHEQUE	20		9845.25
7	07-Apr-14	DD	ANYTOWN INSURANCE CO	32.94		9812.31
8	13-Apr-14	BP	SALLY JONES		100	9912.31
9						
10						

9 We had to change the format slightly, to make it look like this:

	A	B	C	D	E
1	Date	Description	Paid out	Balance	
2	15/03/2014	CASH BARCLAY MAR15 ANYTOWN@16:20	-20	-77	
3	16/03/2014	ANYTOWN BANK LOAN	10000	9923	
4	20/03/2014	INT'L 0002140203 QUICKBOOKS ONLINE LONDON EC4V 6	-15	9908	
5	29/03/2014	CHEQUE	-42.75	9865.25	
6	02/04/2014	CHEQUE	-20	9845.25	
7	07/04/2014	ANYTOWN INSURANCE CO	-32.94	9812.31	
8	13/04/2014	SALLY JONES	100	9912.31	

10 We saved this and called is Transactions2.csv and uploaded this file into QuickBooks.

Upload bank file

1) Download data from your bank:
   - Open a new tab and sign in to your bank.
   - Download transactions: .CSV format only.
   - Close the tab and return to QuickBooks.

2) Select the file to upload.

   Transactions2.csv   [Browse]

11 We have to map out (match) each column of data with something that QuickBooks can recognise.

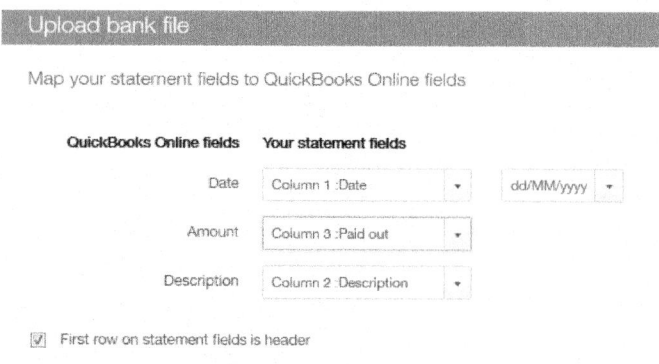

12 We check the entries.

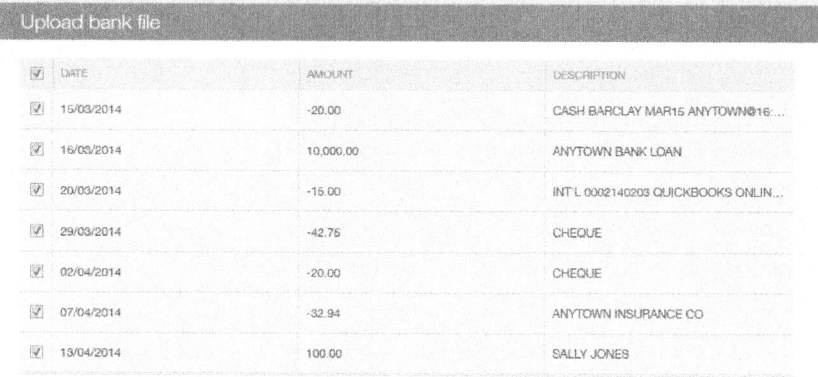

13 QuickBooks asks us if we want to import these 7 entries. We click OK.

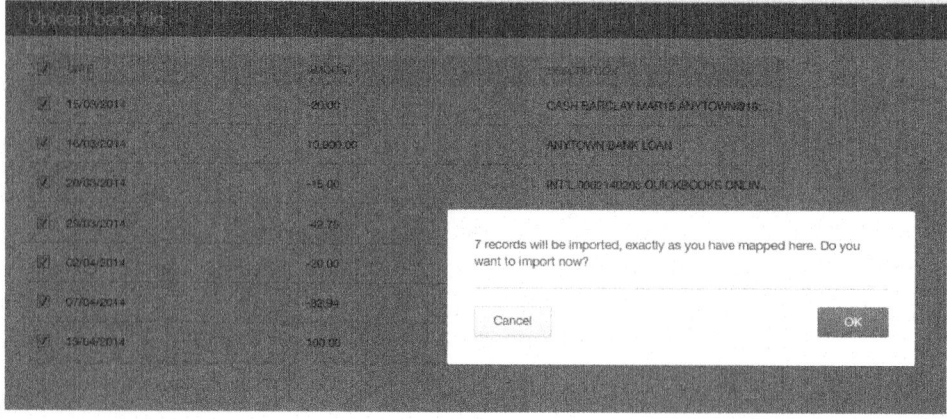

14 QuickBooks confirms the import.

QuickBooks Online Help

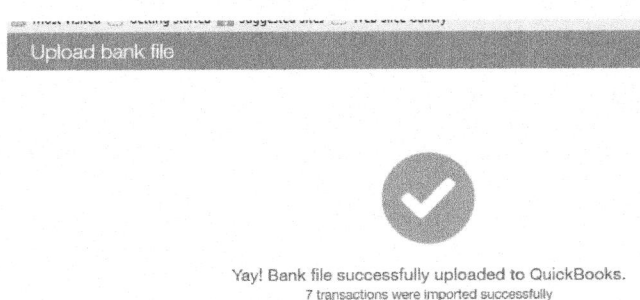

15 Click 'I'm done Lets go" button to confirm.

These entries have now been imported into the system. And on the home page, it says 7 transactions need your attention.

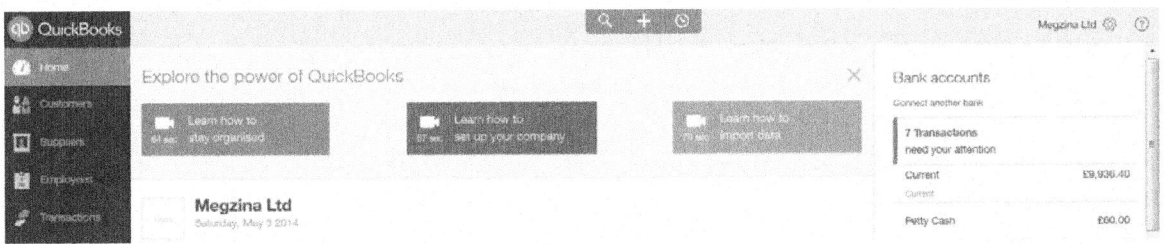

16 Click on the words '7 Transactions' and it brings you to the next screen.

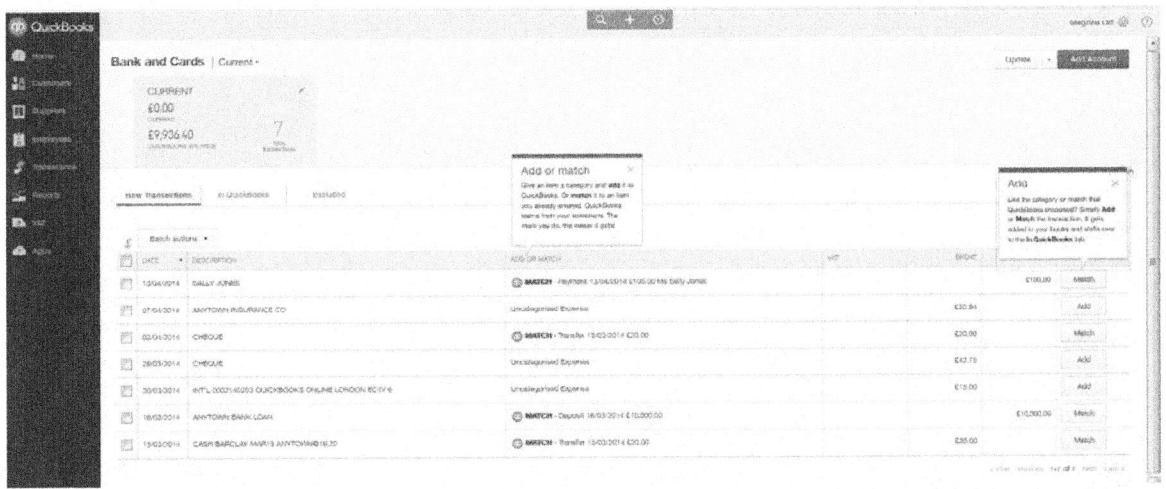

17 You have the option to 'Add or Match'.

18 The first transaction – we can match. The second item (Anytown Insurance) is classed as an 'unclassified expenses' so we click on the tick and click 'Add'.

19 This screen comes up:

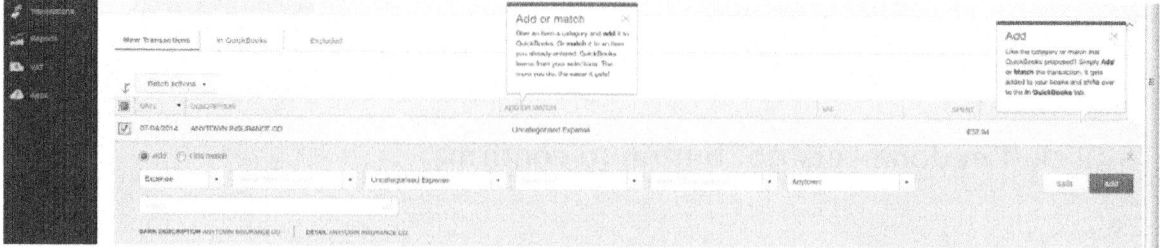

20 From the drop down menu, choose insurance. Insurance is an exempt category (for VAT). And class: office.

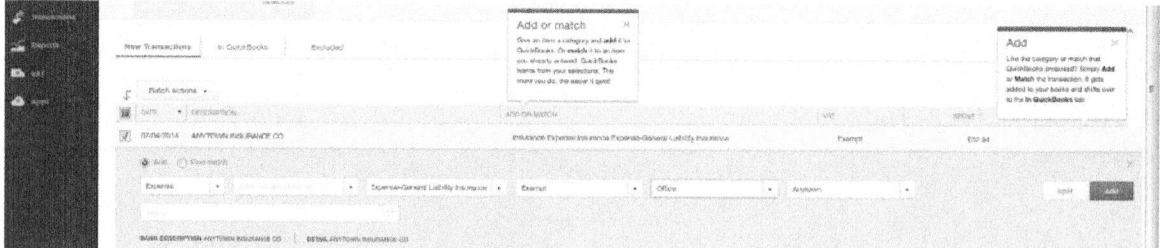

21 Click Add. This transaction is added.

22 The next transaction can be matched.

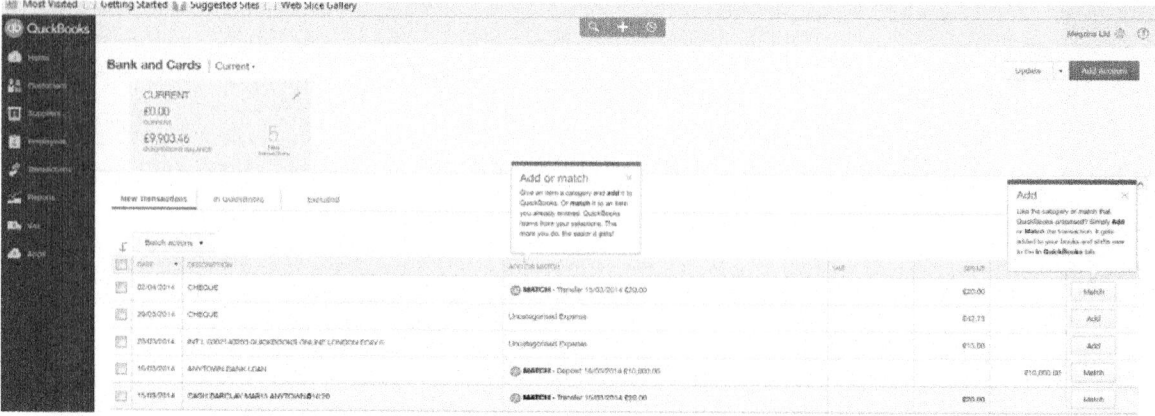

23 The number of 'new transactions' then reduces to 4. To help find matches, you can use 'Find match'. Click on 'Find other matching transactions'.

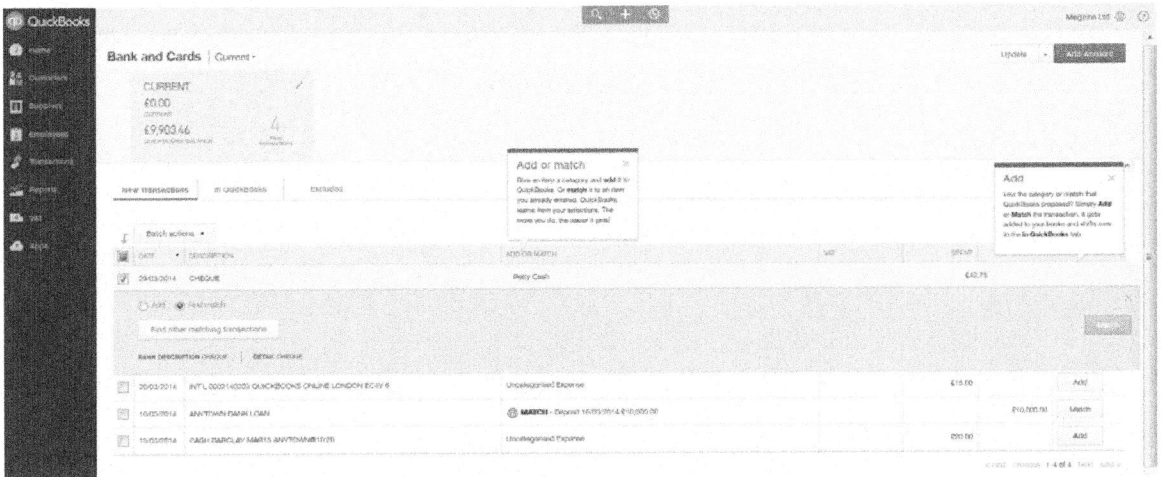

24 A screen pops up. On the left hand side, scroll through the transactions and when you find a match, click 'Add'.

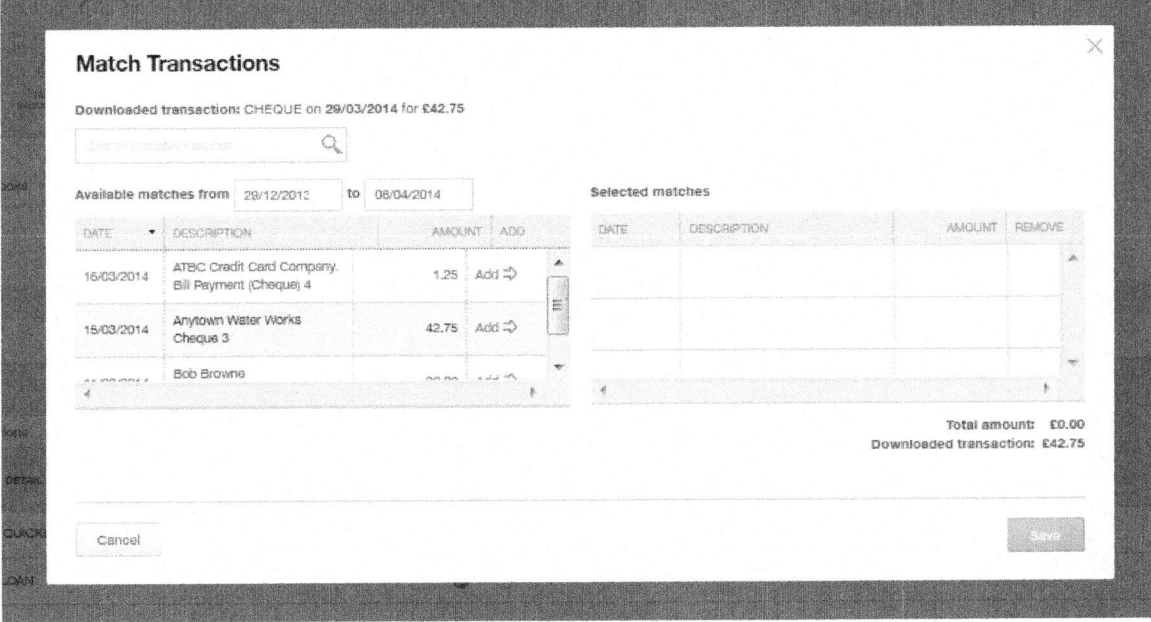

25 When you click 'Add' the transaction from the left moves across to the right.

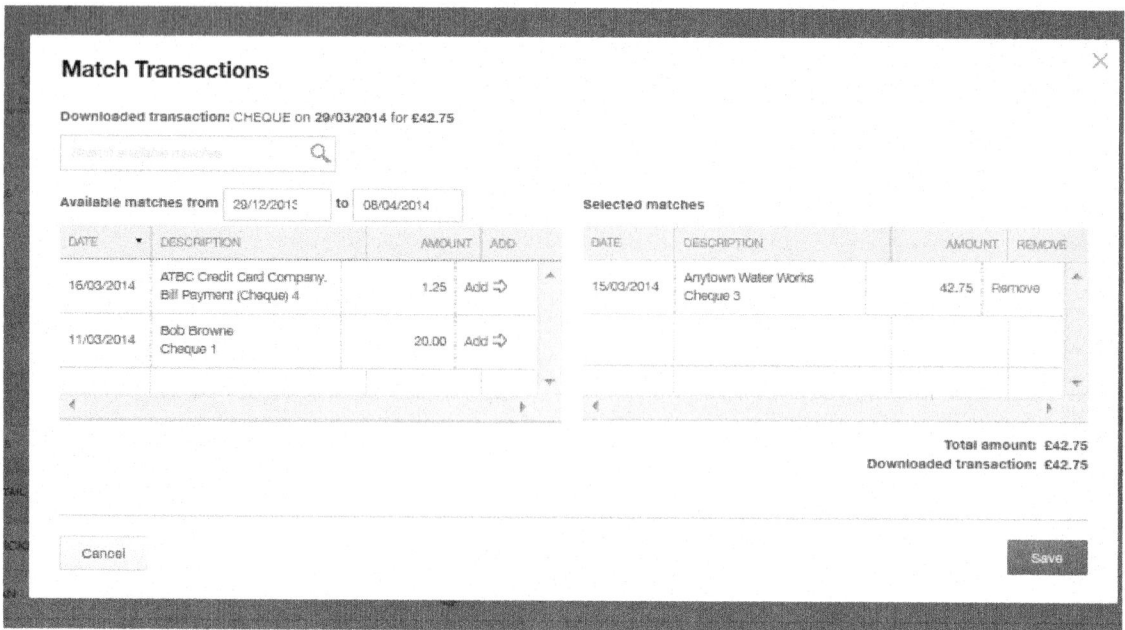

26 Click Save. The transaction has now been matched.

27 The QuickBooks Online transaction needs to be classified to 'dues and subscriptions' it's inclusive of VAT at the standard rate, and goes to the class: Office. Click Add.

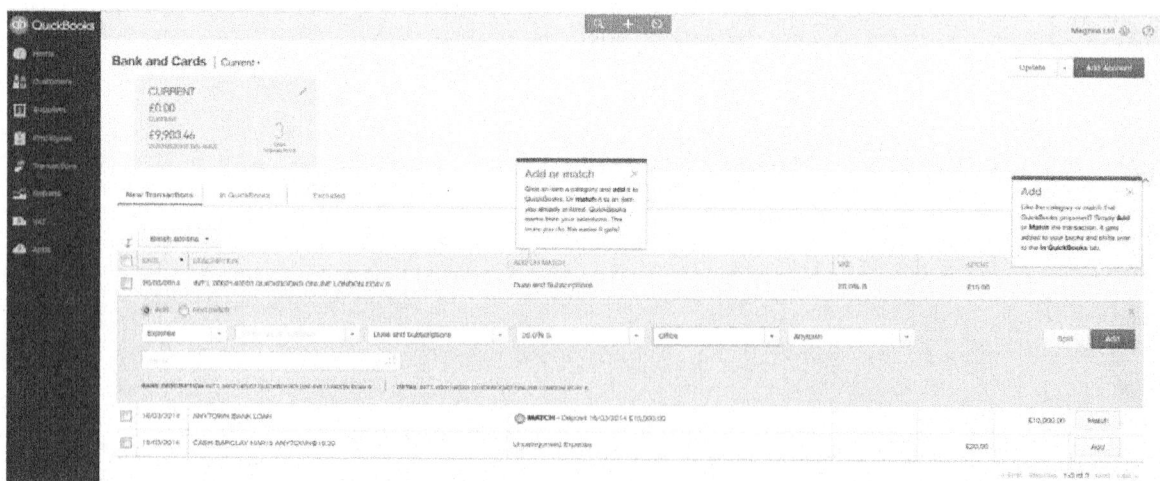

28 The bank loan transaction can be matched. Click Match.

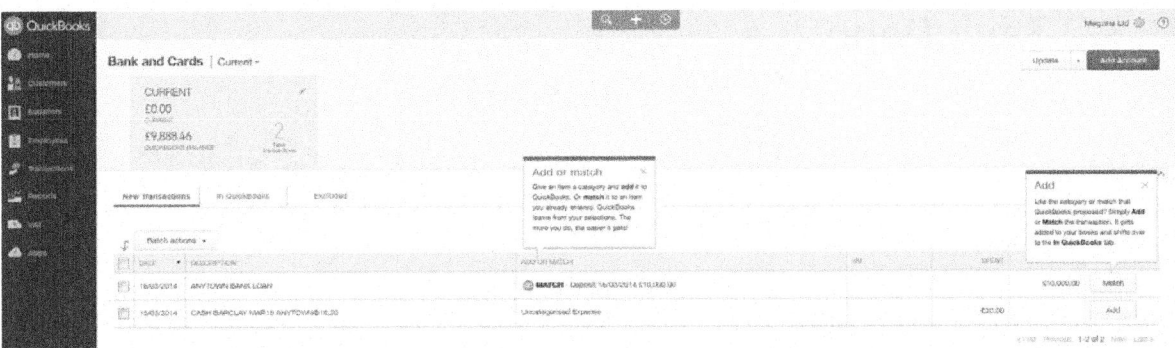

29 The final transaction is £20.00. Click: Find Match. Add the cheque (Bob Brown).

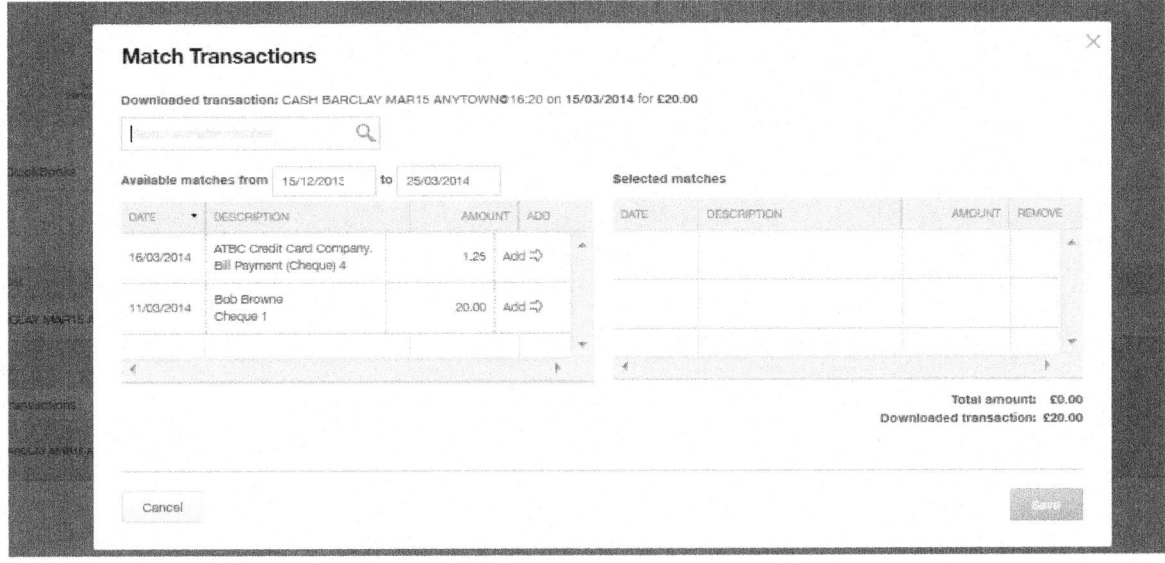

30 All transactions have now been matched.

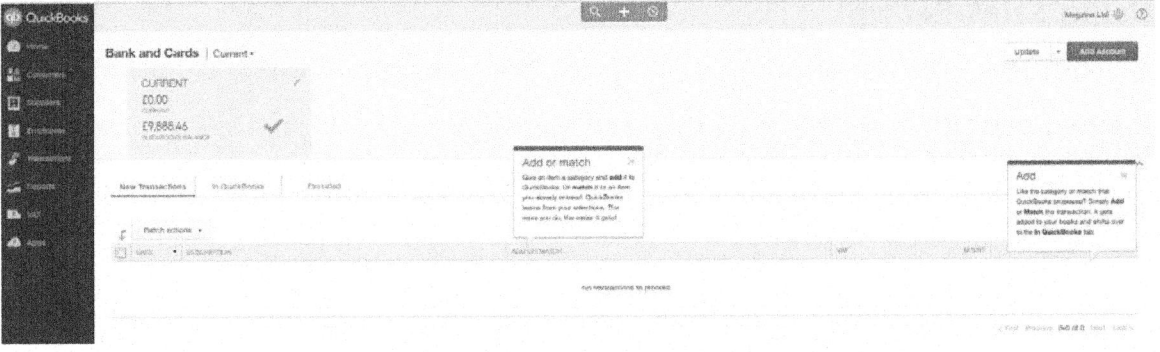

13.2 Bank Deposit

Monies can be received into the bank by using receive payment, Sales receipt, or by journal entry.

Using Receive payment

1 From the Home menu, click '+' in the top middle of the screen and click 'Receive payment'.

2 On the screen which pops us, click the bank account to which the money is to be deposited.

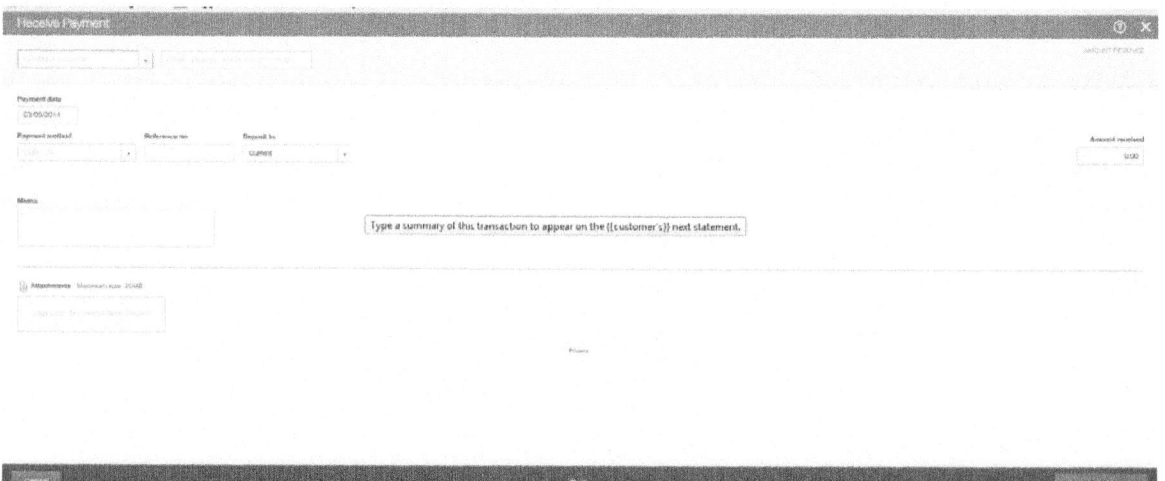

Using Sales Receipt

1 From the Home menu, click '+' in the top middle of the screen and click 'Sales Receipt'.

2 On the screen which pops us, click the bank account to which the money is to be deposited.

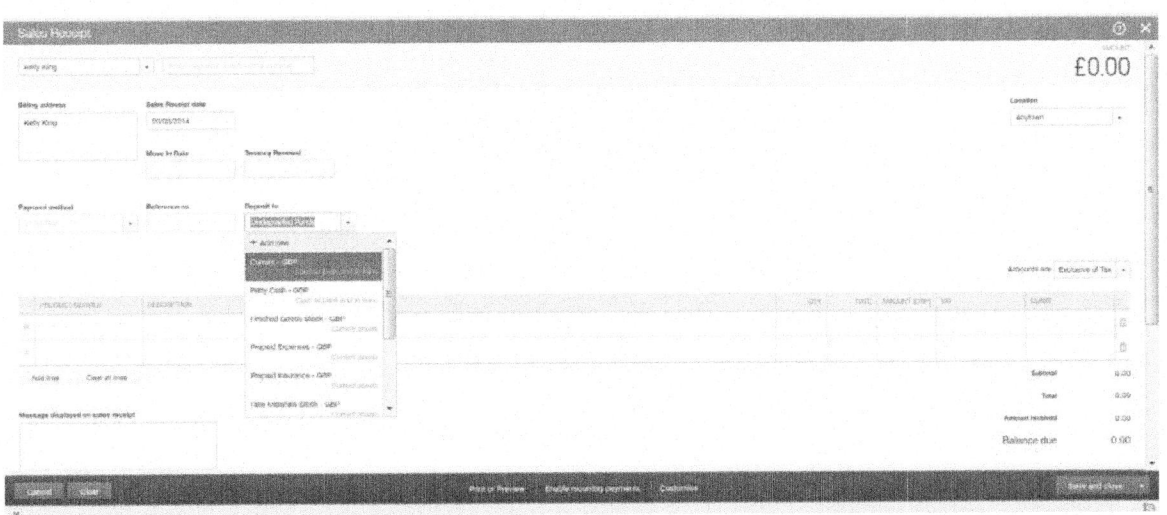

Using Journals

1 From the Home menu, click '+' in the top middle of the screen and click 'Journal Entry'.

2 On the screen which pops us, debit the bank account, and credit the balancing entry.

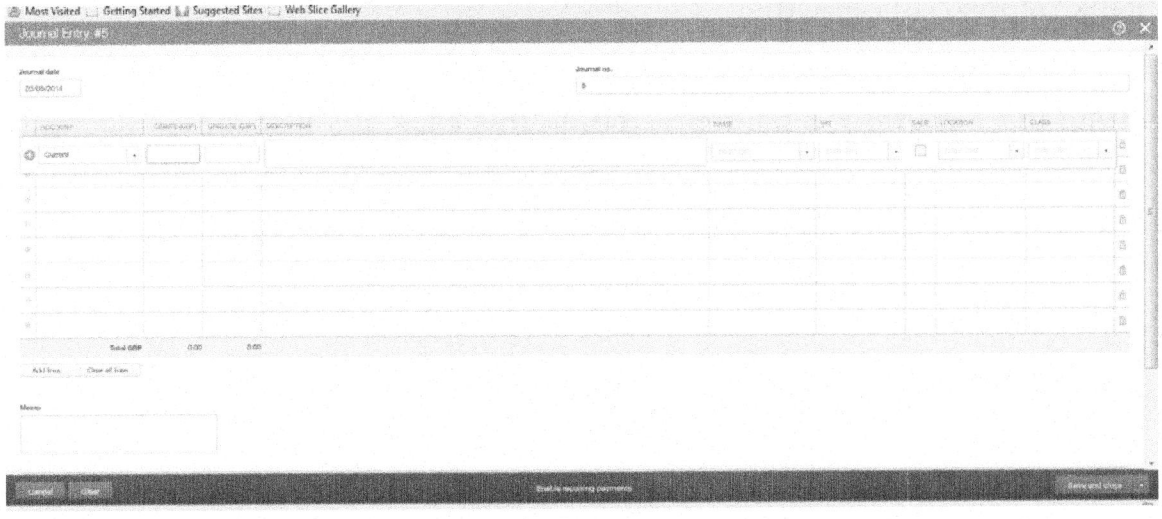

Undeposited Funds

Note, sometimes, when funds are received, it may be 'banked' (on the system) to an account called 'Undeposited Funds'. If this happens, then these funds, then need to be 'deposited' to the bank.

For example, this payment from Sally Jones, was deposited to 'Undeposited Funds'.

1 From the Home menu, click '+' in the top middle of the screen and click 'Bank Deposit' under Other.

2 The screen which automatically shows those existing payments that are sitting there waiting to be deposited. In this case, it's just the £300 from Sally Jones.

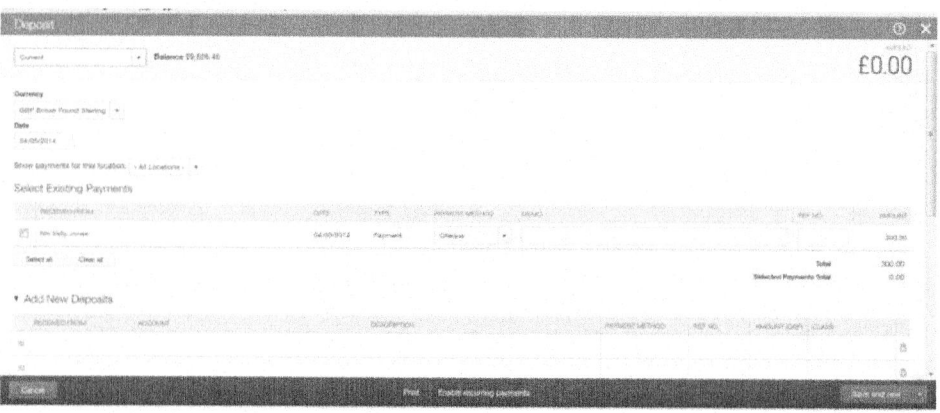

Tick the name, and type in the paying-in slip reference number as: 100200. Click save and close.

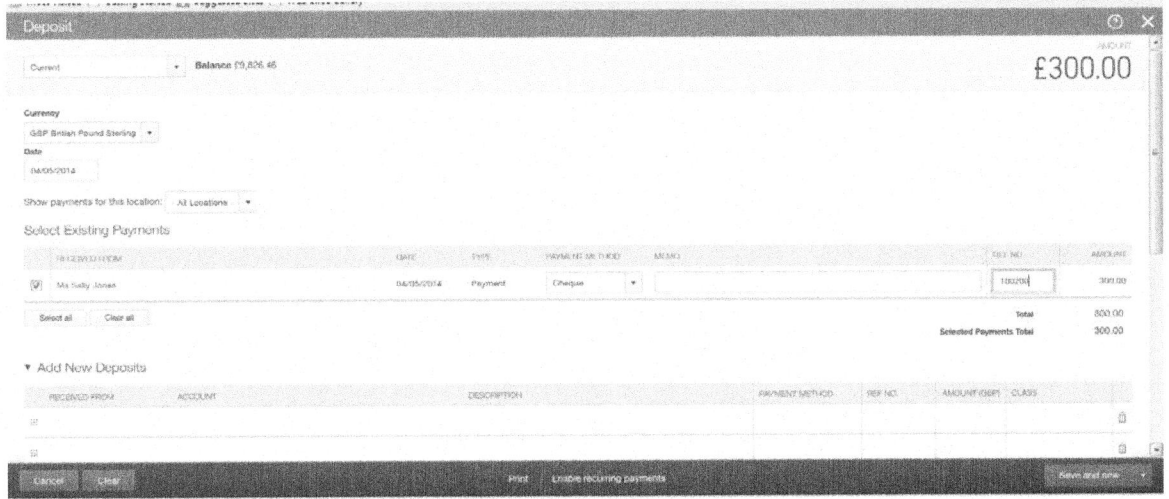

13.3 Transfer

Bank accounts can transfer money between each other. This is another way in which money can be deposited into the account.

To Transfer Between Bank accounts
(e.g. Withdraw £30 from the bank to petty cash)
1 From the Home menu, click '+' in the top middle of the screen and click 'Transfer' under Other..
2 On the screen which pops us, transfer funds from Current Account, to: Petty Cash. Currency GBP. Transfer Amount: £30.00.
3 In the memo type: Cash.
4 Click Save and New.

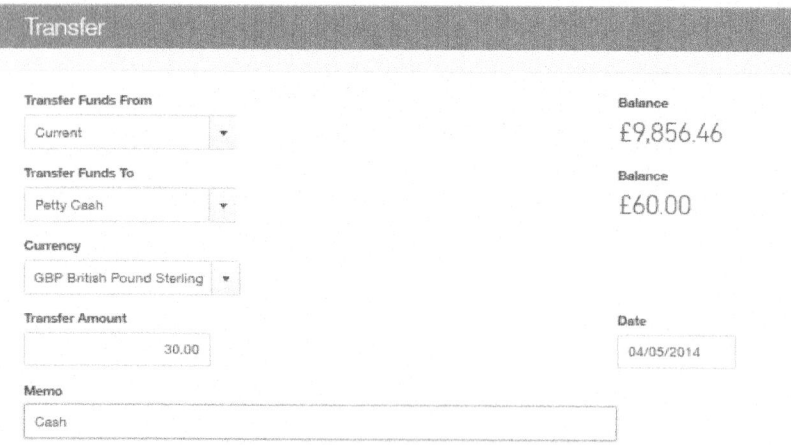

13.4 Bank Reconciliation

A bank reconciliation is useful to perform because it's a means of checking what your QuickBooks system has compared with what your bank statement says.

To do a bank reconciliation:
1 Click on the top right hand corner by the COG / Wheel and choose 'Reconcile' under Tools
2 Click Reconcile Now.

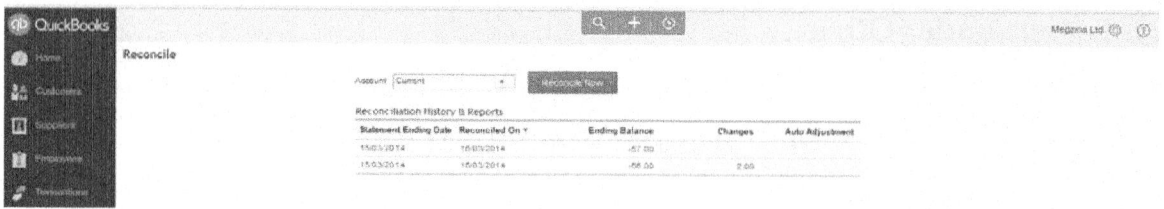

3 You need to have the latest bank statement to hand. The opening balance of the statement should match the figure on the system. If the

account has never been reconciled before, then you need to start at the beginning.

4 Example of a bank statement (downloaded as a CSV file).

	A	B	C	D	E	F
1	Date	Type	Description	Paid out	Paid in	Balance
2	15-Mar-14		CASH BARCLAY MAR15 ANYTOWN@16:20	20		-77
3	16-Mar-14	TRF	ANYTOWN BANK LOAN		10000	9923
4	20-Mar-14	VIS	INT'L 0002140203 QUICKBOOKS ONLINE LONDON EC4V 6	15		9908
5	29-Mar-14		2 CHEQUE	42.75		9865.25
6	02-Apr-14		1 CHEQUE	20		9845.25
7	07-Apr-14	DD	ANYTOWN INSURANCE CO	32.94		9812.31
8	13-Apr-14	BP	SALLY JONES		100	9912.31
9						
10						

5 The opening balance of -57.00 on the system matches the bank statement downloaded. Type in the closing balance of 9912.31.

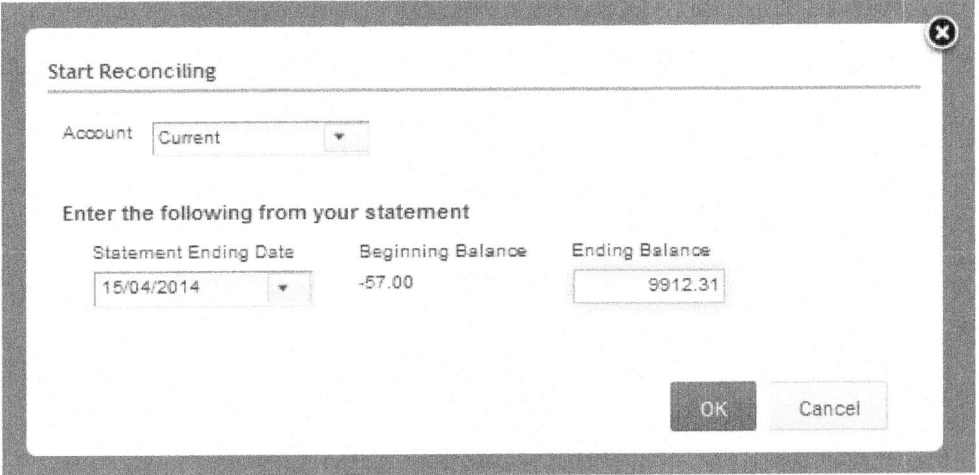

6 Click OK.

7 The system ticked the transactions it recognised automatically. Check that these items are on your bank statement. Note : when you've imported the transactions into the system (as we did in 13.1) the system

recognised the transactions readily, then had we have manually entered in everything.

8 Check that the Difference is at NIL (in the bottom left hand corner). If the reconciliation didn't balance (due to missing transactions), and we had a difference, we would click 'finish later' and add the missing transactions. In this case, all the transactions listed on the bank statement are on the system, and have been ticked. The difference is £0.00.

Edit Information from Statement		Beginning Balance	£ -57.00
		5 Cheques and Payments	£130.69
Service Charge		2 Deposits and Other Credits	£10,100.00
Interest Earned		Statement Ending Balance	£9,912.31
		Cleared Balance	£9,912.31
		Difference	£0.00

9 Click Finish Now.

10 This takes you back to the 'reconcile' page.

QuickBooks Online Help

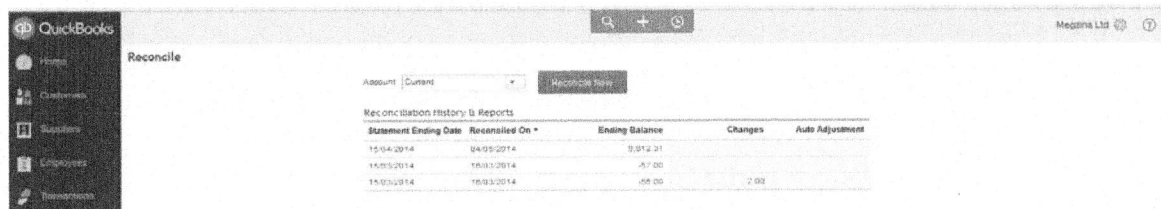

Note, you can click on any of the previous reconciliations to look at or print them.

13.5 Credit Cards

Some businesses use credit cards as this can help to ease the cashflow. From the left hand menu, click Transactions and then Banking.

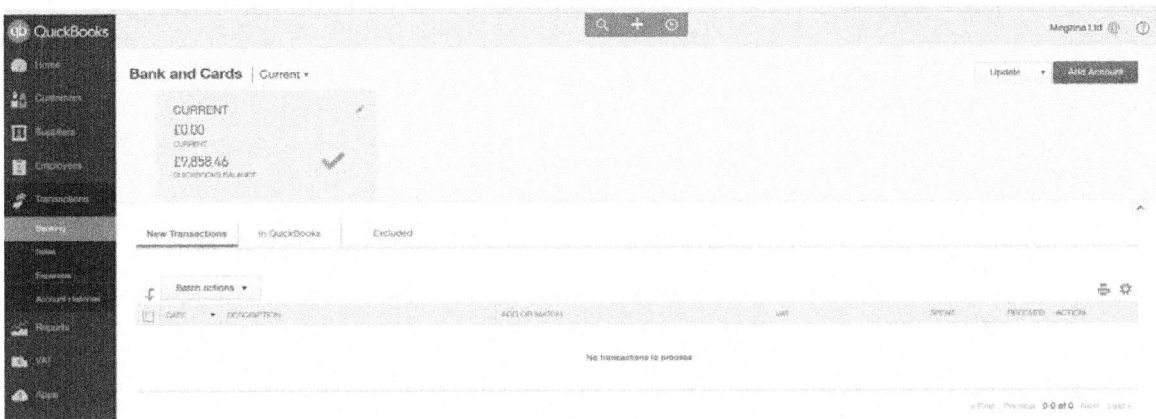

You can 'add account' from the top right hand corner, to add a credit card.

If (for example) you banked with Lloyds Bank, you'd be presented with a screen to log into your Lloyds account.

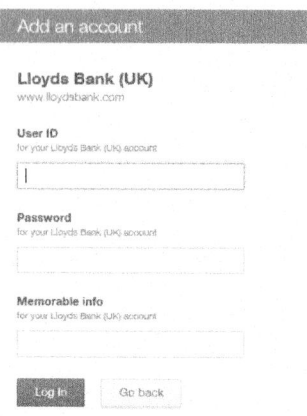

Likewise, if you banked with Barclays, your screen would look like this:

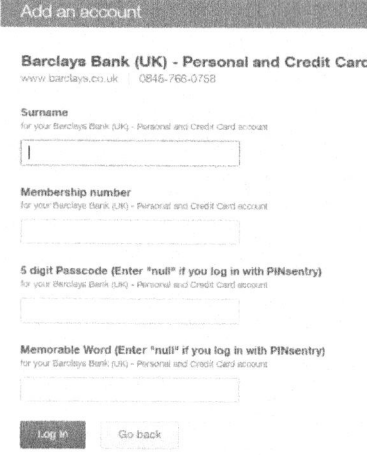

Once you are logged in, your account would be 'connected' with QuickBooks, and the transactions from the system would be 'pulled' into the system when you log into QuickBooks.

Transactions would 'sit' (in the example here there's 148 new transactions to sort out).

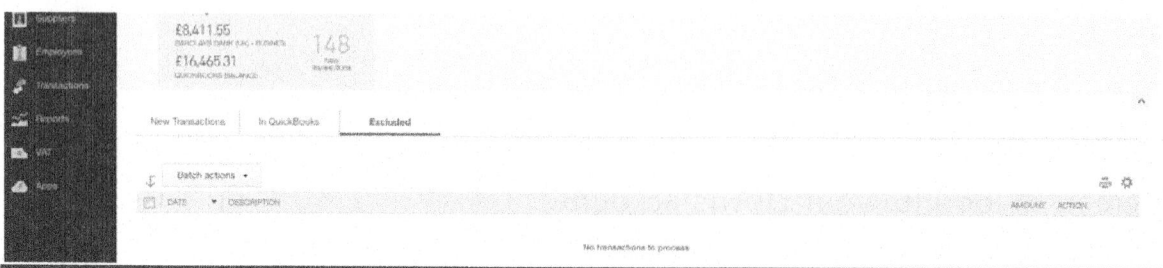

Once they're matched in QuickBooks, they'd appear in the 'in QuickBooks' tab and the outstanding number would reduce. If you wanted the transaction to be excluded, you'd opt to have it excluded.

Importing credit card transactions
Importing credit card transactions works much in the same way as importing bank transactions as in section 13.1.

1 Click on the home page. Click on connect bank from the top right hand corner.

2 Type in the name of your bank and click 'find'. QuickBooks online is connected to many banking institutions.

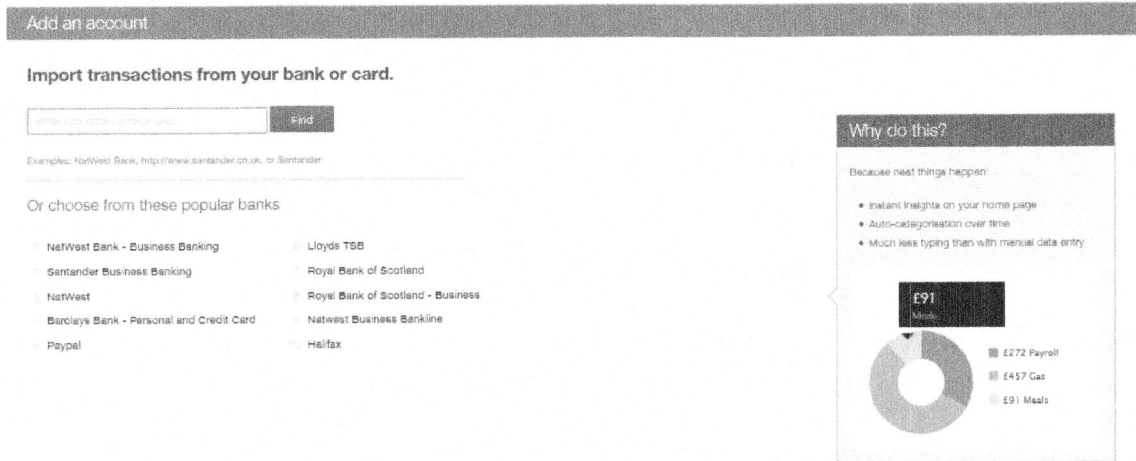

3 Type in the name of your bank, and QuickBooks will come up with its best match.

QuickBooks Online Help

4 Click Manually import a CSV statement. The instructions are:

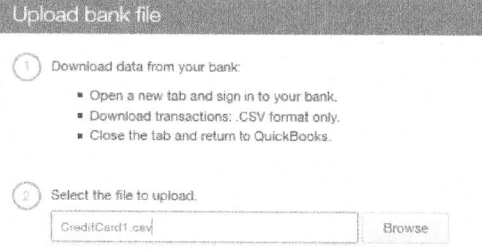

5 Choose the credit card. Click next.

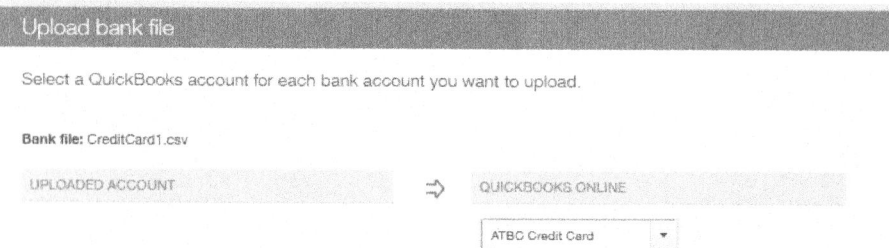

Note, a CSV file will look something like this.

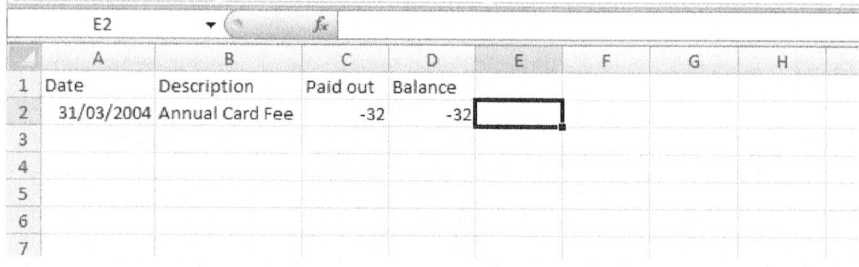

QuickBooks Online Help

6 Ensure the fields are matched up. Then click next.

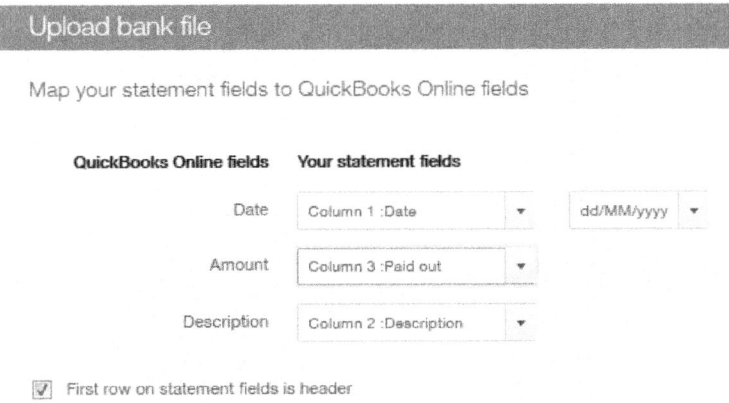

7 The transactions which are imported will be listed.

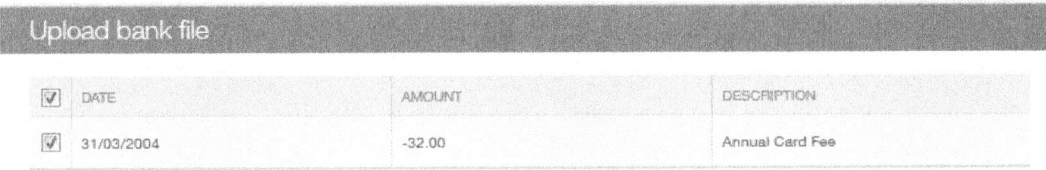

Click next

8 The screen will confirm the number of records that have been imported. In this case one.

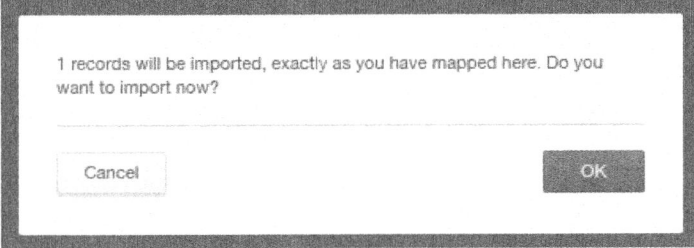

Click Ok

9 When the file is imported successfully, a message will appear on the screen.

QuickBooks Online Help

Click the button: 'I'm Done. Let's go!'

10 Click on credit cards to show the new transactions.

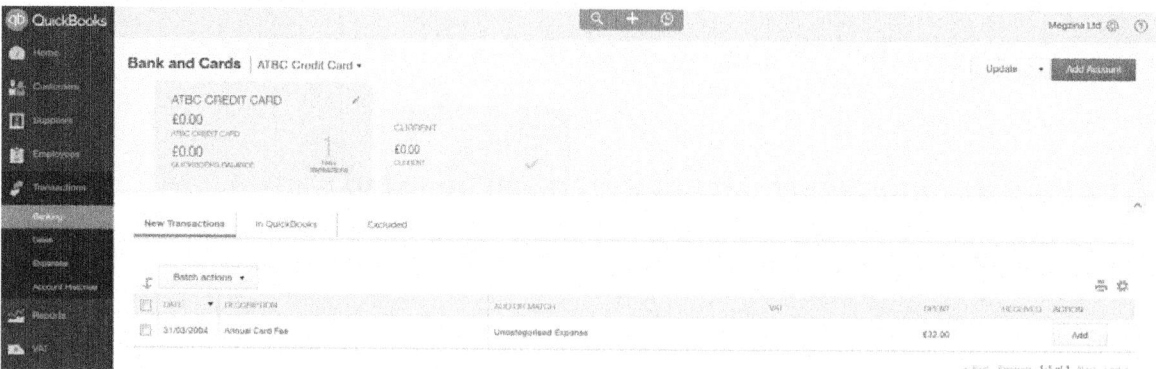

Choose the supplier name (ATBC Credit Card Company), the expense type is dues & subscriptions (it's the annual card fee), it's exempt from VAT. The class is Office.

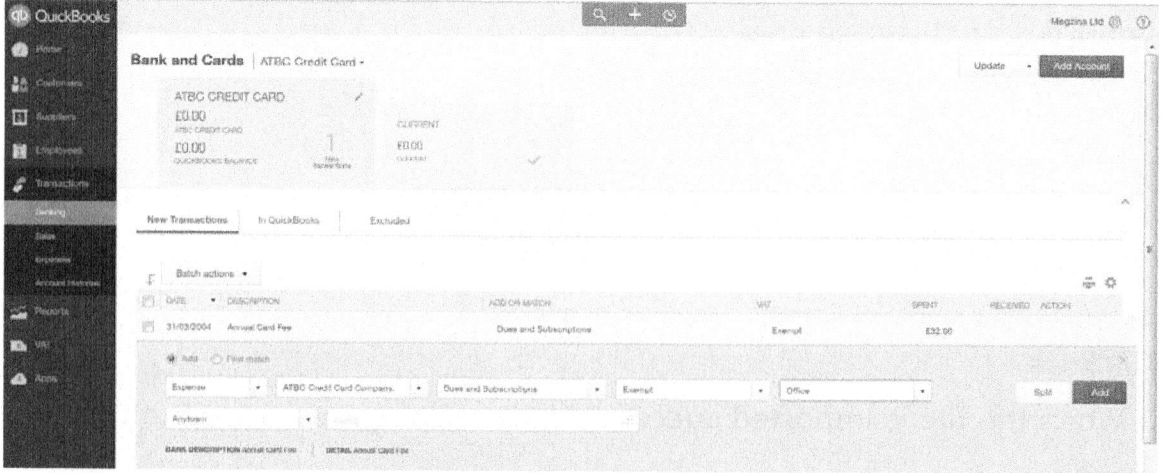

Click Add. The transaction is added.

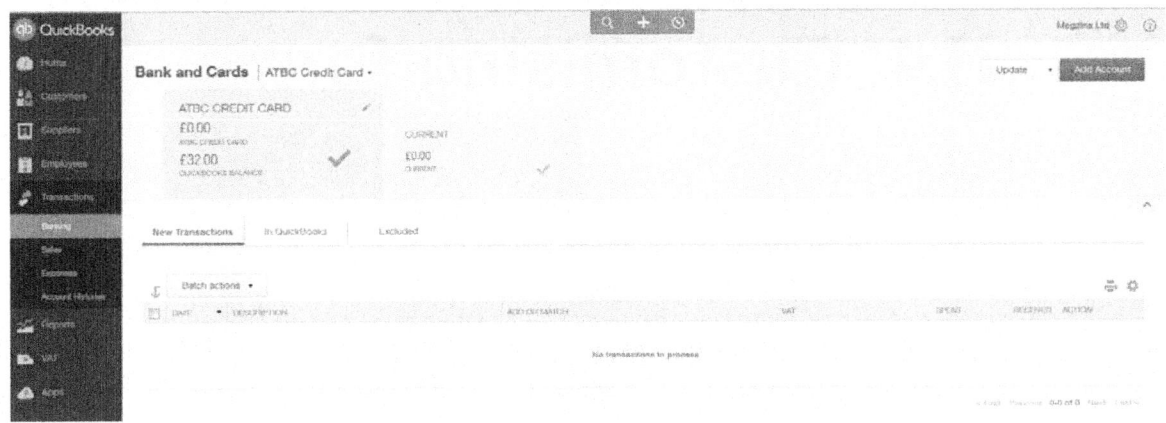

To pay a credit card

1 From the Home menu, click '+' in the top middle of the screen and click 'Transfer'.

2 Transfer funds from Current Account, to the ATBC Credit Card. Currency is GBP. Transfer amount is 32.00. In the Memo type: Pay Balance in Full.

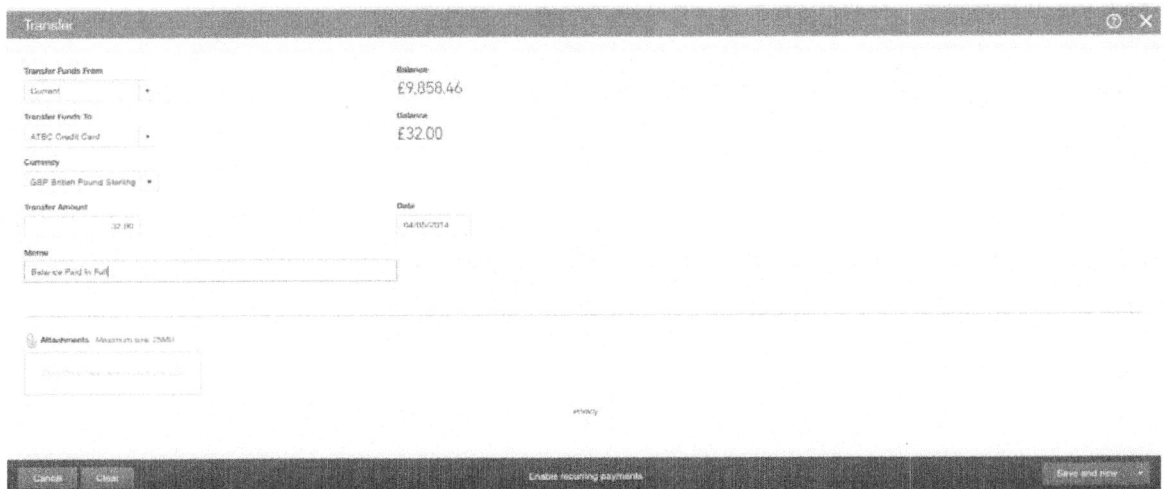

Click save and new.

The card balance on the system will now show NIL.

14: Customising forms

Summary of what is in this chapter:
- 14.1 About QuickBooks forms
- 14.2 Customising an invoice
- 14.3 Customising an estimate or sales receipt
- 14.4 Customising email for sales forms
- 14.5 Creating a statement

14.1 About QuickBooks forms

Each form you use in QuickBooks has its own layout of fields for entering information. If the layout or look/feel of the form doesn't quite meet your needs, you can create your own custom layout and use your version instead. These can be saved as templates for later use. The forms you can customise in QuickBooks are the invoice, the cash sale (sale receipt) and estimate.

14.2 Customising an invoice

QuickBooks lets you customise an invoice form to suit your business. For example you can change the font, the colour and the information which appears.

QuickBooks Online Help

Customising the invoice template

To customise a new invoice template:

1 From the top middle of the home page, click '+'.

2 Click create Invoice (under customers).

3 Bottom middle of the page click *Customise*.

This screen pops up:

4 Style:

    Logo: You can upload a logo (click upload).

    Colour: You can choose between black & white, or (click on the down arrow square colour) to decide on the colour

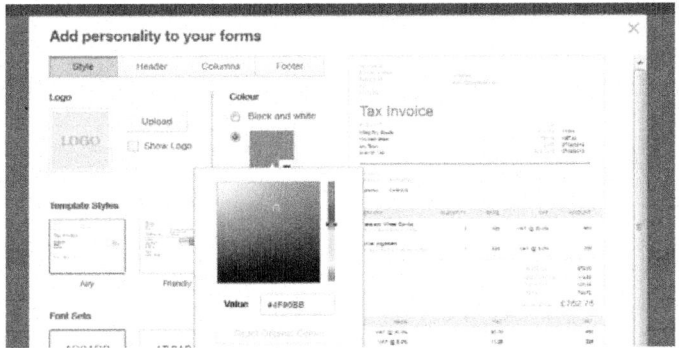

Template Styles: choose from Any, Friendly and Bold

Font Sets: choose from Helvetica and Times

5 Header:

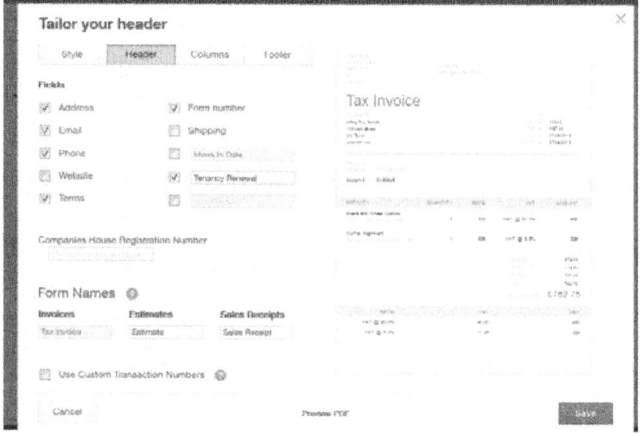

Fields: You can choose which fields are on the form by ticking those which you want to appear e.g. Address, Email, Phone, Website, Terms, Form number, Shipping (and 3 other custom fields).

Companies House Registration Number: Optional to include it.

Form Names: you can customise the names of the forms.

Use Custom Transaction Numbers: tick this box if you want to make your own numbers up.

Notice that as you tick and untick and make your selection, the template example invoice on the right-hand side changes.

6 Columns:

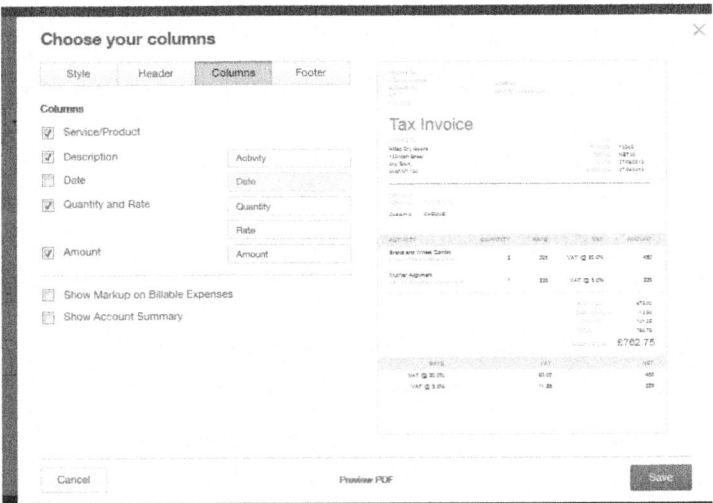

Fields: You can choose which fields are on the form by ticking those which you want to appear e.g. Service/Product, Description, Date, Quantity and Rate, Amount.

There is the option to tick: Show Mark-up on Billable Expenses and Show Account Summary.

7 Footer:

Tick – Show VAT Summary (option is only there if the VAT settings have been switched on).

There's an option to put in a Message to customer on Invoices e.g. bank details and in the footer e.g. Thank you for your business (or some sales/marketing message).

When you've finished making the changes that you want, click save.

14.3 Customising an estimate or sales receipt

To customise an Estimate template:
1 From the top middle of the home page, click '+'.
2 Click Estimate or sales receipt (under customers).
3 Bottom middle of the page click *Customise*.

This screen pops up:

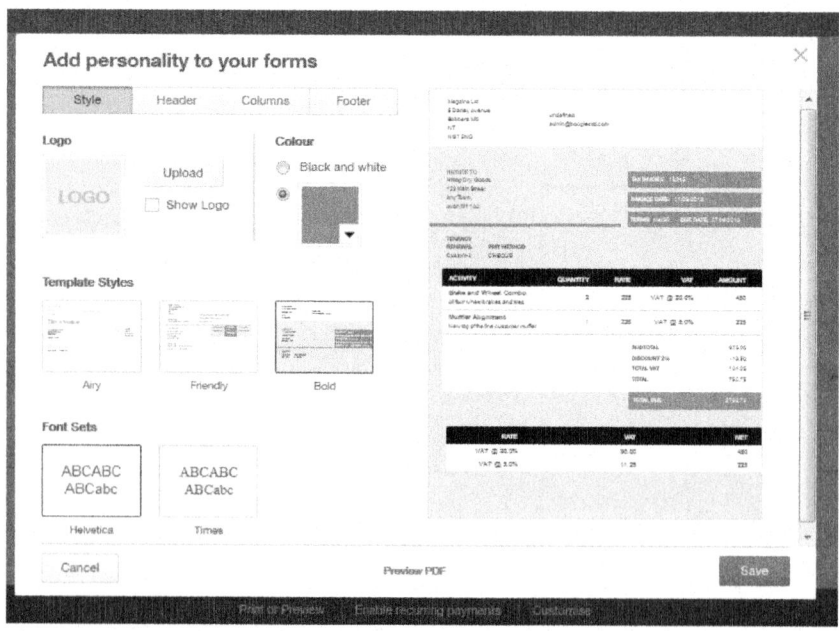

You can customise the estimate and sales receipt in exactly the same way as you would customise the Invoice template.

14.4 Customising email for sales forms

When sending a sales form (invoice, sales receipt or estimate) by email, QuickBooks displays a default message, which you can override on an ad-hoc basis.

To customise the message:

1 Click on the COG/Wheel by the company name.

2 Select *Company Settings*.

3 Click on *Sales* and then *edit* the *Messages*.

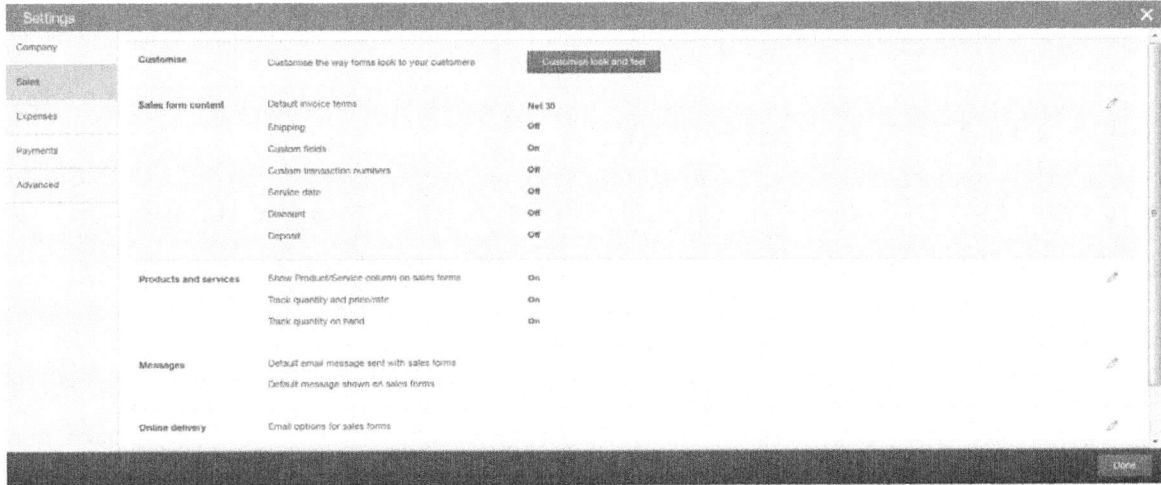

4 The default message can be set for invoices, estimates, credit notes, sales receipts and statements. You can use the given standard message or make up your own. The greeting can be changed from here.

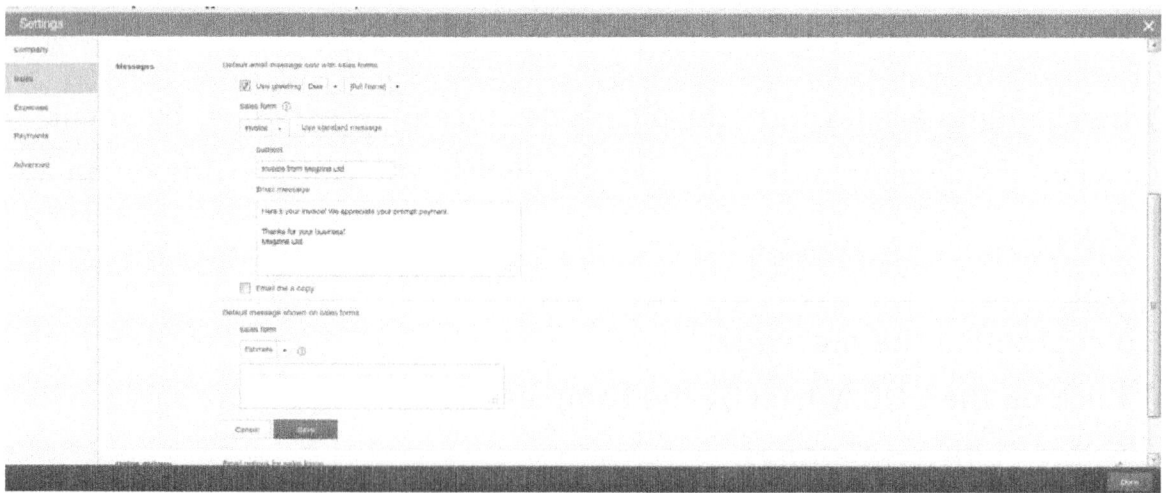

5 Once you've made your selection, click *Save.* And *Done.*

14.5 Creating A Statement

You can send customers a statement to let them know the balance on their account and the transactions which have taken place.

To create a statement:

1 From the Home page, click '+' in the top middle of the screen. From this dropdown menu, select *Statements* from under Other.

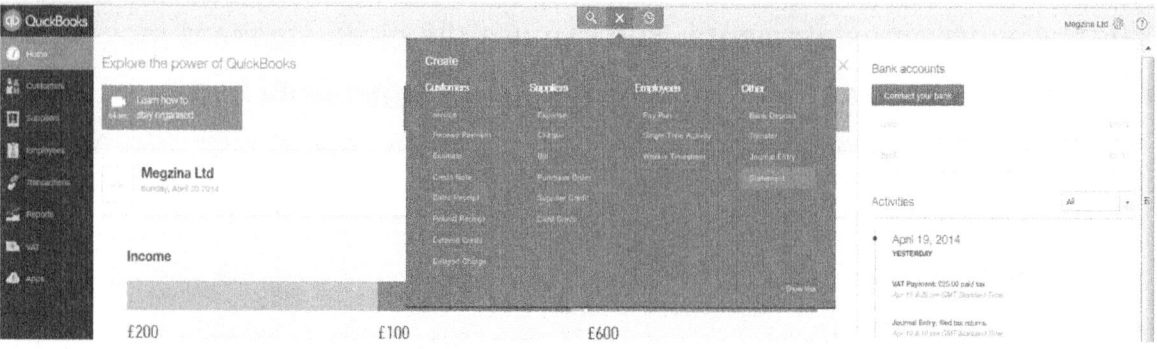

QuickBooks Online Help

2 A form will pop up on the screen, Select the statement date, start date and end date of the period that you want the statement to cover. Click OK.

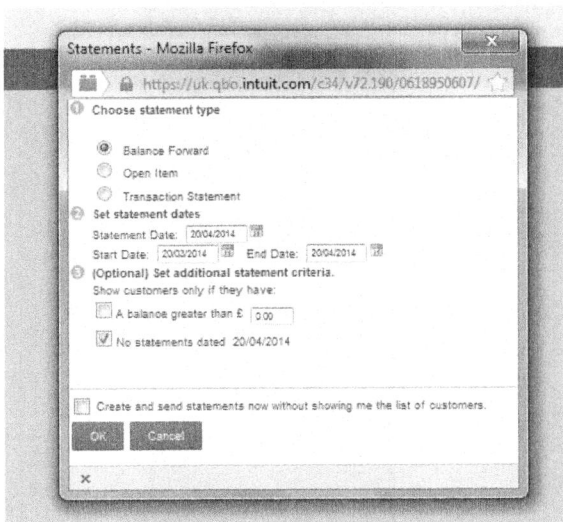

3 Instructions will appear on the screen.

QuickBooks will give you a list of customers who meet the criteria you set for creating statements. (you can change the criteria, by clicking *Change*).

4 Uncheck any customer who should not receive a statement.

5 Make sure the **Delivery Methods** are correct.

6 Optionally, click **Preview** to see how a statement will look after it's created.

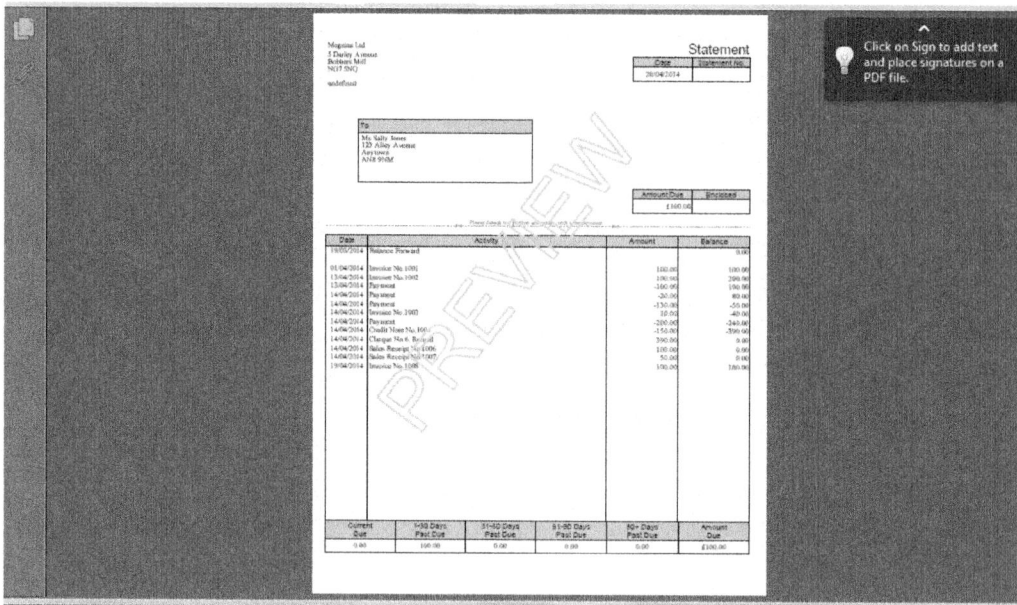

7 Click **Create/Send Selected Statements**.

15: Using sales orders and estimates

Summary of what is in this chapter:
- 15.1 Creating estimates (sales orders)
- 15.2 Creating an invoice from an estimate
- 15.3 Delayed charge
- 15.4 Delayed credits
- 15.5 Displaying reports for estimates

15.1 Creating Estimates (sales orders)

An estimate is a description of work or products that you intend to sell to a prospective customer. "Estimates" in QuickBooks, can also be called "sales order". It is a non-posting transaction, and therefore doesn't have any effect on the financial reports or income and expense balances. Some people will ask you to send them a 'pro forma invoice'. Regardless of what you call the document – QuickBooks has the same process.

To rename the sales order (estimate) as a 'Proforma Invoice'.
1 From the Home menu, click '+' at the top of the page in the middle, and click Estimates.
2 Click customize button at the bottom, select Header.

3 Under 'form names' change the Estimate name to 'Proforma Invoice'.

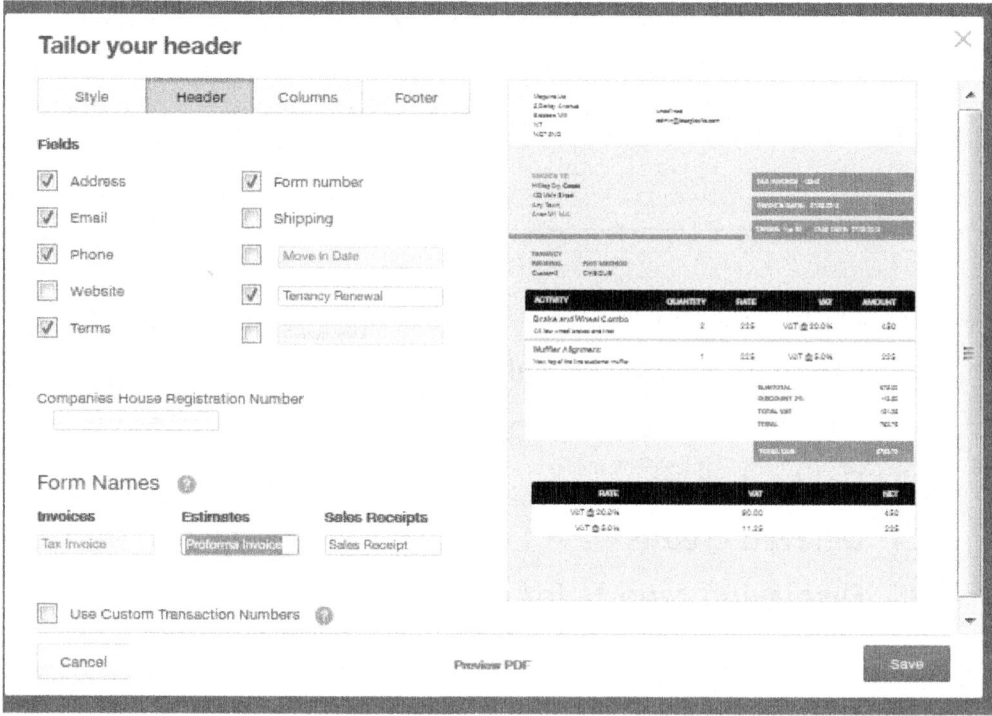

4 Save

Now, when the estimate is printed, the words 'proforma invoice' will be printed (see example:

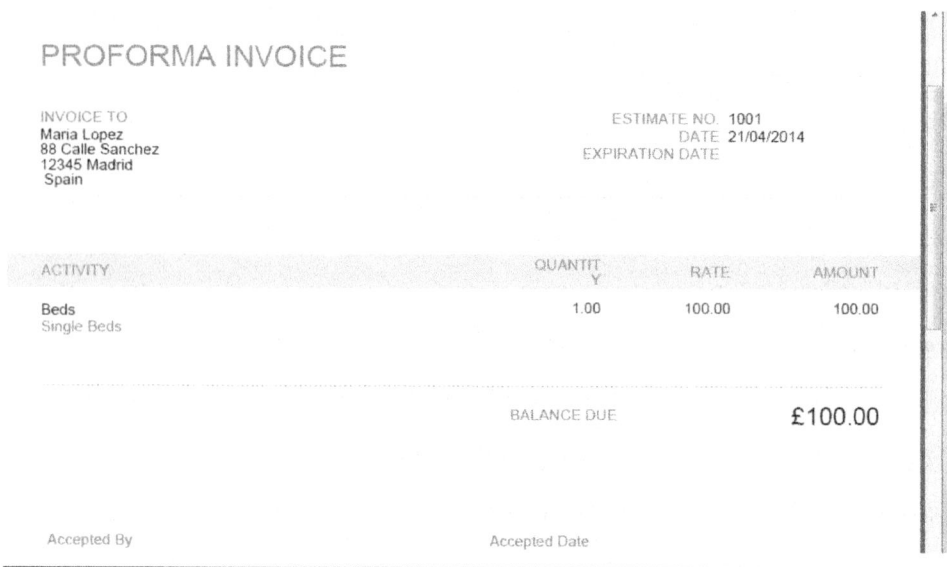

15.2 Creating an invoice from an estimate

If the customer accepts this estimate / pro forma invoice, you can turn it into an invoice and modify it as necessary.

To use an estimate to invoice a customer:

1 Click *customers* from the menu on the left hand side of the screen.
2 Click on the name of your customer in question e.g. *Maria Lopez.*
3 For the estimate/pro forma invoice which we've just created above, on the line, where the TYPE: Estimate is, under ACTION click *Start Invoice* :

4 Save and close.

15.3 Delayed charge

The delayed charge is a way to calculate charges and running total prior to adding everything to an invoice.

To enter a Delayed Charge:
1 From the Home menu, click '+' at the top of the page in the middle, and click Delayed Charge.
2 Choose customer: *Maria Lopez*
3 Product/Service: Hours, Quantity: 2, Rate: 20, VAT: 0% ECG.

QuickBooks Online Help

4 The Form will look like this below:

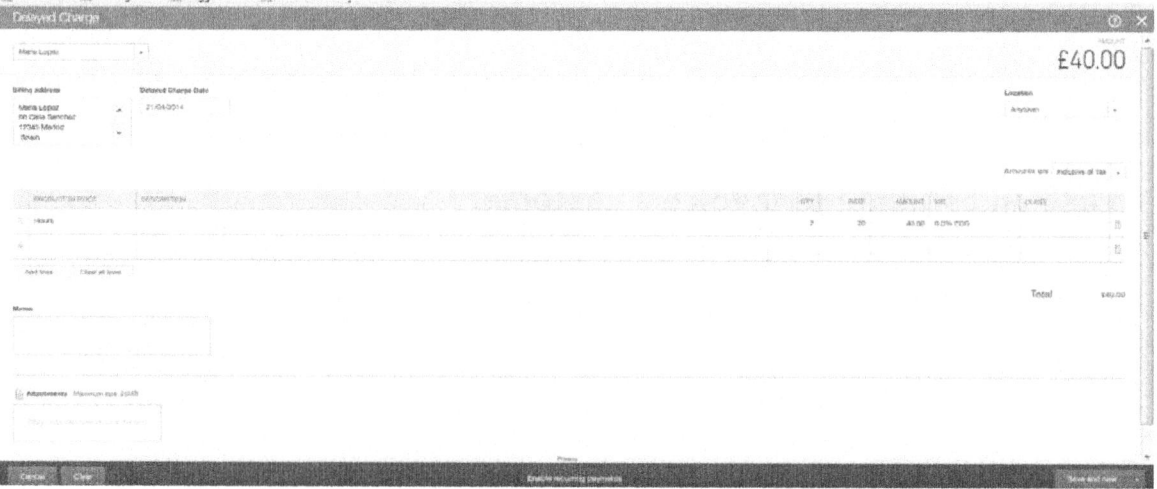

5 Save and close.

If you look at customer Maria – you will see that her pending invoice is unaffected. It remains unchanged. The delayed charge doesn't show as a balance owing on her customer account.

You can use the delayed charge to keep a running total. When you are ready to invoice the customer, you will have all the information ready.

To invoice a customer from a delayed charge:

1 Click *customers* from the menu on the left hand side of the screen.

2 Click on the name of your customer in question e.g. *Maria Lopez*.

3 For the delayed charge which we've just created above, on the line, where the TYPE: Charge is, under ACTION click *Start Invoice* :

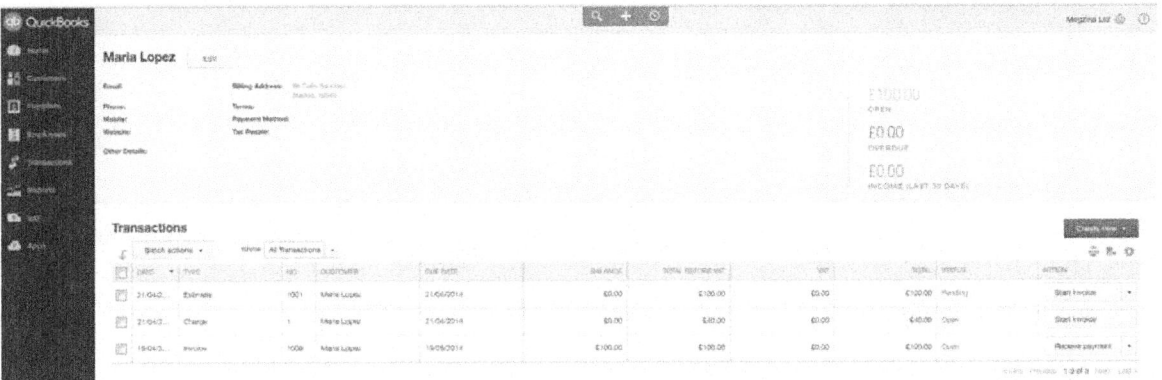

4 Click save and close.

15.3 Delayed credits

The delayed credit is a way to calculate credits and running total prior to adding everything to a credit note.

To enter a Delayed Credit:

1 From the Home menu, click '+' at the top of the page in the middle, and click Delayed Credit.

2 Choose customer: *Maria Lopez*

3 Product/Service: Hours, Quantity: 0.5, Rate: 20, VAT: 0% ECG.

4 The Form will look like this below:

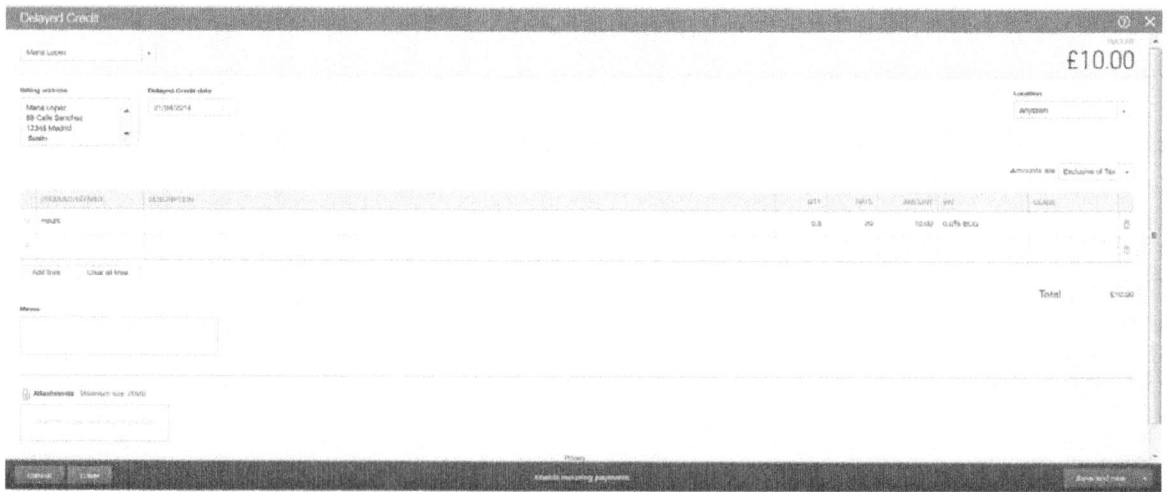

5 Save and close.

You can use the delayed credit to keep a running total. When you are ready to send a credit memo to the customer, you will have all the information ready.

To send a credit memo to a customer from a delayed credit:
1 Click *customers* from the menu on the left hand side of the screen.
2 Click on the name of your customer in question e.g. *Maria Lopez*.
3 For the delayed credit which we've just created above, on the line, where the TYPE: Credit is, under ACTION click *Start Invoice* :

4 Click save and close.

15.5 Displaying reports for estimates

Although the estimate itself doesn't affect the financial reports (it's a non-posting transaction), it can be very useful to know how much is outstanding as an estimate. It could be viewed a 'unbilled' invoices.

1 On the far left hand side, click Reports.
2 In the search bar type in *Estimates* and *estimates by customer* option will appear. Click search.

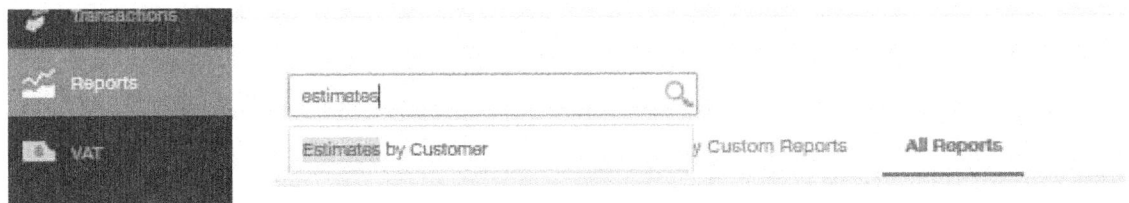

3 A report will appear.

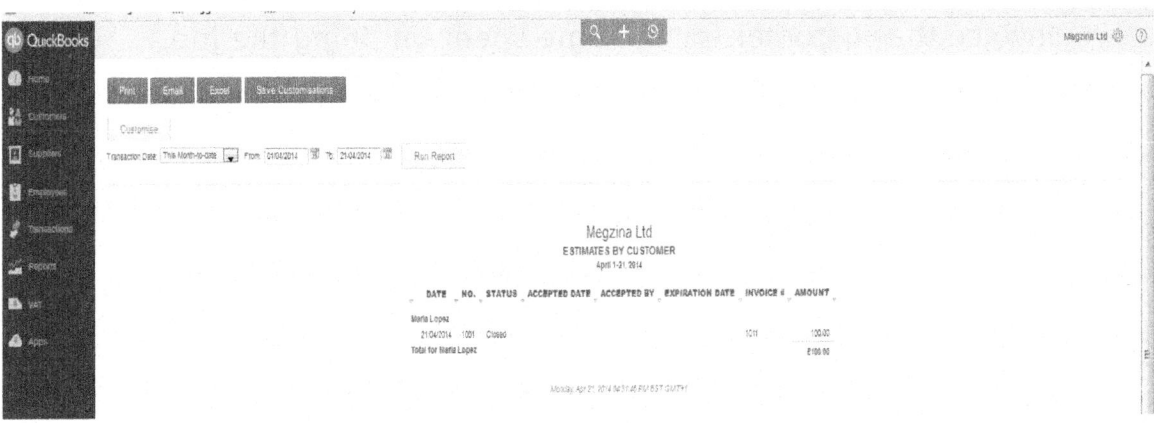

16: Tracking time

> *Summary of what is in this chapter:*
> 16.1 Tracking time
> 16.2 Weekly Timesheet
> 16.3 Invoicing a customer from a Timesheet
> 16.4 Single Time Activity
> 16.5 Displaying project reports for time tracking

16.1 Tracking time

QuickBooks online lets you keep track of the time a person spends on each job. The person could be an employee or subcontractor or owner of the business. You can use time data to:

- Invoice the customer for the time spent on doing the job.
- Report on the number of hours worked – by person or by the customer's job.
- Provide hours worked on an employee's pay cheque, or a cheque to a non-employee (subcontractors, owner, supplier)

Turn on time tracking in QuickBooks
In order to use time tracking, you must first switch it on.

To turn on time tracking:

1 From the top right hand corner, click on the COG / wheel next to the business name.

2 Choose Company Settings.

3 Click Time Tracking, under the Advanced menu.

4 Edit the two options to ON – for: Add Service field to timesheets & Add Customer field to timesheets. Click Save.

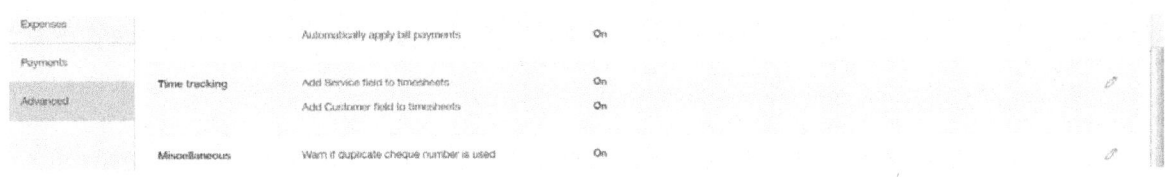

5 Click Done.

Entering time data in QuickBooks

When you track time with QuickBooks, you have a choice of two forms to enter time:
- Weekly Timesheet or
- Single Time Activity

If you want to enter time for multiple days or multiple jobs, then the best one to go for, is the Weekly Timesheet.

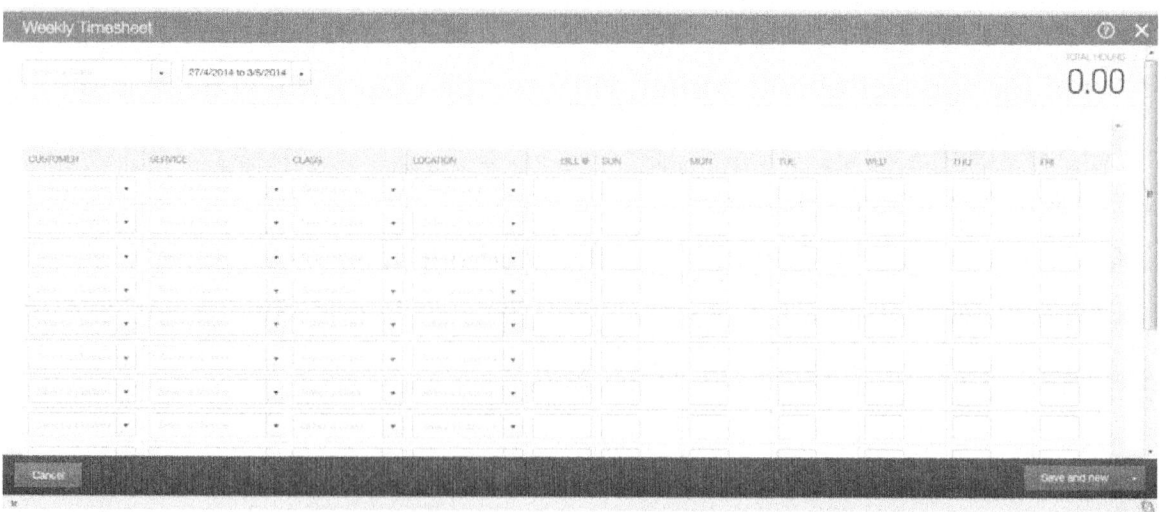

If you tend to enter detailed notes about your activities, or you prefer to enter time data as you complete an activity, use the Single Time Activity form instead.

Information you enter in the Time Activity form displays in the weekly timesheet and vice versa. They're simply different views of the same information.

16.2 Weekly Timesheet

Recording employee time on a weekly timesheet
We shall complete a weekly timesheet for a Chris Jones. And later in this chapter, we'll invoice a customer for the time Chris spent working on a job for that customer.

To enter information on a weekly timesheet:
1 From the home page, click on the "+" and choose Weekly Timesheet from under the employees menu. By default the weekly timesheet form appears. The week begins on a Sunday. If you want to change this, go to Company Settings, and under Advanced > Time Tracking, change the day of the: First day of work week to one of your choice. The current week is displayed by default: 27 April 2014 – 03 May 2014.

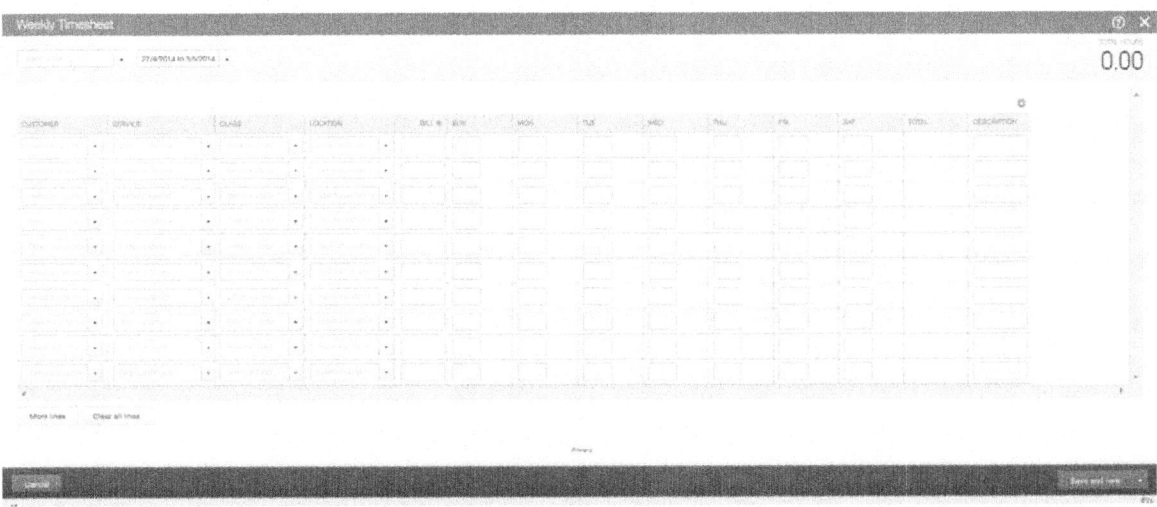

2 In the Select A Name field, click "+ Add New" and type in the name Chris Jones. Type: Supplier. Click Save.

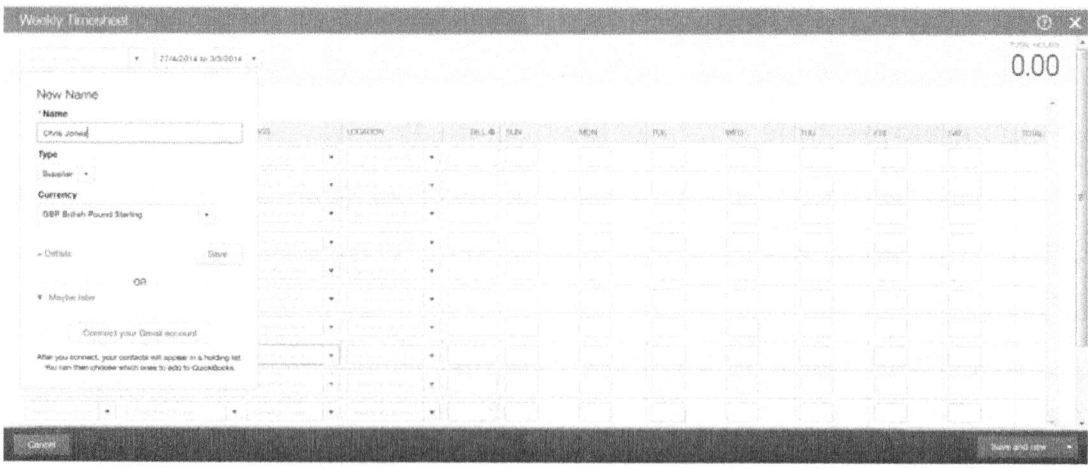

3 QuickBooks will track the time you enter for this supplier and display it when you are ready to pay this supplier.

4 In the Customer field, click 'Add new' and create a customer called Kelly King. Click Save. Tab to the next field (Service).

5 In the Service field, click 'Add New' and tick I sell this product/service to my customers. For Description on sales forms, type in 'Tiling'. Price/rate 40.00. Income account: sales.

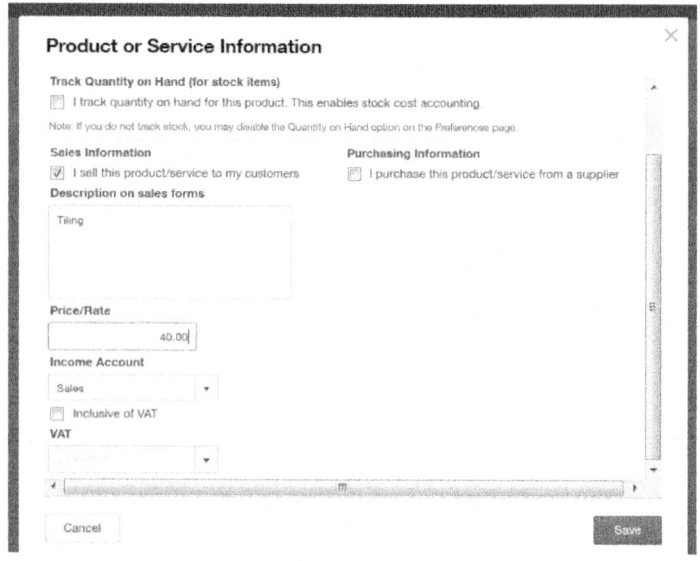

6 Click save.

7 Tab through to location, choose Anytown.

8 In Monday type 4.25 hours (this will automatically revert to 4:15 i.e. 4 hours 14 mins); For Tuesday type 5.5 (this will automatically revert to 5:30 i.e. 5 hours 30 mins). The total at the end of the line will say 9:45.

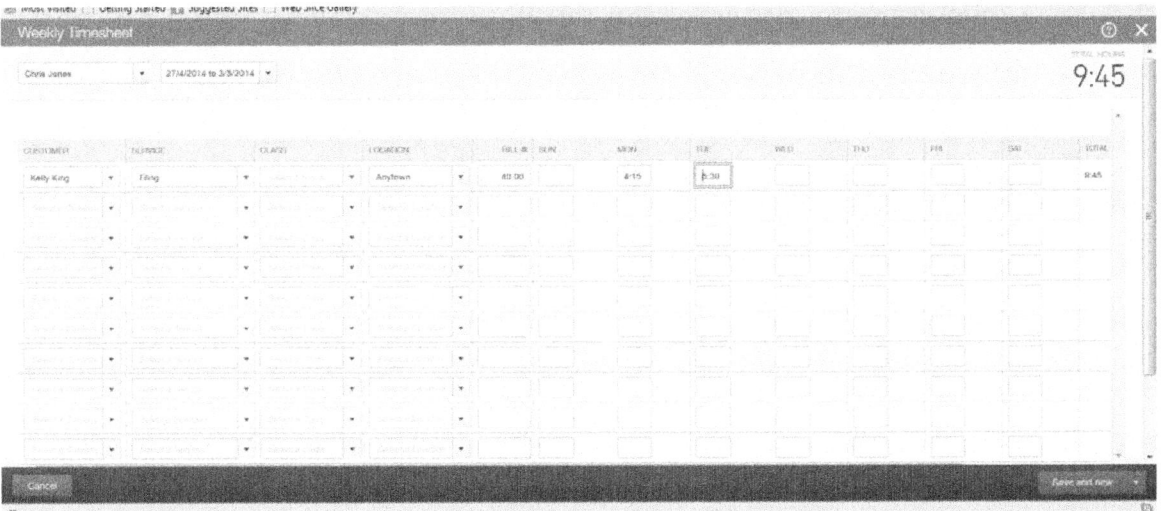

9 Click Save and Close to record the weekly timesheet.

QuickBooks has now recorded the hours that Chris Jones has worked for Kelly King. This time can now be transferred onto an invoice for Kelly King.

16.3 Invoicing a customer from a timesheet

To invoice a customer (Kelly King) from a timesheet created:

1 We created a timesheet for one of our suppliers who worked on the Kelly King job. We now want to invoice Kelly.

QuickBooks Online Help

2 Customers > Kelly King > Create Invoice.

3 On the invoice page, outstanding unbilled items will be listed on the right hand side of the page. In this case, there are two items.

4 You can click on 'Open' to remind yourself of what the item is e.g.

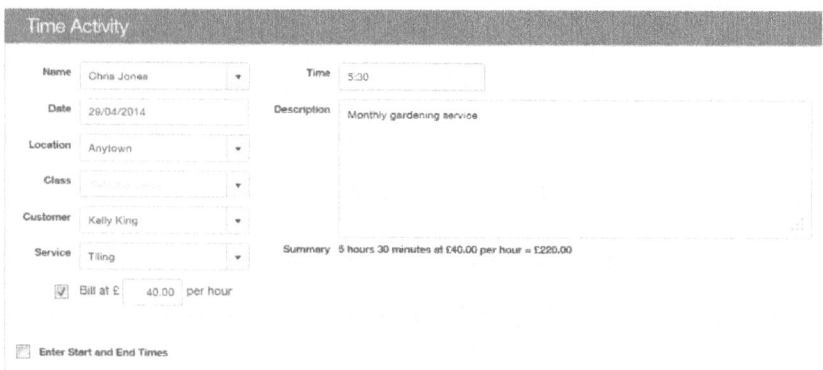

5 You even have the option (by ticking) to Enter Start and End Times. Click save and close to close this screen.

6 Click 'add' on both / all billable items. This will add the two items to the invoice.

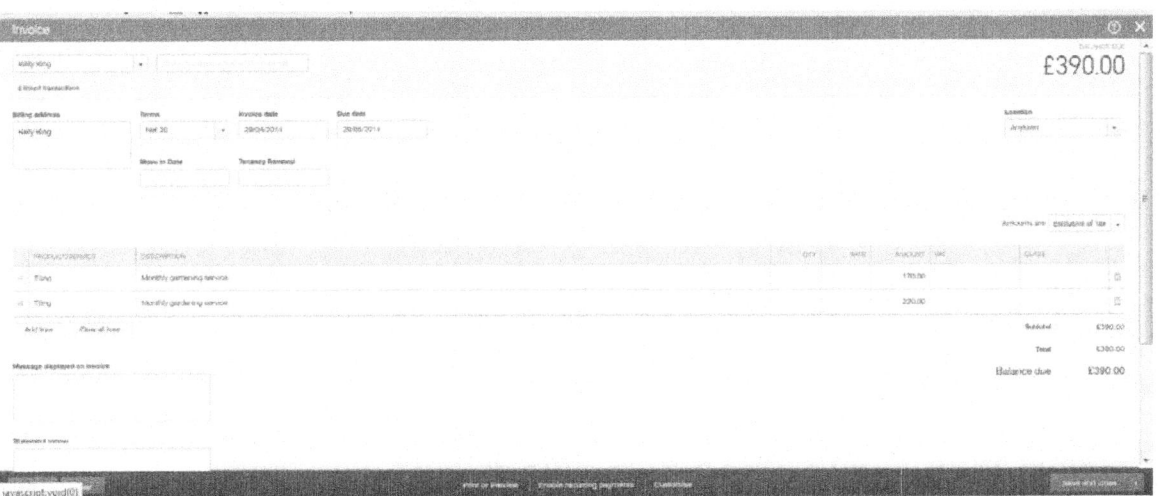

7 Click save and close.

8 Note, if you are VAT registered – you will have to allocate a VAT code to the transaction. In this case, its 20% VAT – (Standard VAT). The invoice looks like this:

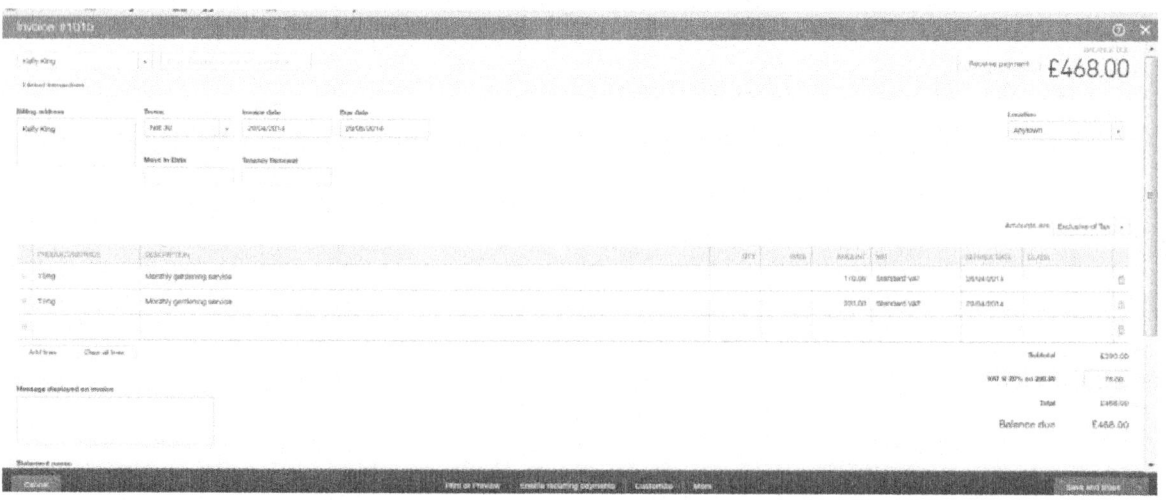

16.4 Single Time Activity

To enter information for a single time activity:

1 From the home page, click on the "+" and choose Single Time Activity from under the employees menu.
2 Name – choose Megzina Magic (employee created in an earlier chapter).
3 Date – 4th May 2014. Location: Anytown. Class: Office. Customer: Kelly King. Service: Gardening. Tick: Bill at 50.00 per hour.
4 Enter start and end times. Start: 10:00am. End: 11:00am. Break: 00:15.
5 The screen should resemble this:

6 Save and close.

16.5 Displaying project reports for time tracking

QuickBooks provides 4 reports on time. You can create these reports by going to reports on the left side menu bar and typing in Time.

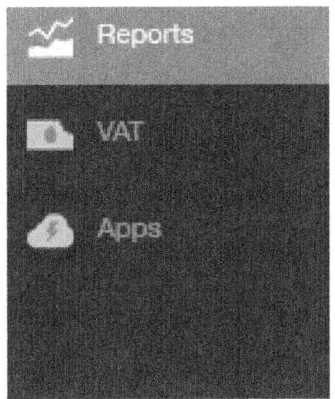 

1 Recent / Edited Time Activities

Lists the 25 products/services (time activities) most recently entered or edited so you can see your employees' latest activities.

Megzina Ltd
RECENT/EDITED TIME ACTIVITIES
Created/Edited: Since April 3, 2014

ACTIVITY DATE	LAST MODIFIED	CLIENT	EMPLOYEE	PRODUCT/SERVICE	MEMO/DESCRIPTION	RATES	DURATION	BILLABLE	AMOUNT
29/04/2014	03/05/2014 06:52:22 PM BST	Kelly King	Chris Jones	Tiling	Monthly gardening service	40.00	5:30	Yes	220.00
28/04/2014	03/05/2014 06:42:17 PM BST	Kelly King	Chris Jones	Tiling	Monthly gardening service	40.00	4:15	Yes	170.00

2 Time Activities by Customer Detail

Lists the products/services (time activities) your employees provided to each customer.

Megzina Ltd
TIME ACTIVITIES BY CUSTOMER DETAIL
Activity: April 2014

ACTIVITY DATE	EMPLOYEE	PRODUCT/SERVICE	MEMO/DESCRIPTION	RATES	DURATION	BILLABLE	AMOUNT
Kelly King							
28/04/2014	Chris Jones	Tiling	Monthly gardening service	40.00	4:15	Yes	170.00
29/04/2014	Chris Jones	Tiling	Monthly gardening service	40.00	5:30	Yes	220.00
Total for Kelly King					9:45		£390.00

3 Time Activities by Employee Detail

Lists the products/services (time activities) provided by each employee, including hourly rate and duration. Note that it's not just employees, but suppliers who show up in this report too.

Megzina Ltd
TIME ACTIVITIES BY EMPLOYEE DETAIL
Activity: April 2014

ACTIVITY DATE	CLIENT	PRODUCT/SERVICE	MEMO/DESCRIPTION	RATES	DURATION	BILLABLE	AMOUNT
Chris Jones							
28/04/2014	Kelly King	Tiling	Monthly gardening service	40.00	4:15	Yes	170.00
29/04/2014	Kelly King	Tiling	Monthly gardening service	40.00	5:30	Yes	220.00
Total for Chris Jones					9:45		£390.00

4 Unbilled Time

Lists products/services (time activities) provided by your employees that have not yet been billed.

Megzina Ltd
UNBILLED TIME
Activity: All Dates

ACTIVITY DATE	POSTING	EMPLOYEE	MEMO/DESCRIPTION	RATE	DURATION	AMOUNT	BALANCE

This report contains no data.

17: Using multiple currencies

Summary of what is in this chapter:

17.1 Turning on multicurrency

17.2 Updating the Currency list

17.3 Setting up foreign accounts

17.4 Creating foreign customers and suppliers

17.5 Creating a foreign invoice

17.6 Entering and paying foreign bills

17.7 Exchange rate gain and losses report

17.1 Turning on multicurrency

If you have customers or suppliers using foreign currencies, then it'll be useful to turn on the multicurrency function. Our home currency is GBP. 1 From the wheel/cog by the name of the company in the top right hand corner, click on the wheel, and under Settings select Currency Centre.

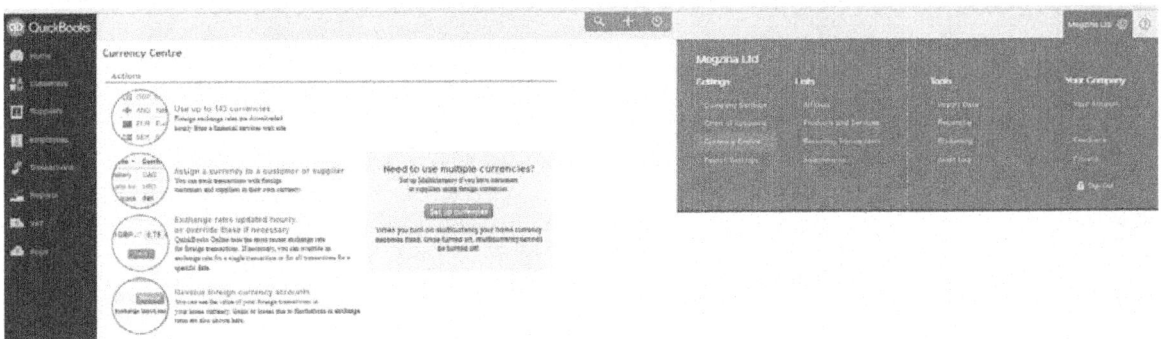

2 Click the blue button – *set up currencies*. Beware: When you turn on multicurrency, your home currency becomes fixed. Once turned on, multicurrency cannot be turned off.

3 QuickBooks online lists 3 currencies – GBP, EUR and USD.

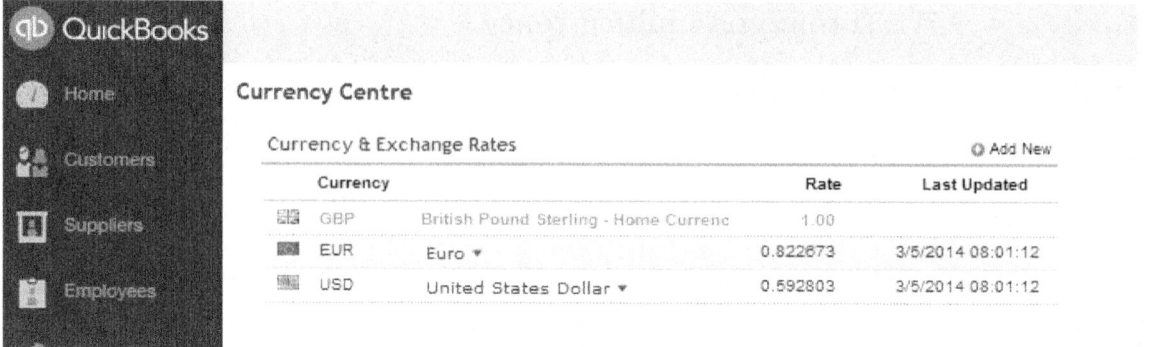

17.2 Updating the Currency list

1 From the currency centre, click "Add New."

2 From the drop down menu add the currency you'd like to add. Choose AUD (Australian Dollar). Add New.

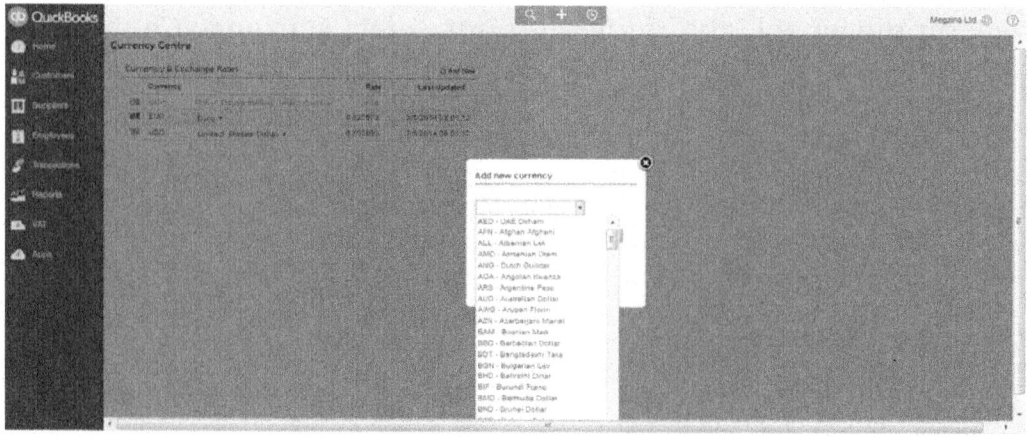

3 If you want to adjust the currency exchange rate – click on the currency (on the down arrow), and the option 'Edit Currency' is displayed.

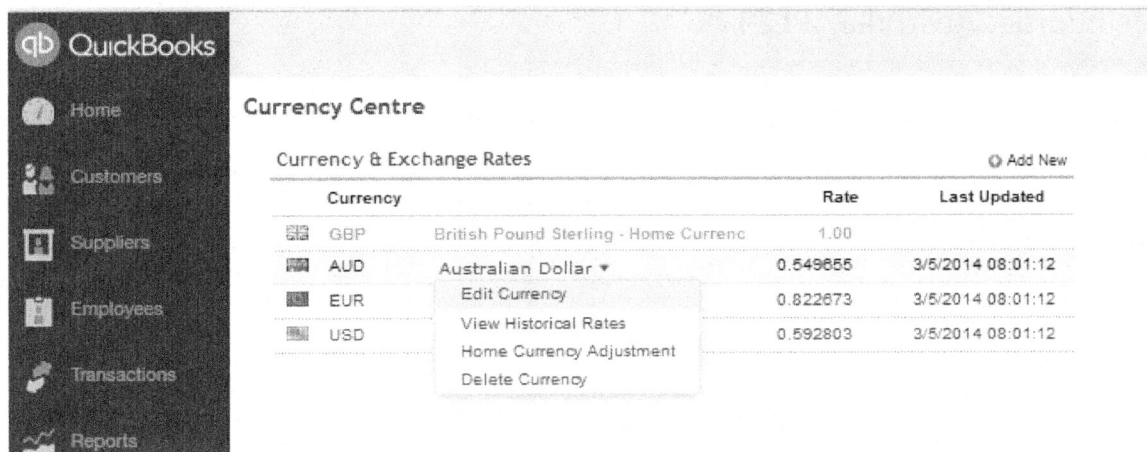

4 On the pop up screen, amend the exchange rate.

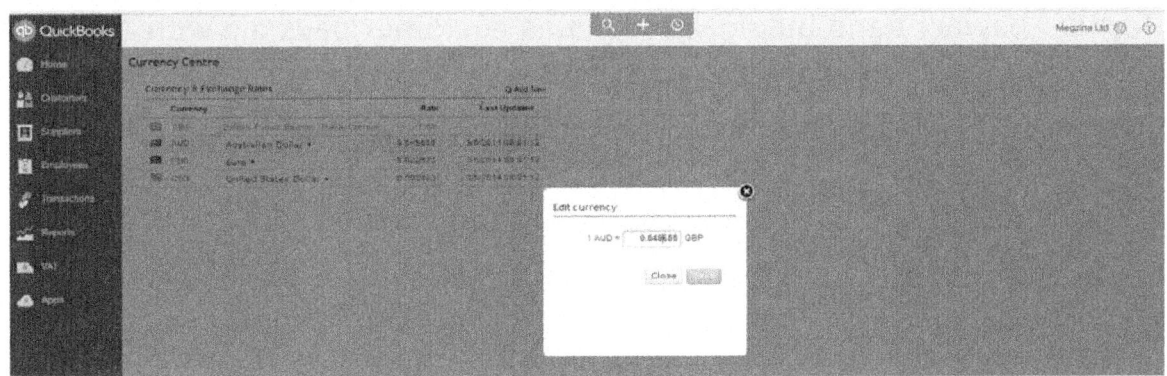

5 Click save.

17.3 Setting up foreign accounts (Customers)

Now that multi currency is switched on, we can set up foreign accounts for customers and suppliers in their home currency.

To set up a foreign customer:

QuickBooks Online Help

1 Go to customers > New Customers

2 Create a New Customer called: Kylie Scott. 10 Ramsay Street, Melbourne, Australia, A12345

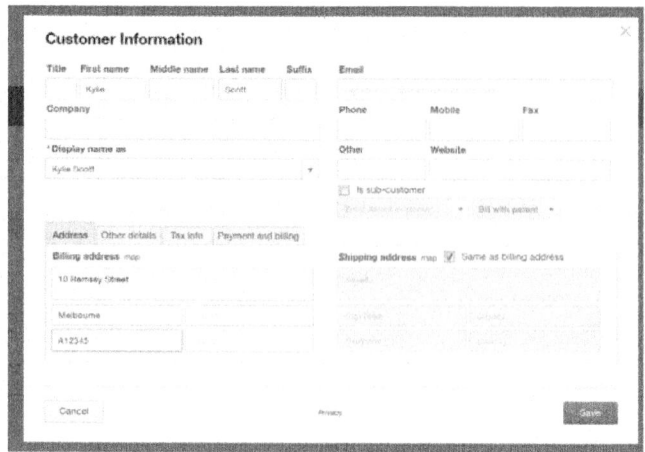

3 Under payment and billing, choose this customer pays me with AUD.

3 Click save.

17.4 Creating foreign suppliers

To set up a foreign supplier:

1 Go to Suppliers > New Supplier

2 Create a New Customer called: Harold Bishop. Bishop Ltd. 88 Cathedral Way, Melbourne, Australia, A67890. Choose: I pay this customer with AUD.

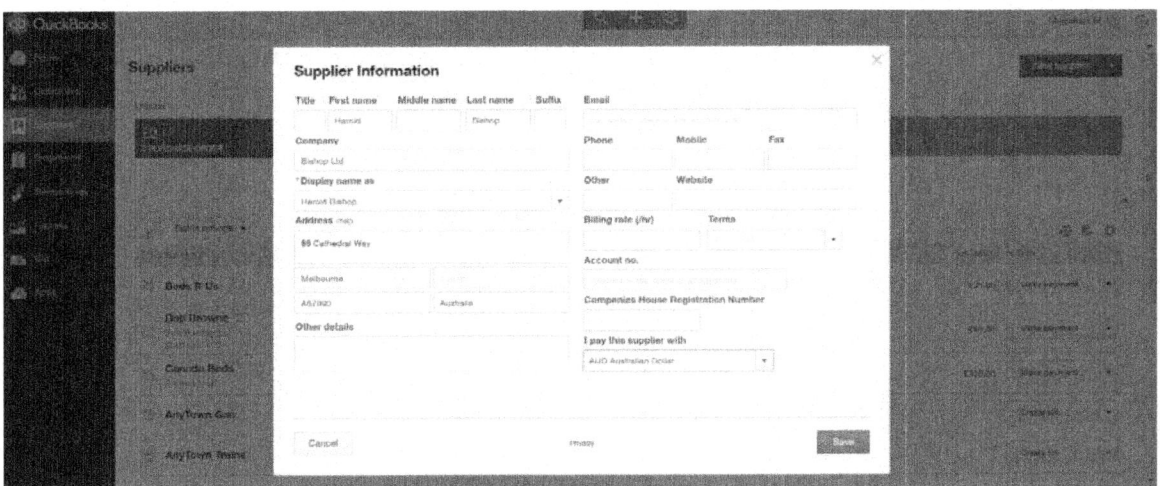

3 Click save.

17.5 Creating a foreign invoice

To create a foreign invoice:

1 Click Customers > choose Kylie Scott (our Australian customer created in 17.3) and click Invoice Customer. The screen which appears is almost identical to the GBP invoice, accept the foreign currency will be shown, and so will the exchange rate.

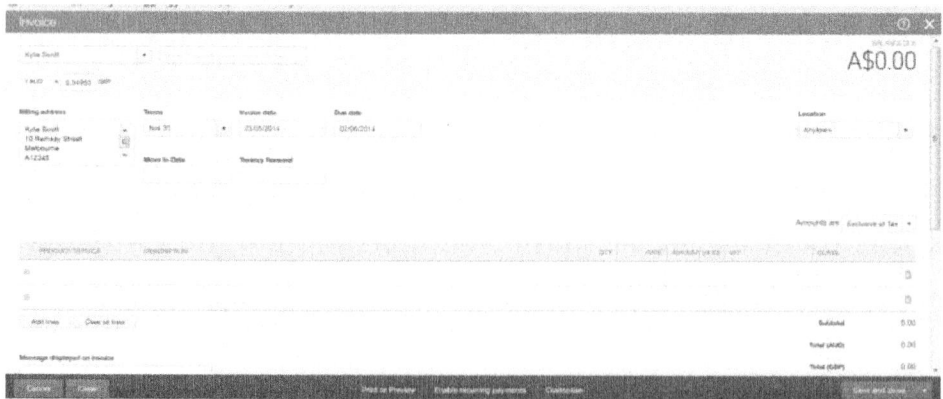

2 Create a new service called 'Removals'. The description is: international removals. Enter the price/rate as 200.00. Click save.

3 This amount is then converted to AUD as at the exchange rate the system has stored. You can manually change the exchange rate in the top left hand corner. QuickBooks will prompt you to ask whether you want the exchange rate to apply for just this transaction or all transactions for AUD going forward.

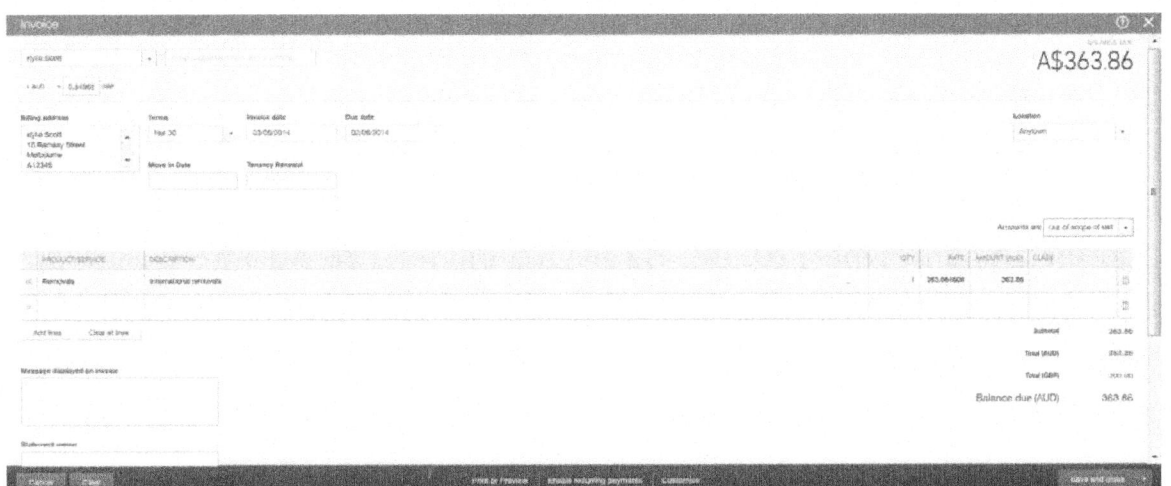

4 Choose the correct VAT if applicable. Save and close.

QuickBooks automatically converts foreign amounts for reports.

This customer balance report shows Kylie King as owing £200.00.

17.6 Entering and paying foreign bills

To enter a foreign bill:

1 Click Suppliers > choose Harold Bishop (our Australian supplier created in 17.4) and click create bill. The screen which appears is almost identical

to the GBP bill, accept the foreign currency will be shown, and so will the exchange rate.

2 Choose Computer and Internet Expenses. In the description, type – copywriter.

3 In the amount, type 120. (We received a bill for 120 AUD from Harold).

4 It's bill no. 569. The bill is outside the scope of VAT. And we class this as 'office'. The screen should resemble this:

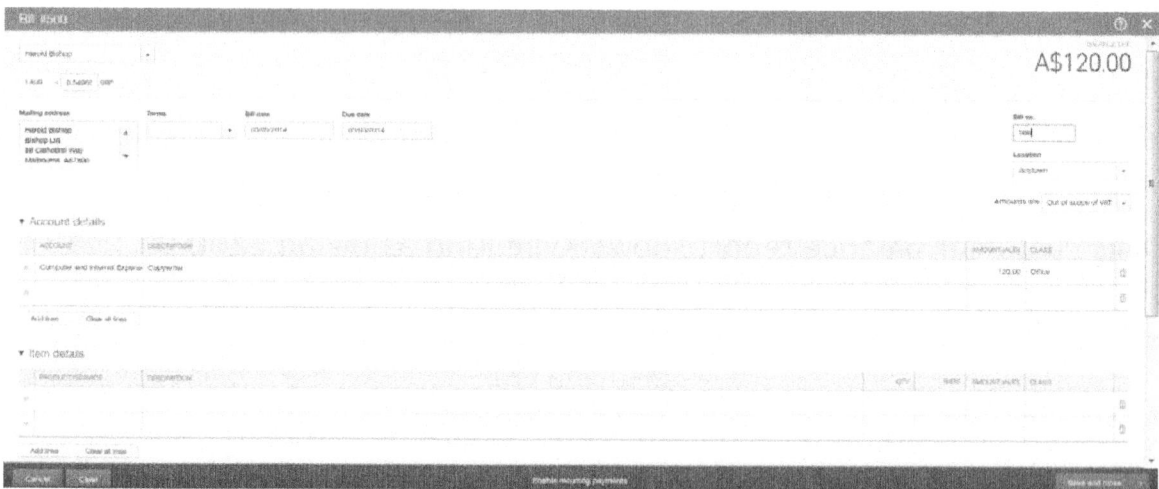

5 Click save and close.

To pay a foreign bill:

1 From the suppliers menu, click on Harold Bishop and Make A Payment. This screen will show:

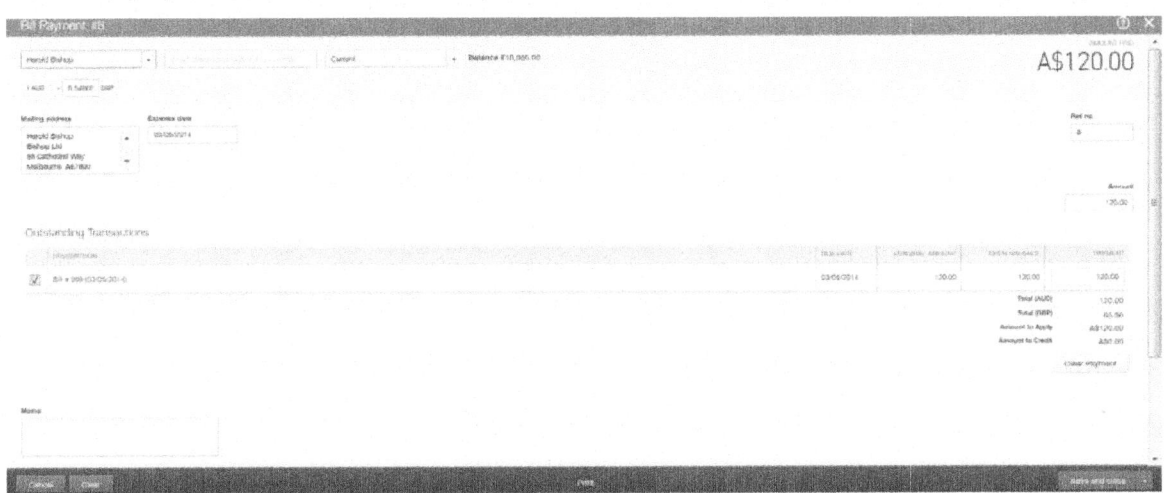

2 This bill is being paid from the Current Account. The currency (exchange rate) is shown as 1 AUD = 0.549655. Currently, the GBP amount is £65.96.

3 If the exchange rate had changed (the pound had weakened against the Australian Dollar) – the actual amount we'd end up paying would increase. For example, change the exchange rate to 0.58. QuickBooks asks us whether we want to save this new exchange rate for all transactions or just this one. Choose only this transaction. Click OK.

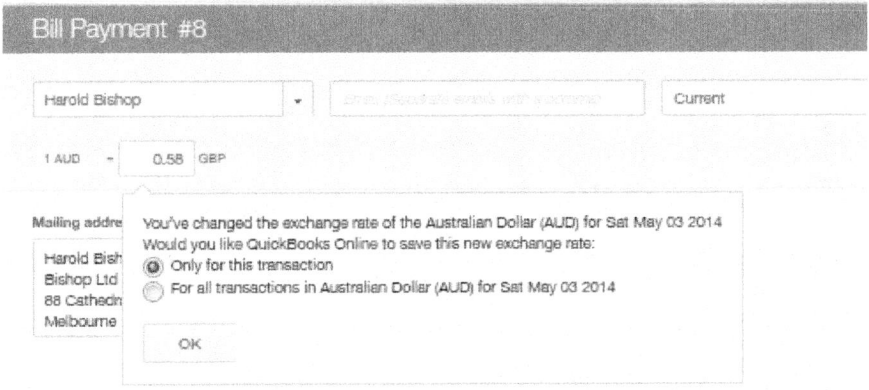

4 The amount we're now paying is £69.60.

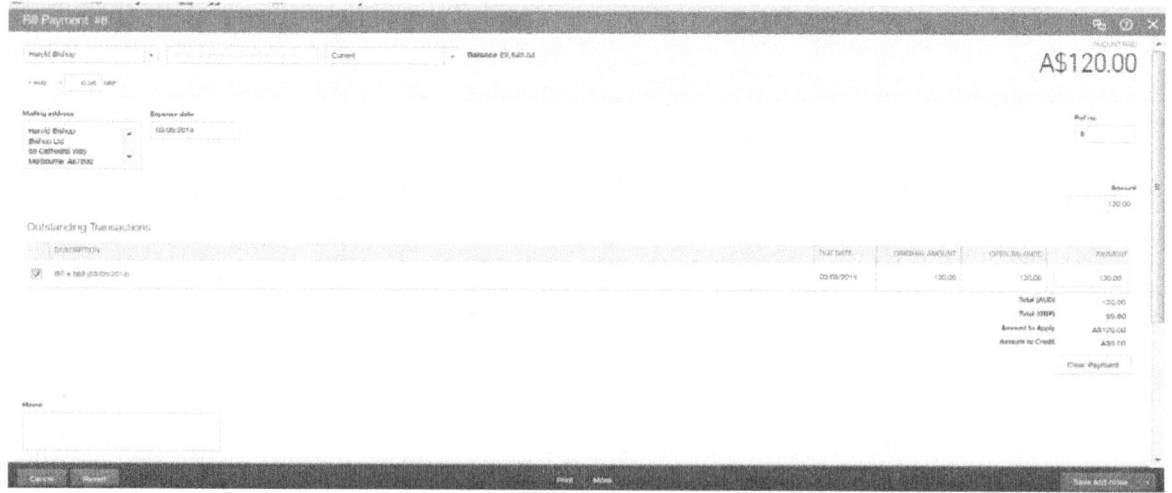

5 Click save and close.

17.7 Exchange rate gain and losses report

If you do business in foreign currencies, changes in exchange rates produce two types of gains and losses:

- **Unrealised** gains and losses - arise on transactions that haven't been completed.
- **Realised** gains and losses - arise once transactions have been completed.

You can run a report for both of the above:
1 Click on Reports from the left hand menu. Type in 'Gains' and look at two reports available:
    1 Realised Exchange Gains & Losses
    2 Unrealised Exchange Gains & Losses

Realised Exchange Gains and Losses - Report

This shows that in our example, for Harold Bishop, we realised a loss of £3.64 due to the exchange rate moving against us.

Megzina Ltd
REALISED EXCHANGE GAINS & LOSSES
May 1-3, 2014

TRANSACTION TYPE	DATE	NAME	CURRENCY	EXCHANGE RATE	REALISED GAIN/LOSS	BALANCE
Bill Payment (Cheque)	03/05/2014	Harold Bishop	AUD	0.58	-3.64	-3.64
TOTAL					£ -3.64	

18: Tracking Finance

Summary of what is in this chapter:
- 18.1 Tracking Finances
- 18.2 Budgeting
- 18.3 Searching transactions

18.1 Tracking finances

QuickBooks has various features which can help you to track and plan the finances of your company.

Statement of Cash Flows Report
1. On the left **Navigation Panel** select **Reports.**
2. On the next screen select the header titled **All Reports**.
3. You should see in the list below the headers an option for **Accountant Reports**, select that option and you should see the **Statement of Cash Flows** report.

This report shows cash generated by your business (operating activities), cash spent on your business (investments) and cash in or out from stock and dividends (financing). Cash is the lifeblood of your business. You need 'cash' to pay people... for staff, your suppliers and your taxes. This report will help you to see how you've been using your cash, and from this you can plan accordingly.

Megzina Ltd
STATEMENT OF CASH FLOWS
January 1 - April 25, 2014

	TOTAL
OPERATING ACTIVITIES	
Net Income	281.67
Adjustments to reconcile Net Income to Net Cash provided by operations:	
Debtors	-330.00
Prepaid Expenses	-3,000.00
Stock Asset	-420.00
Laptop - Office:Depreciation	250.00
Creditors	465.00
ATBC Credit Card	0.00
VAT Control	10.00
VAT Suspense	0.00
ATBC Bank Loan	9,833.33
Net cash provided by operating activities	£7,090.00
FINANCING ACTIVITIES	
Opening Balance Equity	2,976.00
Net cash provided by financing activities	£2,976.00
Net cash increase for period	£10,066.00
Cash at end of period	£10,066.00

18.2 Budgeting

It's important to be able to assess the position that we're in but it's also handy to set goals for the business and to then compare the actual position to the budgeted position. A budget is simply a plan of the anticipated monies coming in and out. In QuickBooks Online Plus, you can create Profit and Loss budgets, which track amounts in income and expense accounts.

To create a budget
1 Click on the COG next to the company name.
2 Choose *Budgeting*, under the Tools menu.

A mini interview screen will them pop up. You have the option to:

1. Create the budget from **scratch**, or from **historical amounts**.
2. Choose whether to **subdivide** your budget based on location, class, or customer.
3. Choose a financial year, and give your budget a unique name.

Before you get started, check the following settings:

- Make sure your financial year starts with the correct month. You can find the Financial Year setting in the Company section of Preferences.
- If you plan to create a budget from historical data, you can run a Profit and Loss Detail report to check that transactions have been assigned to the correct income and expense accounts.

3 Click Next.

4 You'll be given 3 options. Start the budget from:

   a) Actual amounts from either this financial year or last financial year
   b) Scratch. No amounts.
   c) Copy from an existing budget.

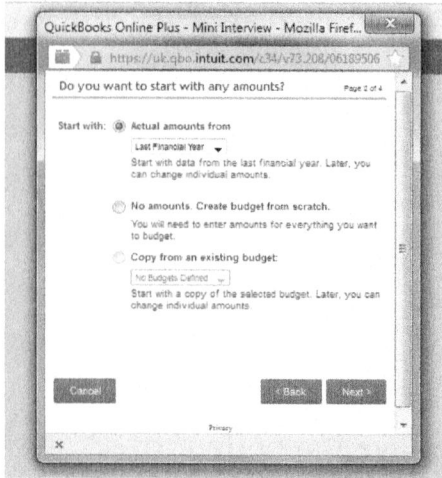

Choose to start the budget from scratch and click *Next*.

5 Every budget tracks amounts in at least two dimensions: accounts and months. You can add a third dimension to your budget by subdividing it. This lets you track separate amounts for each location, each class, or each customer. Click classes. Click Next.

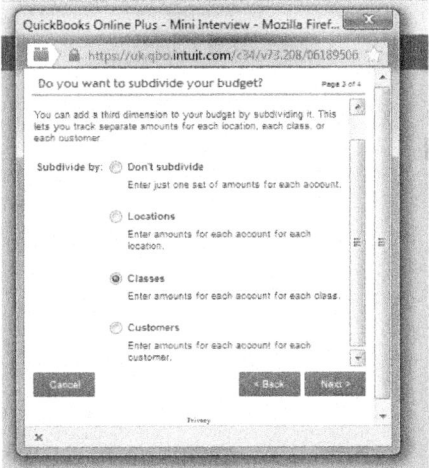

6 Select the financial year from the drop down menu to track for this budget. If the financial year doesn't start with the right month, cancel this interview and go to Preferences. You can change the first month of your financial year in the Company section of Preferences. Click this current financial year e.g. *FY2014 (Jan 2014 - Dec 2014)*.

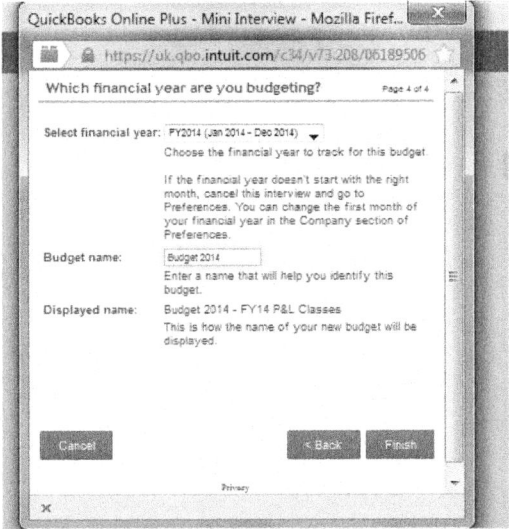

7 Budget name - type in a name for your budget e.g. *Budget 2014.*

8 Displayed name – this is how your budget will be displayed e.g. *Budget 2014 - FY14 P&L Classes.*

9 Click *Finish.*

10 Your template budget will be displayed:

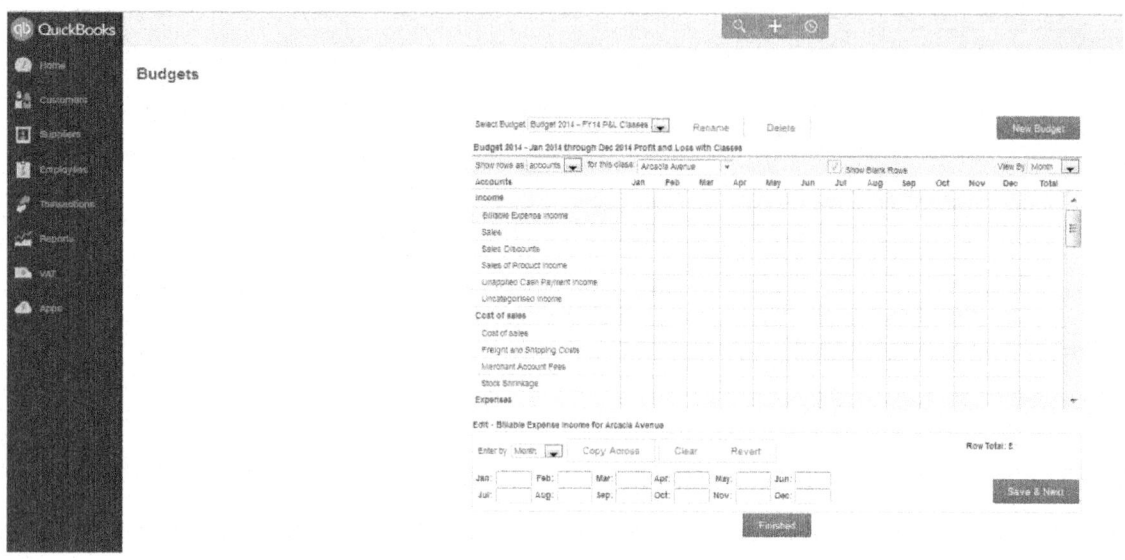

11 Currently, the class showing is Arcacia Avenue, and view is by the month. If we expect sales for the class: Arcacia Avenue to be 1000 per month, we'd click in the square January & Sales and type in 1000. This figure automatically jumps into the January box in the bottom left hand corner.

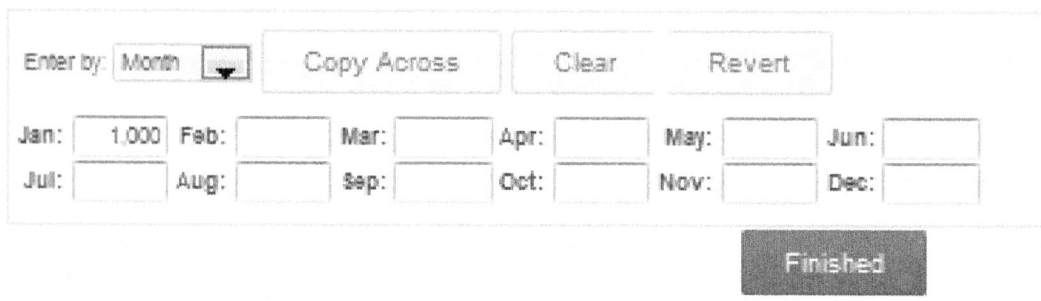

12 Click Copy Across and all months have 1000.

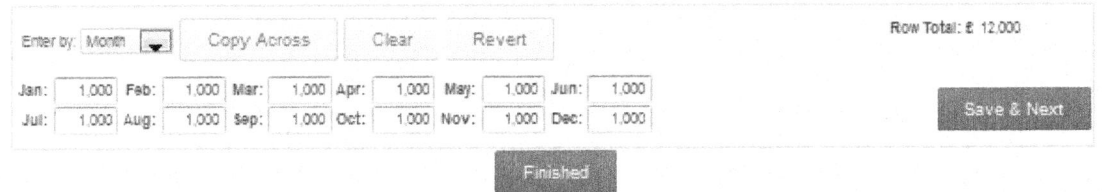

13 The Row Total is automatically calculated to £12000. You can amend any one month individually. Once happy with the figures, click Save & Next.

14 These figures are then imported into the budget.

15 Repeat this process with every line.

16 Once finished, click Finished.

17 You can return to the budget to amend it at any point by clicking on the COG next to the company name. And Choosing *Budgeting*, under the Tools menu.

QuickBooks Online Help

To run a budget report

1 Click on Reports on the far left hand menu.

2 In the search box, type in **Budget.**

3 Two options are displayed: Budget Overview and Budget vs. Actuals. Click Budget Overview.

4 This gives you the budget report – which is the figures you have set.

Megzina Ltd
BUDGET OVERVIEW

	TOTAL
Income	
Sales	12,000.00
Uncategorised income	0.00
Total Income	£12,000.00
Gross Profit	£12,000.00
Expenses	
Total Expenses	
Net Operating Income	£12,000.00
Net Income	£12,000.00

5 Go back, and click Budget vs. Actuals.

Megzina Ltd
BUDGET VS. ACTUALS

	ACTUAL	BUDGET	OVER BUDGET	% OF BUDGET
Income				
Sales	340.00	12,000.00	-11,660.00	2.83333%
Sales of Product Income	200.00		200.00	
Uncategorised Income	0.00	0.00	0.00	
Total Income	£540.00	£12,000.00	£ -11,460.00	4.50%
Cost of Sales				
Cost of sales	70.00		70.00	
Stock Shrinkage	70.00		70.00	
Total Cost of Sales	£140.00	£0.00	£140.00	0.00%
Gross Profit	£400.00	£12,000.00	£ -11,600.00	3.33333%
Expenses				
Interest expense	17.58		17.58	
Motor Expenses	25.00		25.00	
Repair and maintenance	100.00		100.00	
Travel Expense	0.00		0.00	
Utilities	42.75		42.75	
Gas	78.00		78.00	
Total Utilities	120.75	0.00	120.75	0.00
Total Expenses	£263.33	£0.00	£263.33	0.00%
Net Operating Income	£136.67	£12,000.00	£ -11,863.33	1.13892%
Other Income				
Insurance Proceeds Received	260.00		260.00	
Total Other Income	£260.00	£0.00	£260.00	0.00%
Other Expenses				
Ask My Accountant	55.00		55.00	
Depreciation	50.00		50.00	
VAT adjustment	20.00		20.00	
Total Other Expenses	£125.00	£0.00	£125.00	0.00%
Net Other Income	£135.00	£0.00	£135.00	0.00%
Net Income	£271.67	£12,000.00	£ -11,728.33	2.26392%

This report compares the budgeted figures versus the actual figures for the reporting period in question. Plus, it also has a column which is the difference between these two columns (the total over budget), and the last column gives the percentage difference.

6 Note, if you click on Customise, you can customise this report, to add further detail, for example a further sub column with the money remaining and percentage remaining (of budget to be spent) and if you just want to show the rows which are mentioned in the budget, tick: *Only accounts with budgeted amounts.*

7 The report will then look like this:

Megzina Ltd
BUDGET VS. ACTUALS: BUDGET 2014 - FY14 P&L CLASSES
January - December 2014

	ACTUAL	BUDGET	OVER BUDGET	REMAINING	% OF BUDGET	% REMAINING
Income						
Sales	210.00	12,000.00	-11,790.00	11,790.00	1.75%	98.25%
Total Income	£210.00	£12,000.00	£ -11,790.00	£11,790.00	1.75%	98.25%
Gross Profit	£210.00	£12,000.00	£ -11,790.00	£11,790.00	1.75%	98.25%
Expenses						
Total Expenses			£0.00	£0.00	0.00%	0.00%
Net Operating Income	£210.00	£12,000.00	£ -11,790.00	£11,790.00	1.75%	98.25%
Net Income	£210.00	£12,000.00	£ -11,790.00	£11,790.00	1.75%	98.25%

8 Note – there are numerous combinations in which the report can be displayed. By month, by quarter, by totals etc., Experiment with what works best for you. And when you do find the best combination, click *Save Customisations.*

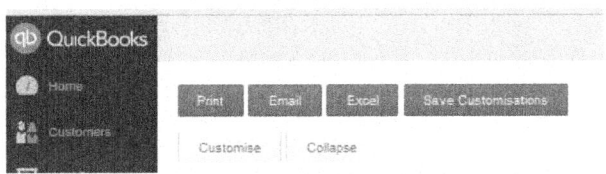

18.3 Searching transactions

Sometimes, we need to back track, and look through transactions that have been put into the system.

To search through transactions:
1 From the Home menu, click on the magnifying glass in the top middle of the search and the 'search transaction bar will open'.
2 To do an advanced search, click on the words 'Advanced Search' and further options will be displayed.

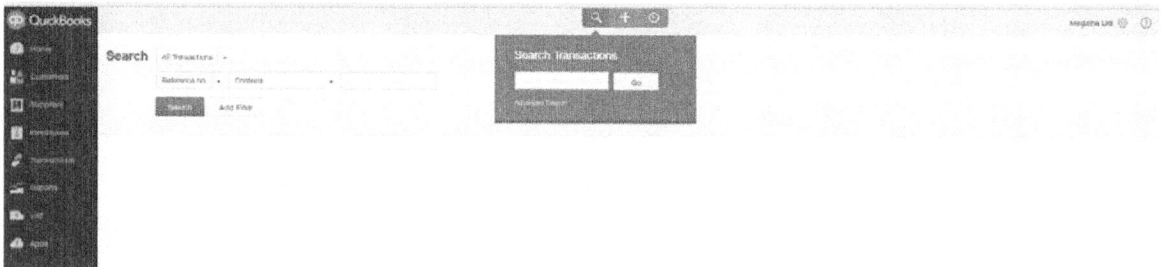

The advanced tool will give you further options. You can search 'all transactions' or (if you know it's a 'bill payment' that you want, you can just select 'Bill Payment' from the dropdown menu and QuickBooks will only search through bill payments – which will be a quicker search. You also have the option to search by amount, name, reference number and various other ways in which you may be able to identify the transaction.
3 Click search

For example – Bills > Supplier > contains or Equals Bob Browne bring up two transactions.

QuickBooks Online Help

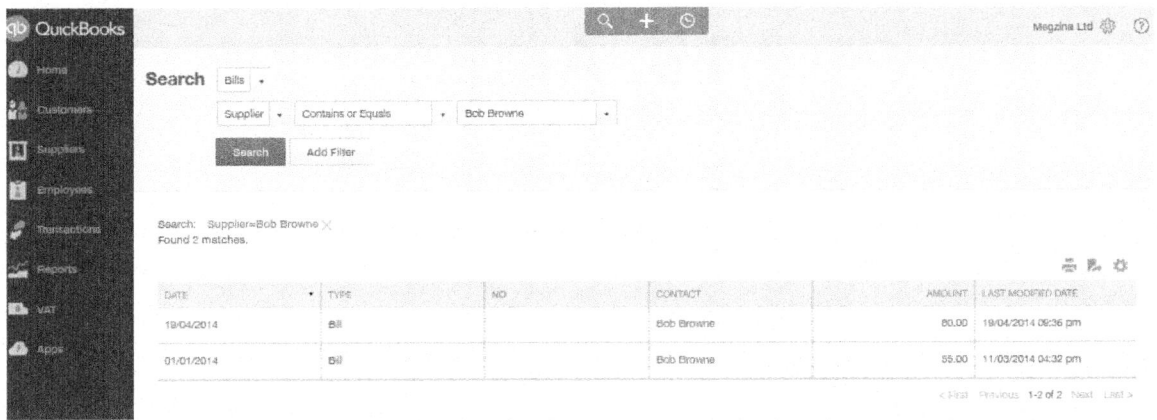

You can then click on a transaction to drill down into it, and it will be displayed on the screen.

e.g.

If there was an error on this form, this could be amended and saved. Otherwise, click Cancel.

19: Apps

Summary of what is in this chapter:
 19.1 Available Apps
 19.2 Import Data

19.1 Available Apps

QuickBooks has partnered with various applications (apps) which can integrate seamlessly with the software. QuickBooks Online is continuously improving, but it doesn't have every single feature which the desktop has, so various apps have been created to fill the gap.

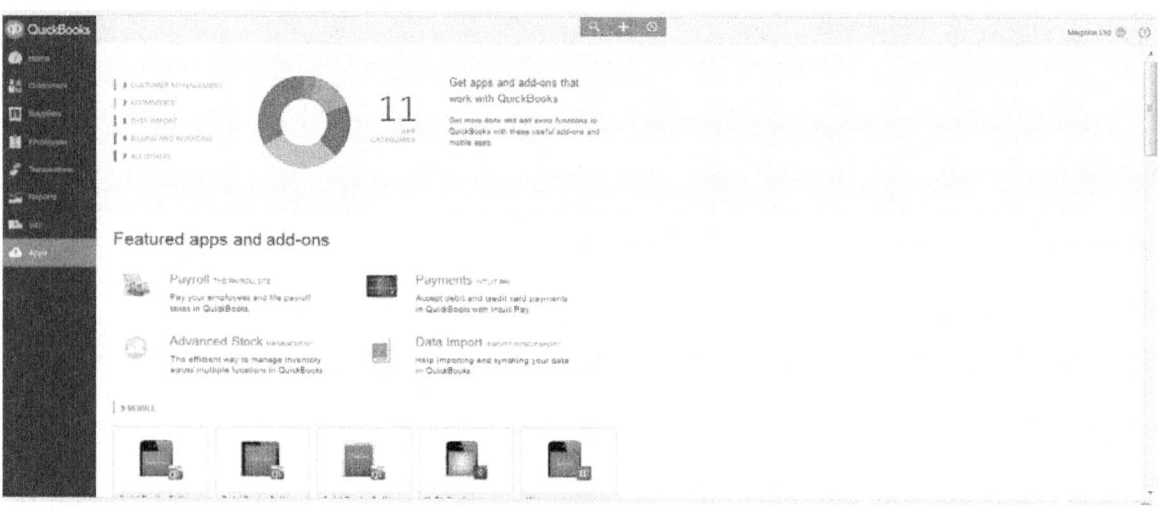

These apps are also handy for mobile devices. There's QuickBooks online for iPad, iPhone and Android.

The currently featured apps and add-ons are:
- Payroll
- Payments
- Advanced Stock
- Data Import

Payroll

If you click on the app – this takes you to the specific website. The payroll site is a site to calculate payroll.

Payments

If you are trading and want to be able to accept card payments (debit and credit card), sign up for Intuit Pay. There are card processing fees, but via intuit, you'll receive a card reader machine, and you'll be able to receive payments on the go.

Advanced Stock

This app gives you an efficient way to manage inventory across multiple locations in QuickBooks.

Data Import

If you click on this app, it takes you to the MoveMyBooks website, the data conversion partner of QuickBooks. This service enables you to import data (historical transactions) from UK versions of Sage and QuickBooks desktop to the UK version of QuickBooks Online.

19.2 Import Data

If you have been running a computerised system of some sort prior to using QuickBooks online, it is possible to be able to import data in and to not have to re-type it.

To import data

1 Click on the COG next to the company name.
2 Click Import *Data*, under Tools. A list of possible data types appears: Customers, Suppliers, Chart of Accounts and Products and Services.

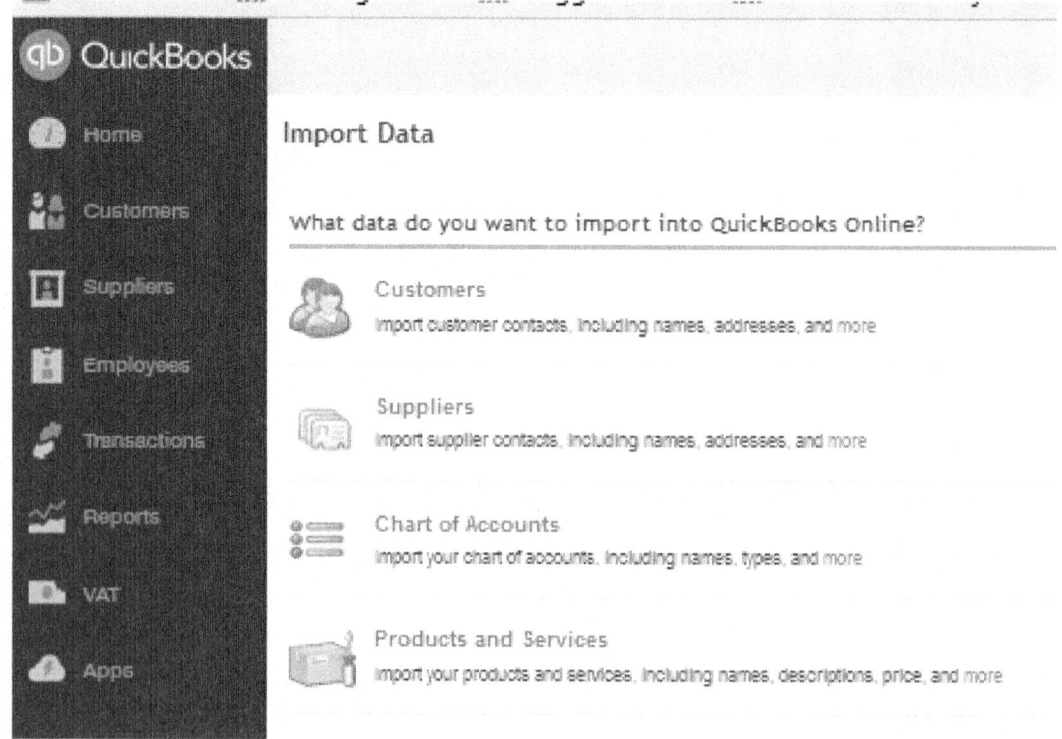

3 Click on Products and Services
4 A checklist screen pops up.

QuickBooks Online Help

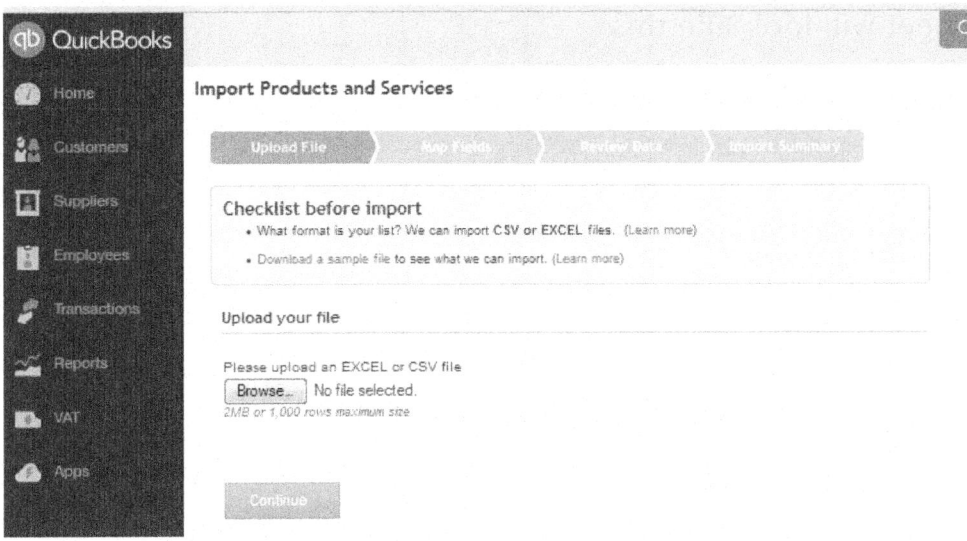

5 Download the sample file. Use it as a template to create your own file (excel or CSV) for the products and services that you want to upload).

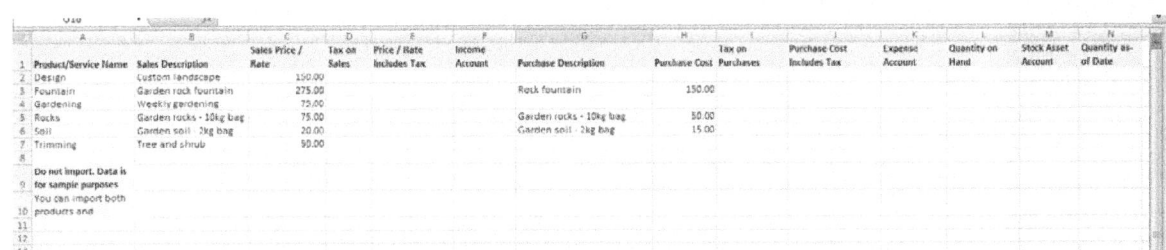

6 Lets create one for the gardening service.

Product/Service Name	Sales Description	Sales Price / Rate
Gardening	Monthly gardening service	50.00

Income Account	Purchase Description	Purchase Cost	Expense Account
Sales	Gardener	28	Janitorial expense

QuickBooks Online Help

Your spreadsheet will look like this:

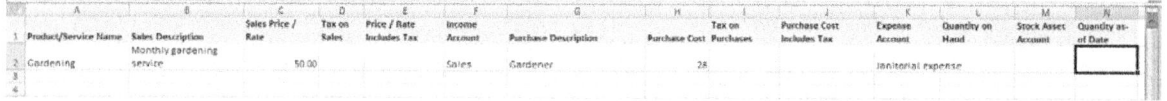

7 Save it as *Products import*.

8 Click *Browse*. Find the file *Products Import* on your system and click *Continue*.

9 QuickBooks will ask you to match the fields.

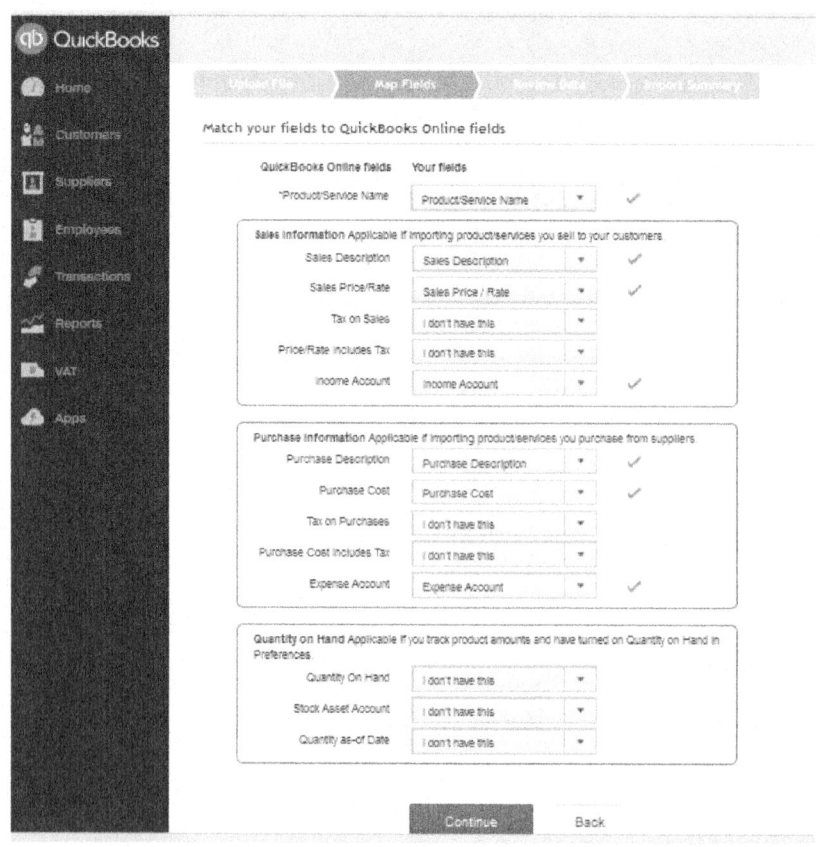

10 Go through the list, choose from the drop down. Click Continue.

11 The rows of data that you want to import will be displayed. If any are incorrect, there'll be a warning sign. The option to change the entry from

the dropdown list will be given. Go through the list and make sure that you are happy with each entry.

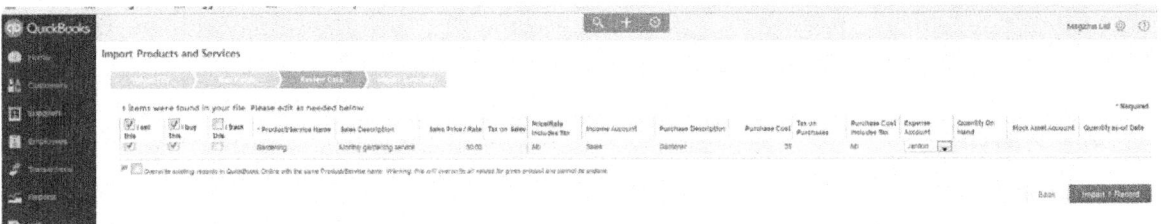

12 Once happy, click *Import 1 Record*. And *OK*.

13 You should see a congratulations screen.

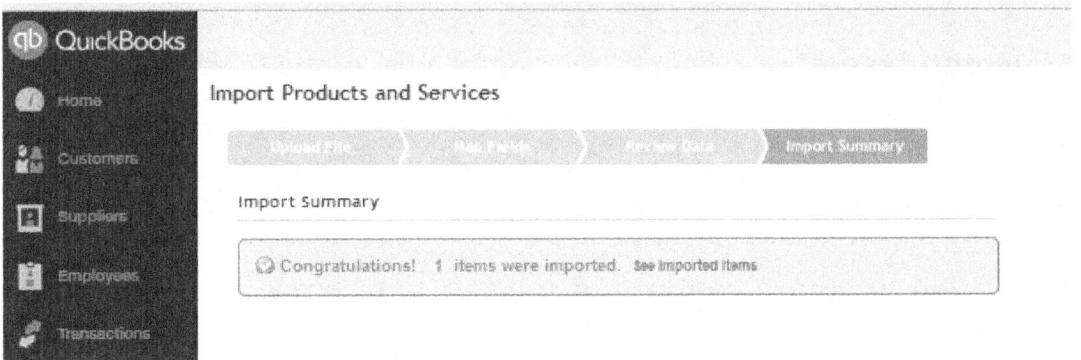

14 And you can see the imported items by clicking on the link. Note – that the Monthly Gardening Service is now added.

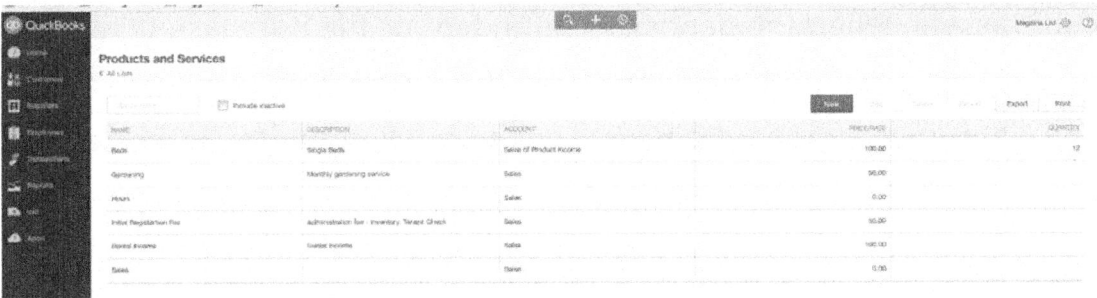

Appendix

Explanation / Uses of each account in the Chart of Accounts:

1 Debtors

- **Debtors'** tracks money that customers owe you for products or services, and payments customers make. QuickBooks Online Plus automatically creates one Debtors account for you. Most businesses need only one. Each customer has a register, which functions like a Debtors account for each customer.

2 Current Assets

- **Allowance for bad debts** - use to estimate the part of your Debtors account that you think you might not collect. Use this only if you are keeping your books on the accrual basis.
- **Called up share capital not paid** - Use to track share capital which has been issued but not yet paid.
- **Development costs** - Use to track amounts you deposit or set aside to arrange for financing, such as an SBA loan, or for deposits in anticipation of the purchase of property or other assets. When the deposit is refunded, or the purchase takes place, remove the amount from this account.
- **Employee cash advances** – use to track employee wages and salary you issue to an employee early, or other non-salary money given to employees. If you make a loan to an employee, use the Current asset account type called **Loans to others**, instead.

- **Investments- other** – use to track the value of investments not covered by other investment account types. Examples include publicly-traded shares, coins, or gold.
- **Loans to officers** - If you operate your business as a Corporation, use Loans to officers to track money loaned to officers of your business.
- **Loans to others** – use to track money your business loans to other people or businesses. This type of account is also referred to as Notes Receivable. For early salary payments to employees, use **Employee cash advances**, instead.
- **Loans to shareholders** - If you operate your business as a Corporation, use Loans to Shareholders to track money your business loans to its shareholders.
- **Other current assets** – use for current assets not covered by the other types. Current assets are likely to be converted to cash or used up in a year.
- **Prepaid expenses** – use to track payments for expenses that you won't recognise until your next accounting period. When you recognise the expense, make a journal entry to transfer money from this account to the expense account.
- **Retainage** – use if your customers regularly hold back a portion of a contract amount until you have completed a project. This type of account is often used in the construction industry, and only if you record income on an accrual basis.
- **Stock** - to track the cost of goods your business purchases for resale. When the goods are sold, assign the sale to a Cost of sales account.

- **Undeposited funds** – use for cash or cheques from sales that haven't been deposited yet. For petty cash, use **Cash on hand**, instead.

3 *Cash at Bank and In Hand*

- **Cash on hand** – use to track cash your company keeps for occasional expenses, also called petty cash. To track cash from sales that have not been deposited yet, use a pre-created account called **Undeposited funds**, instead.
- **Client trust account** - Use for money held by you for the benefit of someone else. For example, client trust accounts are often used by solicitors to keep track of expense money their customers have given them. Often, to keep the amount in a client trust account from looking like it's yours, the amount is offset in a "contra" liability account (a Current Liability).
- **Current** – use to track all your chequing activity, including debit card transactions. Each current account your company has at a bank or other financial institution should have its own Current type account in QuickBooks Online Plus.
- **Money market** – use to track amounts in money market accounts. For investments, see **Current Assets**, instead.
- **Rents held in trust** - use to track deposits and rent held on behalf of the property owners. Typically only property managers use this type of account.
- **Savings** – use accounts to track your savings and CD activity. Each savings account your company has at a bank or other financial institution should have its own Savings type account. For investments, see **Current Assets**, instead.

4 Tangible assets

- **Accumulated amortisation** – use to track how much you amortise intangible assets.
- **Accumulated depreciation** – use to track how much you depreciate a tangible asset (a physical asset you do not expect to convert to cash during one year of normal operations).
- **Accumulated depletion** – use to track how much you deplete a natural resource.
- **Buildings** - use to track the cost of structures you own and use for your business. If you have a business in your home, consult your accountant or the HMRC website for relevant rules and regulations. Use a **Land** account for the land portion of any real property you own, splitting the cost of the property between land and building in a logical method. A common method is to mimic the land-to-building ratio on the property tax statement.
- **Depletable assets** – use to track natural resources, such as timberlands, oil wells, and mineral deposits.
- **Furniture & fixtures** – use to track any furniture and fixtures your business owns and uses, like a dental chair or sales booth.
- **Leasehold improvements** – use to track improvements to a leased asset that increases the asset's value. For example, if you carpet a leased office space and are not reimbursed, that's a leasehold improvement.
- **Machinery and equipment** – use to track computer hardware, as well as any other non-furniture fixtures or devices owned and used for your business. This includes equipment that you ride, like tractors and lawn mowers. Cars and lorries, however, should be tracked with **Vehicle accounts**, instead.

- **Other tangible assets** – use for tangible assets that are not covered by other asset types. Tangible assets are physical property that you use in your business and that you do not expect to convert to cash or be used up during one year of normal operations.
- **Vehicles** – use to track the value of vehicles your business owns and uses for business. This includes off-road vehicles, aeroplanes, helicopters, and boats. If you use a vehicle for both business and personal use, consult your accountant or HMRC to see how you should track its value.

5 Non- current assets

- **Accumulated amortisation of noncurrent assets** – use to track how much you've amortised an asset whose type is **Non-Current Asset**.
- **Deferred tax** – use for tax liabilities or assets that are to be used in future accounting periods.
- **Goodwill** – use only if you have acquired another company. It represents the intangible assets of the acquired company which gave it an advantage, such as favourable government relations, business name, outstanding credit ratings, location, superior management, customer lists, product quality, or good labour relations.
- **Intangible assets** – use to track intangible assets that you plan to amortise. Examples include franchises, customer lists, copyrights, and patents.

- **Investments** – use to track intangible assets that you plan to amortise. Examples include franchises, customer lists, copyrights, and patents.
- **Lease buyout** – use to track lease payments to be applied toward the purchase of a leased asset. You don't track the leased asset itself until you purchase it.
- **Licenses** - to track non-professional licences for permission to engage in an activity, like selling alcohol or radio broadcasting. For fees associated with professional licences granted to individuals, use a **Legal and professional fees** expense account, instead.
- **Organisational costs** – use to track costs incurred when forming a partnership or corporation. The costs include the legal and accounting costs necessary to organise the company, facilitate the filings of the legal documents, and other paperwork.
- **Other non- current assets** - to track assets not covered by other types. Non-current assets are long-term assets that are expected to provide value for more than one year.
- **Other intangible assets** – use to track non-monetary assets that cannot be seen, touched or physically measured that don't fall into the other intangible asset types.
- **Prepayments and accrued income** – use to track payments and income paid in advance to cover costs that will be charged in future years.
- **Security Deposits** – use to track funds you've paid to cover any potential costs incurred by damage, loss, or theft. The funds should be returned to you at the end of the contract. If you

collect deposits, use an **Other current liabilities** account (a Current liability account).

6 Creditors

- **Creditors** tracks amounts you owe to your suppliers. QuickBooks Online Plus automatically creates one Creditors account for you. Most businesses need only one.

7 Credit Card

- **Credit Card** – card accounts track the balance due on your business cards. Create one **Card** account for each card account your business uses.

8 Current Liabilities

- **Client trust accounts – liabilities** – use to offset **Client Trust accounts** in assets. Amounts in these accounts are held by your business on behalf of others. They do not belong to your business, so should not appear to be yours on your balance sheet. This "contra" account takes care of that, as long as the two balances match.
- **Current liabilities** – use to track liabilities due within the next twelve months that do not fit the Current liability account types.
- **Current tax liability** – use to track the total amount of taxes collected but not yet paid to the government.
- **Insurance payable** – use to keep track of insurance amounts due. This account is most useful for businesses with monthly recurring insurance expenses.

- **Line of credit** – use to track the balance due on any lines of credit your business has. Each line of credit your business has should have its own **Line of credit** account.
- **Loan payable** – use to track loans your business owes which are payable within the next twelve months. For longer-term loans, use the Non-Current liability called **Notes payable**, instead.
- **Payroll clearing** – use to keep track of any non-tax amounts that you have deducted from employee payroll payments or that you owe as a result of doing payroll. When you forward money to the appropriate suppliers, deduct the amount from the balance of this account. Do not use this account for tax amounts you have withheld or owe from paying employee wages. For those amounts, use the **Tax and National Insurance payable** account instead.
- **Prepaid expenses payable** - use to track items such as property taxes that are due, but not yet deductible as an expense because the period they cover has not yet passed.
- **Rents in trust – liability** - use to offset the **Rents in trust** amount in assets. Amounts in these accounts are held by your business on behalf of others. They do not belong to your business, so should not appear to be yours on your balance sheet. This "contra" account takes care of that, as long as the two balances match.
- **Short term borrowings** – use to track loans that need to be paid back within 12 months.
- **Tax and national insurance**- use to keep track of tax amounts that you owe to HMRC as a result of paying wages and taxes you have withheld from employee payroll payments. When you

forward the money to HMRC, deduct the amount from the balance of this account.

9 Non-current liabilities

- **Accruals and deferred income** – use at the accounting year end to track expenses for invoices which have not been received by the end of the accounting period.
- **Long term borrowings** – use to track the amount due on long term borrowings.
- **Notes payable** – use to track the amounts your business owes in long-term (over twelve months) loans. For shorter loans, use the Current liability account type called **Loan payable**, instead.
- **Other non-current liabilities** – use to track liabilities due in more than twelve months that don't fit the other Non-Current liability account types.
- **Provision for liabilities** – use to track the funds set aside in anticipation of future expenditures.
- **Shareholder notes payable** – use to track long-term loan balances your business owes its shareholders.

10 Equity

- **Accumulated adjustment** - Some corporations use this account to track adjustments to owner's equity that are not attributable to net income.
- **Called up share capital** - to track share capital which has been issued.
- **Opening balance equity** - QuickBooks Online Plus creates this account the first time you enter an opening balance for a

balance sheet account. As you enter opening balances, QuickBooks Online Plus records the amounts in **Opening balance equity**. This ensures that you have a correct balance sheet for your company, even before you've finished entering all your company's assets and liabilities.

- **Ordinary shares** – use to track its ordinary shares in the hands of shareholders. The amount in this account should be the stated (or par) value of the stock.
- **Owners equity** – use to show the cumulative net income or loss of their business as of the beginning of the financial year
- **Paid- in capital or surplus** – use to track amounts received from shareholders in exchange for shares that are over and above the shares' stated (or par) value.
- **Partner contributions** – use to track amounts partners contribute to the partnership during the year.
- **Partner distributions** – use to track amounts distributed by the partnership to its partners during the year. Don't use this for regular payments to partners for interest or service. For regular payments, use a **Guaranteed payments** account (an Expense account in Payroll expenses), instead.
- **Partners' equity** – use to show the income remaining in the partnership for each partner as of the end of the prior year.
- **Preference shares** – Corporations use this account to track its preferred shares in the hands of shareholders. The amount in this account should be the stated (or par) value of the shares.
- **Retained earnings** – use QuickBooks Online Plus adds this account when you create your company. **Retained earnings** tracks net income from previous financial years. QuickBooks

Online Plus automatically transfers your profit (or loss) to **Retained earnings** at the end of each financial year.
- **Treasury shares** – use to track amounts paid by the corporation to buy its own shares back from shareholders.

11 Income

- **Discounts / refunds given** – use to track discounts you give to customers. This account typically has a negative balance so it offsets other income. For discounts from suppliers, use an expense account, instead.
- **Non- profit income** – use to track money coming in if you are a non-profit organisation.
- **Other primary income** – use to track income from normal business operations that doesn't fall into another Income type.
- **Sales of product income** – use to track income from selling products. This can include all kinds of products, like crops and livestock, rental fees, performances, and food served.
- **Service / fee income** – use to track income from services you perform or ordinary usage fees you charge. For fees customers pay you for late payments or other uncommon situations, use an Other Income account type called **Other miscellaneous income**, instead.
- **Unapplied cash payment income** - reports the **Cash Basis** income from customers' payments you've received but not applied to invoices or charges. In general, you would never use this directly on a purchase or sale transaction.

12 Other income

- **Dividend income** – use to track taxable dividends from investments.
- **Interest earned** - to track interest from cash at bank and in hand accounts, investments, or interest payments to you on loans your business made.
- **Other investment income** - to track other types of investment income that isn't from dividends or interest.
- **Other miscellaneous income** – use to track income that isn't from normal business operations, and doesn't fall into another Other Income type.
- **Tax- exempt interest** – use to record interest that isn't taxable, such as interest on money in tax-exempt retirement accounts, or interest from tax-exempt bonds.

13 Cost of Sales

- **Cost of labour – COS** – use to track the cost of paying employees to produce products or supply services. It includes all employment costs, including food and transportation, if applicable.
- **Cost of sales** – use to track costs related to sales you provide.
- **Equipment rental – COS** – use to track the cost of renting equipment to produce products or services. If you purchase equipment, use a Tangible asset account type called **Machinery and equipment**.
- **Other costs of sales – COS** – use to track costs related to services or sales that you provide that don't fall into another Cost of Sales type.

- **Shipping, freight and delivery – COS** – use to track the cost of shipping products to customers or distributors.
- **Supplies and materials – COS** – use to track the cost of raw goods and parts used or consumed when producing a product or providing a service.

14 Expenses

- **Advertising / promotional** – use to track money spent promoting your company. You may want different accounts of this type to track different promotional efforts (Yellow Pages, newspaper, radio, flyers, events, and so on). If the promotion effort is a meal, use **Promotional meals** instead.
- **Auto** – use to track costs associated with vehicles. You may want different accounts of this type to track petrol, repairs, and maintenance. If your business owns a car or lorry, you may want to track its value as a Tangible Asset, in addition to tracking its expenses.
- **Bad debts** – use to track debt you have written off.
- **Bank charges** – use for any fees you pay to financial institutions.
- **Charitable contributions** – use to track gifts to charity.
- **Cost of labour** – use to track the cost of paying employees to produce products or supply services. It includes all employment costs, including food and transportation, if applicable. This account is also available as a Cost of Sales (COS) account.
- **Distribution costs** – use to track the cost of shipping goods to customers or distributors.

- **Dues and subscriptions** - use to track dues and subscriptions related to running your business. You may want different accounts of this type for professional dues, fees for licences that can't be transferred, magazines, newspapers, industry publications, or service subscriptions.
- **Entertainment** - use to track events to entertain employees. If the event is a meal, use **Entertainment meals**, instead.
- **Equipment rental** - use to track the cost of renting equipment to produce products or services. This account is also available as a Cost of sales account. If you purchase equipment, use a Tangible asset account type called **Machinery and equipment**.
- **Finance costs** - use to track the costs of obtaining loans or credit. Examples of finance costs would be card fees, interest and mortgage costs.
- **Insurance** - use to track insurance payments. You may want different accounts of this type for different types of insurance (auto, general liability, and so on).
- **Interest paid** - use for all types of interest you pay, including mortgage interest, finance charges on cards, or interest on loans.
- **Legal and professional fees** - use to track money to pay to professionals to help you run your business. You may want different accounts of this type for payments to your accountant, attorney, or other consultants.
- **Meals and entertainment** - use to track how much you spend on dining with your employees to promote morale. If you dine with a customer to promote your business, use a **Promotional**

meals account, instead. Be sure to include who you ate with and the purpose of the meal when you enter the transaction.

- **Office/general admin expenses** – use to track all types of general or office-related expenses.
- **Other misc service costs** – use to track costs related to providing services that don't fall into another Expense type. This account is also available as a Cost of Sales (COS) account.
- **Payroll expenses** – use to track payroll expenses. You may want different accounts of this type for things like: Compensation of officers, Guaranteed payments, Compulsory Employers Liability Insurance, Salaries and wages, Payroll taxes
- **Promotional meals – use** to track how much you spend dining with a customer to promote your business. Be sure to include who you ate with and the purpose of the meal when you enter the transaction.
- **Rent or lease of buildings** – use to track rent payments you make.
- **Repair and maintenance** - use to track any repairs and periodic maintenance fees. You may want different accounts of this type to track different type's repair & maintenance expenses (auto, equipment, landscape, and so on).
- **Shipping, freight and delivery** – use to track the cost of shipping products to customers or distributors. You might use this type of account for incidental shipping expenses, and the COS type of **Shipping, freight & delivery** account for direct costs. This account is also available as a Cost of Sales (COS) account.

- **Supplies** – use to track the cost of raw goods and parts used or consumed when producing a product or providing a service. This account is also available as a Cost of Sales account.
- **Taxes paid** - use to track taxes you pay. You may want different accounts of this type for payments to different tax agencies.
- **Travel**– use to track travel costs. For food you eat while travelling, use **Travel meals**, instead.
- **Travel meals** to track how much you spend on food while travelling. If you dine with a customer to promote your business, use a **Promotional meals** account, instead. If you dine with your employees to promote morale, use **Entertainment meals**, instead.
- **Unapplied cash bill payments** - reports the **Cash Basis** expense from supplier payment cheques you've sent but not yet applied to supplier bills. In general, you would never use this directly on a purchase or sale transaction.
- **Utilities** – use to track utility payments. You may want different accounts of this type to track different types of utility payments (gas and electric, telephone, water, and so on).

15 Other expenses

- **Amortisation** – use to track amortisation of intangible assets. Amortisation is spreading the cost of an intangible asset over its useful life, like depreciation of tangible assets. You may want an amortisation account for each intangible asset you have.
- **Depreciation** – use to track how much you depreciate tangible assets. You may want a depreciation account for each tangible asset you have.

- **Exchange gain or loss** – use to track gains or losses that occur as a result of exchange rate fluctuations.
- **Other expenses** – use to track unusual or infrequent expenses that don't fall into another Other Expense type.
- **Penalties and settlements** – use to track money you pay for violating laws or regulations, settling lawsuits, or other penalties.

Explanation of each report:

Seven Types of Reports available:

i. **Business overview** - These reports show different perspectives of how your business is doing:

Profit and Loss - Shows money you earned (income) and money you spent (expenses) so you can see how profitable you are. Also called an income statement.

Profit and Loss Detail - Lists the individual transactions and totals for money you earned (income) and money you spent (expenses).

Profit and Loss by Class - This summarises the income and expenses for each class using income and expense accounts on your chart of accounts. It lets you see if classes are operating at a profit or a loss.

Profit and Loss by Location - This summarises the income and expenses for each location using income and expense accounts on your chart of accounts. It lets you see if locations are operating at a profit or a loss.

Statement of Cash Flows - Shows cash generated by your business (operating activities), cash spent on your business (investments) and cash in or out from stock and dividends (financing).

Balance Sheet - Lists what you own (assets), what your debts are (liabilities), and what you've invested in your company (equity).

Balance Sheet Summary - Summarises what you own (assets), what your debts are (liabilities), and what you've invested in your company (equity).

Audit Log - Shows everything that has happened in your company file so you always know who's been in QuickBooks and what they've done.

Company Snapshot - Displays your income and expenses in year-over-year comparisons using pie charts and bar graphs.

ii. **Manage Accounts Receivable** - These reports let you see who owes you money and how much they owe you so you can get paid:

Customer Balance Summary - Shows each customer's total open balances.

Customer Balance Detail - Lists unpaid invoices for each customer, including invoice date and number, due date, total, and amount owed to you (open balance).

Collections Report - Shows overdue invoices grouped by customer. Includes the due date, days past due, and total for each customer.

Statement List - Lists statements you sent to customers during a selected time period, including the statement date.

A/R Ageing Summary - Shows unpaid invoices for the current period and for the last 30, 60 and 90+ days so you can see how long they've been open (outstanding).

A/R Ageing Detail - Lists all unpaid invoices, grouped by number of days past due. Includes due dates, customer names, amounts, and totals for each billing period.

Invoice List - Shows a chronological list of all your invoices for a selected date range.

iii. **Manage Accounts Payable** - These reports show what you owe and when payments are due so you can take advantage of the time you have to pay bills but still make payments on time:

A/P Ageing Summary - Shows unpaid bills for the current period and for the last 30, 60 and 90+ days so you can see how long they've been open (outstanding).

A/P Ageing Detail - Lists all your unpaid bills, grouped by when the bill was due (ageing period). Includes due dates and amounts.

Bill Payment List - Shows all the bills you paid during a selected date range.

Unpaid Bills - Shows your unpaid bills, their due dates, and days past due so you can avoid late payments.

Supplier Balance Detail - Lists all the bills that make up the total amount you owe each supplier (balance).

Supplier Balance Summary - Shows the total amount you owe each supplier.

iv. **Manage Employees** - These reports help you manage employee activities and payroll:

Time Activities by Employee Detail - Lists the products/services (time activities) provided by each employee, including hourly rate and duration.

Recent / Edited Time Activities - Lists the 25 products/services (time activities) most recently entered or edited so you can see your employees' latest activities.

v. **Review Sales** - These reports group and total sales in different ways to help analyse your sales to see how you're doing and where you make your money:

Sales by Customer Summary - Shows total sales for each customer so you can see which ones generate the most revenue for you.

Sales by Customer Detail - Lists the individual sales transactions for each customer, including dates, types, amounts, and totals.

Sales by Product/Service Summary - Summarises sales for each item on your Product/Service List. Includes quantity, amount, % of sales, and average price.

Sales by Product/Service Detail - Lists sales for each item on your Product/Service List. Includes the date, transaction type, quantity, rate, amount, and total.

Income by Customer Summary - Shows your income minus expenses (net income) for each customer.

Customer Contact List - This report lists each customer's phone number, email and billing address, and other contact information.

Transaction List by Customer - Groups transactions by customer name, so you can see all activity related to each customer.

Sales by Location Summary - This report summarises your unit and sales amounts for all the locations on your Location List.

Sales by Location Detail - This report is a more detailed version of Sales by Location Summary. In addition to the unit and sales amounts for each location, this report lists the transactions that contributed to each total.

Sales by Class Summary - Summarises sales by the categories (classes) you assigned to your transactions; for example, all sales for a particular product line.

Sales by Class Detail - Lists sales for each category (class) you assigned to your transactions. Includes the date, transaction type, product or service, quantity, rate, amount, and balance.

Time Activities by Customer Detail - Lists the products/services (time activities) your employees provided to each customer.

Estimates by Customer - Lists your estimates by customer, and indicates whether estimates were accepted and invoiced.

Unbilled Charges - Lists customer charges (transactions) that you have not yet invoiced.

Unbilled Time - Lists products/services (time activities) provided by your employees that have not yet been billed.

Deposit Detail - Provides detailed information about your deposits, including date, client or supplier, and amount.

vi. **Review Expenses and Purchases** - These reports total your expenses and purchases and group them in different ways to help you understand what you spend:

Expenses by Supplier Summary - This report shows your total expenses for each supplier.

Supplier Contact List - Lists each supplier's name, company, phone number, email, mailing address, and account number.

Purchases by Supplier Detail - Shows your individual purchases and totals for each supplier.

Purchases by Product/Service Detail - Groups your purchases by the items in your Product/Service List.

Cheque Detail - Provides detailed information about each cheque you've written, including date, payee, and amount.

Transaction List by Supplier - Lists all transactions by supplier, so you can view your business activities with a specific supplier.

Open Purchases Order List - Lists your open purchase orders, grouped by supplier. Includes the original amount of each P.O.

Purchases by Class Detail - Classifies your purchases by group (class) so you can track your spending.

Purchases by Location Detail - This report groups the purchase transactions by Location

vii. **Accountants Reports** - These are reports accountants typically use to drill down into your business details and prepare your tax returns:

Account Listing - Provides the name, type, and balance for each account listed in your Chart of Accounts.

Trial Balance - This report summarises the debit and credit balances of each account on your chart of accounts during a period of time.

Profit and Loss - Shows money you earned (income) and money you spent (expenses) so you can see how profitable you are. Also called an income statement.

Transaction Detail by Account - This report lists transactions subtotalled by each account on your chart of accounts. It is like General Ledger without opening balances.

Reconciliation Reports - Lists all reconciliations you've completed and provides links to the individual reconciliation reports.

Journal - This report breaks down every transaction during a period of time into debits and credits and displays them chronologically. Transaction List by Date also lists transactions chronologically, but not as debits and credits.

Balance Sheet - Lists what you own (assets), what your debts are (liabilities), and what you've invested in your company (equity).

General Ledger - For each account in your chart of accounts, the report shows all the transactions that occurred in that account over a period of time. It includes the beginning balance and total for each account.

Recent Automatic Transactions - This report shows the automatic transactions most recently created within the last 4 days.

Transaction List with Splits - This report lists each transaction with its associated split lines.

Statement of Cash Flows - Shows cash generated by your business (operating activities), cash spent on your business (investments) and cash in or out from stock and dividends (financing).

Transaction List by Date - This report lists all the transactions that occurred within a period of time. The report is useful if you need a straight chronological listing of all the transactions your company made.

Recent Transactions - This report shows the transactions most recently modified within the last 4 days.

Index

A

A/R Ageing, 196, 369
absences, 249, 250
accountant, 9, 21, 24, 36, 138, 354, 355, 364
Accounting, *379*
Accounts Receivable, 14, 18, 158, 159, 195, 199, 369
accrual, 21, 22, 36, 199, 204, 238, 239, 351, 352
action, 380
Advance, 254, 257, 260
Amazon, 1
amortisation, 63, 64, 136, 354, 355, 366
apps, 345, 346
Assets, 17, 18, 19, 20, 39, 40, 63, 136, 351, 353
attachment, 48, 79, 87, 109, 131, 133, 156, 158
Attachments, 76, 87, 184
Audit, 195, 369

B

Bad debts, 66, 363
balance sheet, 23, 24, 39, 54, 102, 139, 149, 218, 357, 358, 360
Balance Sheet, 20, 24, 181, 195, 198, 210, 368, 374
Bank, 18, 40, 54, 63, 66, 105, 116, 117, 118, 143, 145, 146, 148, 176, 178, 243, 245, 273, 283, 285, 286, 287, 290, 353, 363
banking, 273, 292
bill, 19, 21, 36, 37, 66, 70, 99, 101, 104, 105, 107, 113, 122, 127, 129, 131, 133, 180, 181, 182, 183, 184, 185, 186, 187, 189, 190, 199, 215, 219, 220, 230, 330, 331, 332, 343, 366, 370
Bill, 46, 77, 107, 130, 131, 132, 182, 188, 196, 219, 220, 321, 343, 370
bonus, 121, 254
Bookkeeper, 379, 382
bookkeeping, *379*
budget, 336, 337, 338, 339, 340, 341, 342, 381
Buildings, 63, 136, 354
business, *379*, 380

C

capital, 20, 63, 65, 136, 149, 351, 359, 360
Cash Flows, 24, 195, 198, 335, 368, 374
cashflow, 181, 290
Certificate, 226
charity, 363, 379
chart of accounts, 17, 39, 43, 44, 45, 51, 54, 61, 62, 67, 68, 91, 102, 141, 149, 218, 368, 373, 374
checklist, 347
cheques, 13, 33, 62, 74, 95, 109, 114, 176, 180, 353, 366
class, 37, 78, 86, 87, 105, 107, 142, 145, 147, 148, 151, 156, 172, 173, 175, 279, 281, 295, 331, 337, 338, 339, 368, 372, 373, 379, 381
classes, 13, 27, 36, 37, 61, 76, 86, 87, 338, 339, 368, 372
commission, 52, 254
Companies House, 36, 299
Contact List, 197, 371, 373

Cost of Sales, 17, 65, 362, 363, 365, 366
Credit Card, 19, 40, 64, 121, 123, 125, 126, 128, 130, 131, 132, 295, 296, 357
credit memo, 153, 171, 172, 174, 311
Credit Note, 77, 172
Creditors, 40, 64, 105, 181, 187, 212, 357
Currency, 37, 38, 124, 286, 296, 324, 325, 326
Current Account, 13, 19, 106, 107, 116, 133, 147, 148, 158, 168, 170, 175, 177, 186, 187, 188, 286, 296, 332, 353
customise, 22, 29, 32, 44, 46, 48, 49, 157, 191, 214, 297, 298, 299, 301, 302, 342

D

Debtors, 18, 40, 41, 63, 105, 159, 173, 212, 351
delayed charge, 308, 309, 310
delayed credit, 310, 311
delete, 43, 91, 92, 161, 185
Deposit, 19, 77, 104, 145, 154, 158, 165, 168, 170, 175, 176, 178, 197, 273, 283, 285, 372
depreciation, 63, 66, 105, 136, 138, 139, 140, 141, 142, 354, 366
direct debits, 13, 110
Discounts, 65, 361
discrepancies, 117, 118
Dividend, 65, 362

E

Email, 1, 299, 379, 382
Employee, 58, 61, 63, 73, 74, 196, 243, 244, 245, 246, 251, 323, 351, 352, 370
Employer Payment Submission, 259
entrepreneur, *379*
Equipment, 18, 40, 65, 66, 362, 364
Equity, 17, 18, 20, 40, 65, 105, 136, 149, 359
error, 344
estimate, 297, 301, 302, 306, 307, 308, 312, 351
exchange rate, 326, 328, 329, 331, 332, 334, 367

F

facebook, 379
finance charge, 129
financial period, 50
financial year, 50, 51, 149, 337, 338, 360, 361
foreign, 46, 324, 326, 328, 330, 331, 333
Foreign exchange, 47
free, 9, 10, 120, 121, 241
freelance, 380
fuel, 231
Full Payment Submission, 259

G

Give As You Earn, 254, 255, 267
goals, 336
Goodwill, 19, 64, 355
Gross pay, 260

H

Help, 8, 15, 59, 150
HMRC, 21, 198, 224, 226, 230, 231, 236, 238, 354, 355, 358
holiday pay, 254

I

Import, 345, 346, 347, 349, 350
Importing, 292
inactive, 91, 92, 93
income tax, 240
Inland Revenue, 258
insurance, 19, 64, 68, 143, 150, 241, 279, 357, 358, 364
interest, 65, 66, 112, 113, 120, 128, 146, 147, 148, 208, 360, 362, 364
internet banking, 110, 273
Investments, 19, 63, 64, 352, 356
invoice, 9, 12, 21, 29, 32, 37, 48, 62, 77, 79, 102, 153, 154, 155, 156, 157, 158, 159, 160, 161, 162, 163, 164, 166, 167, 168, 169, 171, 174, 199, 223, 225, 229, 232, 297, 298, 299, 302, 306, 307, 308, 309, 316, 318, 319, 320, 324, 328, 369
Item, 216, 218, 230

J

journal, 57, 135, 150, 151, 152, 283, 352
Journal Entry, 77, 151, 231, 284

L

liability, *1*
Licenses, 64, 356
lists, 13, 39, 61, 62, 76, 91, 103, 104, 115, 156, 199, 216, 238, 325, 355, 356, 371, 372, 374, 375
loan, 19, 23, 143, 144, 145, 146, 147, 281, 351, 359
Loans, 63, 351, 352
Locations, 37, 76, 82
logo, 28, 79, 157, 298

M

Machinery, 63, 136, 139, 354, 362, 364
Marketing, 379
Markup, 300
Maternity, 247, 248, 250, 253
maternity leave, 248
money, 381
multicurrency, 46, 47, 325

N

National Insurance, 19, 73, 240, 358
Net pay, 260
net profit, 24
net wages, 263, 264
NI deductions, 262
NICs, 240, 260

O

online, 1
Opening Balances, 54
Ordinary shares, 65, 360
overdraft, 379
overtime, 254, 256

P

p32, 258, 262
p45, 240, 246, 269
p60, 271, 272
Partner, 65, 246, 360
patents, 355, 356
paydate, 257
PAYE, 240, 243, 259, 260, 261
payroll, 26, 57, 135, 143, 150, 196, 240, 241, 243, 265, 269, 271, 346, 358, 365, 370
payroll expenses, 260, 261
payroll liabilities, 260, 261
payroll taxes, 240, 261
payslip, 253, 255, 256, 257, 258
pension, 247
Petty Cash, 18, 19, 42, 105, 107, 108, 158, 175, 179, 286, 353
phone, 383

plan, 181, 335, 336, 337, 355, 356
preferences, 26, 46, 48, 72
Prepayments, 18, 64, 356
price, 52, 139, 156, 162, 329, 371
Pro Advisor, 9
profit and loss, 22, 23, 24, 194, 207, 218
Proforma Invoice, 306, 307
published, 1
purchase order, 217, 218, 219
Purchase Order, 77, 104, 217, 218

Q

qualify, 248
QuickInsight, 191, 212
QuickReport, 192, 202, 218

R

Reconcile, 103, 111, 118, 128, 287
Reconciling, 95, 109, 111, 127, 128
Recurring, 76, 77, 98, 160, 161, 185
refunds, 65, 361
reminder, 9, 77, 160
Remittance Advice, 188
remittance advices, 57
report, 20, 21, 22, 24, 36, 116, 118, 129, 152, 191, 192, 194, 195, 198, 199, 200, 201, 203, 204, 205, 207, 208, 209, 210, 211, 212, 213, 214, 219, 222, 233, 236, 237, 238, 239, 312, 323, 324, 330, 333, 335, 337, 341, 342, 368, 371, 372, 373, 374, 375
reporting, 22, 208, 223, 239, 342
reports, 9, 22, 23, 88, 93, 116, 150, 163, 191, 192, 194, 195, 196, 197, 198, 199, 205, 206, 208, 209, 210, 212, 219, 224, 237, 238, 239, 306, 312, 313, 322, 330, 333, 361, 366, 368, 369, 370, 371, 372, 373, 374
Retained Earnings, 102, 149
revenue, 24, 371
review, 1

S

sales order, 306
sales receipt, 77, 154, 155, 158, 164, 179, 232, 283, 297, 301, 302
SAP, 240
Save As You Earn, 254
scheduled, 77, 160, 185, 207, 208
school, 381
Self Employed, 382
service, 379
Single Time Activity, 313, 314, 315, 321
SMP, 240, 248, 250
sole trader, 26, 149
SPP, 240, 248, 249, 251
SSP, 240, 248, 249
statement, 9, 13, 22, 23, 24, 48, 54, 79, 110, 111, 112, 113, 114, 115, 116, 117, 119, 121, 123, 126, 127, 128, 129, 156, 274, 287, 288, 289, 293, 297, 303, 304, 305, 354, 368, 369, 374
statements, 1, 54, 56, 112, 116, 120, 302, 304, 369
Statutory Maternity Pay, 248
Statutory Paternity Pay, 252
Statutory Sick Pay, 248
stock, 9, 18, 19, 63, 105, 135, 136, 215, 216, 217, 219, 221, 222, 335, 346, 352, 360, 368, 375
subaccounts, 68, 69
subcontractors, 313

T

Tax, 19, 64, 65, 72, 223, 227, 245, 252, 358, 362
Tax and National Insurance, 261, 265, 266, 358
taxable, 254, 362
taxes, 19, 34, 135, 240, 265, 266, 335, 357, 358, 365, 366
Telephone, 383
template, 157, 160, 161, 298, 299, 301, 339, 348, *380*
Terms, 61, 76, 84, 131, 299
Time Tracking, 314, 316
training, 9, 379
Trial Balance, 198, 373
twitter, 379

U

Unbilled, 197, 323, 372
unscheduled, 76, 77, 160
user ID, 236, 271

V

VAT, 12, 46, 47, 72, 135, 194, 198, 223, 224, 225, 226, 227, 228, 229, 230, 231, 232, 233, 234, 235, 236, 237, 238, 239, 279, 281, 295, 300, 308, 310, 320, 330, 331
Vehicles, 44, 63, 105, 355
videos, 15, 27

W

wages, 249, 351, 358, 365
weekly timesheet, 315, 316, 318
world, 380
writing, 1

Z

zero-rate, 225

About The Author

Born in Nottingham, UK, Lisa Newton moved to London to study Accounting with Marketing at Middlesex University. Graduating with a first class honours degree, she then went on to do an MSc in Investment Management at City University. In the same month of the Masters graduation ceremony at City, Lisa formed Boogles Ltd with £150. Her mum put in £50, and Lisa used £100 of her overdraft.

Boogles primarily began as a bookkeeping service and has since expanded, and moved into other markets – such as bookkeeping franchise, bookkeeping training courses and products such as maths books & games for kids.

A strong supporter of women in business and entrepreneurial people, Lisa is an Ambassador for Enterprising Women (the UK campaign to give women confidence and ambition to be enterprising - to have ideas and to make them happen). She is a member of the ICB & AAT.

Lisa is a serial entrepreneur and holds various directorships in various industries including telecoms, software, hair & beauty as well as finance. She has won various awards in Business including: Young Entrepreneur of the Year Award 2007 with Precious Online and in 2008 Enterprising Business Award and has been nominated and a finalist in numerous others including her bookkeeping business Boogles Ltd being short listed to the final 5, out of 14,500 entries for Best Bookkeeping Practice Lucas Awards in 2009 and 2011 and Boogles Ltd being short listed for Best Accounting Franchisor in 2011 by the BKN awards. In 2012 & 2013 Boogles won the BKN Best Accounting Franchisor award. In 2013 Lisa was nominated and shortlisted to final 3 – for Bookkeeper of the Year – ICB Luca Awards.

Lisa supports the charity The MS Society. A trainer, speaker, writer, consultant and an avid net-worker, Lisa enjoys meeting people and working on projects with like-minded individuals. More about the author can be found at: www.LisaNewton.co.uk

Email me: lisa@lisanewton.co.uk
Follow me on twitter: @lisa_newton1
Connect on FaceBook: www.facebook.com/booglesb

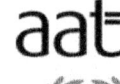

OTHER BOOKS BY THE AUTHOR

How To Start Your Own Bookkeeping Business

How to start your own bookkeeping business is an action-packed, tip-filled, no-nonsense approach to how to start, what to do, things to look out for, pitfalls to avoid and its guidance will help you to avoid the expensive, painful time-consuming mistakes which most freelance independent bookkeepers make...
Author: Lisa Newton.
Published: 2012
ISBN: 978-1477580660

97 Ways To Market Your Accountancy Business

Do you want to take your business 'to the next level'? You'll only be able to do this, if you have more clients, and clients will only find out about you through marketing. This book gives you 97 Ways to market – split by easy to hard methods, and cheapest to most expensive ideas.
Author: Lisa Newton.
Published: 2013
ISBN: 978-148 188 2118

The 21st Century Business Model

Ignore the New World Order at your COST! This book looks at what elements make up the type of business, which will work best in the 21st century. Have you ever thought about going into business and wondered what the best type of business is? Do you want a success template to follow? Are you just not satisfied with the results your own business is giving you, but can't quite put your finger on it? The 21st Century business owner understands that the world has changed. They know that when they understand the new rules of this game - they'll be far ahead of the rest. And that good fortune favours the brave.
Author: Lisa Newton
Published: 2011
ISBN: 978-0-9564252-8-7

Cosmic Ordering With Vision Boards

Think It. See It. Get It! You may have heard of 'The Secret´ and ´the law of attraction´. What this book is all about, is applying the law of attraction and manifesting what you want, through placing orders with the universe through vision boards. The book outlines in detail how to create a board, what works, and (very importantly) what to do if you don't achieve the results that you want. There is a process to remove the blocks and to allow the energy to flow.
Author: Lisa Newton.
Published: 2013
ISBN: 978-1492113607

Make The Most of Your Money

How to budget, save and manage your finances. This book looks at how to make the most of your money. Often the harder you work, the less you have to show for it. This book covers the issue of money. All the stuff you should have been taught in school including income, stocks, bonds, assets, reducing debt, mortgages, loans.
Author: Lisa Newton.
Published: 2013
ISBN: 978-1481990639

Money Maths With Boogles: Workbook 1: Getting To Know Your Numbers: 5-6 yrs

Boogles the calculator has put together this action packed workbook - full of examples and exercises using maths and money. Maths and being able to understand money are key skills that will help you throughout your life. Teachers / Parents / Carers: You can photocopy the sheets for class exercises / homework / extra practice. Play the Boogles Maths game online at www.Boogles.Me.uk
Author: Lisa Newton.
Published: 2013
ISBN: 978-1482017359

QuickBooks Online Help

To order any of these books please fill in the form below:

No. of copies	Title	Price	Total
	Make The Most Of Your Money	£ 8.99	
	Boogles And The Self Employed Consultant	£ 4.99	
	Bookkeeping Made Simple	£ 4.99	
	How To Start Your Own Bookkeeping Business	£ 14.99	
	97 Ways To Market Your Accountancy Business	£ 12.99	
	The Mumpreneur & The Bookkeeper	£ 4.99	
	How To Write A Book In Two Weeks (Or Less)	£ 3.99	
	The 21st Century Business Model	£ 4.99	
	Cosmic Ordering With Vision Boards	£ 6.99	
	What Fat People Should East To Lose Weight	£ 5.99	
	Money Maths With Boogles: Workbook 1: Getting To Know Your Numbers (5-6yrs)	£ 4.99	
	Money Maths With Boogles: Workbook 2: (7-9 yrs)	£ 4.99	
	Money Maths With Boogles: Workbook 3: (9-11 yrs)	£ 4.99	
	For P&P add **£2.50** for the first book, **£1** for each extra book		
	GRAND TOTAL		£

PLEASE FILL IN, IN CAPITAL LETTERS

Name: _____

Address: _____

_____

City: _____ Country: _____

Postcode / Zip: _____

Daytime Tel. No./Email: _____ (in case of query)

Four ways to pay:

1. Telephone the Boogles Hotline on **+44 (0) 20 3371 8894**. Receptionists are there 24 hours a day, 7 days a week. And leave a message with them 'I'd like to order' and we'll call you back. Please have your card (debit or credit card handy).

2. I enclose a Cheque made payable to **Boogles** for
£ _____

3. Please send a payment **via PayPal** to info@booglesltd.com (or just email us and ask for a payment request)

4. Please charge my Visa [ ]   MasterCard [ ]   Amex [ ]   Maestro (issue no. __) [ ]

Card number: ____/____/____/____/___
Expiry date: __/__   Start date: __/__
Last three digits on back of the card: ___

Signature: _____

Please return forms to: (Photocopies acceptable)

Direct Mail Dept., Boogles Book Publishing, Ground Floor, Unit PG04, 23-28 Penn Street, Hoxton, London, England, United Kingdom N1 5DL
Enquiries to: book@booglesltd.com

Boogles Ltd (directly or via its agents) may mail, email or phone you about promotions or products.
[ ] Tick box if you do not want these from us

www.LisaNewton.co.uk